Impressionist Paris.
A Panoramic View of Paris in French Impressionism

IMPRES
PARIS

SIONIST

A Panoramic View of Paris
in French Impressionism

Edited by Frouke van Dijke

HANNIBAL   KUNSTMUSEUM DEN HAAG

FOREWORD

p. 9

THE MYTH OF PARIS

p. 13

PARIS 1867 – A TURNING POINT

p. 73

THE PARISIENNE

p. 119

A CITY AT WAR

p. 163

FRÉDÉRIC BAZILLE

p. 112

GUSTAVE CAILLEBOTTE

p. 36

MARY CASSATT

p. 146

PAUL CÉZANNE

p. 30

EDGAR DEGAS

p. 158

ÉDOUARD MANET

p. 44, 106, 150

CHARLES MARVILLE

p. 48

CLAUDE MONET

p. 94

CAMILLE PISSARRO

p. 26

AUGUSTE RENOIR

p. 200

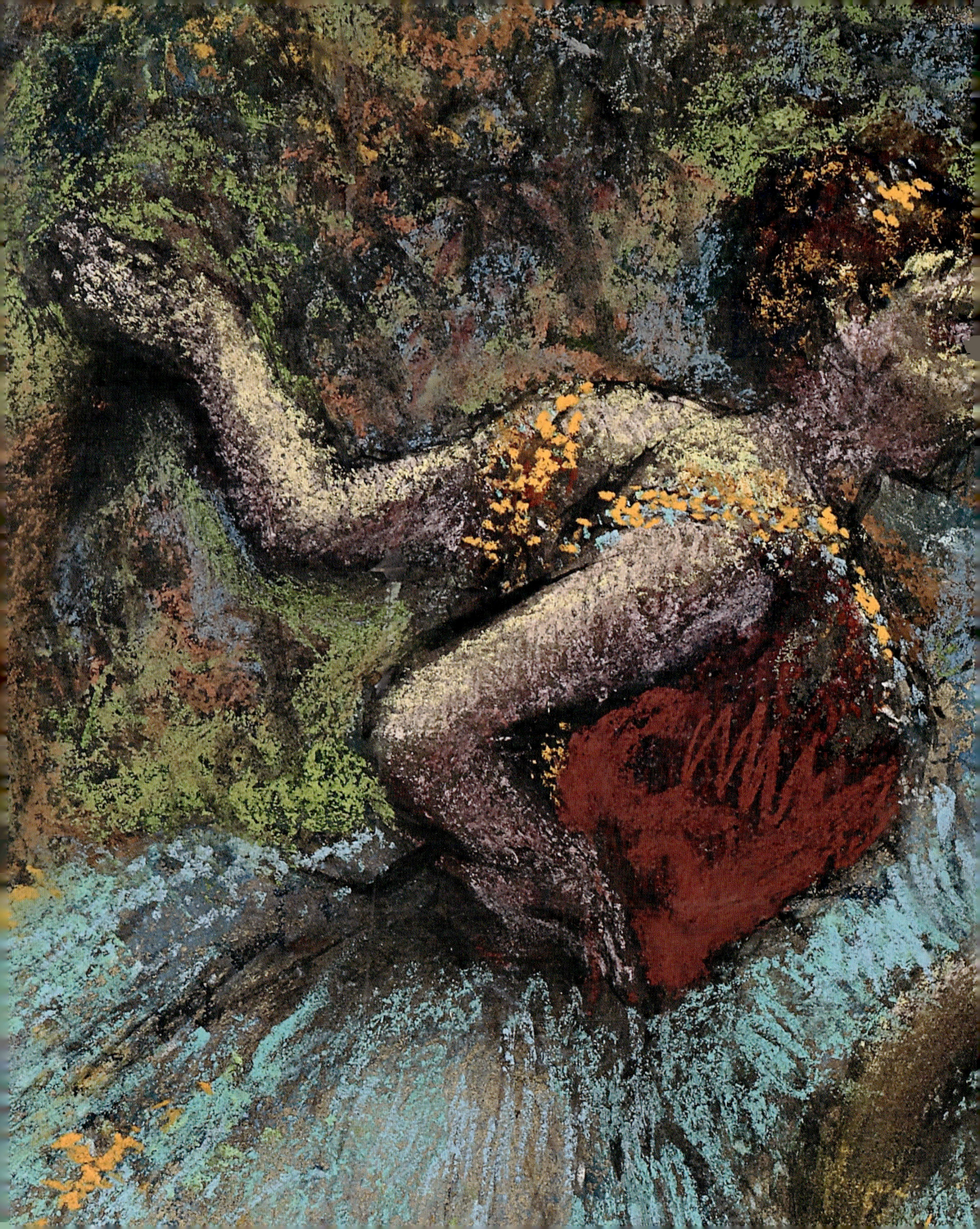

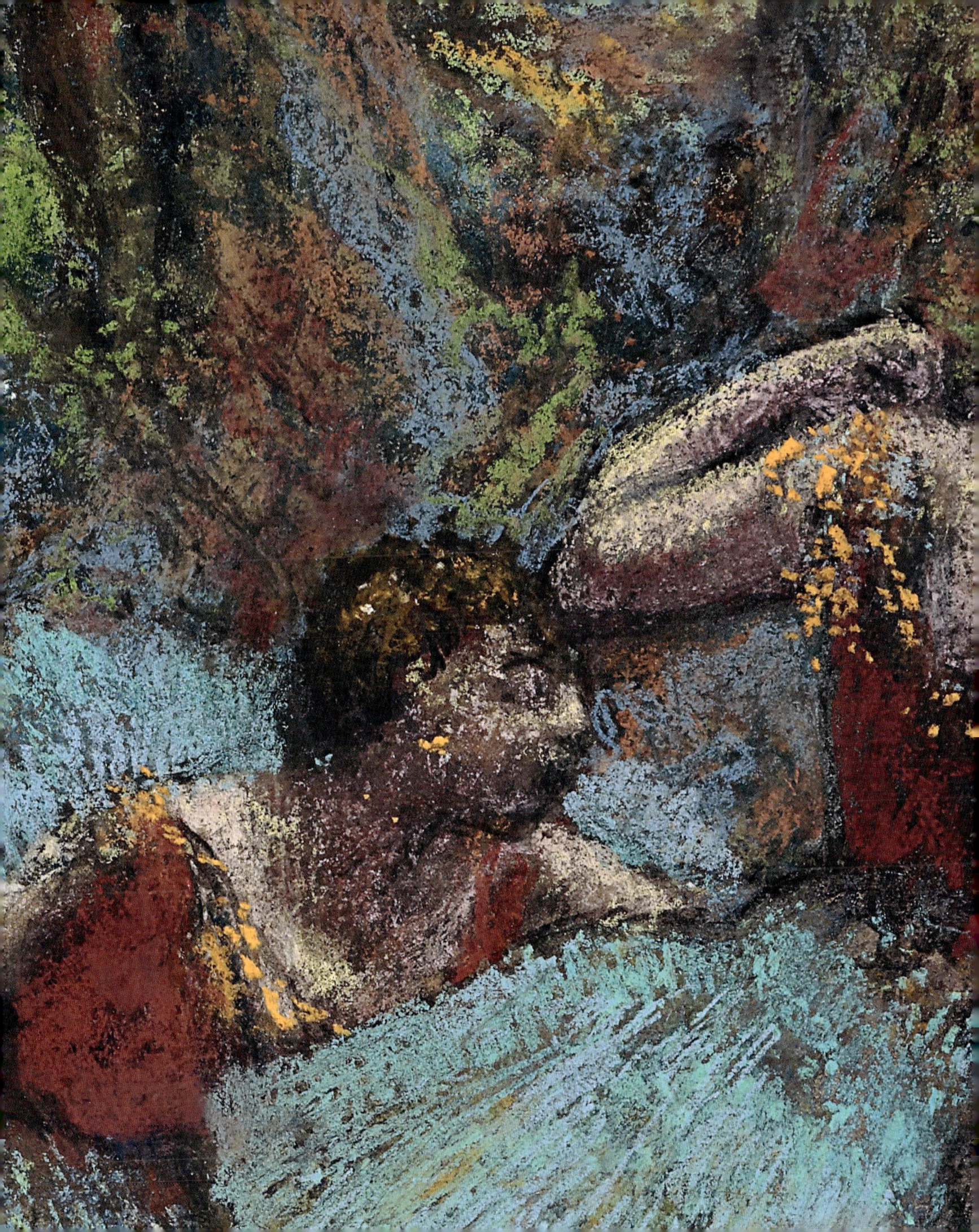

FOREWORD

The Impressionists are known as painters of modern life, a reputation they owe primarily to their depictions of Paris. We are lucky enough to have one of the finest examples of an Impressionist Paris cityscape, *Quai du Louvre* by Claude Monet, in the collection of the Kunstmuseum Den Haag. The painting is not only one of the highlights of our collection, but it also marks a pivotal moment in art history. It is one of three cityscapes that Monet painted from the balcony of the Louvre in 1867. Thanks to a unique partnership with the Alte Nationalgalerie in Berlin and the Allen Memorial Art Museum at Oberlin College, Ohio, the Kunstmuseum is reuniting these three remarkable paintings. As a young artist, Monet turned his back on the hallowed old masters in the Louvre, choosing instead to paint modern life on the streets. For this reason, art historian Linda Nochlin character-ised his three cityscapes as a true turning point in history. With this gesture, Monet settled his dues with the museum – and the stuffy past this institution stood for – and focused entirely on the future.

From the balcony, Monet looked out over a transformed city. Much of medieval Paris had been demolished to make way for new boulevards, squares and apartment buildings. Parks brought nature to the city, and theatres made the new Paris a cultural centre. This was the Paris we know and admire today. But progress had a downside. Modernisation also meant housing shortages, the expulsion of the poor and the exploit-ation of migrant workers: a harrowing process that we now term gentrification. Today's challenge of making cities liveable for everyone has many similarities with the Paris of the French Impressionists. Perhaps by reflecting on the past, the museum can use this exhibition to contribute to making better decisions for the future.

An exhibition as ambitious as *New Paris: From Monet to Morisot* could not have been realised without the tireless support and dedication of all involved. First, I would like to thank Andria Derstine, director of the Allen Memorial Art Museum, and Ralph Gleis, new director of the Albertina Museum in Vienna and former director of the Alte Nationalgalerie, for their positive response to the Kunstmuseum's proposal to reunite Monet's three cityscapes. In addition, I am grateful to all the museums, libraries, archives and collectors for their generosity in lending their precious artworks. Their exception-al loans have made their way to The Hague thanks to the indemnity granted by the Cultural Heritage Agency of the Netherlands. The same generosity has been shown by our sponsors. I would like to express my sincere thanks to the Turing Foundation, the Cultuurfonds, the Stichting Zabawas and the Gravin van Bylandt Stichting for their financial support of this project.

I would like to thank Tim Bisschop for the design of this beautiful book, and the team at Hannibal Books for its editing and production. And I am grateful to the authors Alexander Eiling, Judit Geskó, Kimberly A. Jones, Daniel Koep, Vera Merks, Paul Perrin, Michael Philipp and Joke de Wolf for their excellent contributions. In the Kunstmuseum's galleries, their stories are given wonderful form thanks to the design of Roland Buschmann. In addition, I express my gratitude to Gerard Forde for his excellent translations. Finally, I would like to thank Frouke van Dijke, curator of this exhibition, and all my colleagues at the Kunstmuseum for their enthusiasm and dedication.

Margriet Schavemaker
General director
Kunstmuseum Den Haag

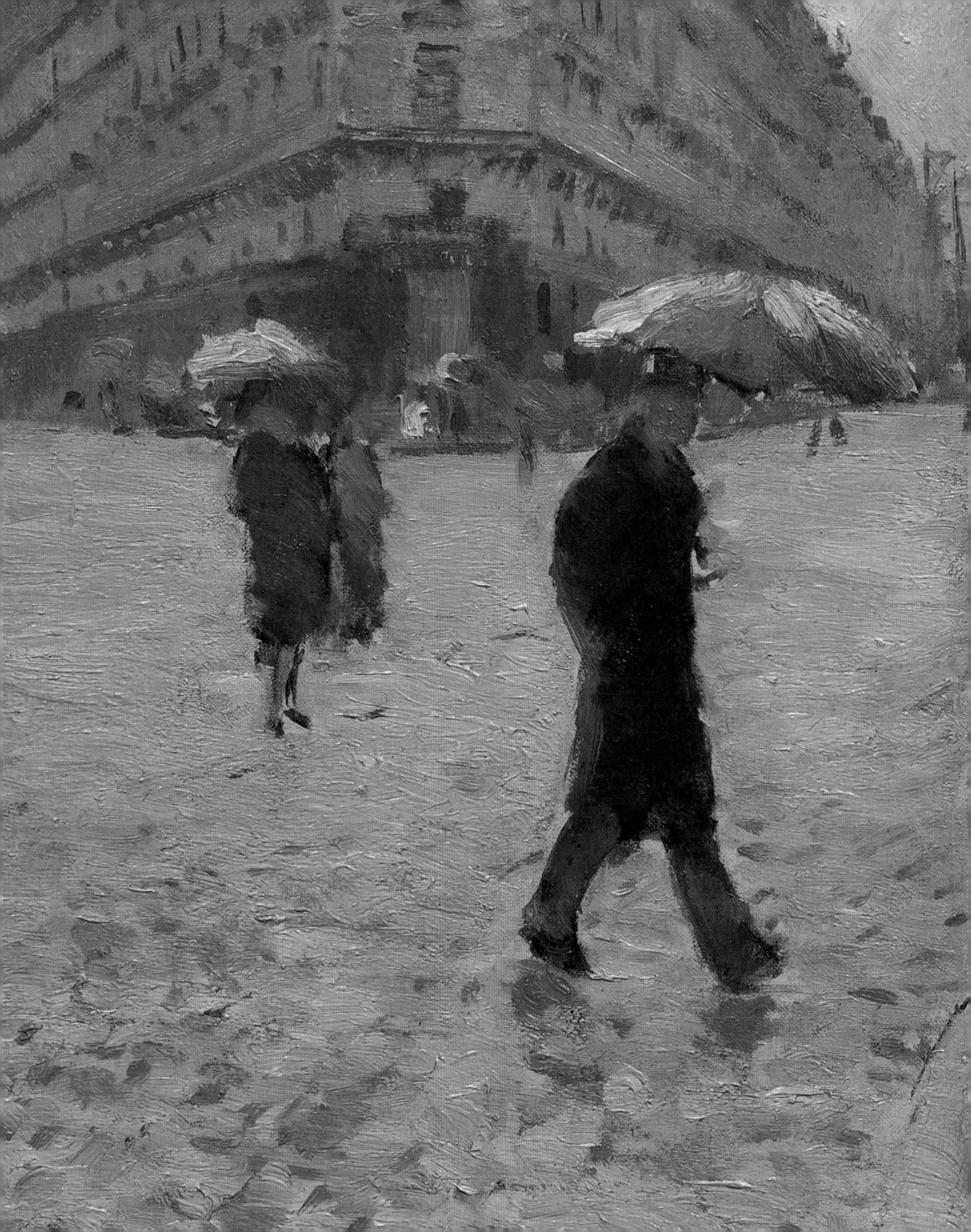

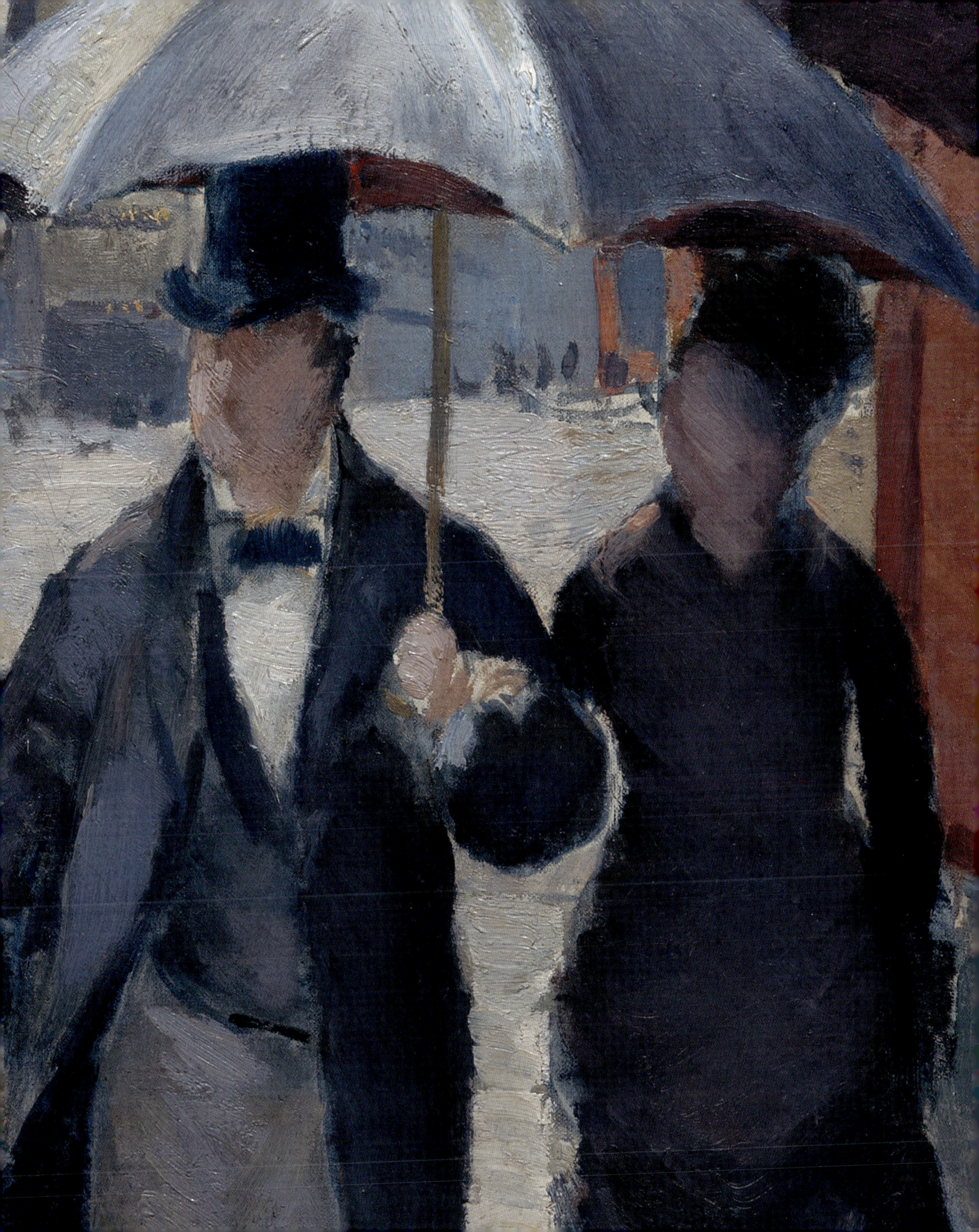

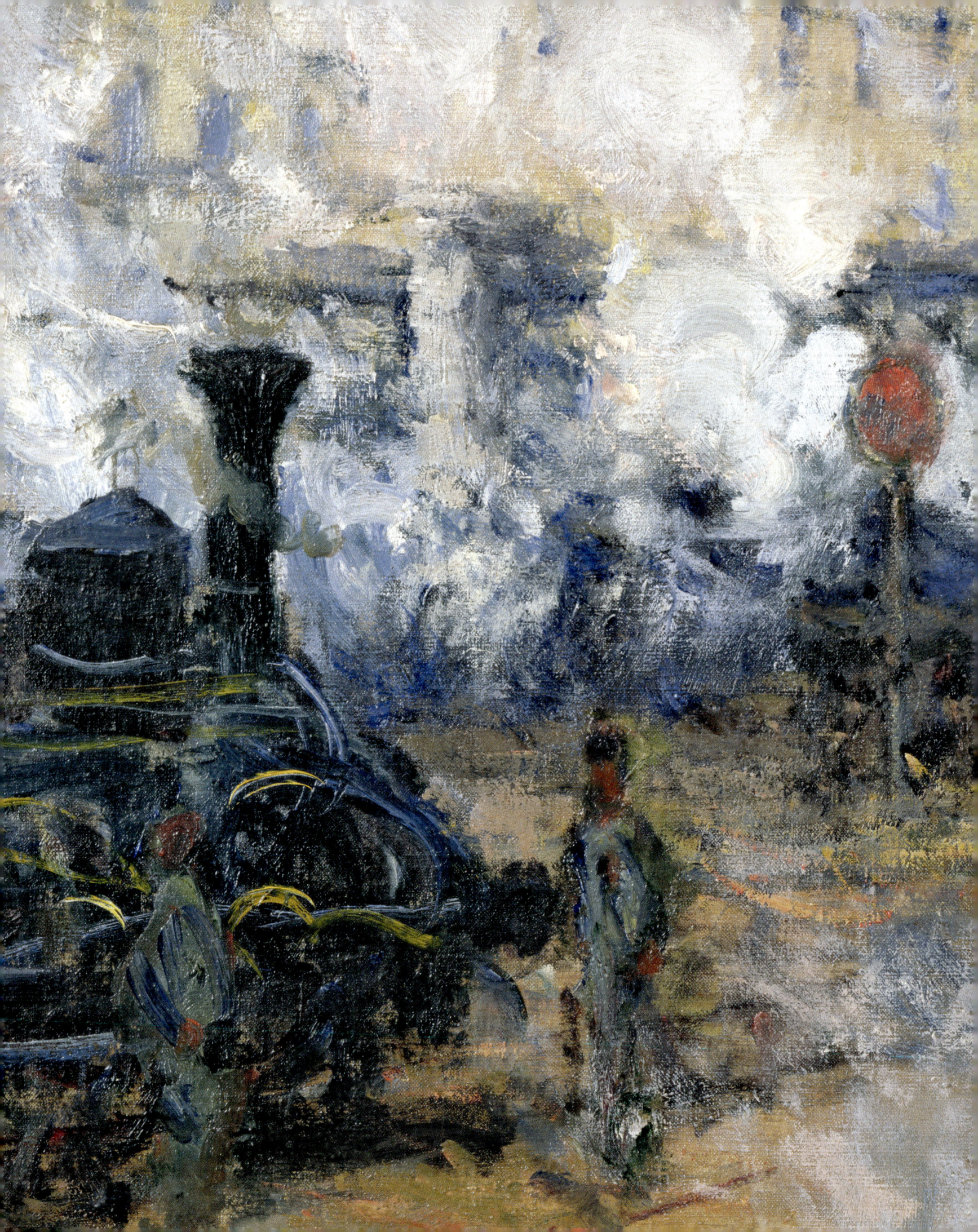

THE MYTH OF PARIS

Frouke van Dijke

Paris is the city of contrasts – heaven and hell, mansions and basement dwellings – the city of great lives and menial jobs.[1]

Edmond Texier, 'Les petites industries', in *Paris guide*, 1867

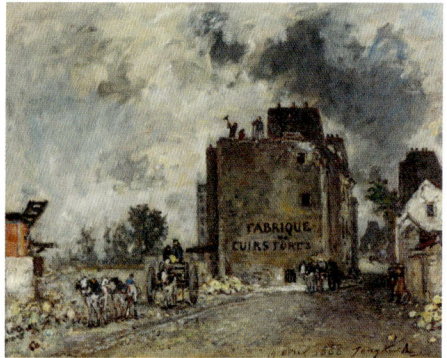

Fig. 1   [p. 59]

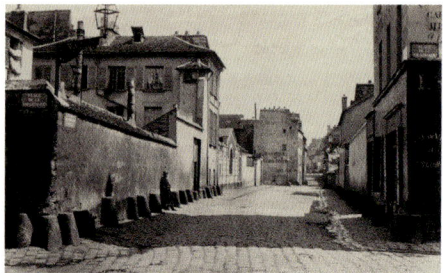

Fig. 2   [p. 58]

Fig. 1
Johan Barthold Jongkind (1819–1891), *Demolition of the Rue des Francs-Bourgeois-Saint-Marcel*, 1868

Oil on canvas, 33.9 × 41.9 cm, Kunstmuseum Den Haag. Acquired with the support of the Rembrandt Association

Fig. 2
Charles Marville (1813–1879), Rue des Francs-Bourgeois-Saint-Marcel, as seen from the Place de la Collégiale, 5th/13th arrondissement, Paris, 1865–68

Albumen print, 21.7 × 36.2 cm, Musée Carnavalet – Histoire de Paris

Silhouetted against a cloudy spring sky that threatens rain, on a rooftop on the former rue des Francs-Bourgeois-Saint-Marcel (now boulevard Saint-Marcel) on the Left Bank, a group of men with hammers and pickaxes are chipping away at a building, brick by brick. The painted sign 'Fabrique de cuirs forts' (Hard leather factory) is visible on the facade, which – like the rest of Paris – is being demolished at a steady pace. Below, more workmen are removing the rubble from the street by horse and cart [fig. 1].

The scene was recorded in 1868 by the Dutch painter Johan Barthold Jongkind. Six years earlier, he had met the talented 22-year-old Claude Monet in Normandy and had advised him to paint outdoors as much as possible, leading Monet later to point to the Dutchman as his mentor. Before the Impressionists depicted Paris, Jongkind was already walking through the streets of the French capital with his sketchbook. Moreover, his painting *Demolition of the Rue des Francs-Bourgeois-Saint-Marcel* foreshadows typical Impressionist features: Jongkind painted the scene quickly but accurately with loose brushstrokes and strong contrasts between light and dark. Alongside his signature, he inscribed the date – 19 April 1868 – thus creating not only a modern cityscape, but also a document of the times: a page from the visual diary of a city in transition.

The Impressionists met each other in Paris in the 1860s, the heyday of Haussmann's urban renewal. Tens of thousands of masons, roofers and carpenters were constructing not only new houses and streets, but also the myth of Paris: the city of light, beauty and romance. And the Impressionist painters also played their part. Their cityscapes depict a city where the facades glisten, the streets are swept, and the sun (almost) always shines. This was exactly the image Haussmann had in mind with his all-encompassing design for a new Paris. But the creation of all this beauty went hand in hand with exploitation and oppression. Haussmann may have given Paris a new visage, but it was a city with two faces.

A centre of civilisation

On 22 June 1852, Emperor Napoleon III made Georges-Eugène Haussmann prefect of the Seine department, giving him responsibility for the entire department, including the city of Paris. The appointment was linked to a clear mission: Napoleon III wanted a large-scale redevelopment of his capital. The emperor, who had until recently led the country as president, seized absolute power in 1851 through a coup d'état, enabling him to fulfil his childhood dream of following in the footsteps of his famous uncle, Napoleon Bonaparte. The establishment of the Second Empire was intended to restore not only the honour and glory of France, but also that of the Bonaparte lineage. And so, under the pretext of a civilising

offensive, Napoleon III colonised large parts of North Africa, Asia and South America, conquered trading posts and had the Suez Canal dug by thousands of forced labourers in order to secure control of the international market.[2] Amid this aggressive expansionism, the emperor focused his attention on Paris. The capital must fulfil its role as the symbolic centre of this new world power, or as Victor Hugo put it in 1867: 'Paris is the centre of civilisation.'[3]

These were rather grand words for a city that had for decades been choking on its own misery. In 1862, Haussmann reported that more than half of Parisians – about a million people – lived on bread rations. The city recorded the highest mortality rate in France, which continued to rise due to various epidemics.

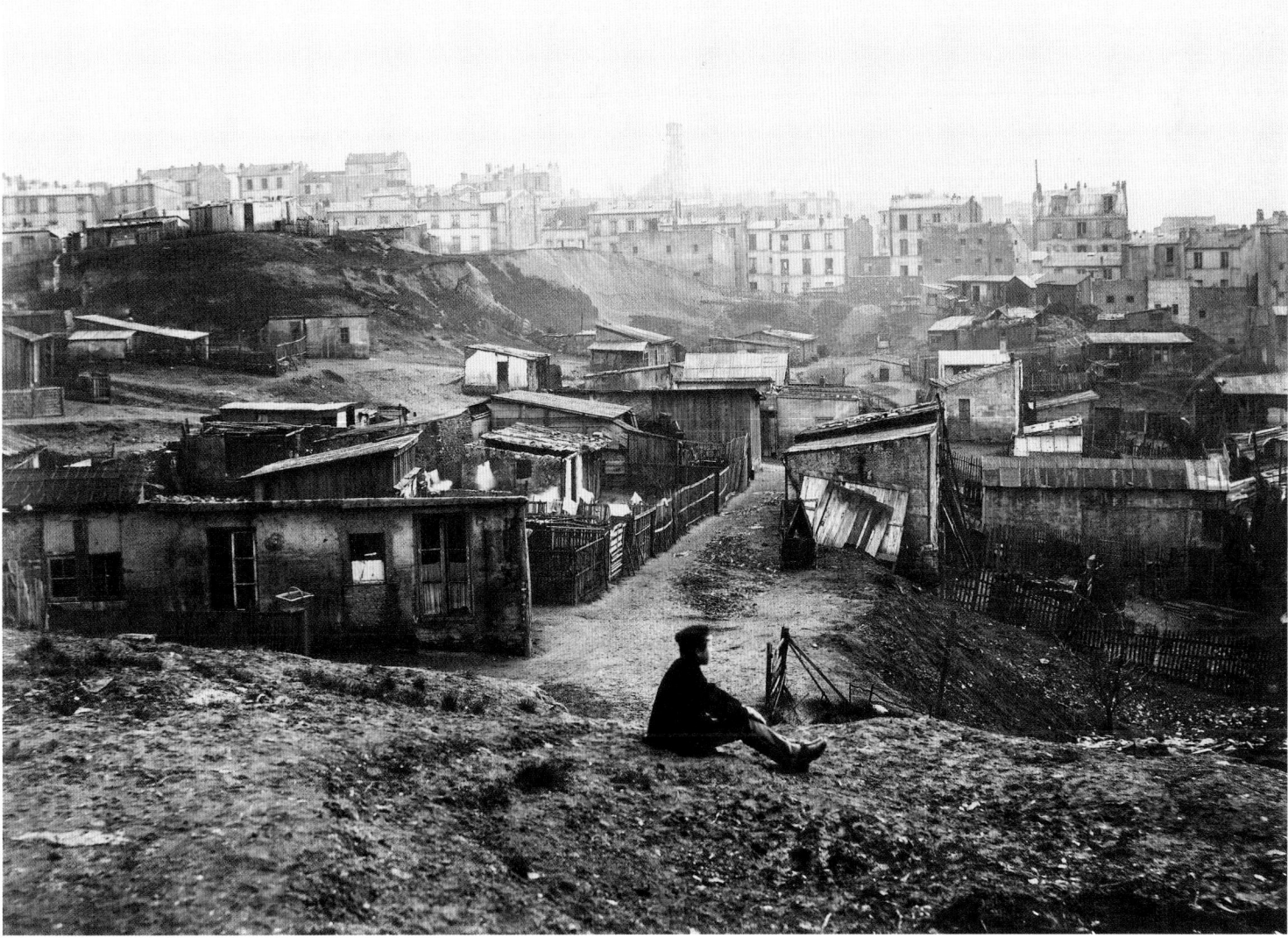

Fig. 3

Fig. 3
Charles Marville (1813–1879),
Top of the rue Champlain (view to the right) (20th arrondissement), 1877–78
Albumen silver print from glass negative,
26 × 36.6 cm, Musée Carnavalet – Histoire de Paris

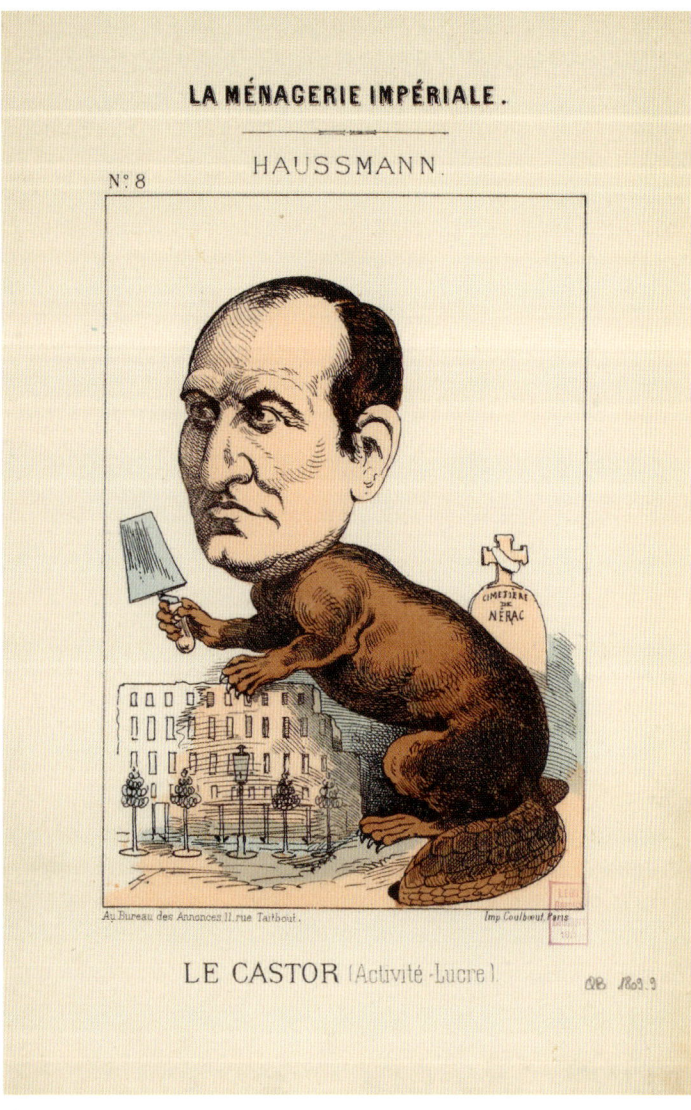

LA MÉNAGERIE IMPÉRIALE.

N° 8   HAUSSMANN.

Au Bureau des Annonces,11.rue Taitbout.   Imp.Coulbœuf,Paris

LE CASTOR (Activité -Lucre).   CB 1860.9

Fig. 4

Some 40,000 people had succumbed to cholera in the previous 20 years. The Seine was both a water supply and a sewer, a foul-smelling river full of excrement and food waste mixed with chemicals from the laundries located along its banks. The small island at its centre, the Île de la Cité, was home to 14,000 people, living in cramped conditions.[4] The city itself was like a patchwork of islands, the tangle of unplanned streets and alleyways so dense that the route from one arrondissement to another was like navigating a maze.

In this respect, Napoleon's vision of Paris cannot be dismissed as one man's megalomaniac project. Indeed, the emperor was not the first to devote himself to transforming the city. Since the Enlightenment, philosophers had regarded the pitiful city as a utopian experiment: a testing ground where well-considered reorganisation could result in a better society. But it was Haussmann who translated these ideas into a grand, comprehensive and strategic plan, implemented at breakneck speed.

Throughout Paris the sound was heard of shovels breaking ground and chisels against brick. Haussmann built houses, schools and hospitals, police stations and fire stations, covered markets and department stores, and laid out squares and parks. Thanks to the wide streets, daylight and oxygen finally streamed in through the windows. Gas lamps and the first experiments with electric lights brought the excitement and thrill of nightlife. New theatres and museums made Paris a centre of culture. Haussmann untangled the city and drew a clear street plan with wide boulevards that cut their way straight through the centre. In all these respects, his eye for detail was unparalleled, ensuring, for example, that the population density – the highest in Europe – was almost the same in each district. The maximum height of buildings, the corresponding proportions of windows and doors and the design of lampposts, newspaper kiosks, benches and even the gutters: everything was a carefully considered component in Haussmann's city as *gesamtkunstwerk*.

This radical transformation garnered praise from some quarters, but also created unrest among Parisians, who no longer recognised their familiar surroundings. Cartoons depicted Haussmann as an overly destructive beaver who left no corner of the city untouched [fig. 4]. Viewed from above the city, the sight evoked a feeling of powerlessness in the photographer and balloonist Nadar: 'These rascals have destroyed, ransacked everything in our country, even the memory.... And, old Parisians... awake each morning like the traveller who arrived yesterday in a foreign city...'[5] By the time Victor Hugo somewhat pompously described Paris as the centre of civilisation, Haussmann had indeed skilfully erased any memory of the city's history of poverty and disease. The great clean-up was complete and with the Universal Exposition of 1867 Napoleon III invited the world to his house-warming party. Visitors were able to inspect every nook and cranny of the new Paris, whether looking down from Nadar's hot-air balloon or on a spectacular tour of the sewer system deep beneath the newly paved streets.[6]

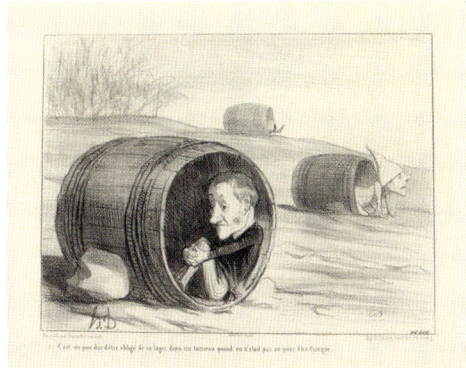

Fig. 5 [p. 67]

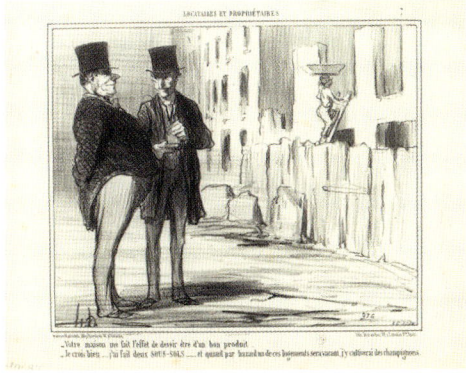

Fig. 6 [p. 66]

Fig. 4
Louis Valentin Émile de La Tremblais (1821–1892),
Haussmann/The Beaver (Profitmaking Activity)
In: Paul Haldol (1835–1875), *La Menagerie Imperiale*, 1870–71,
Bibliothèque nationale de France

Fig. 5
Honoré Daumier (1808–1879), From the
series *Tenants and Owners*: 'It's a bit hard
to be obliged to live in a barrel when
one wasn't born to be a cynic', 1854
Lithograph, 27.6 × 35 cm, Musée Carnavalet – Histoire de Paris

Fig. 6
Honoré Daumier (1808–1879), From the series
Tenants and Owners: 'Your house seems
to me to be a good product. – I think so...
I made two basements... and when by chance
one of these accommodations is vacant,
I will grow mushrooms there', 1856
Lithograph, 27.1 × 35.8 cm, Musée Carnavalet – Histoire de Paris

Urban colonisation

The Universal Exposition was not only the city's calling card but also a celebration of industry, where France and foreign nations exhibited their latest inventions and feats of technology. Industrialisation was the catalyst for the new Paris, the engine behind the growing population and the newly acquired wealth of the bourgeoisie. While this elite of industrialists, engineers, bankers and stockbrokers may have lacked noble titles, they certainly had no shortage of money or leisure time. They were a new type of city dweller with new needs, their lives revolving around consumption: imbibing culture in the theatres, eating in restaurants, drinking in bars and nightclubs, and shopping for the latest fashions in department stores. They were the proprietors of Haussmann's Paris, which was designed largely to cater to their lifestyle.

All this was at the expense of the other half, or perhaps the majority, of Parisians: the lower middle classes, the workers, the immigrants. Their homes were demolished and the new apartments built in their place were unaffordable. The 14,000 people on the Île de la Cité were forced to move out. Although Haussmann was concerned with the aesthetics of his city down to the smallest detail, he left the actual construction to the free market. This led to large-scale expropriation and speculation, with slum neighbourhoods bought up, gentrified and sold again at exorbitant prices.[7] Savvy entrepreneurs took their chances. The main character of Émile Zola's novel *The Kill* (1872) is one such speculator, the wily Saccard, who works his way up through the world of real estate via a combination of insider knowledge and bluff. The game had few winners and many losers. In her book *Dividing Paris* (2022), Esther da Costa Meyer characterises the gentrification process as nothing less than a 'brutal act of colonization' of the city.[8] Much of the city's original population was forced to leave, and previously autonomous surrounding villages such as Batignolles, Montmartre and Montparnasse were annexed in 1860, an administrative intervention that in some cases split existing communities in two.[9] The new suburbs now had to pay taxes to Paris. These were partly invested in the beautification of the city centre, in return for which these neighbourhoods received the poor who were driven from the heart of the city and had to suffer the stench of the tanneries and the pollution of the match factories, crucial industries that the inhabitants of the city centre would rather be rid of.

Why expel these labourers 'after making them contribute generously to the embellishments of the city of Paris for 20 years', a group of workers asked themselves in 1867 in a report on various trades in France, published on the occasion of the Universal Exposition.[10] They felt neither nostalgia for the old Paris nor love for the new: 'We do not regret those sordid old homes, poorly lit and unhealthy.... But neither do we like these splendid buildings where the stairs are polished, and the corridors are of stucco: where the bourgeois of the third floor no longer sees the oeuvrier [worker] go by in his working clothes.'[11]

In Haussmann's apartment buildings, different classes lived alongside each other with as little contact as possible. In most cases, the ground floor was intended for shops or employees. The floors above were occupied by the bourgeoisie. The longest climb was, of course, reserved for the poorest residents. The *sixièmes* (sixth-floor rooms) were small, uncomfortable spaces directly under the roof that were freezing cold in winter and boiling hot in summer. Some people made the best of it. For example, a handyman from Montparnasse reported that the residents on the uppermost floors of several adjoining buildings had demolished the walls between them, creating a kind of alley. There, high above Haussmann's street plan, they had created a parallel Paris that met *their* needs.[12]

Art and class

The cartoonist Bertall took a slice through an apartment building to illustrate a cross-section of Parisian society [fig. 7]. His drawing shows the contrast between the comfortably furnished homes of the middle classes and the bare rooms on the top floor, where Bertall depicts a poor couple who cannot feed their children, a poet sheltering from a leaking roof and... two penniless artists.

The Impressionists found themselves in a very particular position, navigating between the different classes in a way that few other Parisians could, with one foot in the elite salon and the other in cafés in the working-class neighbourhoods where they could find affordable spaces to live and work. To keep costs down, Monet, perennially short of money but always immaculately dressed, shared a studio with his friends Frédéric Bazille and Auguste Renoir. Most of the Impressionist artists were born into bourgeois families that were either comfortably off or even extravagantly wealthy. Some no longer received financial support from their families because of their unconventional career choice, while others, such as Gustave Caillebotte, Edgar Degas and Berthe Morisot, were able to hold on to their avant-garde ideals thanks to their well-to-do backgrounds.

The Impressionists were not blind to the city's social divisions. In 1863, the wealthy Bazille was surprised at 'how the people living in smart neighbourhoods are crassly ignorant of everything except the races and the theatre'.[13] Not long thereafter, he made a large painting of an Italian street musician [fig. 8]. Her age is difficult to estimate since her face has both childlike and adult features. With a violin in her hand, she stands at the intersection of two streets, with the city looming behind her squat figure. Around the same time, Auguste Renoir also painted a monumental portrait of a violin-playing artiste, in this case a clown, probably from the popular Cirque Napoléon [fig. 9]. Both artists took their example from Édouard Manet, who in the 1860s was mainly interested in figures on the fringes of society: rag-pickers, street vendors and vagabonds, who for centuries had defined the city's streetscape. But Haussmann's attention was focused largely on the new elite and soon the Impressionists' interests shifted along with it, resulting in numerous depictions of horse racing and the theatre.

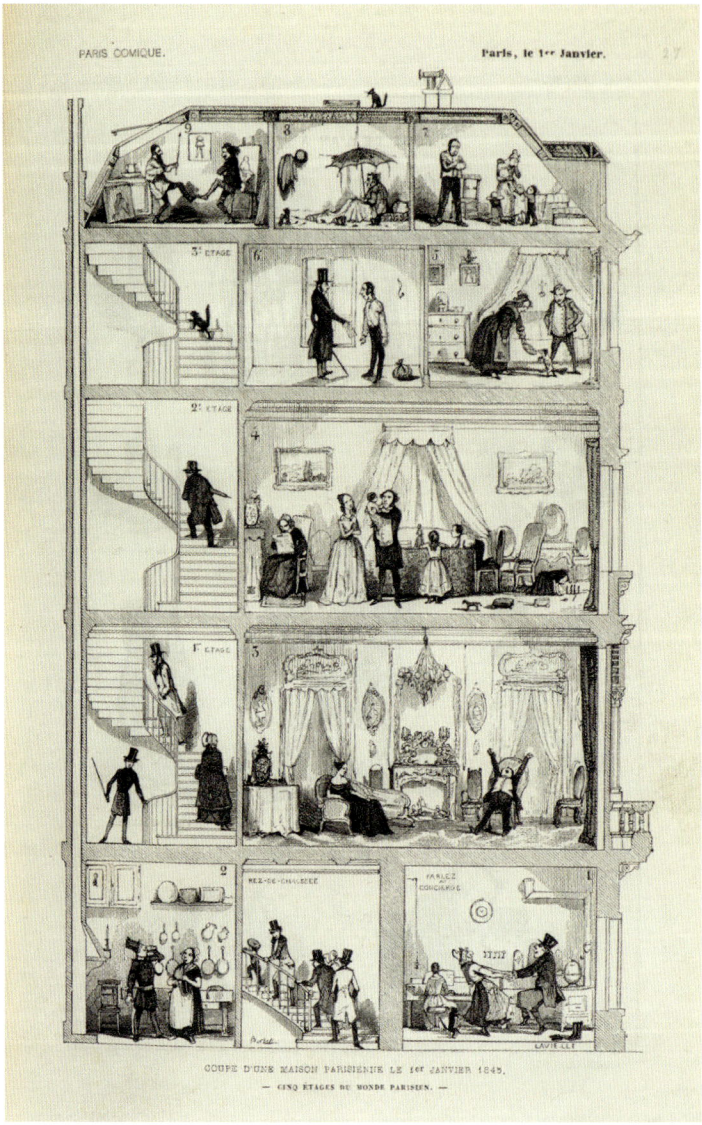

Fig. 7

Fig. 7
Bertall (1820–1882), Section of a Parisian house on 1 January 1845 – five floors of the Parisian world
In: George Sand et al., *Le Diable à Paris, Paris et les Parisiens*, Paris, 1845

Fig. 8
Frédéric Bazille (1841–1870), *Little Italian Street Singer*, 1866
Oil on canvas, 131 × 98 cm, Musée Fabre de Montpellier

Fig. 9
Auguste Renoir (1841–1919), *The Clown*, 1868
Oil on canvas, 193.5 × 130 cm, Kröller-Müller Museum, Otterlo

Fig. 10
Édouard Manet (1832–1883), *A Game of Croquet*, 1873
Oil on canvas, 72.5 × 106 cm, Städel Museum, Frankfurt am Main, property of the Städelscher Museums-Verein e.V.

Fig. 11
Claude Monet (1840–1926), *The Tuileries*, 1876
Oil on canvas, 54 × 73 cm, Musée Marmottan Monet, Paris, Gift of Eugène and Victorine Donop de Monchy, 1940

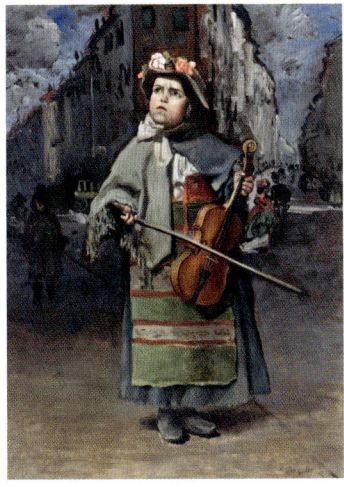

Fig. 8 [p. 64]

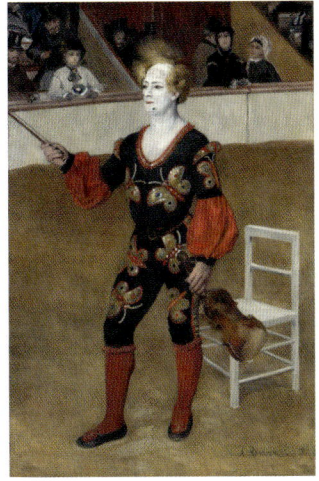

Fig. 9 [p. 65]

greening of public spaces.[17] Nothing was too extravagant for the emperor: artificial waterfalls and ponds, rock formations, and an army of botanists who forced thousands of exotic plants into the French soil with great skill and ingenuity. These public parks were popular with the Impressionists. Caillebotte and Monet, who both loved gardening, returned time and again to the flower beds of Parc Monceau, established by the Duke of Chartres.

In 1876, Monet captured the enviable view from the fifth-floor apartment of the art collector Victor Chocquet, looking out over the garden of the old Tuileries Palace [fig. 11]. This now public park had formerly been open to the public only a few days a year. But the *pièce de résistance* of Parisian parks was the Bois de Boulogne, a grand former hunting ground in the wealthy west of the city, where the bourgeoisie gathered to walk, ride horses and network. It was a favourite subject of Morisot, who lived only a stone's throw away.

The right to saunter

It was no coincidence that the Impressionists' careers began in Paris. In addition to access to the best art training and exhibition opportunities, the city provided abundant inspiration. The early cityscapes of Manet, Monet and Renoir are linked to the vision of Charles Baudelaire, the poet who had a love-hate relationship with Paris. Baudelaire saw the city as the modern landscape and believed that the artist should respond to it. The Industrial Revolution had replaced the cliffs with apartment blocks and the forests and meadows with urban parks. For Baudelaire, modern art was about capturing the 'transient' and the 'fleeting'. And what environment embodied this phenomenon better than the ever-changing streets of Paris?[14] Sauntering was the essence. The arrival of pavements and attractive shop windows radically altered the use of public space. Whereas the elite once ventured out only by horse and carriage – and commoners on foot – strolling had become a popular activity among the middle classes.[15] Baudelaire characterised the painter of modern life as a *flâneur*: a figure who wanders aimlessly through the streets, without a mapped-out route or predetermined plan, with the sole purpose of absorbing the city's impressions.

The Impressionists observed urban life on café terraces and in the theatre. They painted picnics and boat trips: the leisure activities of the rich middle classes, to which they belonged. This is exemplified in *A Game of Croquet* [fig. 10] in which Manet has depicted his friends playing the popular ball game in the garden of the Belgian painter Alfred Stevens. He had bought a stately house on rue des Martyrs, equipped with an English landscaped garden. He lived there for only for a few years, because his house too was eventually demolished. 'Behind every house there was a garden,' Renoir later recalled bitterly about the lost Paris.[16] His house on place du Carrousel was demolished to make way for the expansion of the Louvre.

Renoir's resentment is somewhat misplaced. A private garden in Paris was an exception. Moreover, the city's parks were privately owned. Napoleon III was aware of the value of nature in the city, also for the working classes. One of the most important nineteenth-century urban interventions in the capital was the

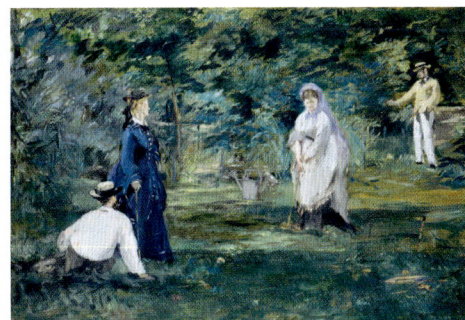

Fig. 10 [p. 45]

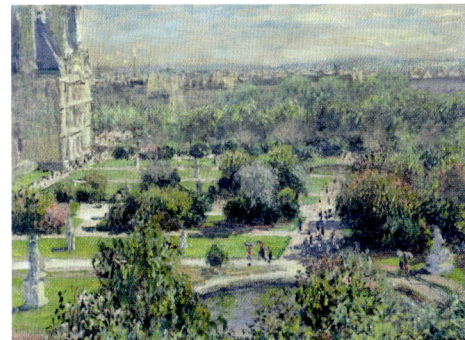

Fig. 11 [p. 197]

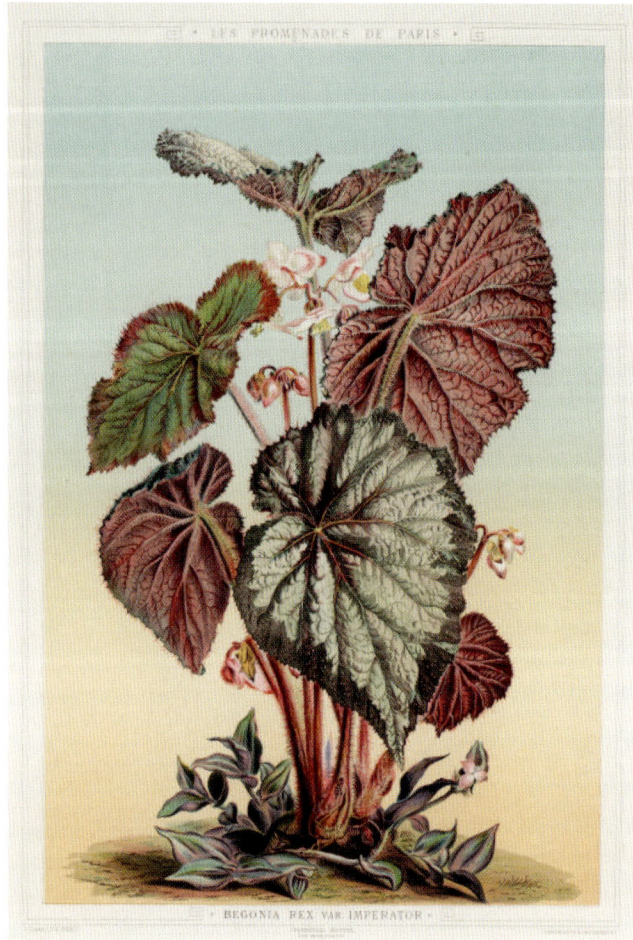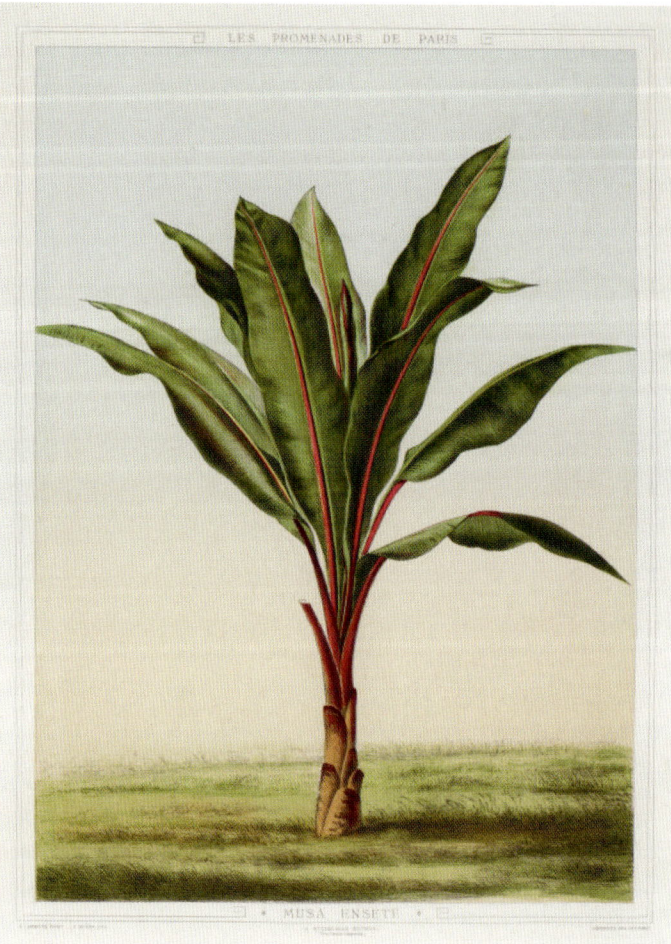

Fig. 12

Fig. 12
Two prints depicting the plants
of the Bois de Boulogne
From: Adolphe Alphand, *Les Promenades de Paris*, 1867–73,
Lithograph, 45 × 63 cm, Kunstmuseum Den Haag

Fig. 13
Claude Monet (1840–1926),
The Pont de l'Europe. Gare Saint-Lazare, 1877
Oil on canvas, 65 × 81 cm, Gift of Eugène and Victorine
Donop de Monchy, 1940, Musée Marmottan Monet, Paris

Fig. 14
Gustave Caillebotte (1848–1894),
Paris Street. Rainy Day, 1877
Oil on canvas, 54 × 65 cm, Musée Marmottan
Monet, Paris, Michel Monet bequest, 1966

The public urban park is a fascinating phenomenon. Here a mixing of classes took place that led to some nervousness among the elite. In her article 'La rêverie à Paris' (1867), George Sand made a case for the importance of daydreaming, regardless of rank or position. She praised Paris as the capital of the *flâneur*, mainly thanks to its parks. Here the landscape stimulates the imagination. Under the motto 'luxury for everyone!', Sand declares sauntering (one's head full of creativity and free from worries) as a basic right.[18] Despite Napoleon III's progressive point of departure, Paris showed little eagerness when it came to the democratisation of these urban oases. High fences and the enforcement of regulations were designed to keep out and demotivate the unwanted stroller. The Bois de Boulogne was difficult to reach on foot, while the omnibus was more expensive on Sundays – the only day off for workers – than on weekdays. Workers did not saunter, they walked, every day and for hours, from the suburbs to the city centre because the horse-drawn tram was too expensive, or its timetable did not correspond with their working hours.[19]

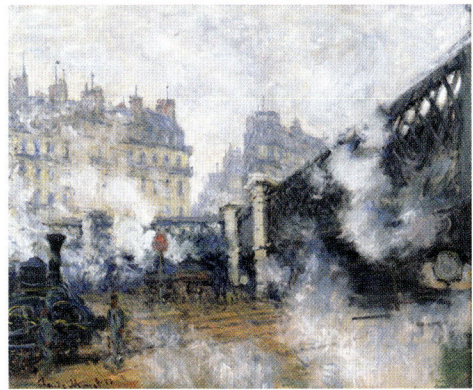

Fig. 13 [p. 95]

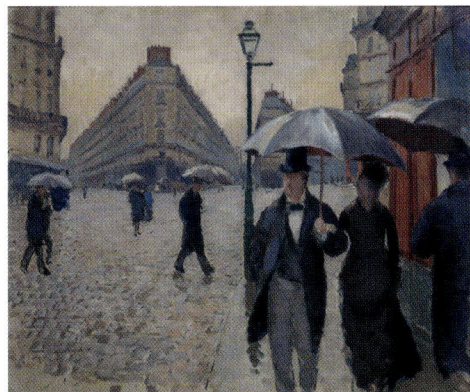

Fig. 14 [pp. 134–135]

Sand praises the hardworking gardeners who maintained the beauty of the Bois de Boulogne, but forgets the foreign labourers who helped to shape Paris's parks. She compares her visit to the greenhouses full of exotic flowers, agaves and banana trees to a tale from *The Thousand and One Nights*. The flora came partly from French colonies such as Algeria, where botanical gardens provided a supply of plants and animals. The Parisian park was thus part of the emperor's colonial ambition. The message was clear: everything exotic can be tamed thanks to superior French engineering.[20] Even Sand, a woman with radically progressive ideals for her time, was trapped in this colonial perspective when she expressed her admiration for the 'tropical forms' of the Bois de Boulogne, for which courageous French naturalists had braved 'distant worlds' and the 'harmful appetite of wild animals and native cannibals, some of whom are fond of white flesh in tomato sauce'.[21]

Embracing the new Paris

The desire for nature was fuelled by the rise of industry. While Haussmann kept the city centre as free as possible from factories, the railways symbolised progress and modernity. In the *Paris guide* of 1867, Léon Say describes the railway stations as the real gateways to Paris, while not hiding his disdain for the working class: 'The other [gateways] are only service entrances for market gardeners, quarrymen, for a few backward messengers.'[22] Particularly in the 8th arrondissement, around Gare Saint-Lazare, the Impressionists celebrated the new world of steel, steam and cast iron as the visual language of the future.

Initially, the young Impressionists preferred to stroll around the old and familiar Paris. Renoir in particular was less than charmed by the uniformity of Haussmann's new edifices, complaining that the multiplicity of the city's striking buildings had been exchanged for one and the same facade: 'cold and lined up like soldiers at a review'.[23] Most of Monet and Renoir's early cityscapes depict locations around the Pont Neuf, despite its name the oldest bridge in Paris. When Monet painted three different views from the balcony of the Louvre in 1867, he focused on several historic monuments that Haussmann had spared from demolition. But the new Paris eventually seduced the Impressionists. Monet painted a series of views near the railway tracks of Gare Saint-Lazare with the modern lattice pattern of the cast-iron Pont de l'Europe prominently featured [fig. 13]. The master of capturing an atmosphere was clearly drawn to this peculiar mix of heavy metal and immaterial clouds of steam. Even more than Monet, the lesser-known Impressionist Armand Guillaumin considered this area his home. Unlike his colleagues, Guillaumin came from humble origins. He worked as a ticket seller for the railways, and later in the department of bridges and hydraulic engineering at the city hall.[24] His paintings, depicting industrial activity along the Seine, including smoking factory chimneys and cranes, fitted seamlessly with his background.

But no one embraced Haussmann's Paris more warmly than Caillebotte. As one of the youngest and richest of the Impressionists, he embodied the bourgeois, moving in the highest circles regardless of his artistic ambitions. In 1877, he painted the work *Paris Street. Rainy Day* [fig. 14], a departure from the

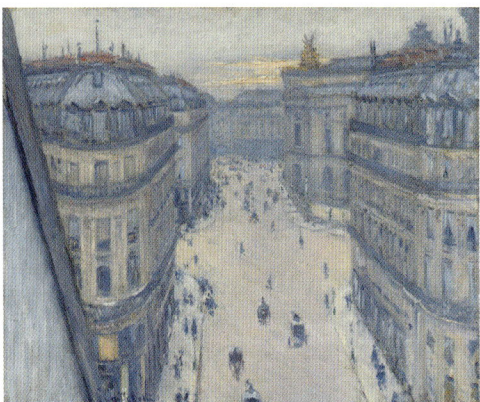

Fig. 15   [pp. 38–39]

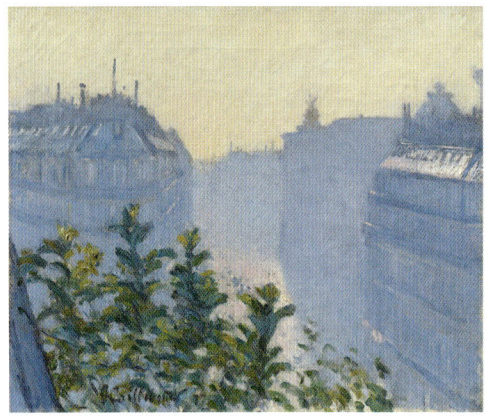

Fig. 16   [p. 37]

usual sunny Impressionist views of the city.²⁵ Caillebotte does not specify the exact intersection, so recently constructed it did not yet bear a name. We now know it to be the area around the place de l'Europe but, above all, Caillebotte's cityscape symbolises every new, identical-looking street in Paris.²⁶ Shortly afterwards, he moved with his brother to a luxury apartment on boulevard Haussmann, named after the prefect himself. From their balcony, he painted several views of the city's new skyline, including the gleaming gold sculptures on the facade of the new Opéra Garnier [figs. 15–16].

Caillebotte was fond of playful perspectives, giving the Impressionist cityscape a new dimension. His painting *View Seen Through a Balcony* (1880) provides the merest glimpse of the street scene, viewed through the decorative metalwork of a typical Haussmannian balcony [fig. 17]. This point of view reflects Caillebotte's interest in modern photography, his background as an engineer and his social origins. Caillebotte, Monet, Renoir and Pissarro often painted their views of Paris from a comfortable apartment, either their own or one made available to them by one of their hospitable clients. This choice was, of course, partly based on practical considerations: an interior or a balcony offered the opportunity to work in peace. Moreover, painting on the street sometimes required a permit. But the bird's-eye view is also the perspective of the bourgeois, who sees and experiences Paris from the vantage point of his own class. For them, the myth of Paris was often a reality.

This does not mean that the Impressionists were blind to the other side of Paris. Caillebotte painted not only views from bourgeois apartments, but also shirtless men on their knees scraping a parquet floor. Degas depicted the strong upper arms of women starching businessmen's white collars. But they are exceptions to the rule. Some art historians have accused the Impressionists of being complicit in the gentrification of Paris through their sunny and therefore promotional images of Haussmann's city. But the ideas of the emperor and the prefect also stemmed largely from good intentions: necessary reforms, whose execution sadly was dominated by the needs, interests and taste of the rich. The temptation of their Paris was too great, the myth too enchanting.

Fig. 15
Gustave Caillebotte (1848–1894),
Rue Halévy, View from the Sixth Floor, 1878
Oil on canvas, 59.5 × 73 cm, Museum Barberini, Potsdam

Fig. 16
Gustave Caillebotte (1848–1894),
Rue Halévy, View from the Balcony, 1877
Oil on canvas, 54 × 65.5 cm, Museum Barberini, Potsdam

Fig. 17
Gustave Caillebotte (1848–1894),
View Seen Through a Balcony, 1880
Oil on canvas, 65.6 × 54.9 cm, Van Gogh Museum, Amsterdam.
Purchased with support from the VriendenLoterij, the Vincent
van Gogh Foundation, the Mondriaan Fund, the Rembrandt
Association, thanks in part to the Culture Fund, and the VSB Fund

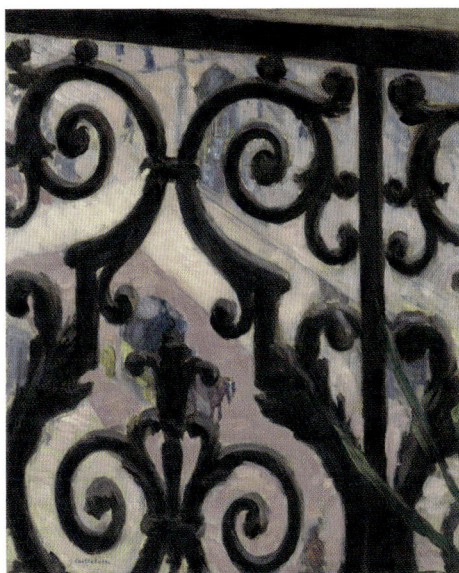

Fig. 17 [p. 34]

1 Edmond Texier, 'Les petites industries' in *Paris guide par les principaux écrivains et artistes de la France*, vol. 2 (Paris, 1867), p. 963.

2 Emmanuelle Guenot, 'Napoleon III and France's Colonial Expansion: National Grandeur, Territorial Conquests and Colonial Embellishment 1852–70', in Robert Aldrich and Cindy McCreery (eds.), *Crowns and Colonies: European Monarchies and Overseas Empires* (Manchester, 2016), pp. 211–220.

3 Victor Hugo, 'Introduction', in *Paris guide par les principaux écrivains et artistes de la France*, vol. 1 (Paris, 1867), p. XIX.

4 David H. Pinkney, *Napoleon III and the Rebuilding of Paris* (Princeton, NJ, 1972), pp. 87–88.

5 Nadar, *Sous l'incendie* (Paris, 1882), p. 5. This text is almost universally misquoted in the literature on nineteenth-century Paris.

6 Esther da Costa Meyer, *Dividing Paris: Urban Renewal and Social Inequality, 1852–1870* (Princeton, NJ, 2022), p. 194.

7 Da Costa Meyer 2022 (note 6), p. 2.

8 Da Costa Meyer 2022 (note 6), p. 305. For her explanation see p. 298, 305–306.

9 Da Costa Meyer 2022 (note 6), p. 305. For her explanation see p. 298, 305–306.

10 Da Costa Meyer 2022 (note 6), p. 284.

11 Da Costa Meyer 2022 (note 6), p. 284.

12 Leslie Page Moch and Rachel G. Fuchs, 'Getting Along: Poor Women's Networks in Nineteenth-Century Paris', in *French Historical Studies*, vol. 18, no. 1 (spring 1993), p. 43.

13 Jean-Claude Yon, 'Self-Portrait as a Theater-Goer: Bazille and Show Business in Paris Based on His Letters', in Michel Hilaire and Paul Perrin (eds.), *Frédéric Bazille and the Birth of Impressionism*, exh. cat. Musée Fabre (Montpellier, 2016), p. 64.

14 Charles Baudelaire, *Œuvres complètes de Charles Baudelaire: III, L'art romantique* (Paris, 1885), p. 68.

15 Priscilla Parkhurst Ferguson, Paris as Revolution: *Writing the Nineteenth-Century City* (Berkeley, CA, 1994), p. 94.

16 Renoir quoted in Da Costa Meyer 2022 (note 6), p. 278.

17 Colta Ives, *Public Parks, Private Gardens: Paris to Provence*, exh. cat. New York (The Metropolitan Museum of Art), 2018.

18 George Sand, 'La rêverie à Paris', in *Paris guide* 1867 (note 1), p. 1202. For an analysis of Sand's article see: Gideon Fink Shapiro, *The Promenades of Paris: Alphand and the Urbanization of Garden Art, 1852–1871*, PhD dissertation, University of Pennsylvania, 2015, p. 73.

19 Da Costa Meyer 2022 (note 6), p. 244, 317.

20 Da Costa Meyer 2022 (note 6), p. 240.

21 Sand 1867 (note 18), p. 1200.

22 Léon Say, 'Les chemins de fer', in *Paris guide* 1867 (note 1), p. 1657.

23 Quoted in James H. Rubin, *Impressionism and the Modern Landscape: Productivity, Technology and Urbanization from Manet to Van Gogh* (Berkeley, Los Angeles & London, 2008), p. 34.

24 Rubin 2008 (note 23), p. 70.

25 An oil study of this painting can be found in Musée Marmottan Monet, Paris.

26 Gloria Groom and Kelly Keegan, *Caillebotte Paintings and Drawings at the Art Institute of Chicago*, digital catalogue (Art Institute of Chicago), 2015, p. 3.

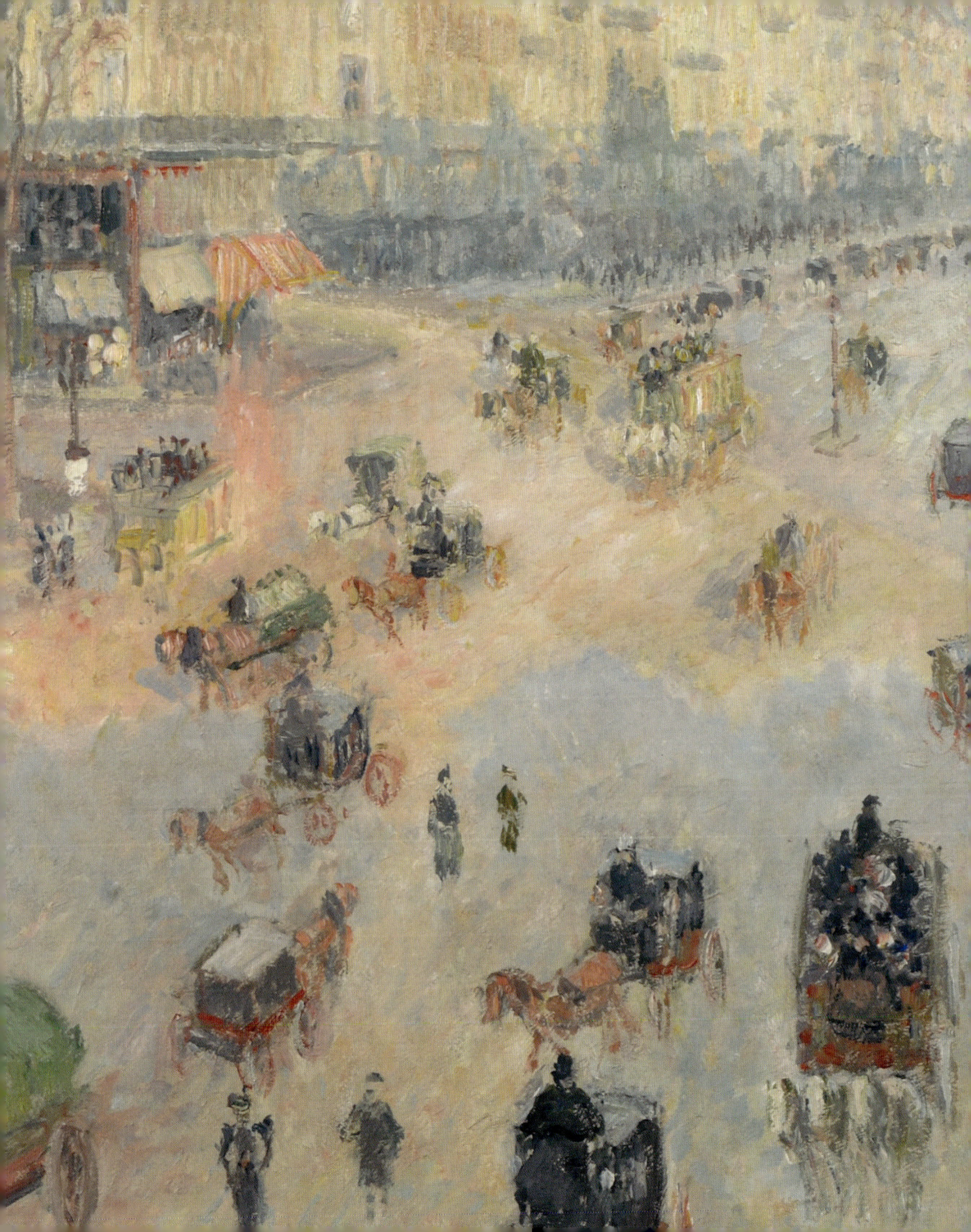

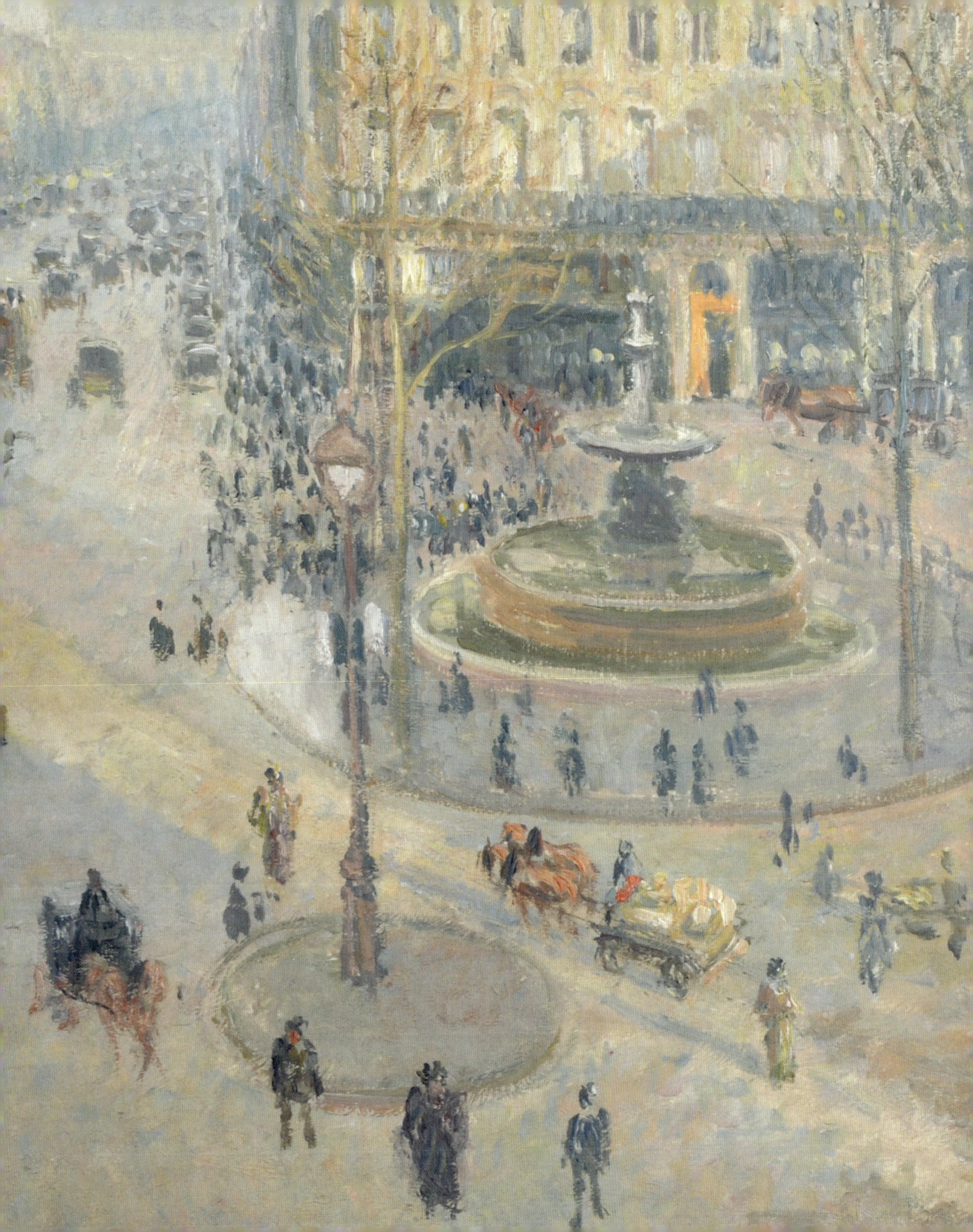

CAMILLE PISSARRO (1830–1903)

L'Avenue de l'Opera, 1898
Le Boulevard Montmartre, Mardi Gras, Sunset, 1897
Boulevard Montmartre, Dusk, 1897

On a sunny winter's morning in early 1898, Camille Pissarro painted the view from his room at the Hôtel du Louvre, located on the corner of the place du Palais Royal in Paris, where he stayed from the winter of 1897 to the spring of 1898. Pissarro looked out on the place du Théâtre français and the avenue de l'Opéra, where the Palais Garnier (also known as the Opéra Garnier) stands at the end of the wide boulevard. This newly built opera house served as the focal point for the surrounding streets in the chic quartier de l'Opéra.[1] The construction of the avenue de l'Opéra, formerly the boulevard Napoléon, was completed in 1877. In a letter to his son Lucien, Pissarro describes the view of the avenue thus: 'It may not be very aesthetic,... but [in fact] so silvery, so bright, so vibrant with life.'[2]

For many years, Pissarro had mostly painted landscapes and scenes of peasant life. In the last years of his career, he travelled to large cities such as London, Rouen and Paris. There he discovered a new theme: the cityscape, in which the energy of the city and its inhabitants is central.[3] However, Pissarro did not participate in the bustling life of the city himself, but instead painted it from a distance. Tormented by a recurring eye infection, he had been advised by his doctor to avoid wind and bright light.

Although he took this advice with a pinch of salt, Pissarro made many of his paintings from the windows of apartments and hotel rooms where he stayed temporarily.[4] This position allowed him to take a step back, as it were, to rise above the teeming city and experiment with different vantage points and perspectives.[5] Below him, pedestrians and traffic swarmed around the two round-abouts on the place du Théâtre français before disappearing into the adjacent streets.

From his room in the Hôtel du Louvre, Pissarro attentively observed the lively city from morning to night and the changes it underwent with the coming and going of the seasons. The sun rose from behind the hotel, in the lower right of the composition. The carefully chosen shades of warm yellow, orange and silvery blue bring the ever-changing atmosphere to a pause. The movement of the busy city and its inhabitants is thus briefly halted on this early winter morning.

Pissarro painted 15 paintings from his hotel room, like a series of snapshots.[6] He exhibited some of them in June 1898 at the famous gallery of the art dealer Paul Durand-Ruel, who, like Pissarro himself, considered these cityscapes a high point in his career as a painter.[7]

[VERA MERKS]

1   Caroline Shields, 'Geographies of Impressionism in the Age of Industry: An Introduction', in Caroline Shields (ed.), *Impressionism in the Age of Industry* (New York, 2019), p. 24.
2   Joachim Pissarro and Claire Durand-Ruel Snollaerts, *Pissarro, Critical Catalogue of Paintings*, vol. III, no. 1171 (Paris, 2005), p. 728.
3   Pissarro and Durand-Ruel Snollaerts 2005 (note 2), p. 122.
4   Pissarro and Durand-Ruel Snollaerts 2005 (note 2), p. 122.
5   Joachim Pissarro, *Camille Pissarro* (London, 1993), p. 264.
6   Richard R. Brettell and Joachim Pissarro, *The Impressionist and the City: Pissarro's Series Paintings* (New Haven, CT, 1992), p. xxviii.
7   Christopher Lloyd and Anne Distel, *Pissarro* (Boston, 1980), p. 142.

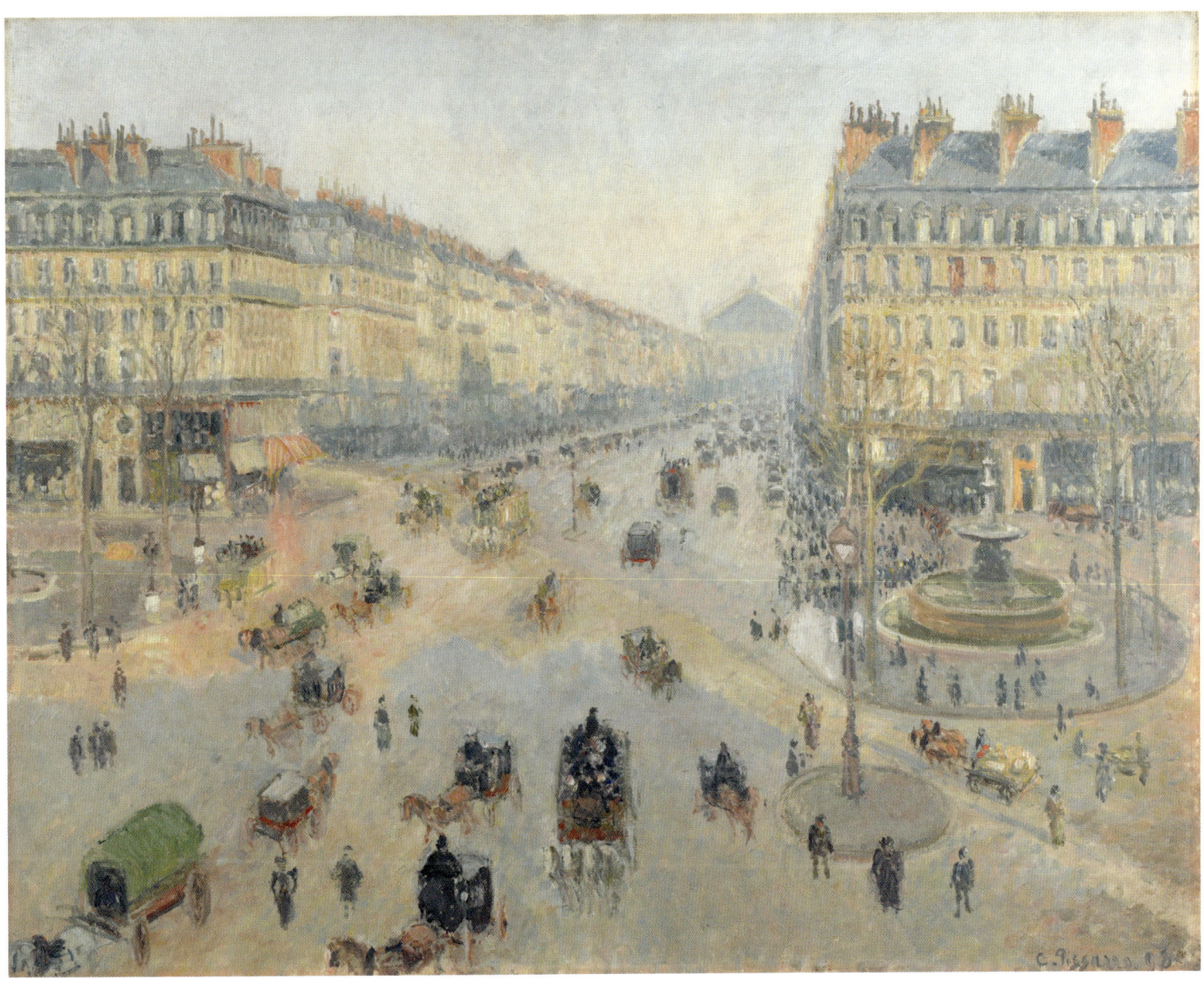

Camille Pissarro (1830–1903), *L'Avenue de l'Opéra*, 1898
Oil on canvas, 73.3 × 92.3 cm, Musée des Beaux-Arts, Reims

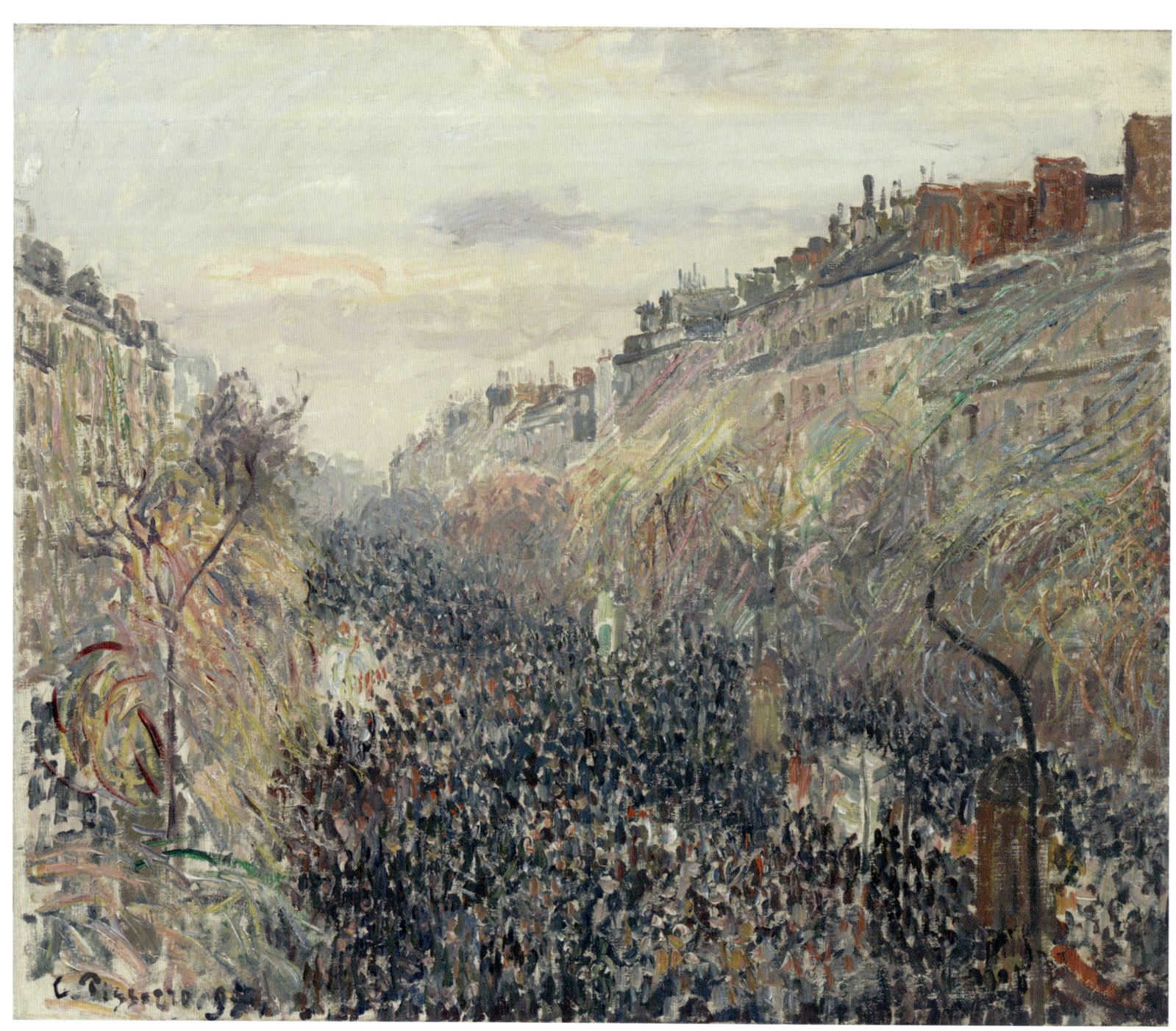

Camille Pissarro (1830–1903), *Le Boulevard Montmartre, Mardi Gras, Sunset*, 1897
Oil on canvas, 54 × 65 cm, Kunst Museum Winterthur. Acquired in 1947

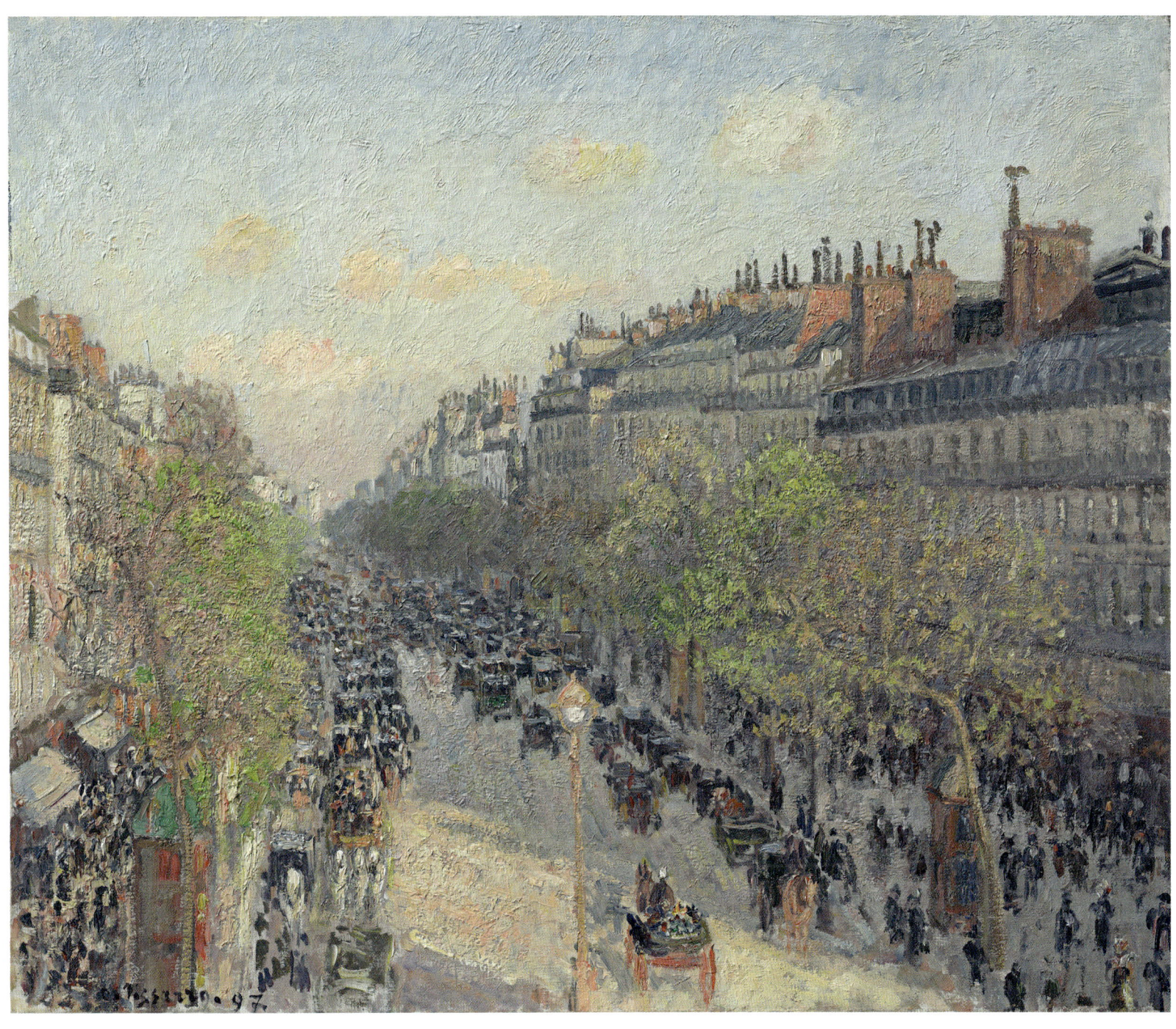

Camille Pissarro (1830–1903), *Boulevard Montmartre, Dusk*, 1897

Oil on canvas, 54 × 65 cm, Museum Barberini, Potsdam

PAUL CÉZANNE (1839–1906)

At Quai de Bercy in Paris, c. 1875–76

Paul Cézanne did not paint *At Quai de Bercy in Paris* in the open air – as was usual among the Impressionists – but in his studio. His canvas is a copy of a painting that his colleague, the Impressionist Armand Guillaumin, had made a little earlier on the north bank of the Seine. The two painters met in 1861 at the Académie Suisse in Paris and remained friends throughout their lives. They often walked together through the new Paris. Both exhibited at the first Salon des Refusés in 1863, and in 1874 they participated in the first Impressionist exhibition. In 1873, while staying at the estate of Dr Gachet, the physician who treated Vincent van Gogh during his final years, Cézanne made a portrait of his friend Guillaumin, sitting relaxed in a meadow. The small etching is a lasting testimony to their friendship.

The painting shows the beginnings of the modernisation of the quai de Bercy. A floating crane rises high into the sky above the five arches of the Pont National. Next to it is a barge, probably transporting building materials. A man with a horse-drawn cart and another with a wheelbarrow are working on the construction of the embankment.

The period after the monarchy of Napoleon III marked the birth of the Third Republic. In 1875, the National Assembly approved a constitution that provided for the democratic election of a senate and a president. With the organisation of several vast Universal Expositions and the construction of the metro, Paris experienced enormous industrial and technological progress. It was the beginning of the Belle Époque, whose prosperity also stemmed from France's relentless colonial expansion.

The atmosphere of change in the metropolis is palpable in the painting. The two artists' painting styles are also innovative. A comparison between the two works shows that Cézanne went a step further than Guillaumin. His colours are brighter and more contrasting, the black is more intense, the contours are stronger and more clearly defined. In contrast to Guillaumin's original, Cézanne does not allow the figures, horses and working materials to blend completely with their environment. He gives the cloud formations a concrete form with parallel, diagonal brushstrokes. In this way, he searches for a way to capture a fleeting atmosphere in a solid painterly structure.

Cézanne strove to replace the spontaneous snapshots of Impressionism with images that make tangible the organising principles that structurally underlie all visible phenomena. More so than the Impressionists, he sought balance in his compositions. He did so by reducing scenes to more geometric forms and planes. As a 'Post-Impressionist' he would become a role model for the later Cubist artists and would have a lasting influence on twentieth-century modern art.

[DANIEL KOEP]

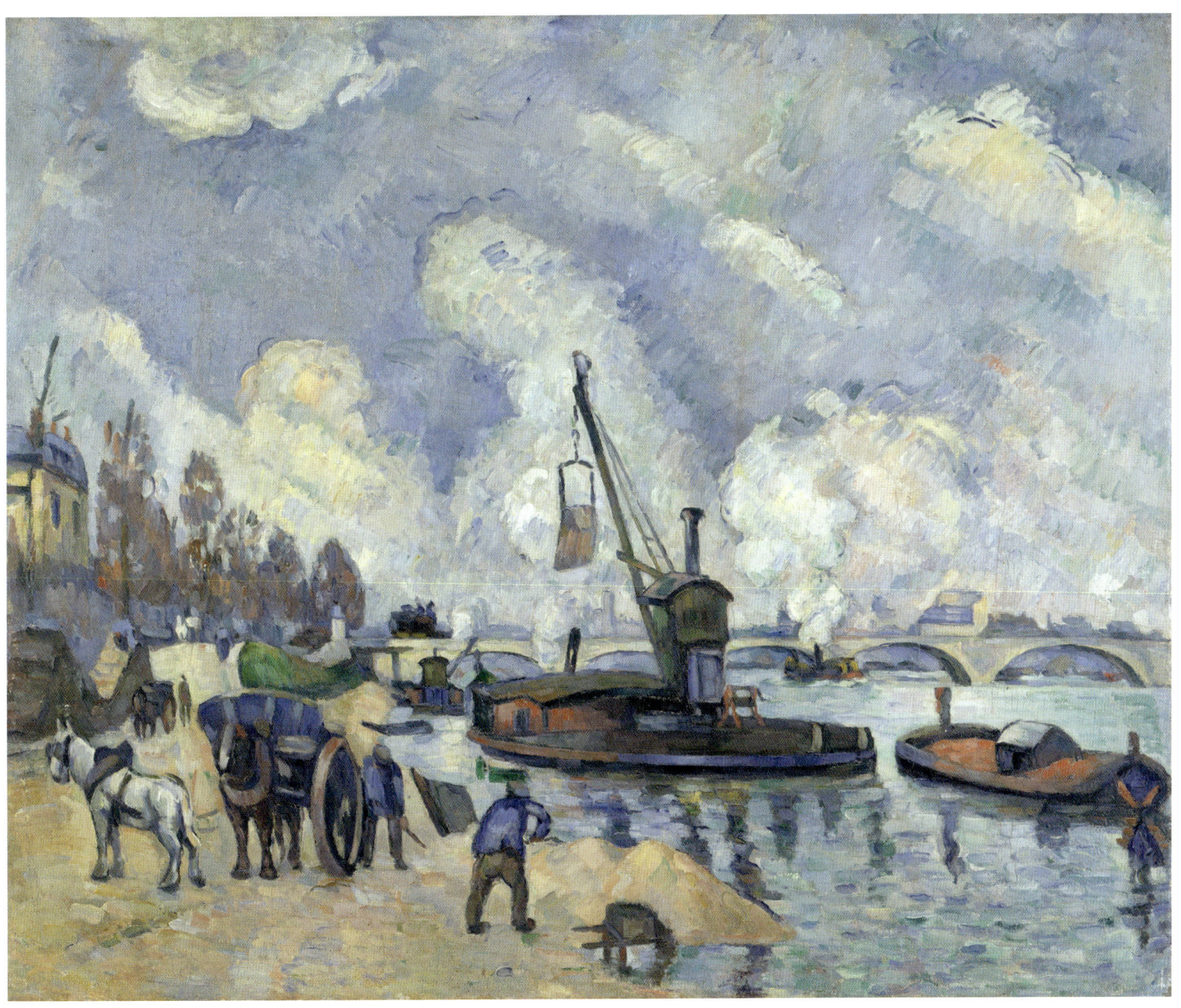

Paul Cézanne (1839–1906), *At Quai de Bercy in Paris*, c. 1875–76
Oil on canvas, 59.5 × 72.5 cm, Hamburger Kunsthalle

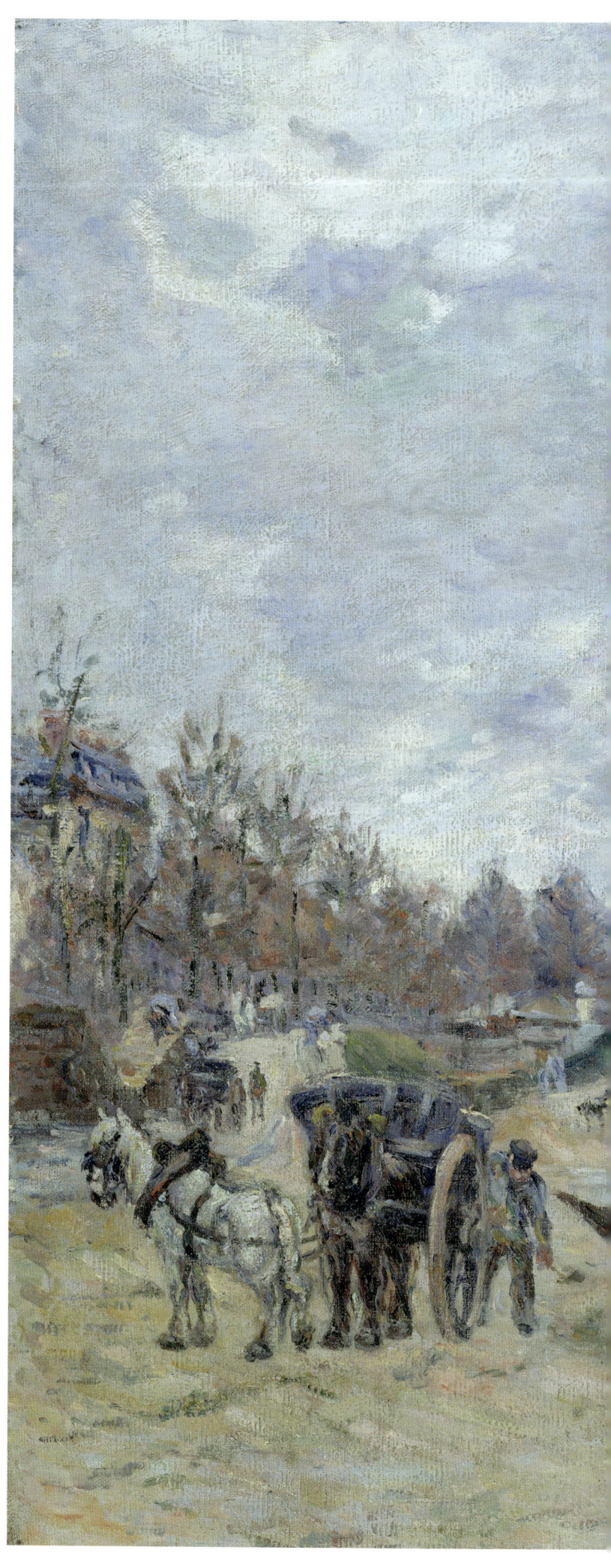

Armand Guillaumin (1841–1927), *At Quai de Bercy in Paris*, c. 1874

Oil on canvas, 56.1 × 72.4 cm, Hamburger Kunsthalle.
Acquired with funds from the Campe Historical Art Foundation, 1983

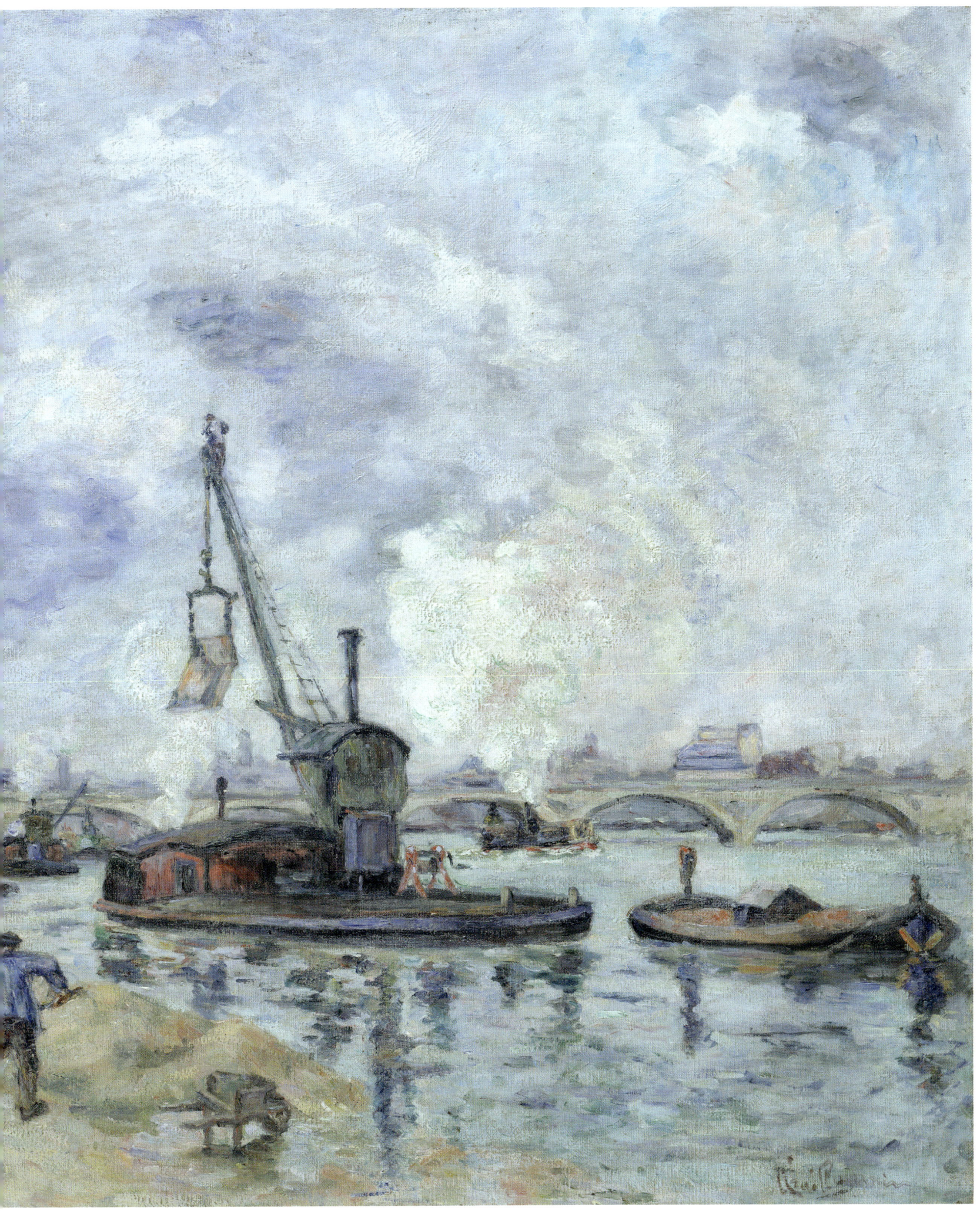

Gustave Caillebotte (1848–1894), *View Seen Through a Balcony*, 1880

Oil on canvas, 65.6 × 54.9 cm, Van Gogh Museum, Amsterdam. Purchased with support from the VriendenLoterij, the Vincent van Gogh Foundation, the Mondriaan Fund, the Rembrandt Association, thanks in part to the Culture Fund, and the VSB Fund

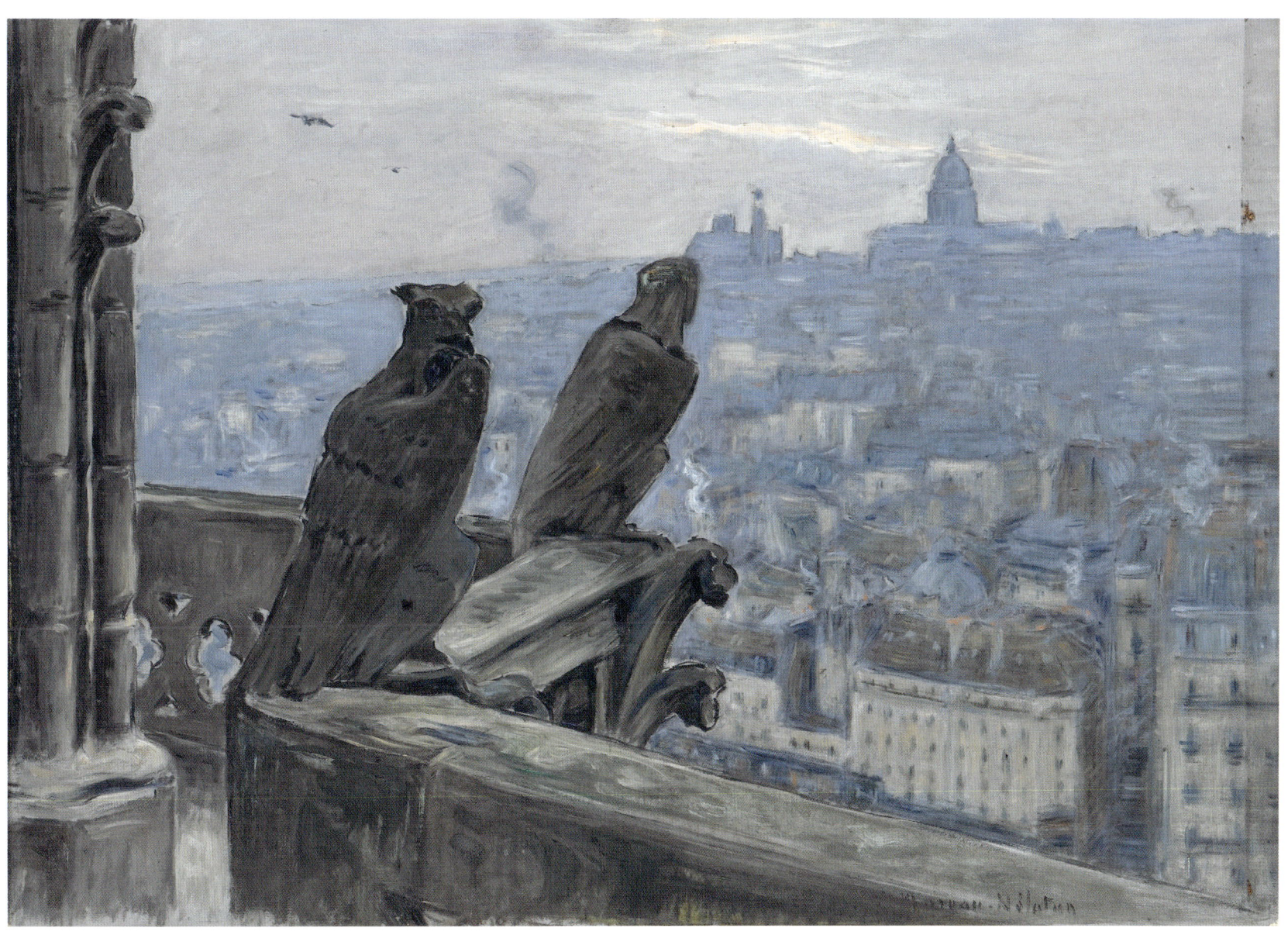

Etienne Moreau-Nélaton (1859–1927), *Paris Seen from Notre-Dame*, c. 1898

Oil on canvas, 61.5 × 88.3 cm, Staatsgalerie Stuttgart. Gifted by the artist 1901

GUSTAVE CAILLEBOTTE (1848–1894)

Rue Halévy, View from the Balcony, 1877
Rue Halévy, View from the Sixth Floor, 1878

Many of Gustave Caillebotte's cityscapes have a daring vantage point, are painted from surprisingly close up, or contain remarkable details. Caillebotte fundamentally changed the view of the city from a balcony, a motif that Claude Monet had introduced into Impressionist painting. His *Rue Halévy, View from the Sixth Floor* offers a spectacularly steep view from a mansard roof on to a wide street that leads our gaze to the distance. The height of the recently built apartment blocks with classicist sandstone facades and zinc roofs is further emphasised by the Lilliputian pedestrians and carriages sketched with loose blue-black brushstrokes. The buildings' architectural unity was more important to Caillebotte than the passers-by, whose fleeting depiction is reminiscent of Monet's painting *Boulevard des Capucines* (Nelson-Atkins Museum of Art, Kansas City), painted just a few years earlier.

Caillebotte had taken up residence in a building at the end of rue La Fayette, where it meets boulevard Haussmann, and looked southwest down rue Halévy. This street had been built only 20 years earlier after the demolition of old buildings. The neighbourhood in the 9th arrondissement is dominated by the Opéra Garnier, commissioned by Napolean III in 1858 and inaugurated in 1875. On the right of the painting, we can see one of the gilded group of figures that surmounts the opera house. Caillebotte was not interested in the magnificent neo-baroque building itself, but in the image of the modern metropolis as Baron Haussmann had planned it and as it had taken shape here for the wealthy bourgeoisie. While the evening sun creates a harmonious play of pastel pink and violet shades, the height of the viewpoint creates a sense of elevation. This is reinforced by the sloping roofline on the left, which indicates that the painter is standing on a balcony. It is clear that the bold perspective is the artist's decision and that he involves the viewer in it.

The emphasis on the painter's position is even stronger in *Rue Halévy, View from the Balcony*, painted a year earlier at the same location. Here, the blue-green leaves of the plants in the foreground partially obstruct the view. In any case, the street blurs in the violet morning light in which a pale sun makes the zinc roofs glisten. The palette evokes a calm, pleasant atmosphere that gives no hint of the bustling city below.

Shortly after the paintings were created, in 1879, the 31-year-old Caillebotte moved into an apartment in the block on the right with access from 31 boulevard Haussmann. There he made more paintings with a view of the wide, tree-lined street from the balcony. The fortune he had inherited meant he could afford an apartment on one of the most beautiful new streets in Paris. But the choice of this address also testifies to his positive attitude towards urban modernity.

[MICHAEL PHILIPP]

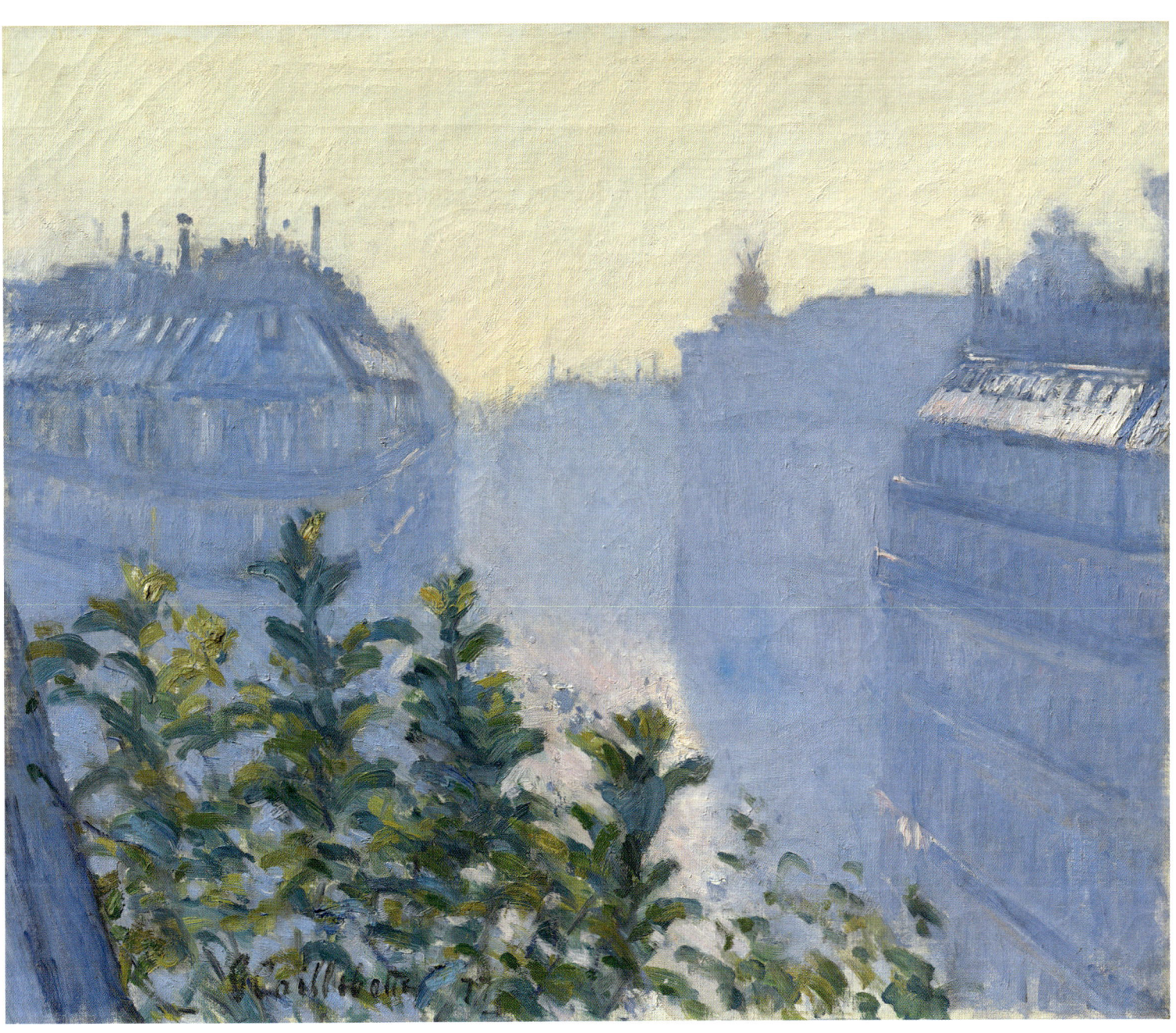

Gustave Caillebotte (1848–1894), *Rue Halévy, View from the Balcony,* 1877
Oil on canvas, 54 × 65.5 cm, Museum Barberini, Potsdam

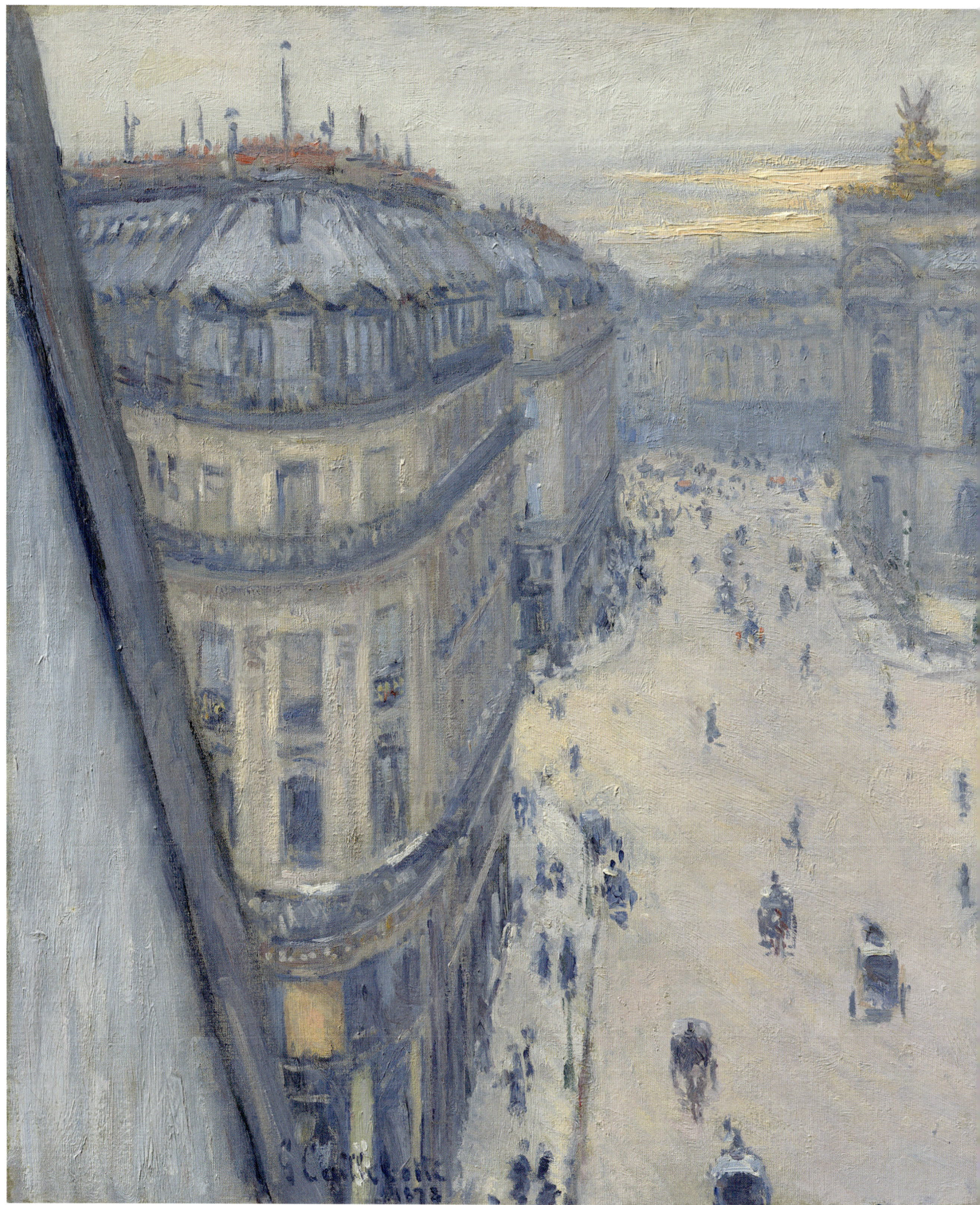

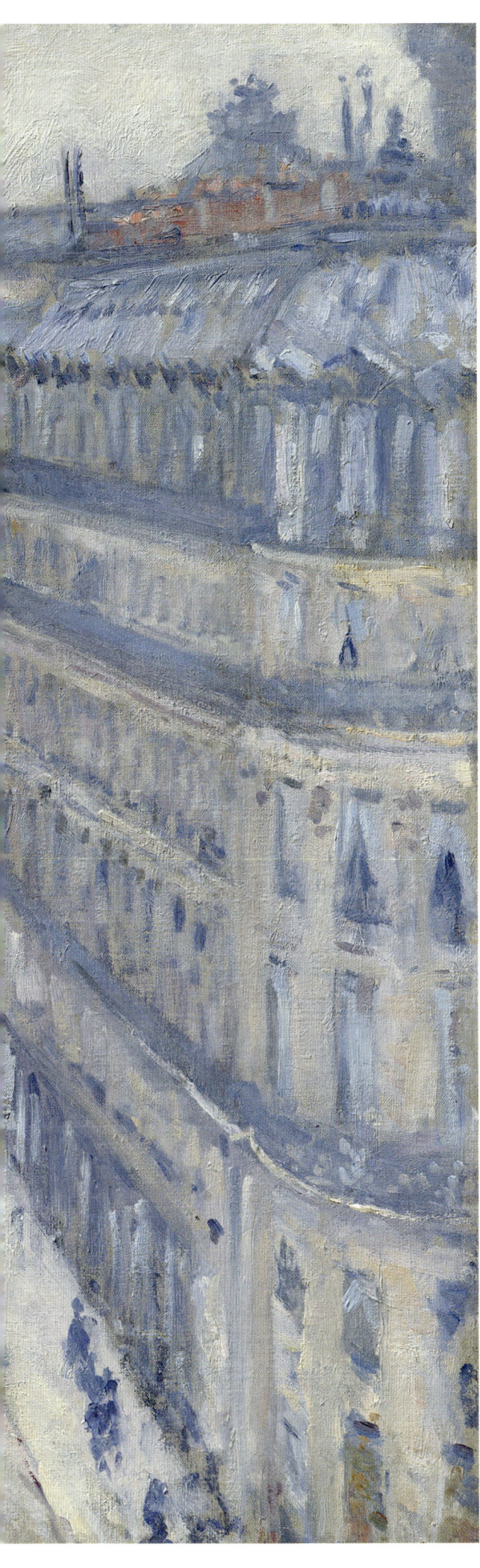

Gustave Caillebotte (1848–1894), *Rue Halévy, View from the Sixth Floor*, 1878
Oil on canvas, 59.5 × 73 cm, Museum Barberini, Potsdam

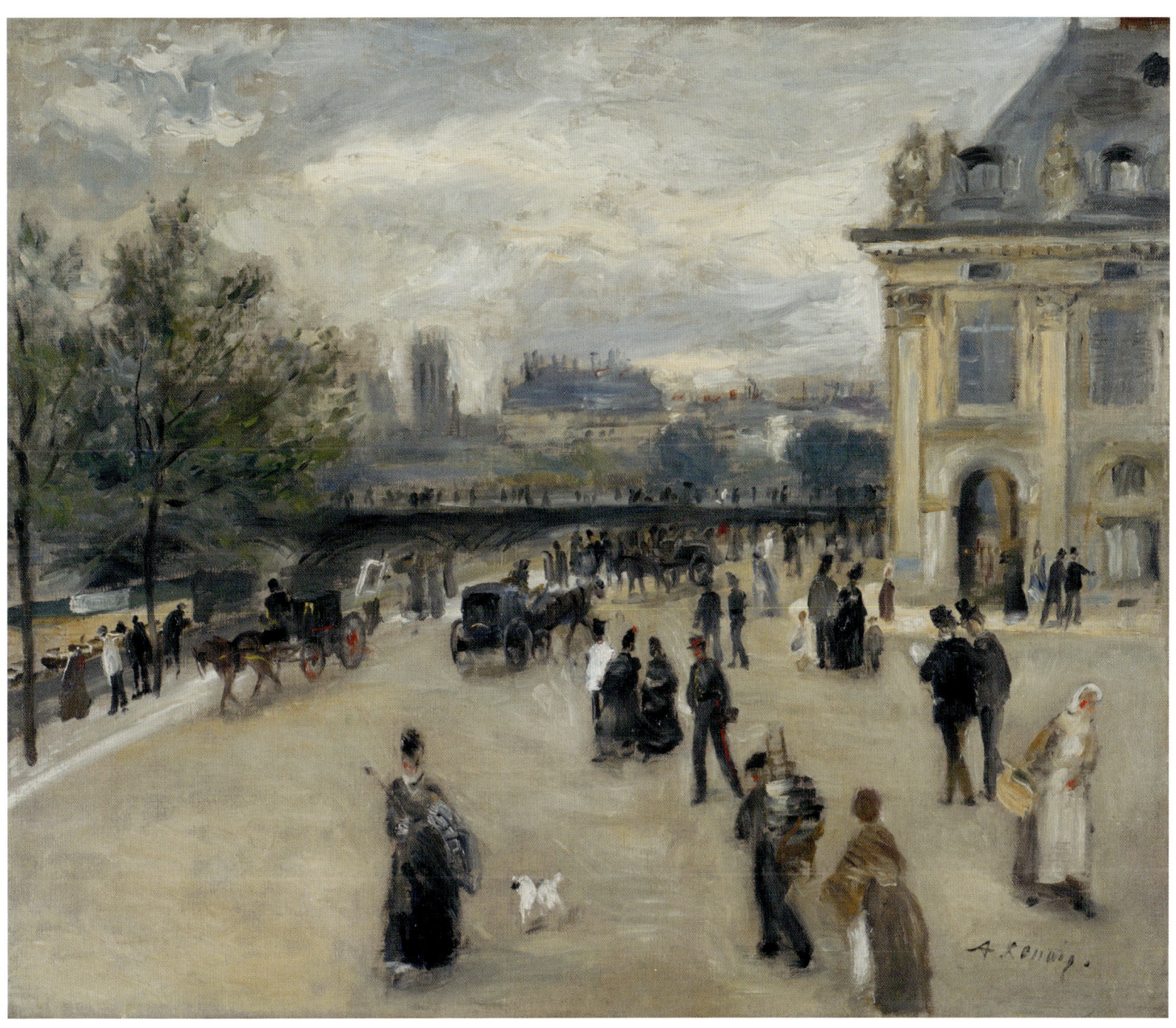

Auguste Renoir (1841–1919), *The Institute at the Quai Malaquais, Paris*, 1875
Oil on canvas, 46 × 56 cm, Private collection, courtesy of Connery & Associates

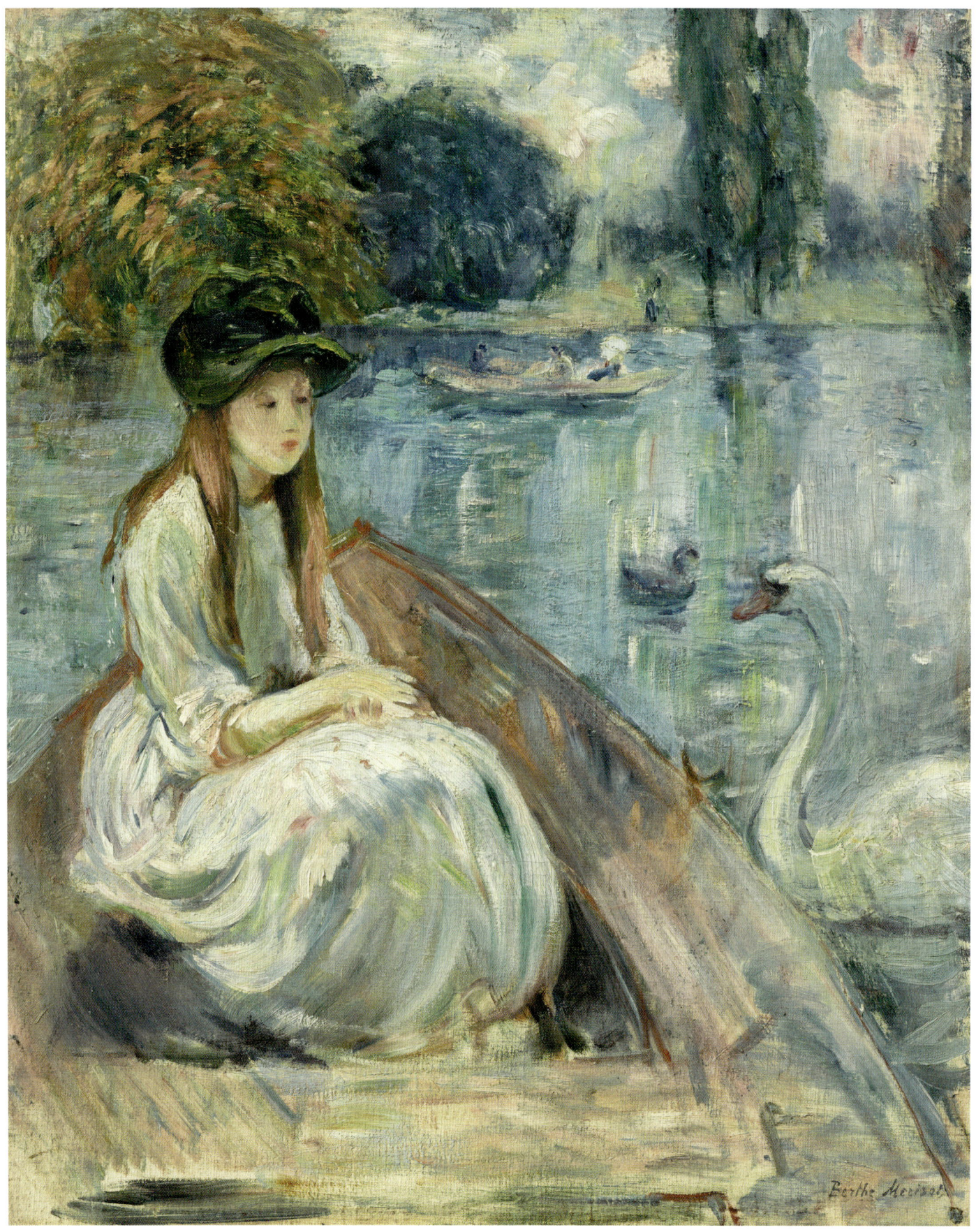

Berthe Morisot (1841–1895), *Jeanne Fourmanoir on the Lake*, 1892
Oil on canvas, 61 × 50.5 cm, FAMM Museum, Mougins, The Levett Collection

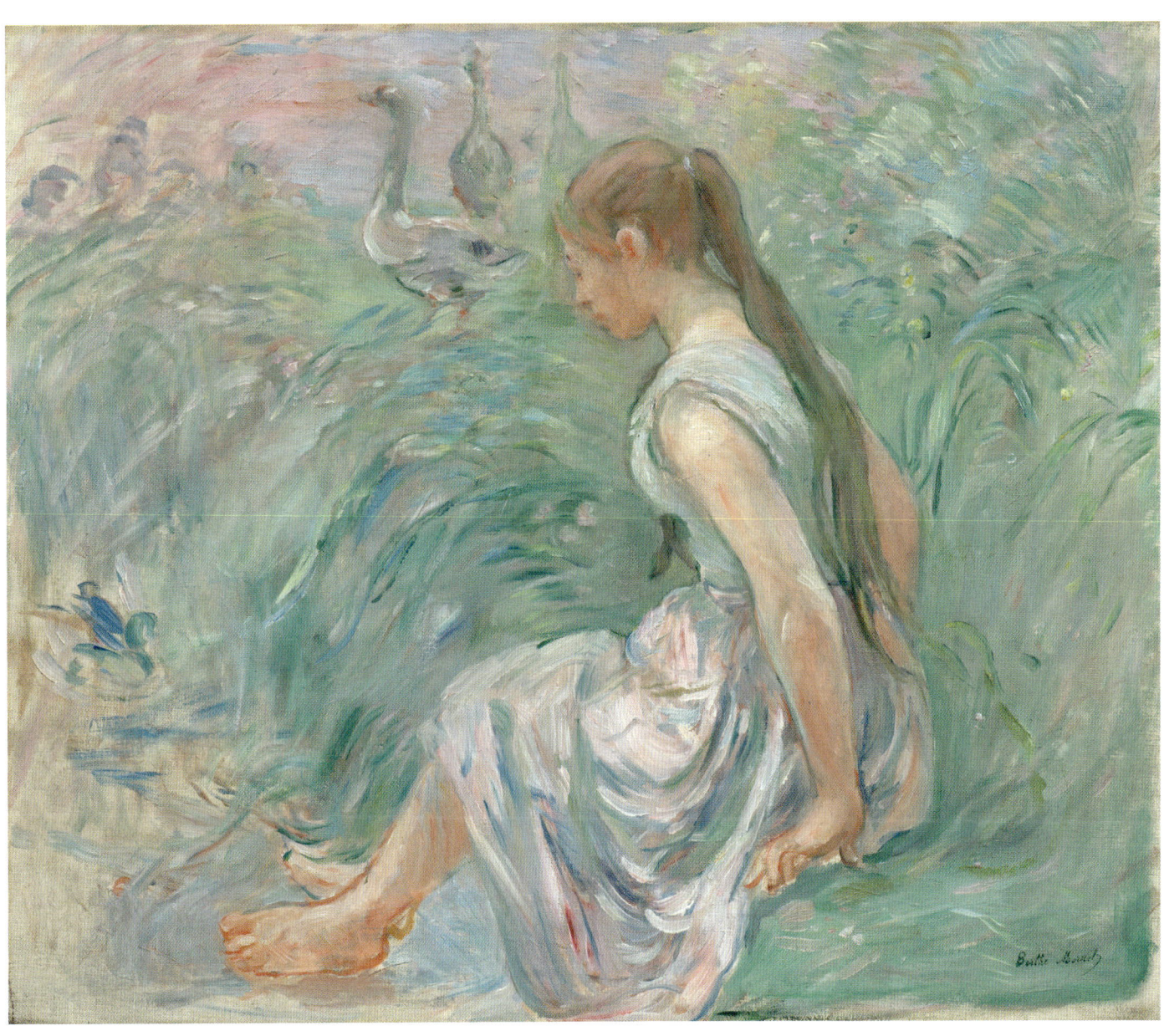

Berthe Morisot (1841–1895), *Peasant Woman with Geese at the Water's Edge*, 1893
Oil on canvas, 46 × 54 cm, Private collection

ÉDOUARD MANET (1832–1883)

A Game of Croquet, 1873

A Game of Croquet is one of the few paintings in which Édouard Manet comes very close, stylistically and thematically, to the work of his Impressionist colleagues. He painted it in 1873, a year before their controversial first group exhibition in Nadar's studio, but did not show the canvas there. The public only got to see it in 1884 at the major retrospective exhibition after Manet's death.

The scene is probably set in the garden of Alfred Stevens, a Belgian artist who was a friend of Manet. Stevens is most likely the man sitting on the grass on the left, watching the ladies playing. The woman in the blue dress is the red-haired Victorine Meurent, dancer, artist and Manet's favourite model in the 1860s – she posed for both the controversial painting *Olympia* and the scandalous *Le Déjeuner sur l'herbe*. Victorine watches Alice Legouvé (or Lecouvé), a model for Stevens and later for Manet, who is about to hit a ball through the last hoop towards the barely visible end post on the far right. Manet's friend Paul Roudier seems completely unimpressed by the ladies' performance – he is feeding the ducks in the background – but attracts everyone's attention with his bright yellow jacket and dazzling white trousers.

The distance between the figures and their arrangement in a diagonal line gives the composition a rather unnatural and posed feel. This is further reinforced by the watering can that stands somewhat forlornly in the middle of the composition. The painting is often cited in the literature as a striking example of Manet's turn to painting *en plein air* ('in the open air'). However, that process proceeded in fits and starts. From 1870, Manet gradually turned away from studio painting and works with historical connotations and quotes from old masters. He increasingly painted his landscapes in the open air. They include garden and beach scenes with family members or friends of the artist as central figures. There has always been some doubt as to whether Manet really made *A Game of Croquet* outdoors. The work is painted in an extremely sketchy *plein-air* style, which does not necessarily mean that Manet painted the subject with rapid brushstrokes. Technical research has shown that the picture was painted in several sessions. The artist was known for the well-considered placement of his brushstrokes, which were designed to give the impression of a wet-in-wet painting technique, intended to emphasise his virtuosity. Moreover, Manet was fond of word play and it is not impossible that he flirted here with the partial homophony of *croquet* and *croquis* (sketch).

Croquet, reimported to France from England – at the time, the only mixed outdoor sport – had become a popular pastime of the Parisian middle classes. Manet had already painted *The Croquet Party* (Nelson-Atkins Museum of Art, Kansas City), featuring friends and family members, in 1871, but that scene is set in the public garden of the casino in the fashionable seaside resort of Boulogne-sur-Mer. In the painting in the Städel Museum, Manet moved the scene to a private garden. By including his friends Stevens and Roudier alongside female models, he gave his composition the slightly provocative quality of a dressed-up version of *Le Déjeuner sur l'herbe*.

[ALEXANDER EILING]

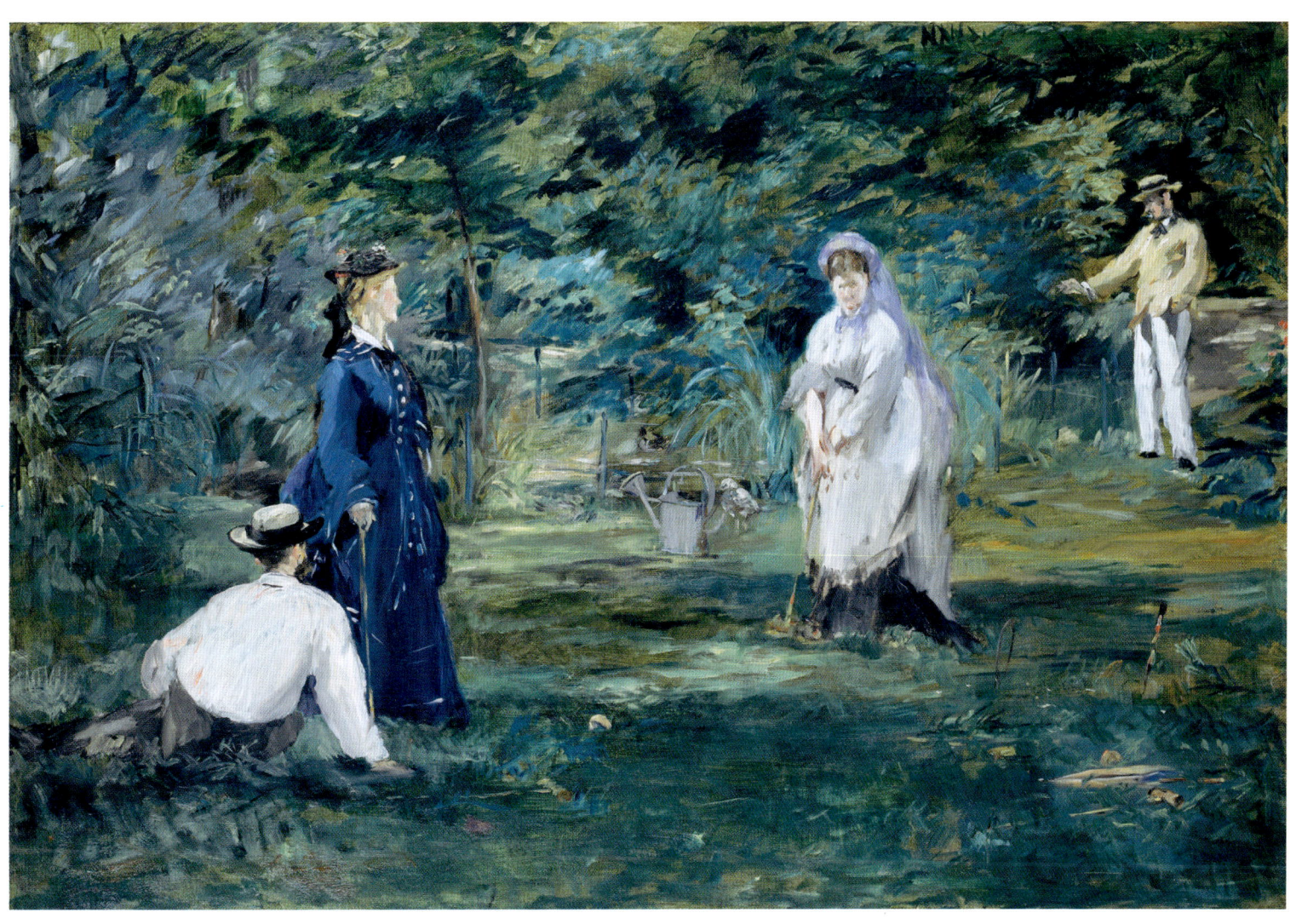

Édouard Manet (1832–1883), *A Game of Croquet*, 1873
Oil on canvas, 72.5 × 106 cm, Städel Museum, Frankfurt am Main, property of the Städelscher Museums-Verein e.V.

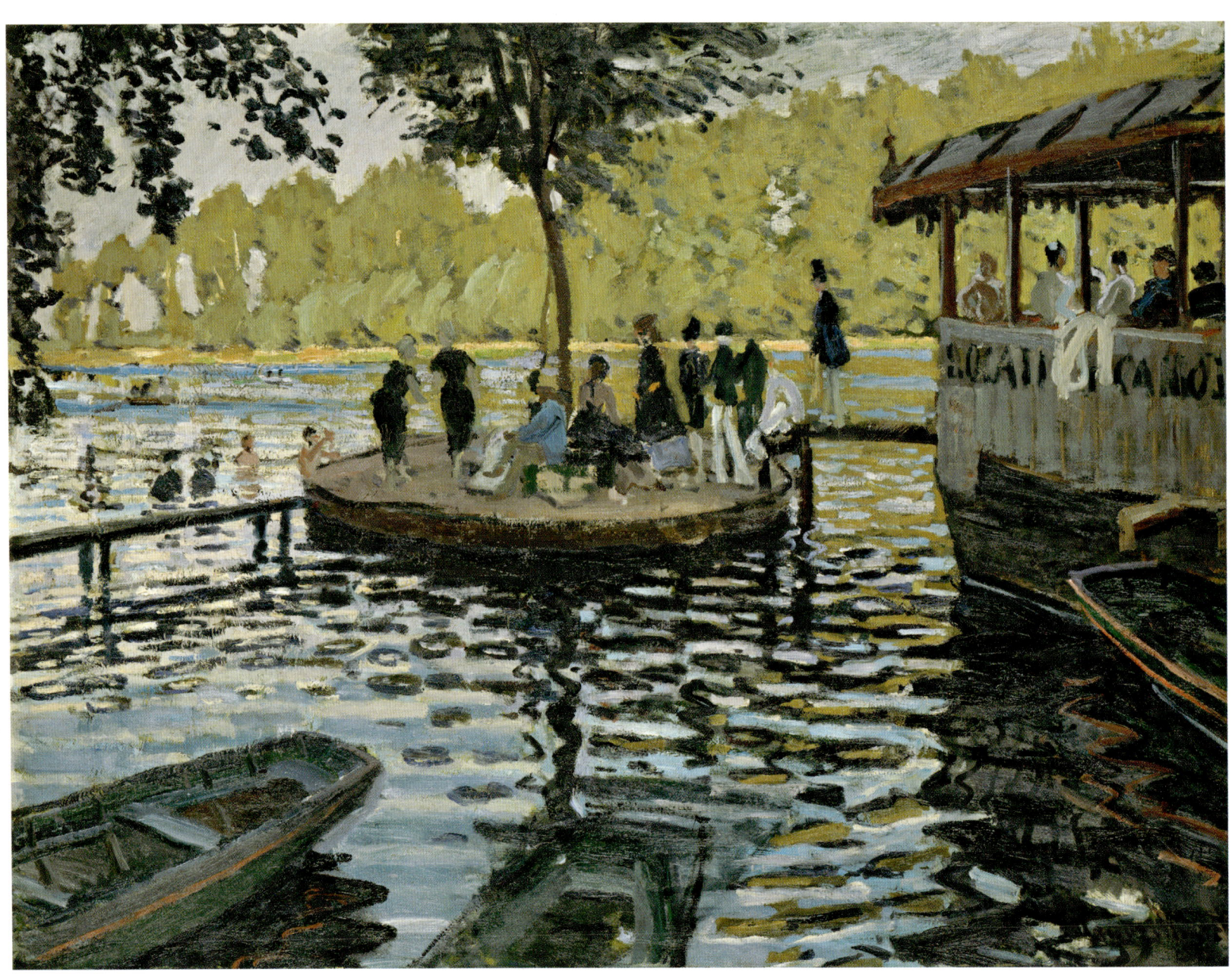

Claude Monet (1840–1926), *La Grenouillère*, 1869
Oil on canvas, 74.6 × 99.7 cm, Metropolitan Museum of Art, New York

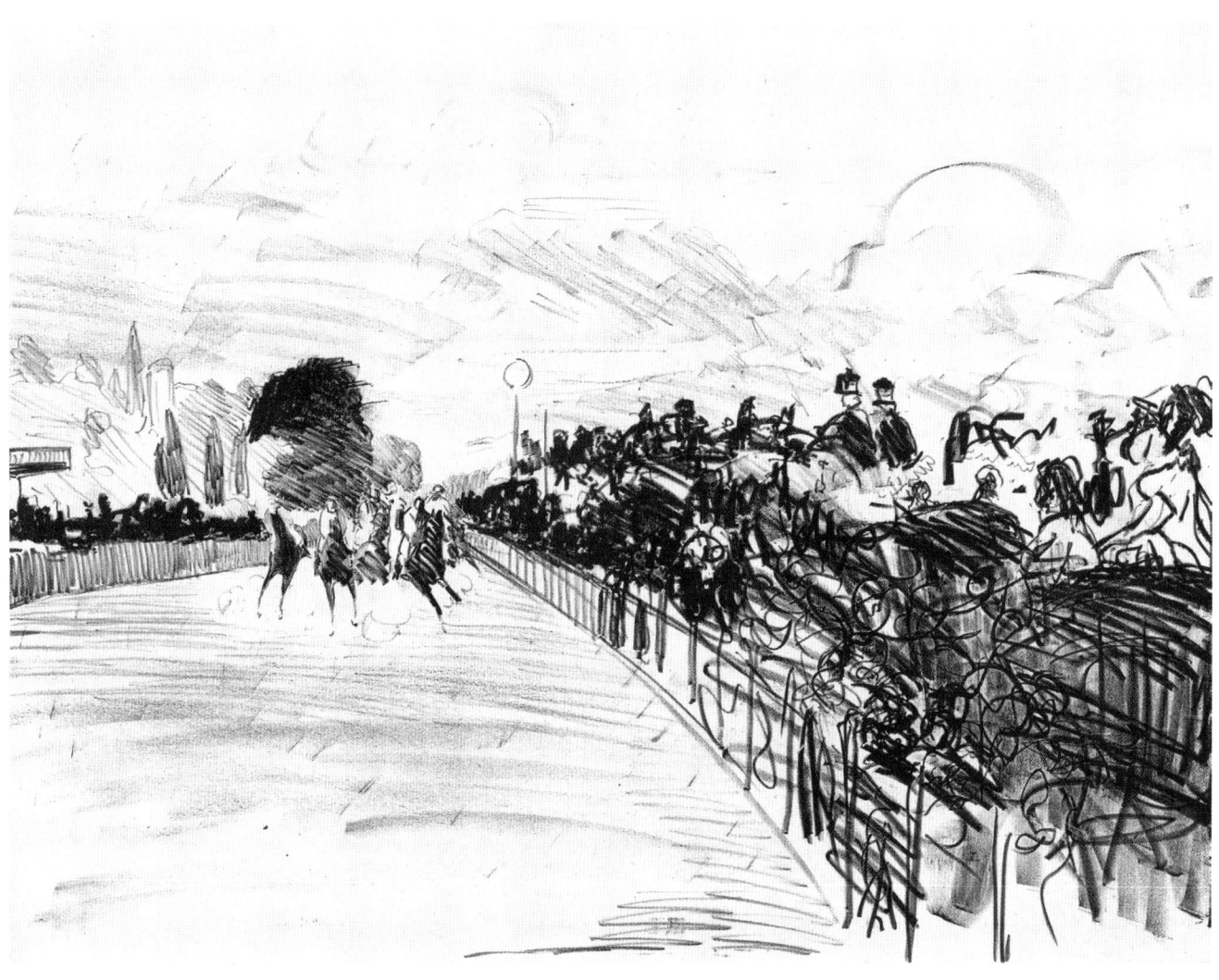

Édouard Manet (1832–1883), *The Races (Les courses)*, Paris 1865–72 (posthumous edition 1884)

Lithograph on paper, 42.4 cm × 54.6 cm, Van Gogh Museum, Amsterdam (Vincent van Gogh Foundation)

CHARLES MARVILLE (1813–1879)

From 1865 onwards, Charles Marville and his assistants must have walked through Paris with a heavily laden cart. The city council had commissioned him to photograph the streets that were to be demolished as part of Haussmann's transformation. It was a major commission: by 1869, Marville had taken at least 300 photographs of the capital's streets. In the run-up to the Universal Exposition in 1878, after the fall of Napoleon III, a second series followed, showing the newly completed boulevards and squares.

Marville's cart contained a large camera and a mobile darkroom. Plastic negatives did not yet exist, so he worked with glass plates measuring 30 by 40 centimetres, which he covered with light-sensitive chemicals just before taking the photo. The plate had to be developed immediately. This complicated technique meant that Marville could take only a few shots per day. He usually set up his camera at the end of a street, enabling him to record all the buildings on both sides. The streets in the densely populated neighbourhoods that had to make way for the new boulevards were busy, full of traffic and people, but the long exposure time – sometimes as long as 30 seconds – meant that any fast-moving vehicle or pedestrian did not register on the plate, giving the impression of empty streets. The sharpness of the prints is still astonishing. If you look closely, you can even read the posters on the walls. And occasionally you see a curious local resident hanging out of a window to observe the photographer with his mysterious machine.

Marville had prior experience of photographing buildings for the city government, proudly calling himself 'photographe de la ville de Paris'. He was born in 1813 into a working-class Parisian family as Charles-François Bossu. In his recently discovered will, he indicates that he chose a pseudonym at the age of 18 because he had been bullied about his surname as a schoolboy: Bossu means hunchback.[1] It is one of the few personal details known about him. Although Marville associated with famous fellow photographers and the highest Parisian officials and was commissioned to portray famous artists and architects, he remained resolutely in the background. He lived with Jeanne-Louise Leuba, who called herself Madame Marville despite not being married to him. Apart from his photographs in books and magazines and approximately 1,500 prints, the only personal documents that have survived are a few invoices and reminders. Nonetheless, we are still able to trace his career.

Like many photographers of his generation, Marville trained as an illustrator. He made wood engravings for romantic travelogues and stories before switching to photography around 1851. He took photographs of landscapes and churches for Louis Désiré Blanquart-Evrard from Lille, the very first publisher of photo books. In 1855, Marville exhibited six of these images at the first photography exhibition in the Netherlands, in Amsterdam and then The Hague. He increasingly received commissions from architects; for example, he photographed almost all the new buildings and projects by Gabriel Davioud, the architect responsible for the renovation of Paris's squares and monuments under Haussmann. From 1853 until his death, Marville also worked repeatedly for Eugène Viollet-le-Duc, the restoration architect who was also active in the city council.

In some cases, the city architects needed Marville's photographs to keep track of the progress of construction work.[2] Images were also used in albums that the city government or Napoleon III could use to show how the modernisation of Paris was progressing at the Universal Expositions. In 1858, Marville received his first major commission from the City of Paris, to photograph the recently renovated Bois de Boulogne, for which he was even given his own temporary photography studio. He probably won the commission because Davioud was involved in the construction of the park. Marville took about 70 photos of the ponds, waterfalls, newly planted trees, artificial rock formations, paths and buildings. The photo album was shown at the 1862 International Exhibition in London and the 1867 Universal Exposition in Paris. The images were widely praised by the critics, with two photographs from the series being considered 'the most complete landscapes in the exhibition'.[3] The images were also used as the basis for the prints in *Les Promenades de Paris*, an album about the construction of green areas in the French capital that the city council published in 1867.

The Bois de Boulogne was the first project of the new Paris to be completed. The park became a popular subject for photographers who wanted to sell their prints to tourists and other interested parties. The overcrowded narrow streets with open sewers were another matter. Initially, Marville's images were intended only for the Service du Plan, the city's cartographic service. It used the photos to keep track of all the work and possibly as evidence in legal cases. Marville's original commission from the city council around 1865 has not been preserved. In 1866, Haussmann spoke in the city council about a special committee to collect maps, scale models, drawings and other objects to show at the 1867 Universal Exposition, but in the end the presentation never took place. A fire at the Hôtel de Ville in 1871 destroyed Marville's first photographs and a large part of the image archive. Fortunately, Marville had kept his negatives safely at home and he suggested making new prints. In the meantime, some streets had disappeared and the photos, originally intended for internal use

only, had acquired historical significance. The new museum of the history of Paris, the later Musée Carnavalet, also showed interest in the photos. The city council eventually ordered three prints of each image.

In the lead-up to the Universal Exposition of 1878, the city was once again being reshaped, and unfinished prestige projects, such as the avenue de l'Opéra, were completed in record time. Marville was once again there on behalf of the city. In the photograph he took on 24 February 1876, you can see the workers in the foreground posing, leaning against their pickaxes. To the side, two men in top hats and suits look approvingly at the camera. A mammoth task had been completed. Thanks to Marville, the whole world could witness this when his photos were shown at the 1878 Exposition. The photographer himself lived just long enough to see it. He died a year later, after a short illness.

[JOKE DE WOLF]

1   See the biography in Sarah Kennel (ed.), *Charles Marville: Photographer of Paris*, exh. cat. (Washington National Gallery of Art), 2013.
2   Joke de Wolf, *Le Nouveau Paris: Charles Marville Photographs the City Transformation*, Rijksmuseum Studies in Photography, vol. 18 (Amsterdam, 2017).
3   Edmond Fierlants, 'La photographie à l'exposition universelle de Londres', *Le moniteur de la photographie*, no. 17 (15 November 1862), p. 197.

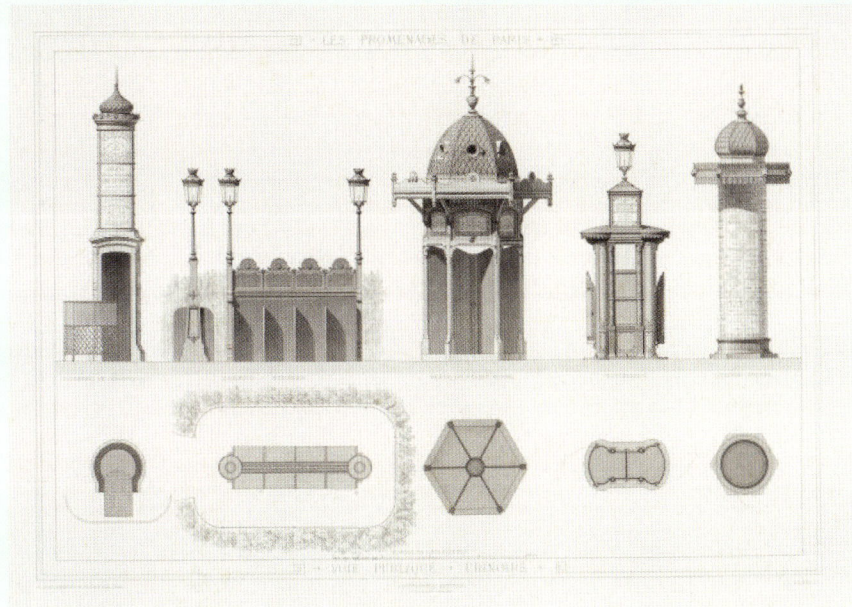

Public road – urinals
From: Adolphe Alphand, *Les Promenades de Paris*, 1867–73, Lithograph, 45 × 63 cm, Kunstmuseum Den Haag

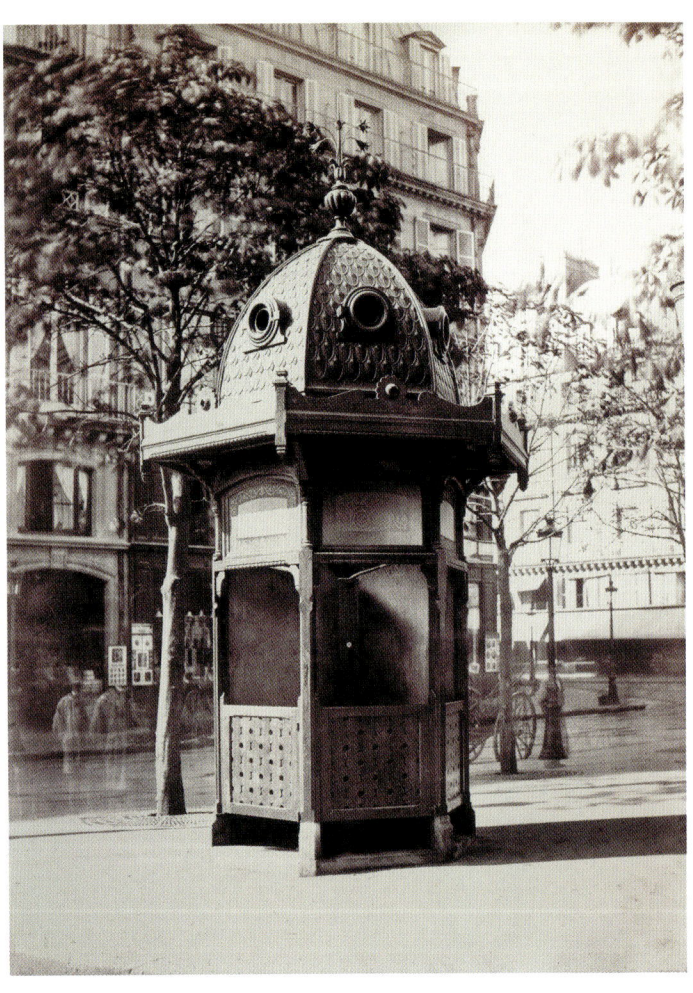

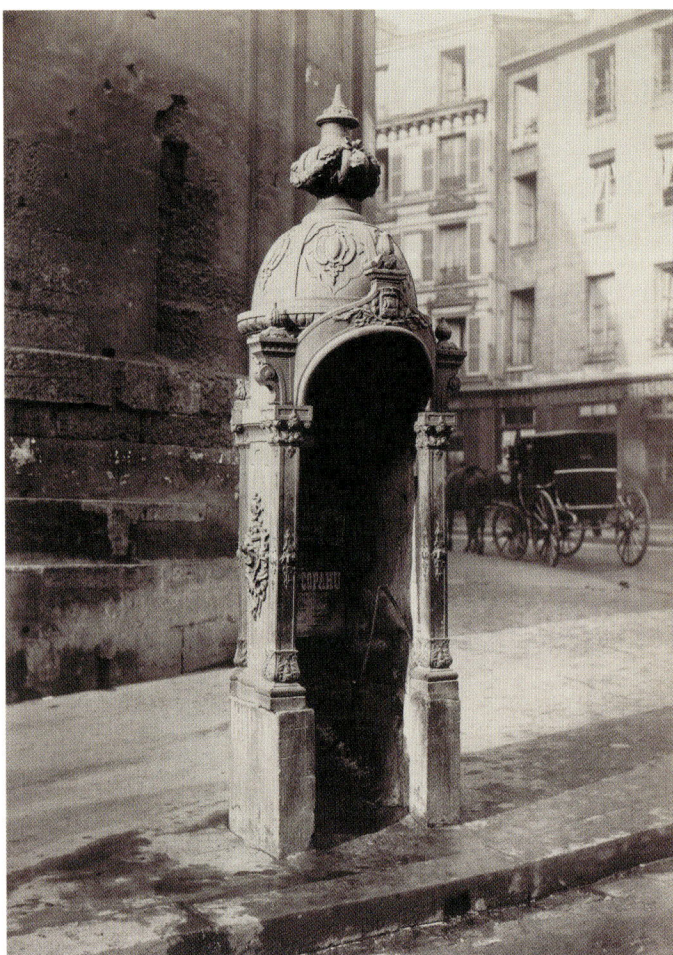

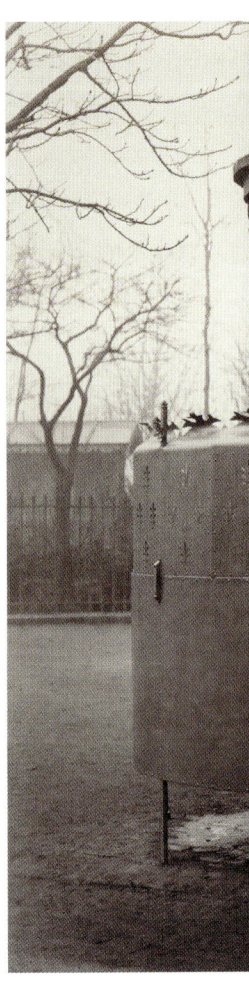

Charles Marville (1813–1879),
Urinal kiosk, Place du Théâtre
français, 1st arrondissement,
Paris, 1858–78

Albumen print, 36.2 × 26.8 cm,
Musée Carnavalet – Histoire de Paris

Charles Marville (1813–1879),
Urinal, rue du Faubourg Saint-
Martin, 10th arrondissement,
Paris, 1858–78

Albumen print, 36.4 × 26.9 cm,
Musée Carnavalet – Histoire de Paris

Charles Marville (1813–1879),
Urinal with screen, Square
des Batignolles, 17th
arrondissement, Paris, 1858–7

Albumen print, 33.5 × 24.2 cm,
Musée Carnavalet – Histoire de Paris

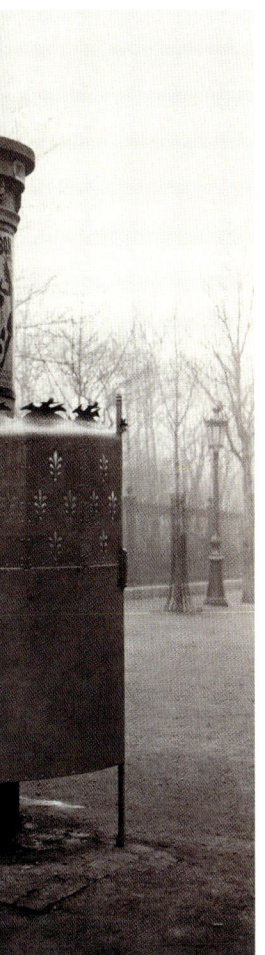
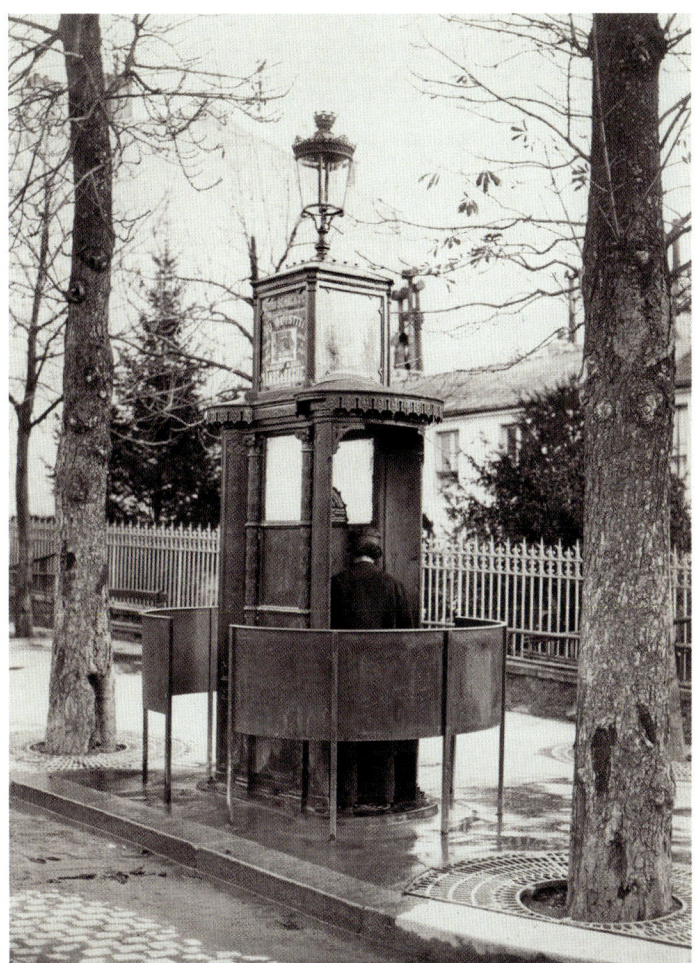
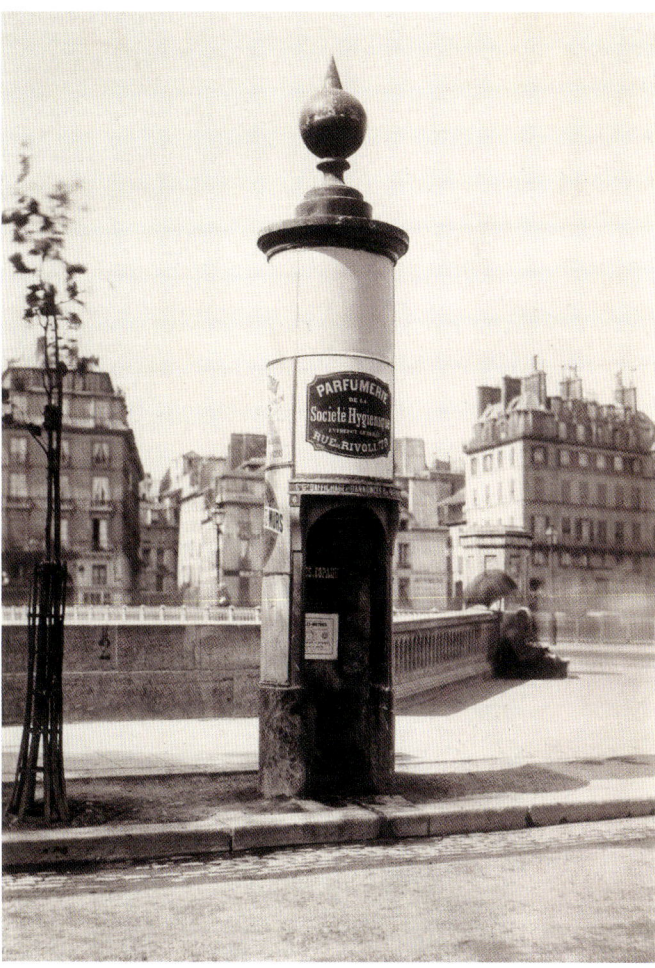

Charles Marville (1813–1879),
Cast-iron urinal with screen,
chaussée de la Muette, 16th
arrondissement, Paris, 1858–78
Albumen print, 36.7 × 27 cm,
Musée Carnavalet – Histoire de Paris

Charles Marville (1813–1879),
Vespasienne (urinal), Pont
d'Arcole, 4th arrondissement,
Paris, 1858–71
Albumen print, 34.7 × 25.1 cm,
Musée Carnavalet – Histoire de Paris

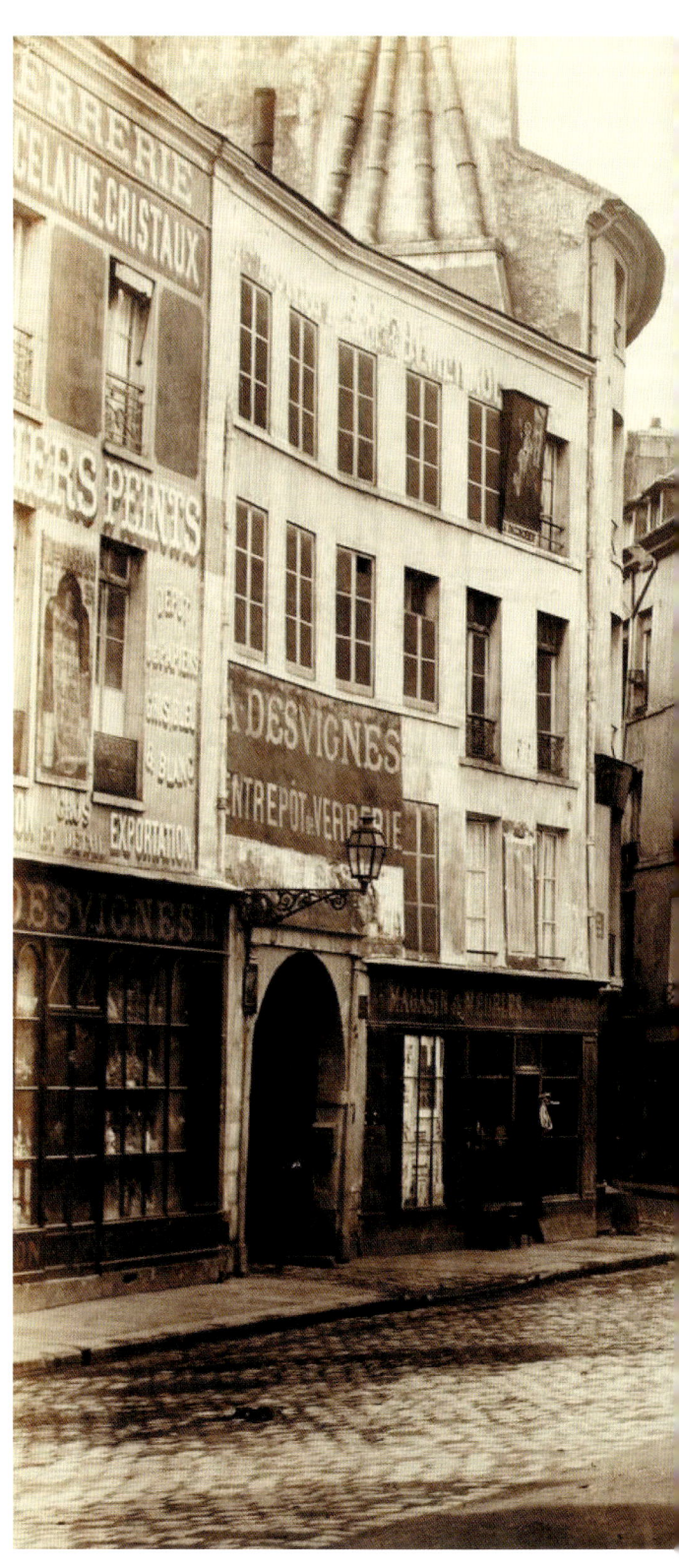

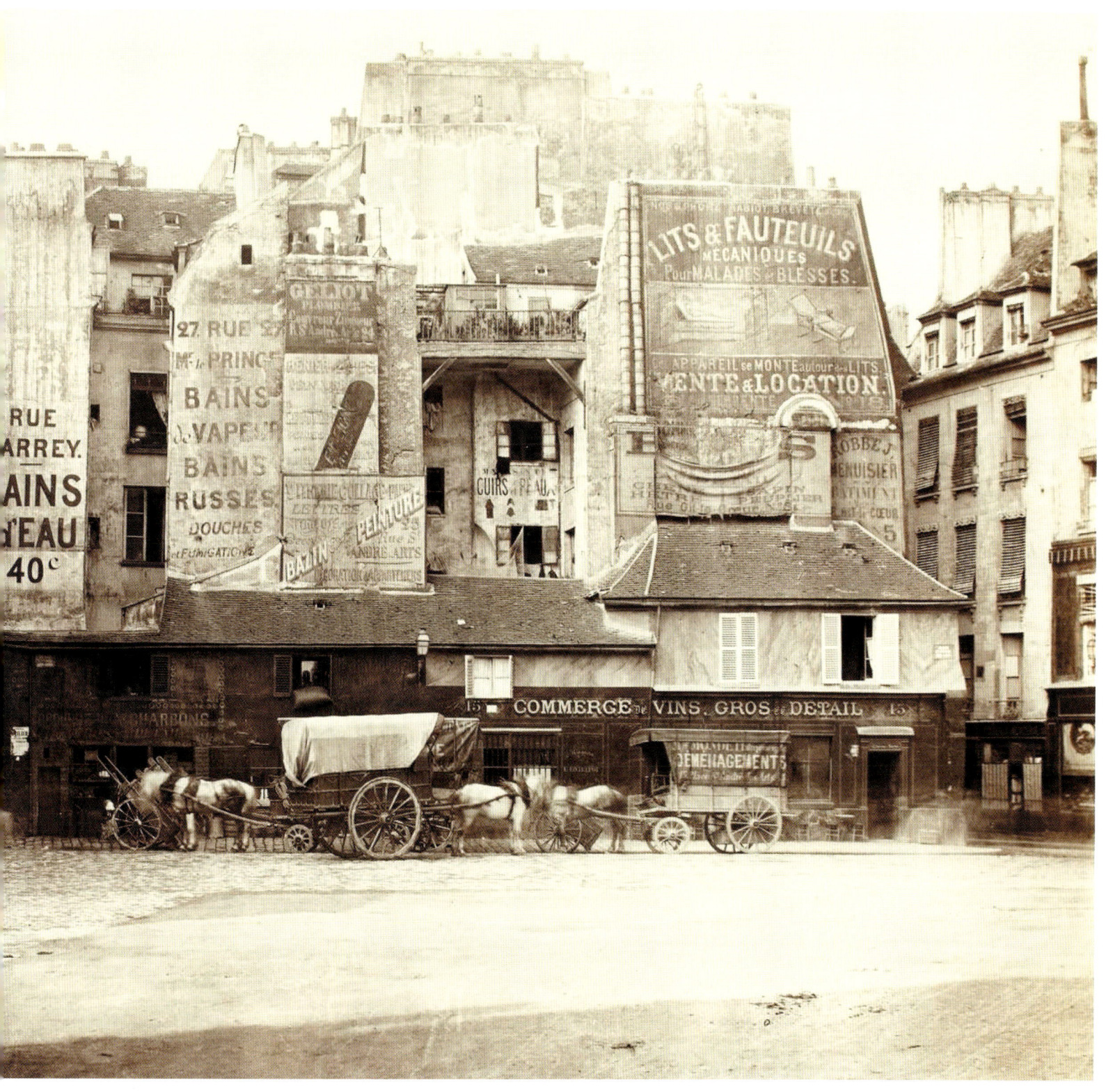

Charles Marville (1813–1879), Place Saint André des Arts, 6th arrondissement, Paris, 1865–68   Albumen print, 22.8 x 36.6 cm, Musée Carnavalet – Histoire de Paris

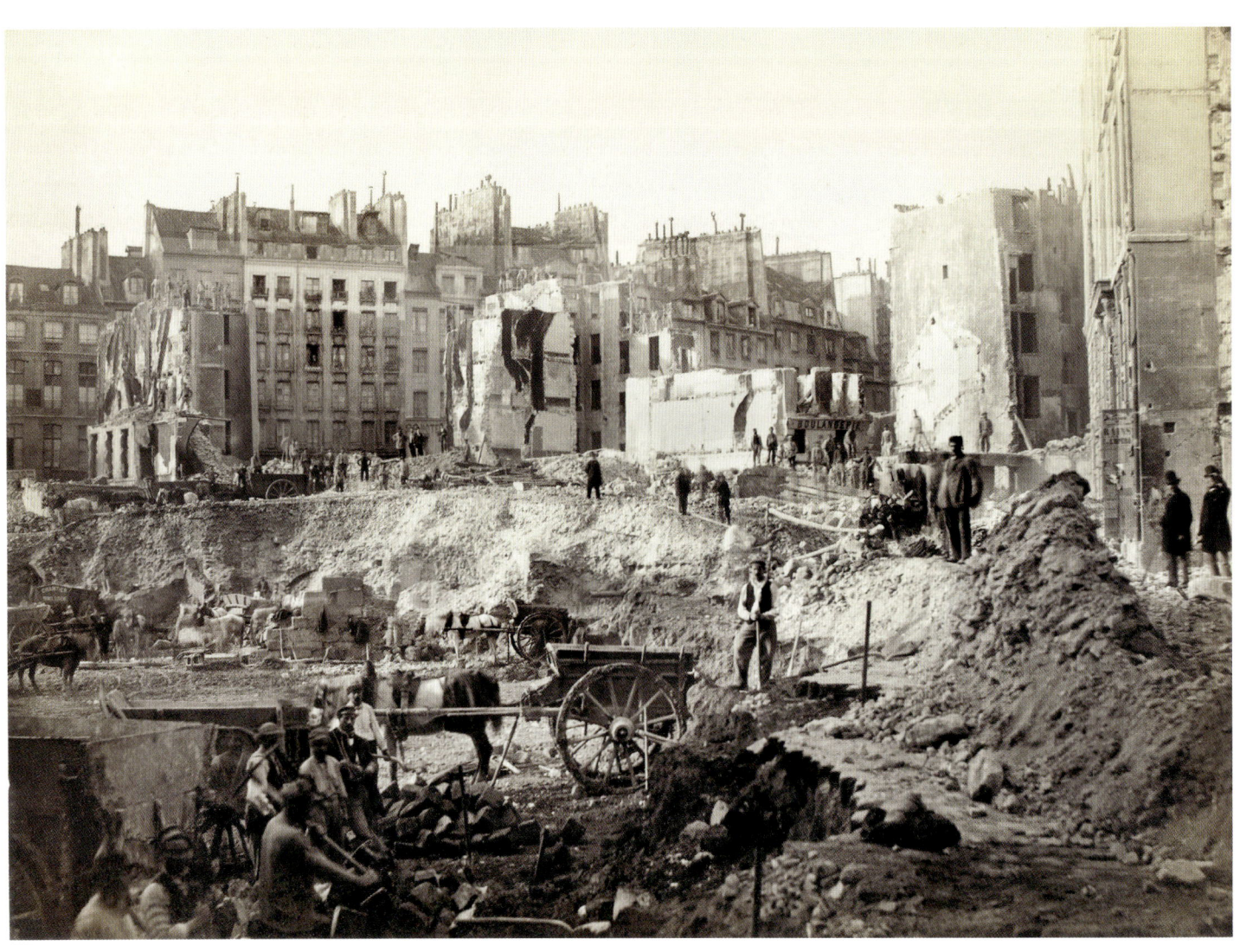

Charles Marville (1813–1879), Construction of the Avenue de l'Opéra in Paris. Excavation of the Butte des Moulins, 24 February 1876

Albumen print, 25.8 × 35.9 cm, Loan from the Rijksmuseum, Amsterdam

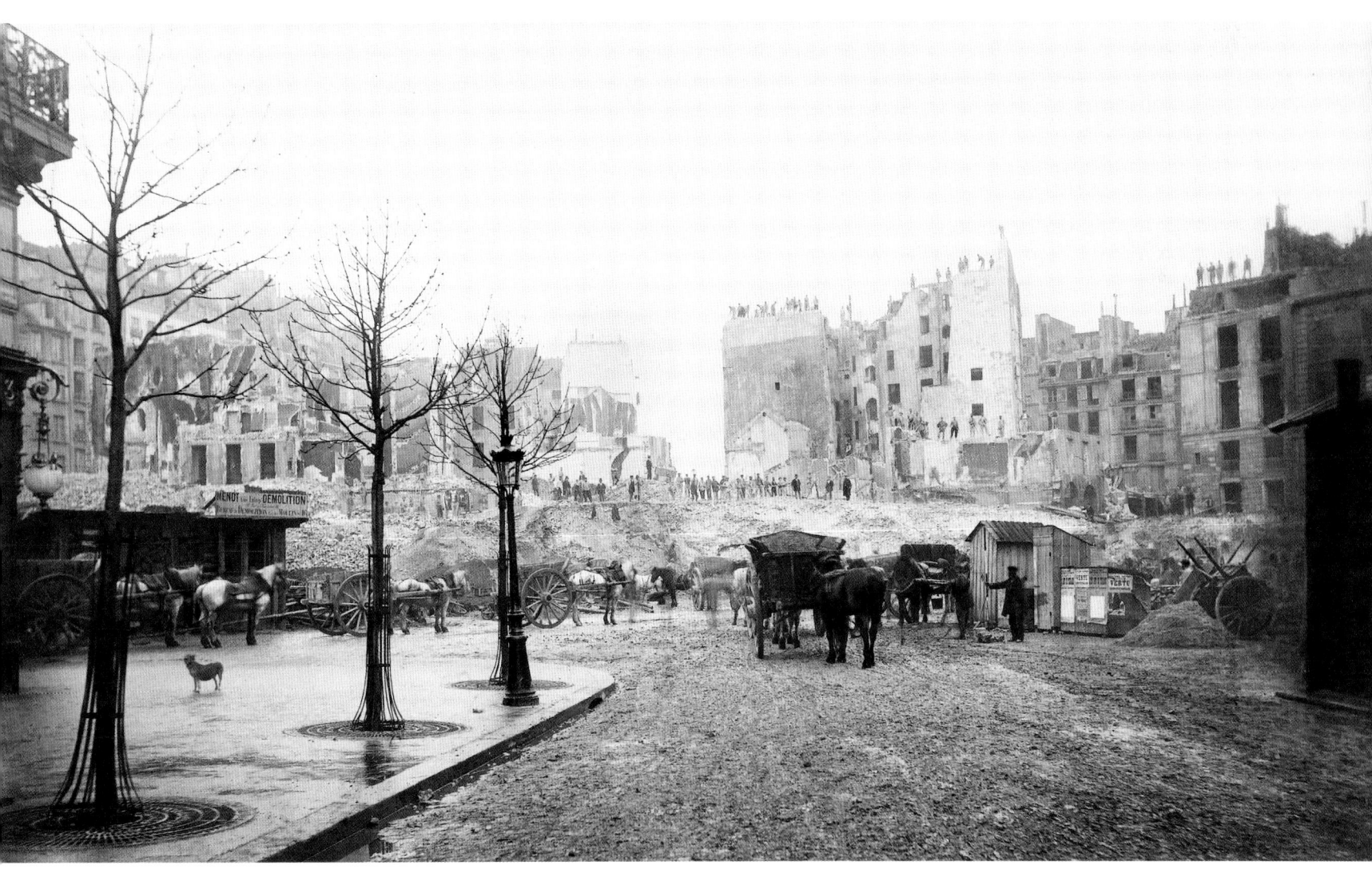

Charles Marville (1813–1879), Opening of the Avenue de l'Opéra. Butte des Moulins (from rue Saint-Honoré), between December 1876 and February 1877

Albumen print, 20.5 × 36.1 cm, Musée Carnavalet – Histoire de Paris

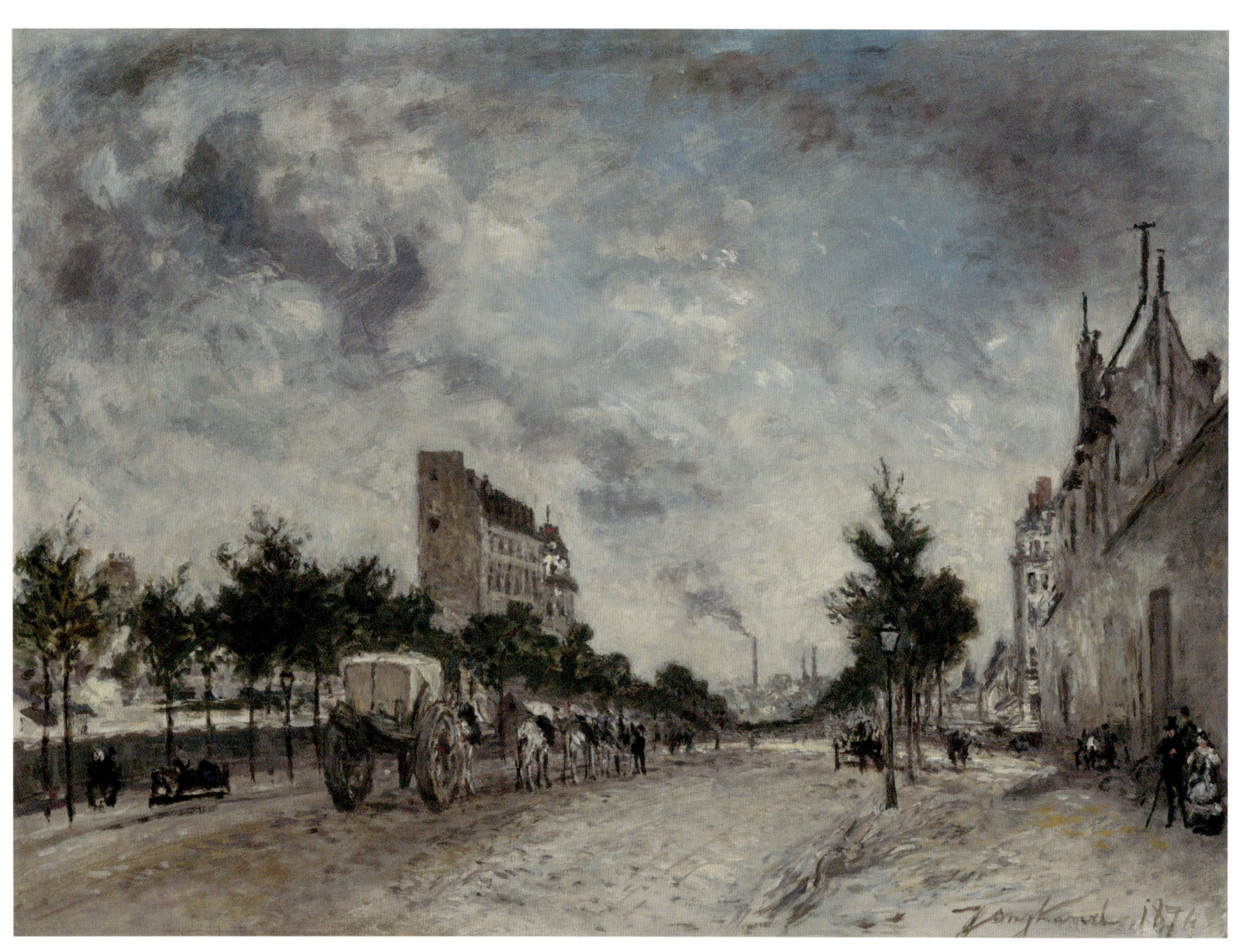

Johan Barthold Jongkind (1819–1891), *The New Boulevard de Port Royal, Paris*, 1874

Oil on canvas, 34 × 47 cm, Private collection

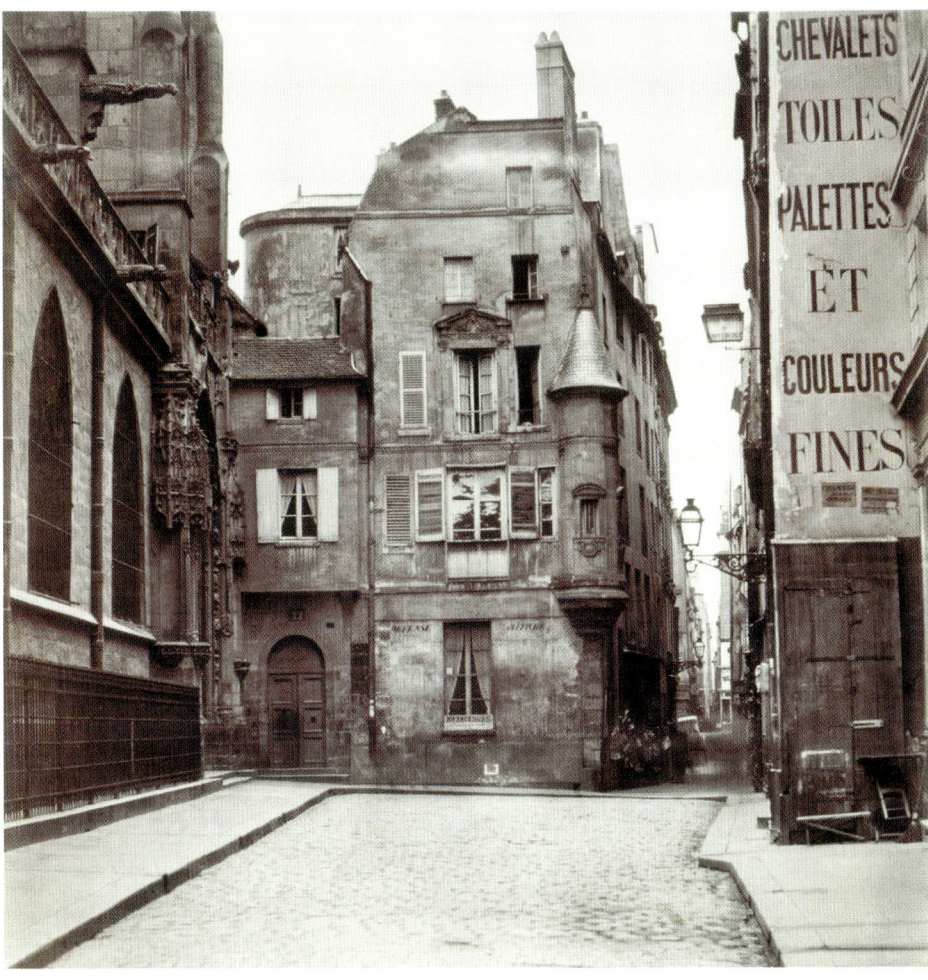

Charles Marville (1813–1879), Rue des Prêtres-Saint-Germain-l'Auxerrois, 1st arrondissement, Paris, 1865–68

Albumen print from a negative on wet collodion glass, 27 × 27.1 cm, Musée Carnavalet – Histoire de Paris

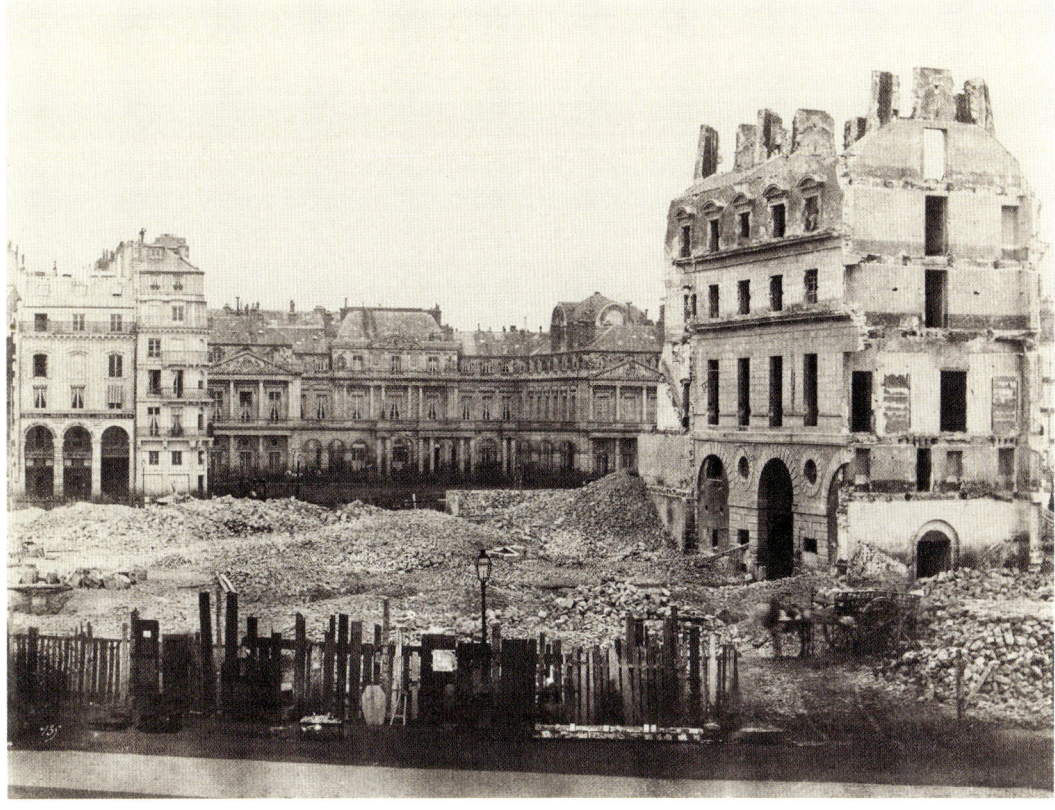

Charles Marville (1813–1879), Palais-Royal, 1st arrondissment, Paris, 1852–54

Albumen print, 16 × 21.5 cm, Musée Carnavalet – Histoire de Paris

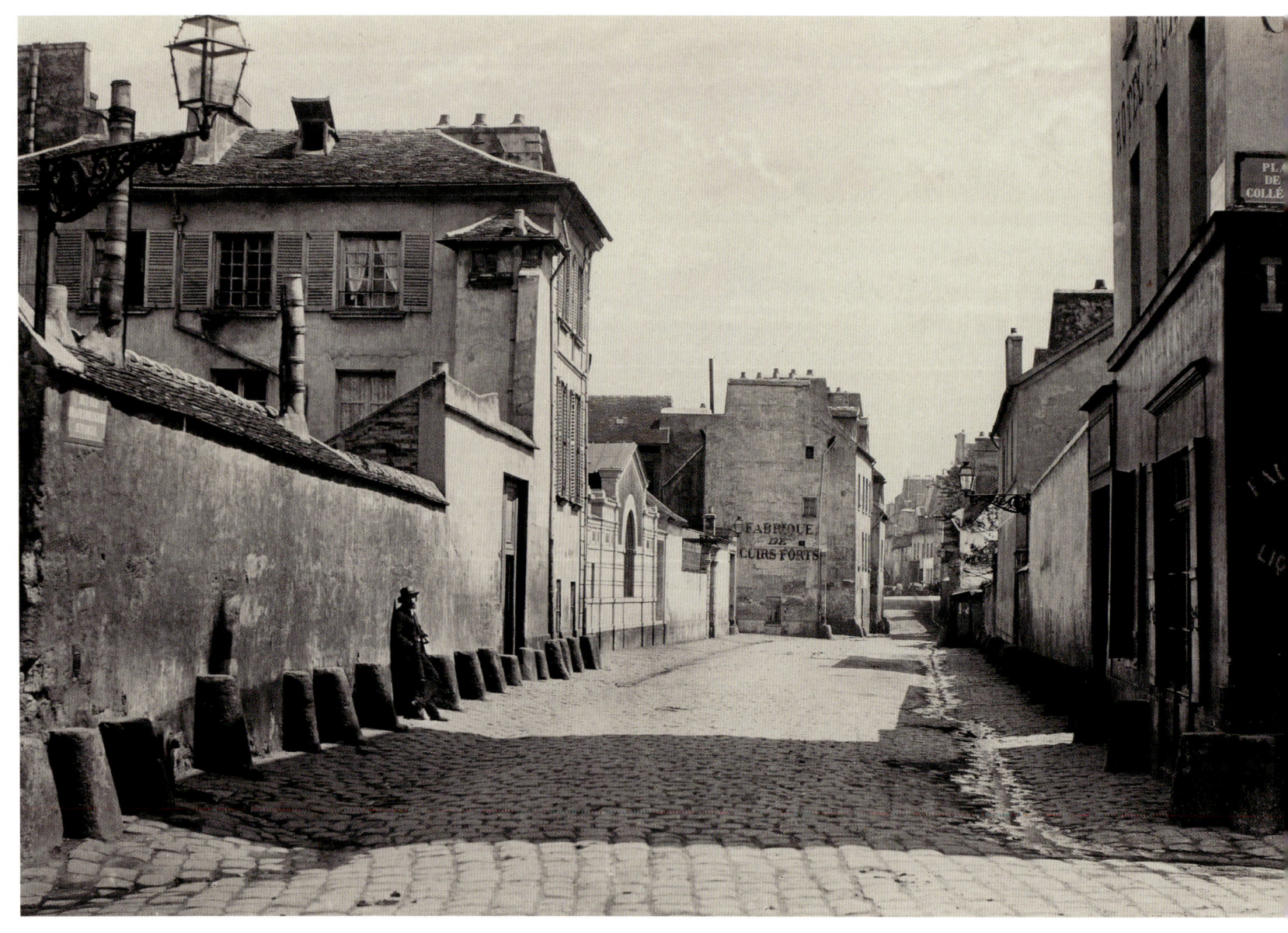

Charles Marville (1813–1879), Rue des Francs-Bourgeois-Saint-Marcel, as seen from the Place de la Collégiale, 5th/13th arrondissement, Paris, 1865–68
Albumen print, 21.7 × 36.2 cm, Musée Carnavalet – Histoire de Paris

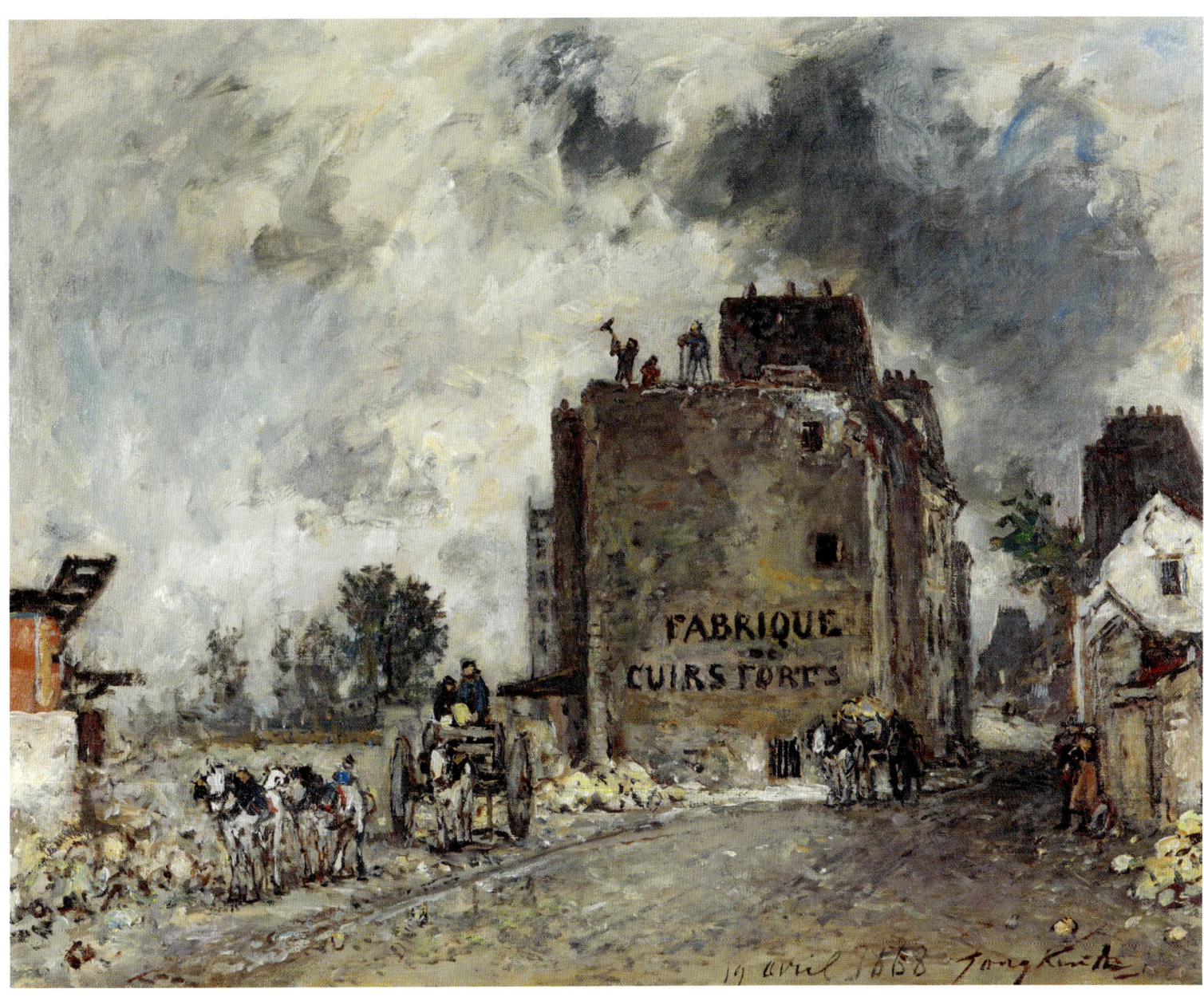

Johan Barthold Jongkind (1819–1891), *Demolition of the Rue des Francs-Bourgeois-Saint-Marcel*, 1868
Oil on canvas, 33.9 × 41.9 cm, Kunstmuseum Den Haag. Acquired with the support of the Rembrandt Association

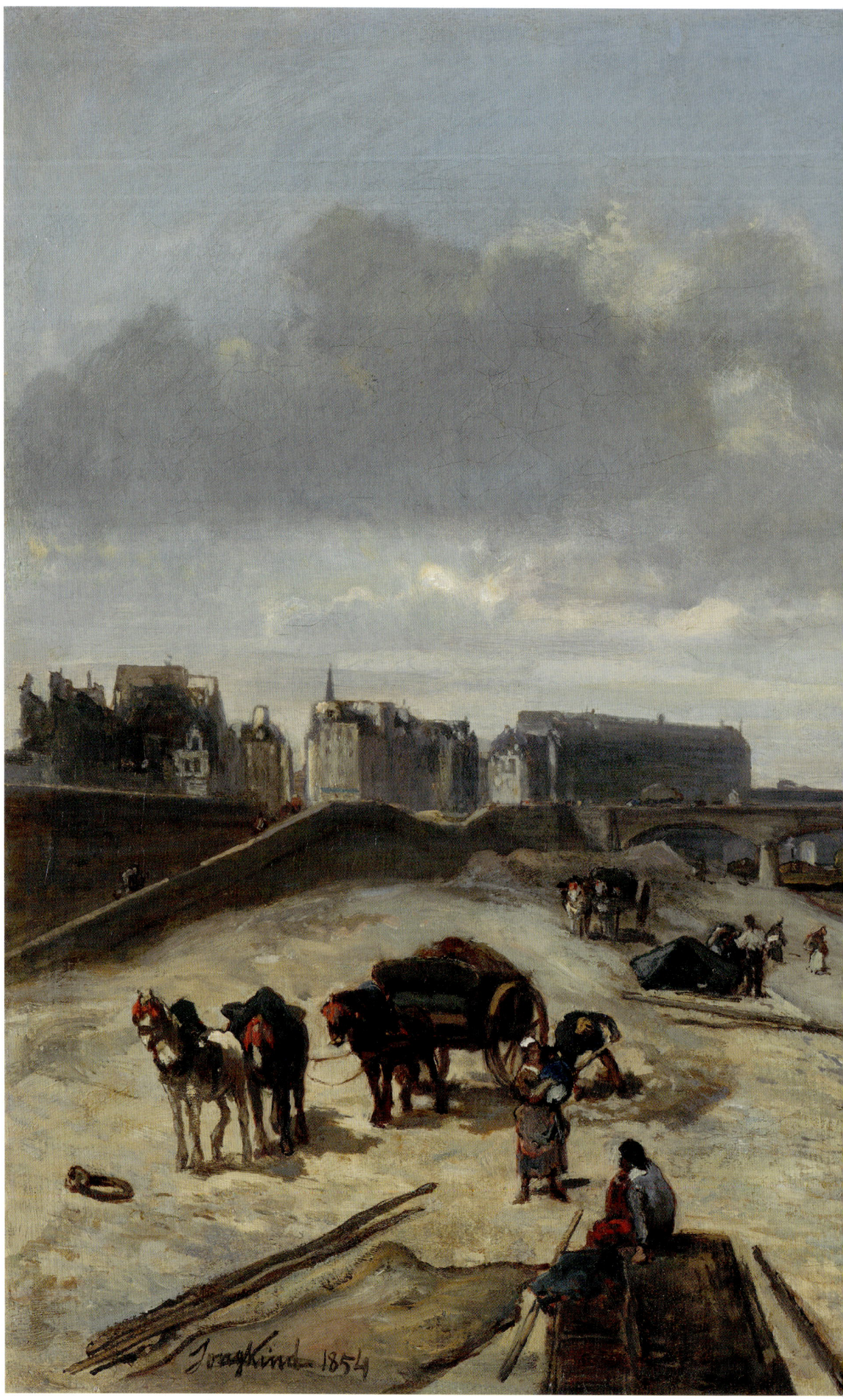

Johan Barthold Jongkind
(1819–1891), *The Chapel of
Notre Dame Seen from the
Pont de la Tournelle*, 1854

Oil on canvas, 43.9 × 65.4 cm,
Kunstmuseum Den Haag. Long-term
loan from a private collection

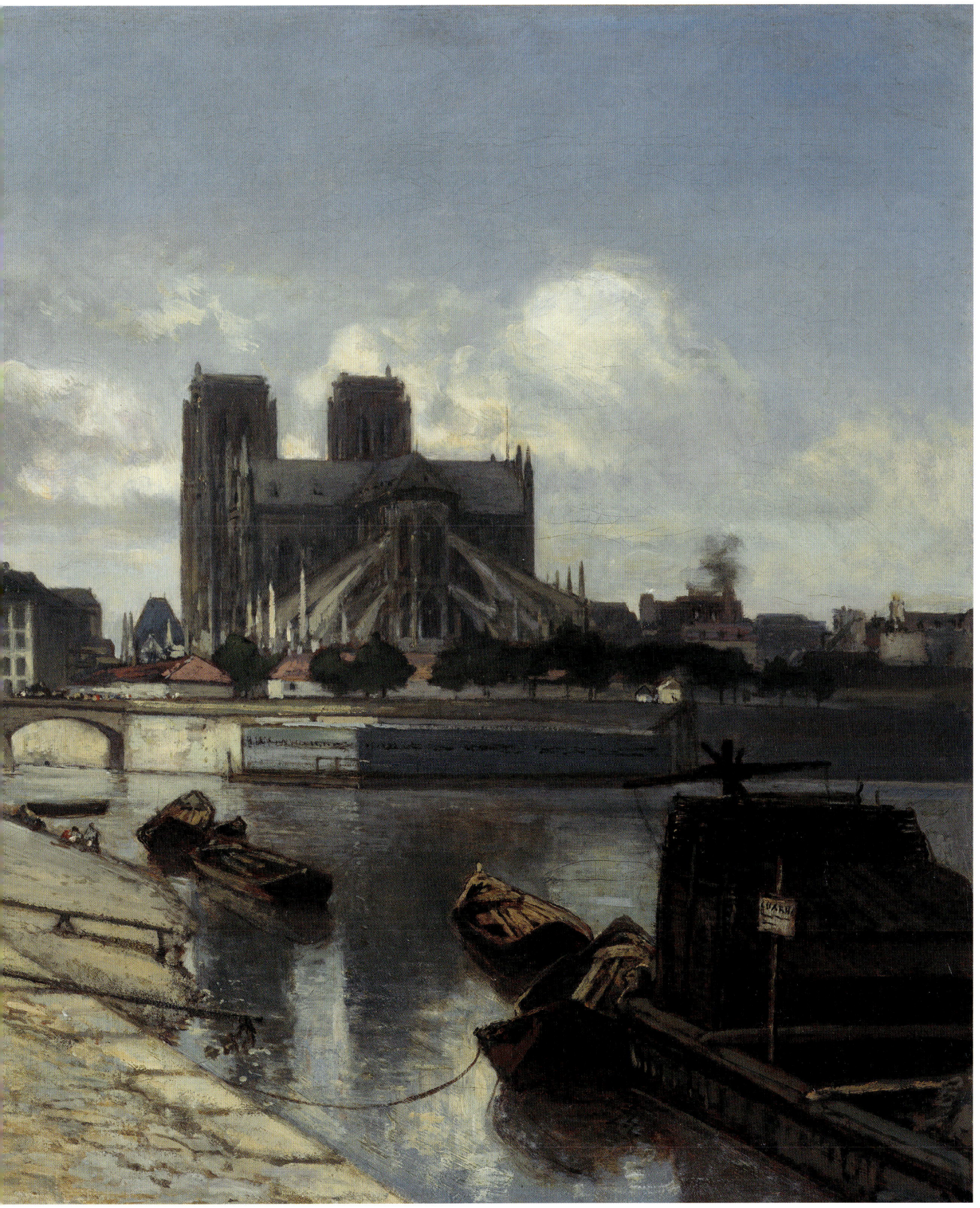

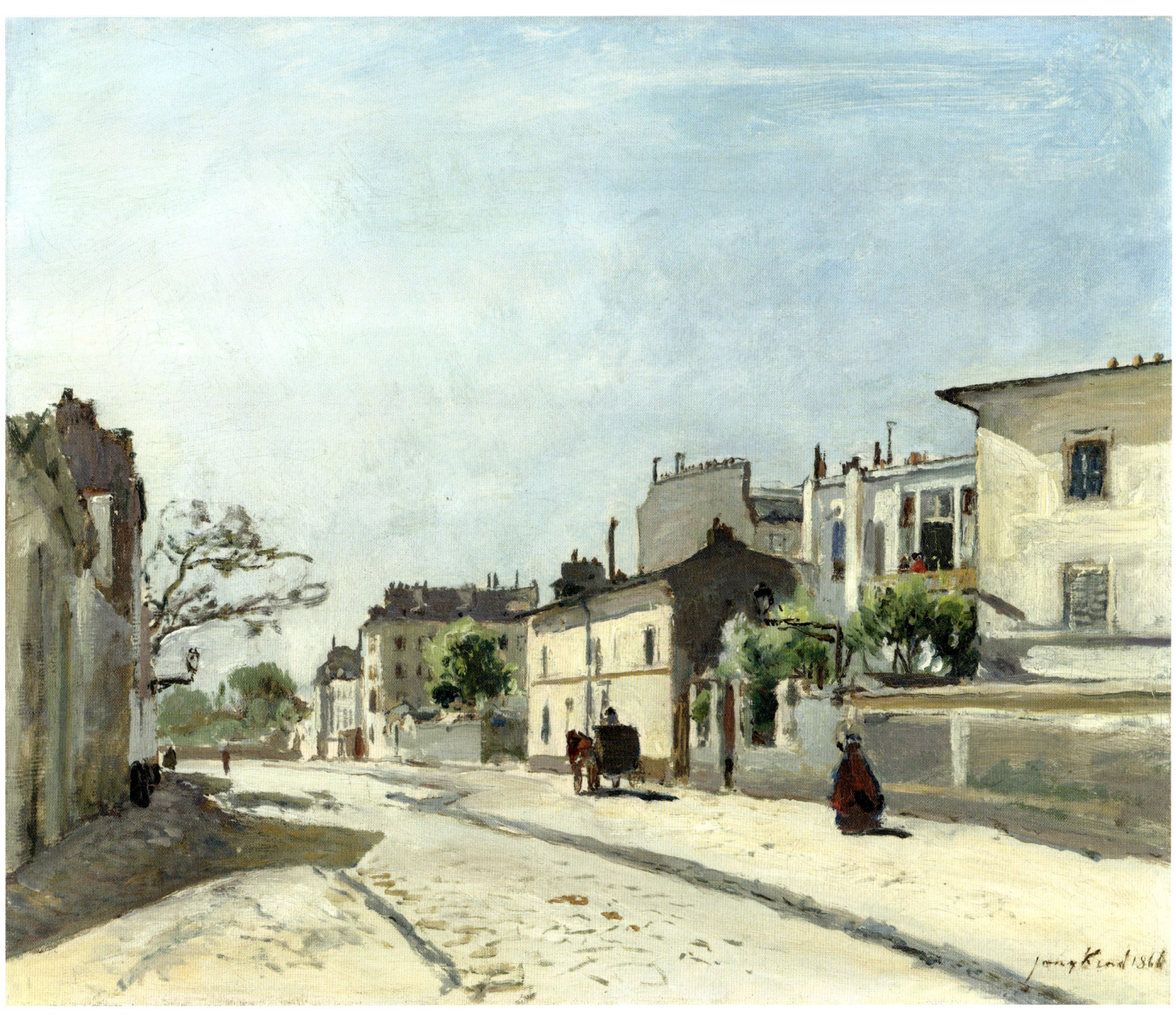

Johan Barthold Jongkind (1819–1891), *Rue Notre-Dame, Paris*, 1866

Oil on canvas, 38.7 × 47.6 cm, Rijksmuseum, Amsterdam. Acquired with the support of the VriendenLoterij, the Rijksmuseum Fund and the Rembrandt Society, partly thanks to the Cultuurfonds

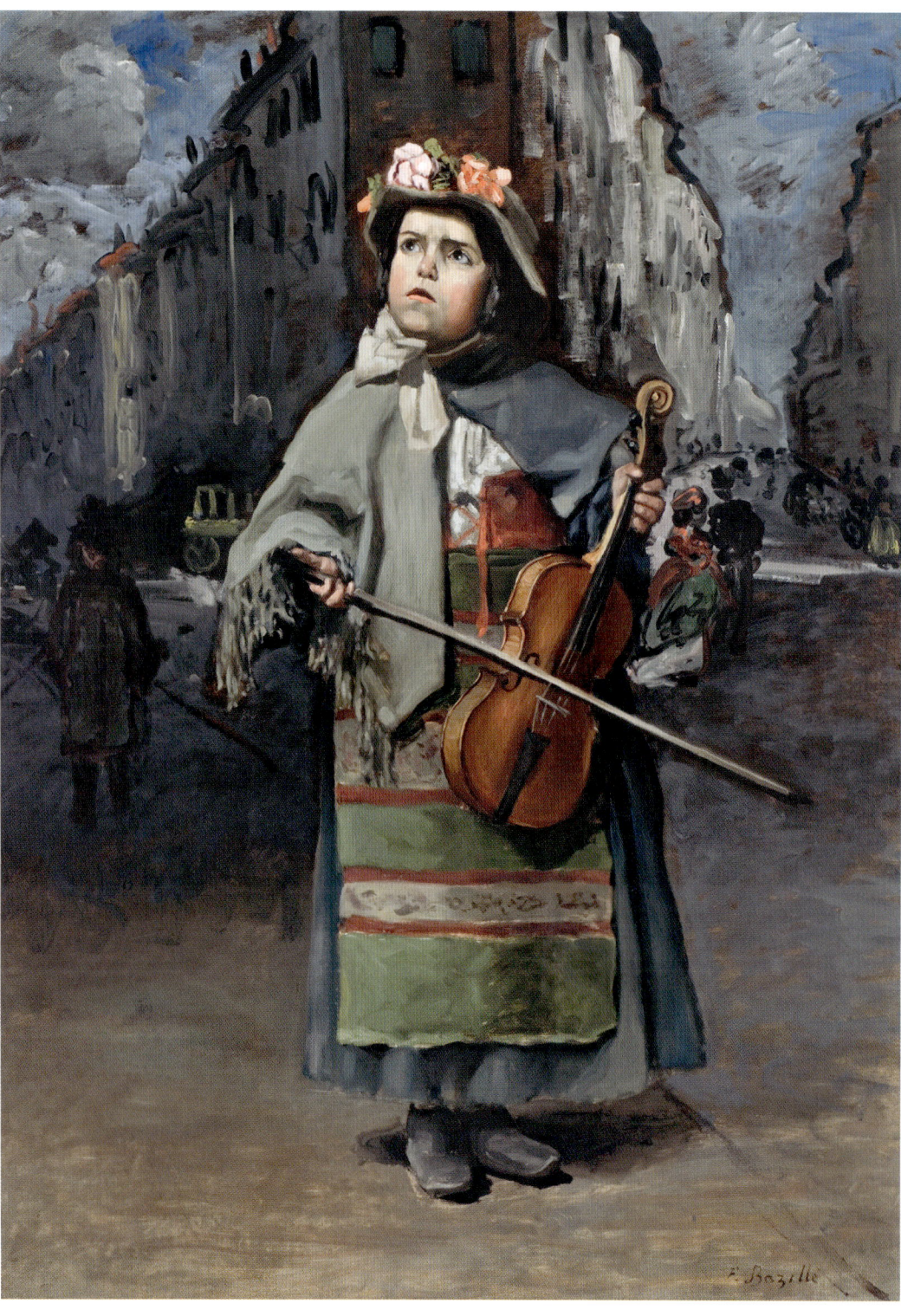

Frédéric Bazille (1841–1870), *Little Italian Street Singer*, 1866
Oil on canvas, 131 × 98 cm, Musée Fabre de Montpellier

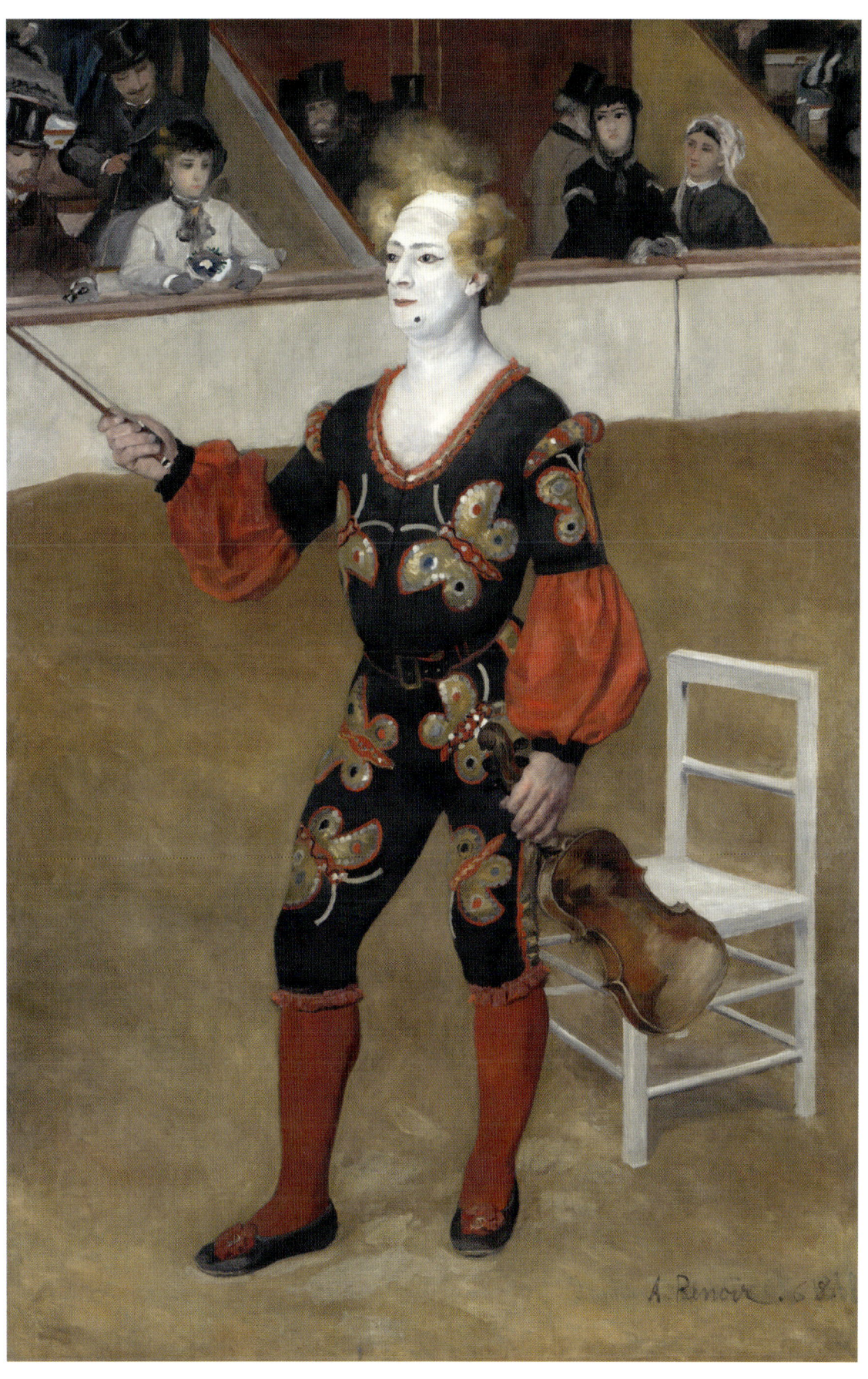

Auguste Renoir (1841–1919), *The Clown*, 1868
Oil on canvas, 193.5 × 130 cm, Kröller-Müller Museum, Otterlo

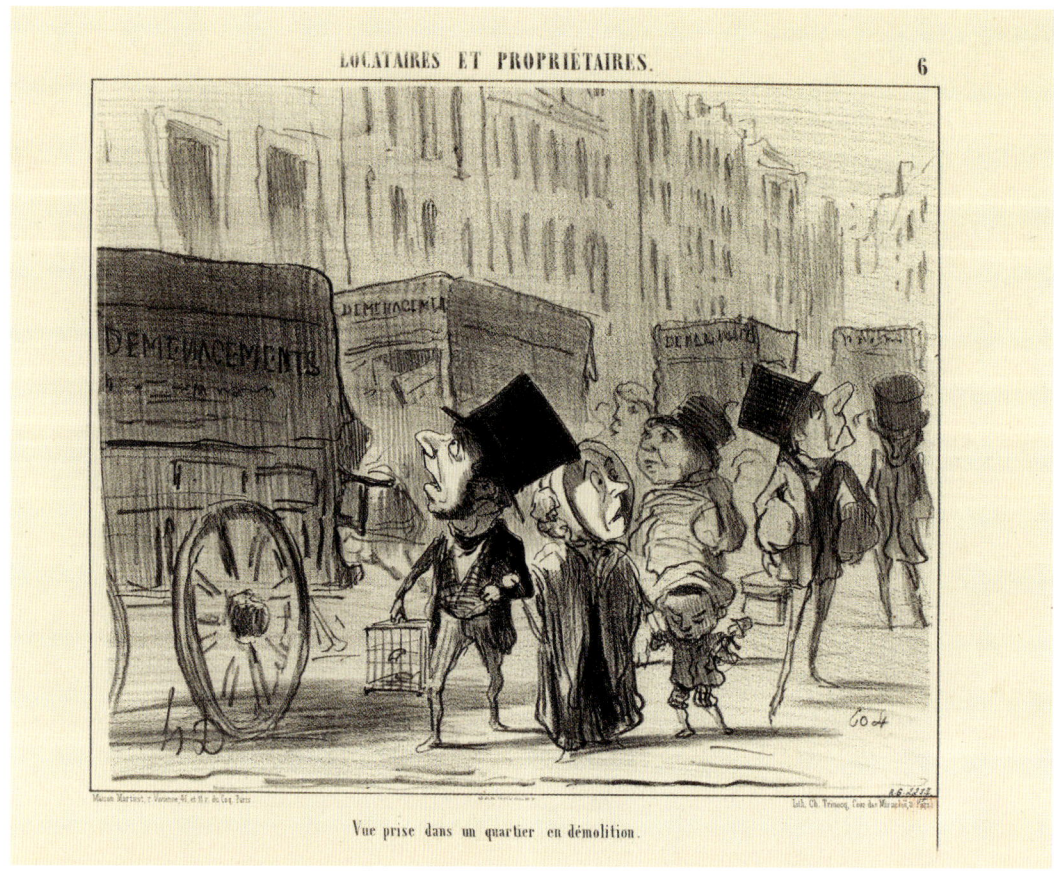

Honoré Daumier (1808–1879), From the series *Tenants and Owners*: 'View of a neighbourhood being demolished', 1854
Lithograph, 27.2 × 34.8 cm, Musée Carnavalet – Histoire de Paris

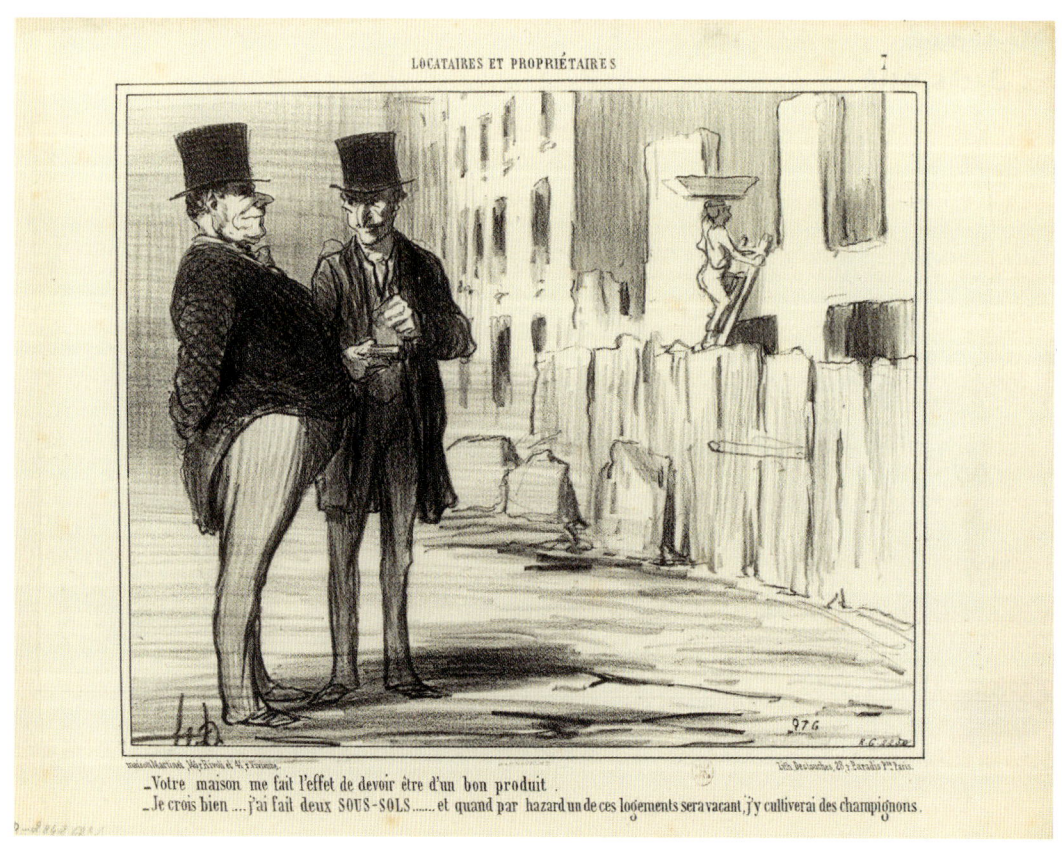

Honoré Daumier (1808–1879), From the series *Tenants and Owners*: 'Your house seems to me to be a good product. – I think so... I made two basements... and when by chance one of these accommodations is vacant, I will grow mushrooms there', 1856
Lithograph, 27.1 × 35.8 cm, Musée Carnavalet – Histoire de Paris

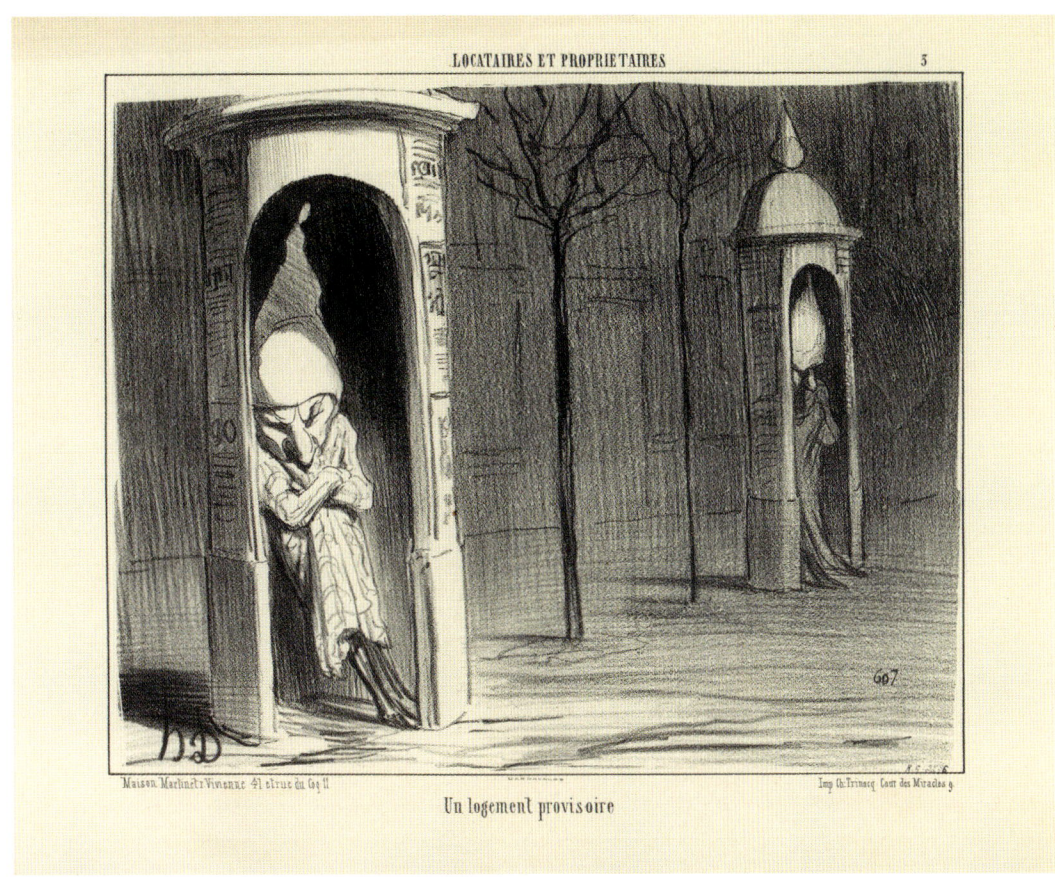

Honoré Daumier (1808–1879), From the series *Tenants and Owners*: 'A temporary accommodation', 1854

Lithograph, 27.8 × 35.1 cm, Musée Carnavalet – Histoire de Paris

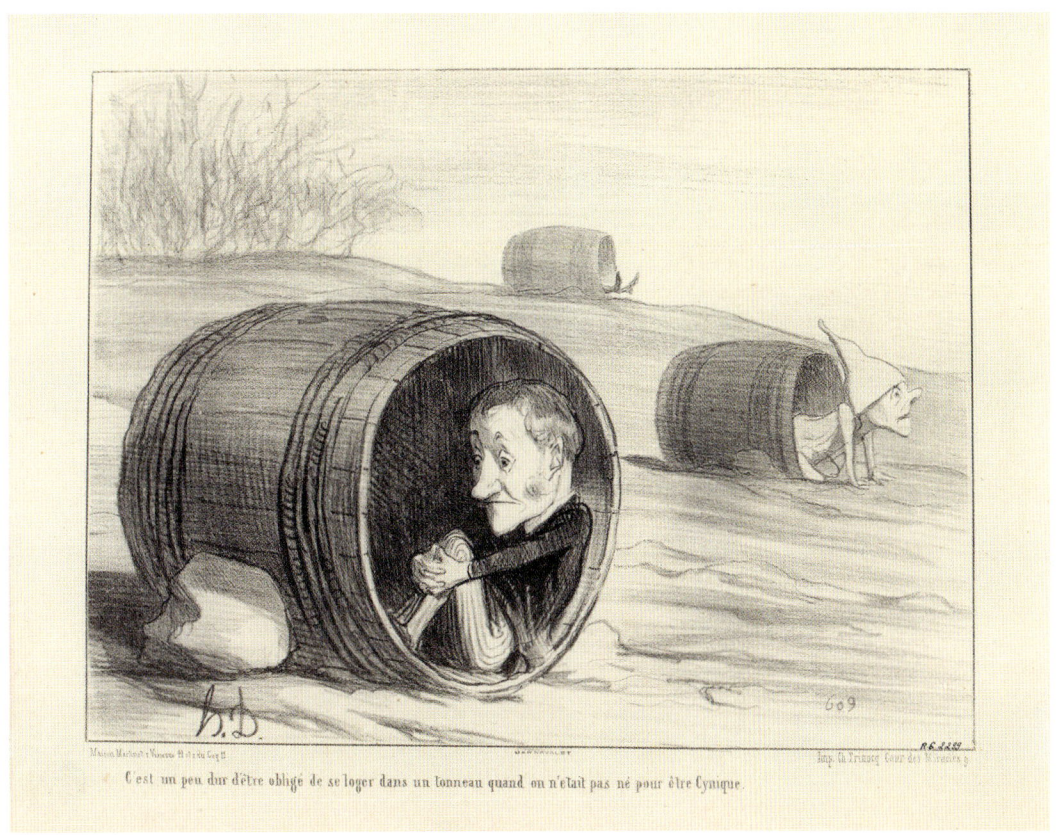

Honoré Daumier (1808–1879), From the series *Tenants and Owners*: 'It's a bit hard to be obliged
to live in a barrel when one wasn't born to be a cynic', 1854

Lithograph, 27.6 × 35 cm, Musée Carnavalet – Histoire de Paris

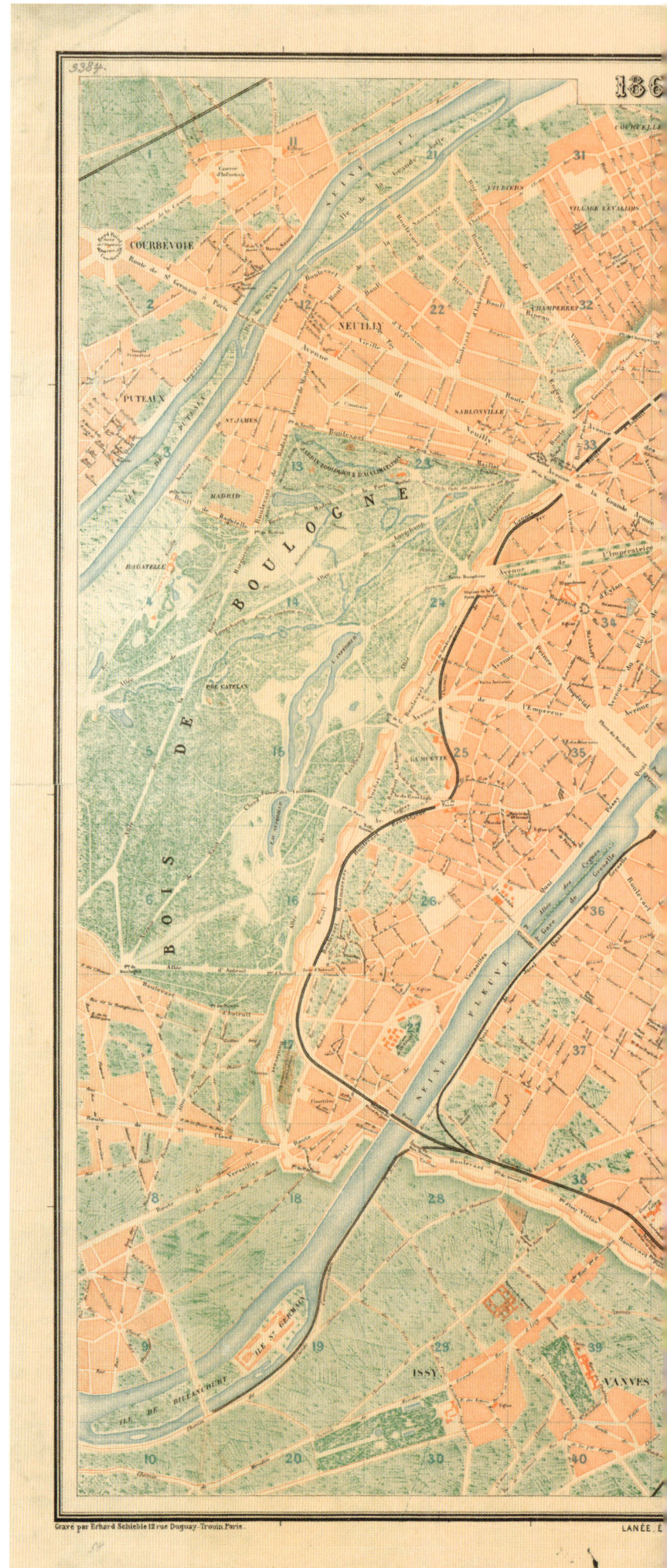

Erhard Schieble (1821–1880), City map 'Le Paris de Napoléon III', 1867

Engraving, c. 1:17 000, 57 × 79 cm, Staatsbibliothek zu Berlin

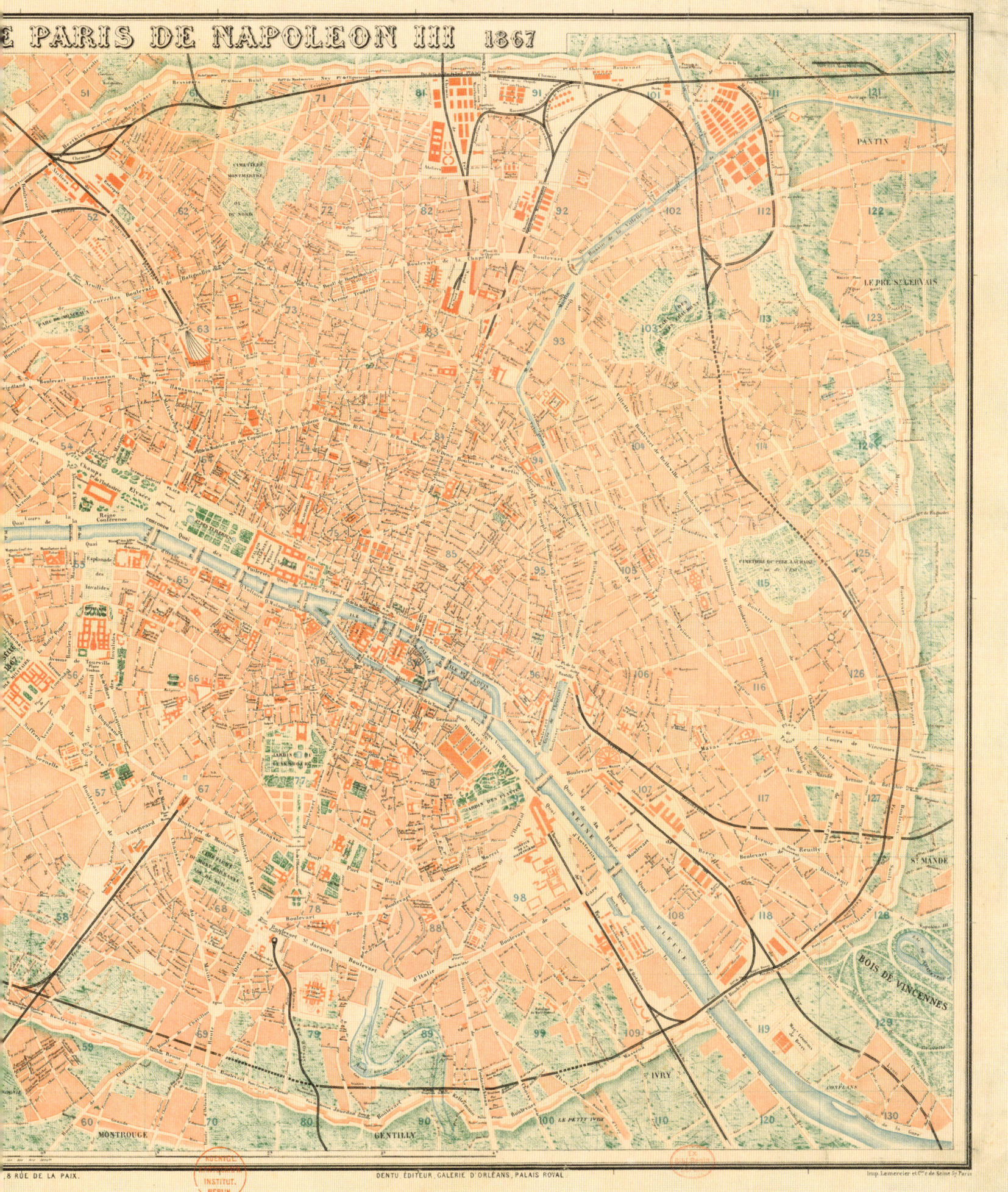

E PARIS DE NAPOLEON III   1867

8 RUE DE LA PAIX.   DENTU ÉDITEUR, GALERIE D'ORLÉANS, PALAIS ROYAL.   Imp. Lemercier et C.ie r de Seine 57 Paris

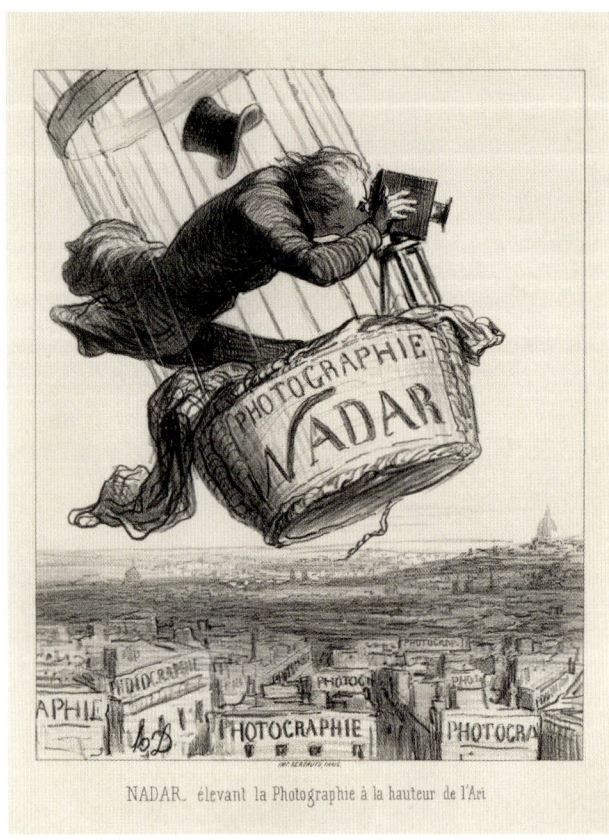

Honoré Daumier (1808–1879), Nadar Elevating
Photography to the Height of Art, 1862

Page from *Le Boulevard*, Lithograph, 26.7 × 22.1 cm,
Bibliothèque nationale de France

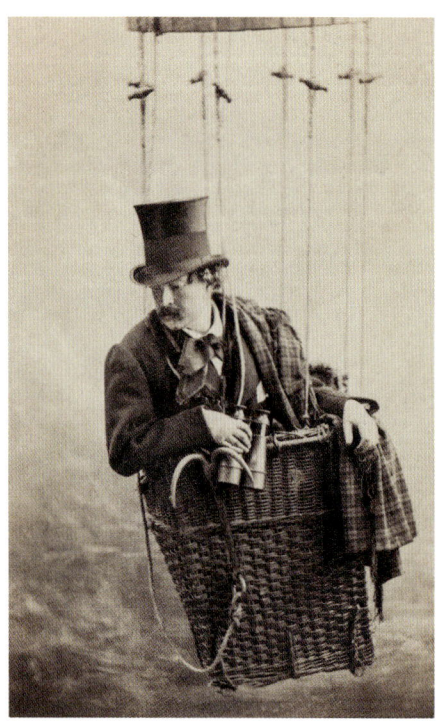

Photo Studio of Nadar, Portrait of
Nadar (Félix Tournachon), 1860–1890

Albumen print, 8.5 × 5.5 cm,
Musée Carnavalet – Histoire de Paris

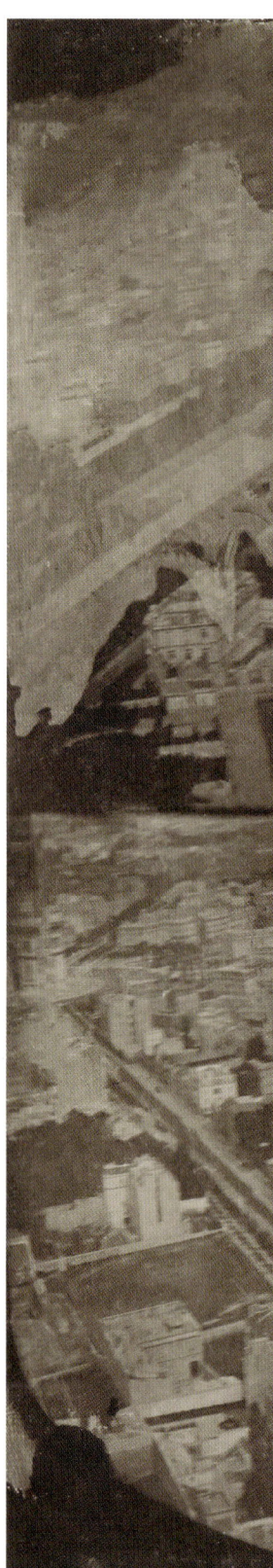

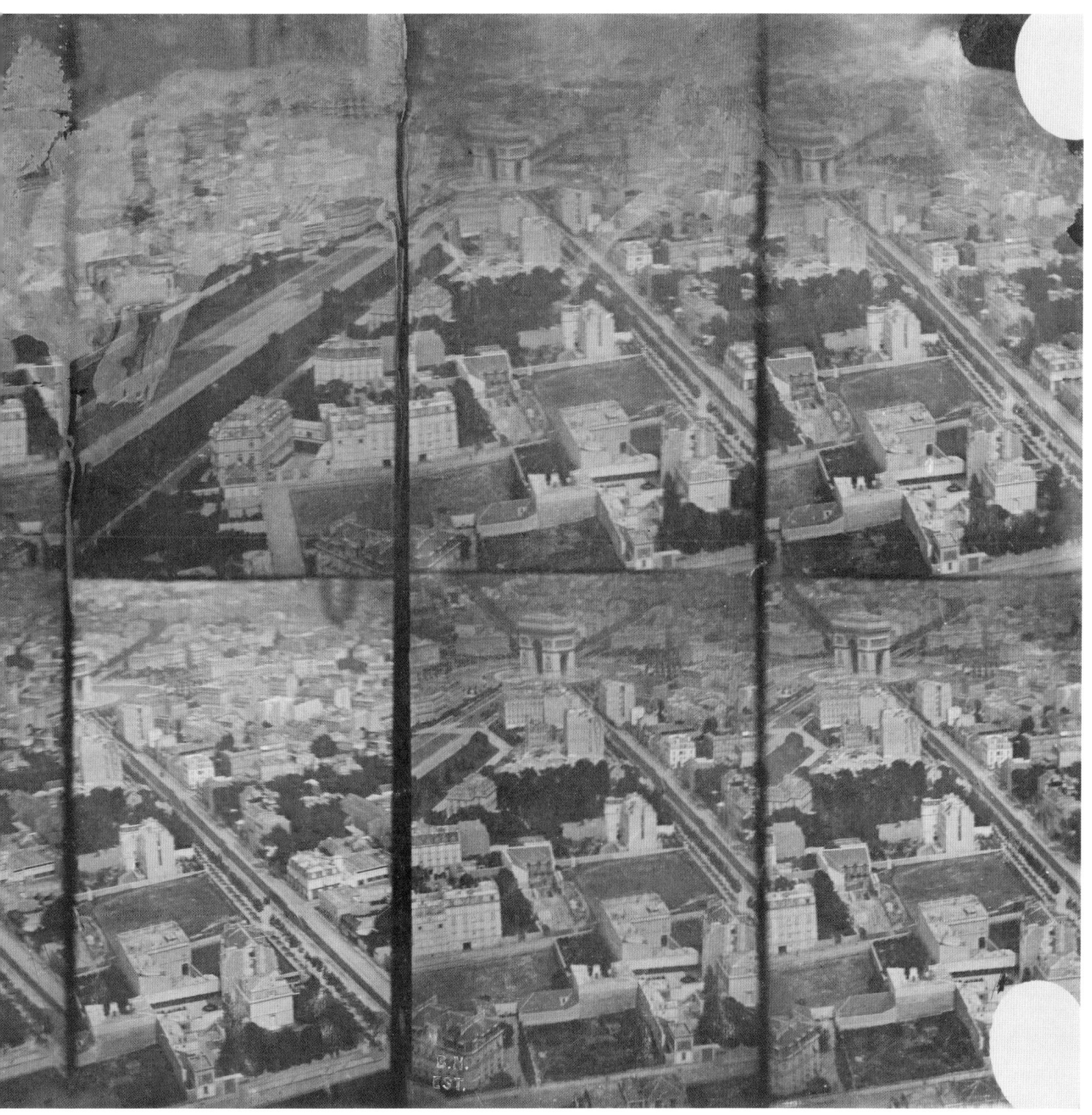

Nadar (1820–1910), Aerial views of the Étoile district in Paris, 1868
Photo (unknown technique), 23 × 28.8 cm. Bibliothèque nationale de France

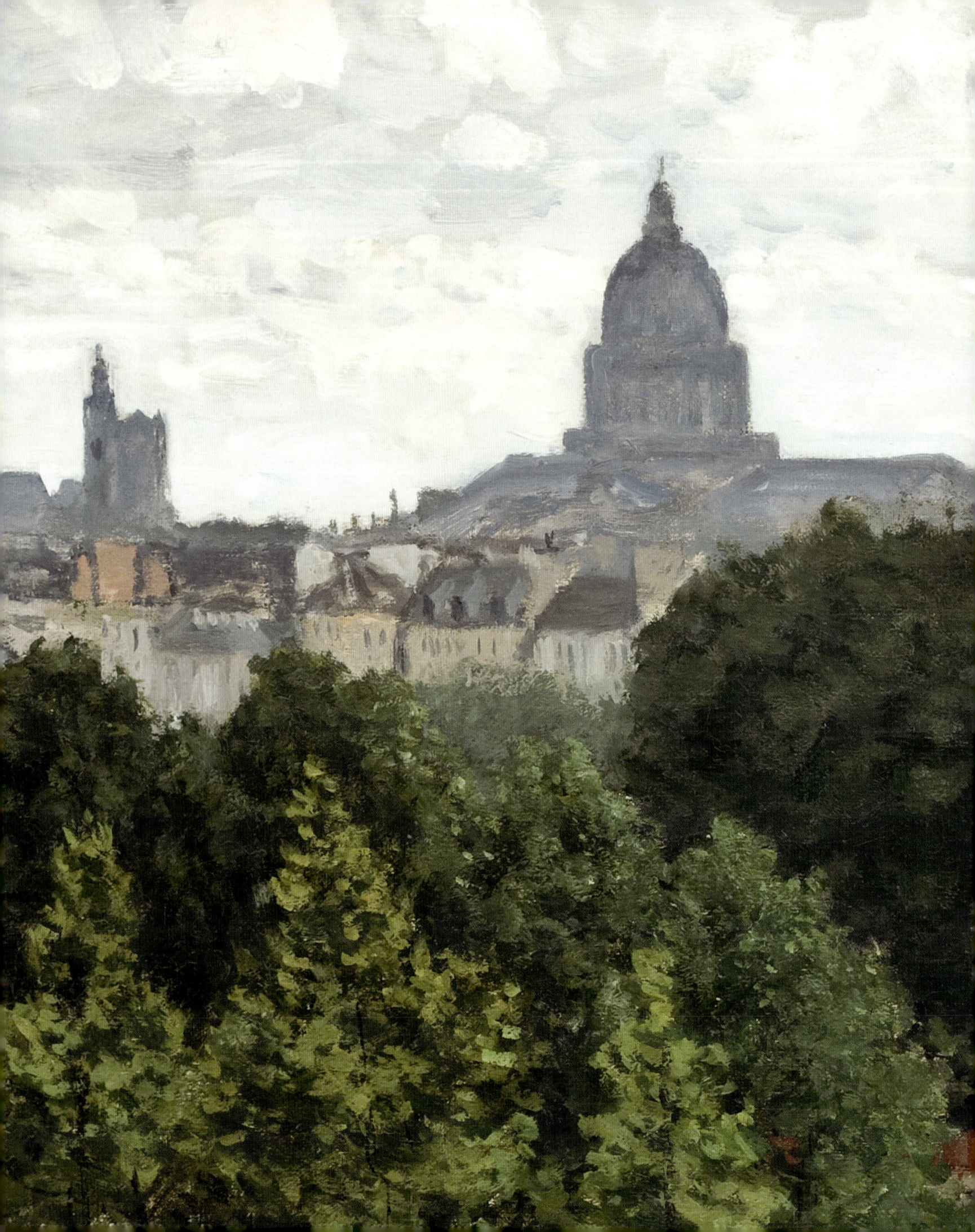

PARIS 1867 – A TURNING POINT

Frouke van Dijke

1 January
'One o' clock in the morning. 1867, what do you have in store for us?"[1]

Edmond and Jules de Goncourt, *Journal*

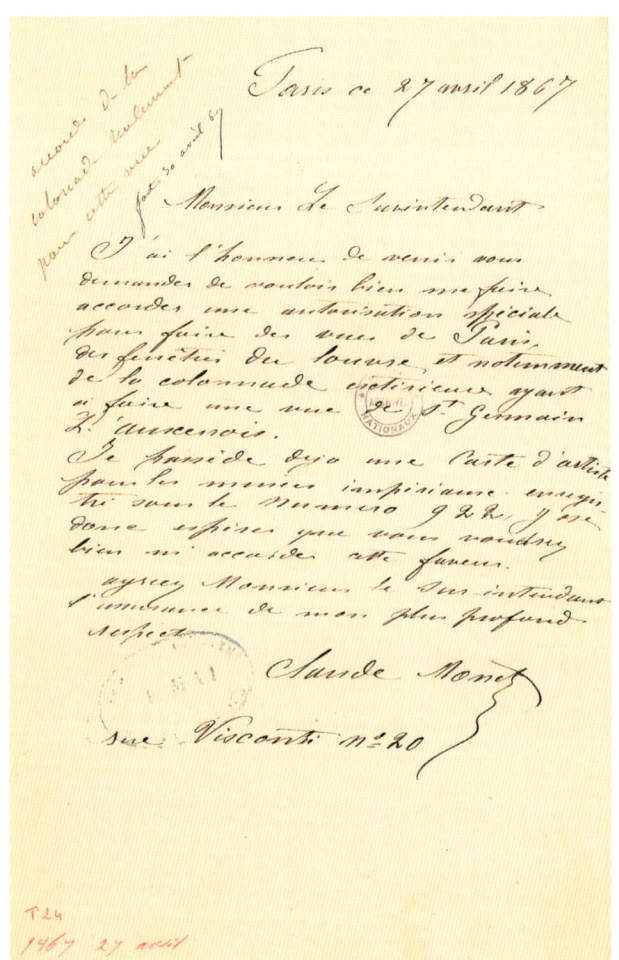

Fig. 1

Fig. 2

Fig. 1
Letter from Claude Monet to Comte de Nieuwerkerke,
director of the Louvre, 27 April 1867
Archives nationales

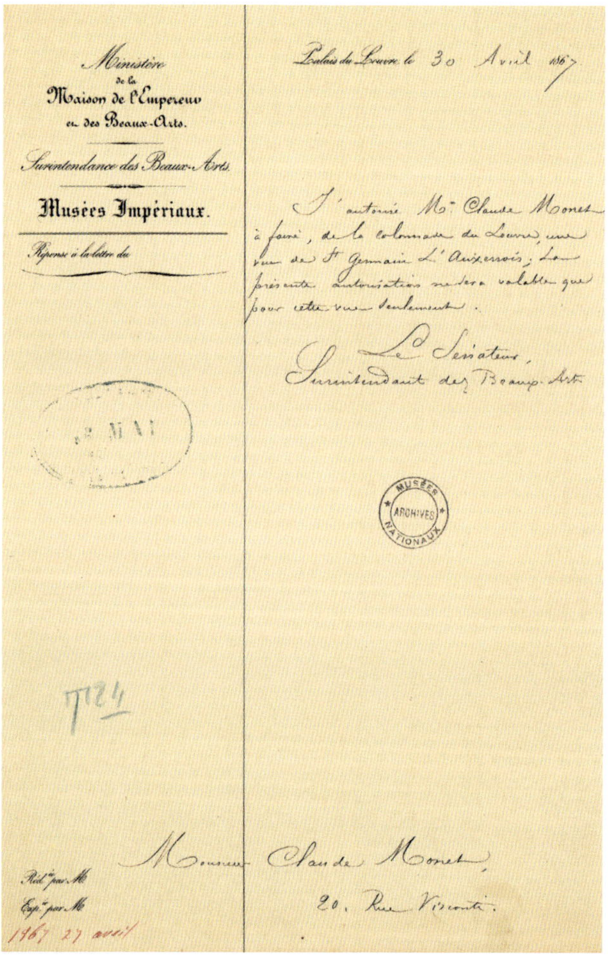

Fig. 2
Permission for Claude Monet to paint from
the balcony (the colonnade) of the Louvre,
from Comte de Nieuwerkerke
Archives nationales

The invention of the paper clip, the first passage through the Suez Canal, the patenting of dynamite, the publication of the first volume of Karl Marx's *Das Kapital*, the founding of Canada: 1867 was an eventful year. The physicist and chemist Marie Curie was born in Warsaw on 7 November that year, while the poet and art critic Charles Baudelaire died in Paris on 31 August. In Missouri, the infamous American outlaw Jesse James robbed another bank. Profit: $4,000. Loss: three human lives. In January, Emperor Kōmei of Japan succumbed to smallpox in Tokyo, and on 6 June Tsar Alexander II of Russia narrowly escaped death in a failed attempt on his life in Paris. He was there on the occasion of the Universal Exposition, which, with around ten million visitors, 41 participating countries and more than 50,000 exhibitors, could justifiably call itself the largest event of 1867.[2]

That spring, more than a month after the exhibition's opening, on the other bank of the Seine, about three and a half kilometres from the exhibition grounds, 26-year-old artist Claude Monet had taken up position on the east balcony of the Louvre.[3] His artist's card – number 922 – granted him permission to paint in the Louvre, but he had more ambitious plans. In a letter sent at the end of April to the museum's director, Émilien de Nieuwerkerke, he requested official access to the balcony in order to paint 'views of Paris' [figs. 1–2].[4] The request was granted and resulted in three cityscapes: a view of the Church of Saint-Germain-l'Auxerrois, one of Quai du Louvre, the busy street between the museum and the Seine, and one of the formal lawn and flower beds of the Jardin de l'Infante (Garden of the Princess). These were Monet's first cityscapes of Paris [figs. 3–5].

Could Monet have been aware of the great significance of his undertaking at that moment? Probably not. The young painter had other things on his mind: his lover, Camille Doncieux, was pregnant, his pockets were empty and his father – who disapproved of the relationship – had decided to cut off his funds for a while. To make matters worse, all the works he had recently submitted to the annual Salon had been rejected by the jury. Monet was not in a good position. Nevertheless, looking out over the city, he must have had a certain sense of excitement about the future. In Paris in 1867, revolution was in the air: all the ingredients were present for the birth of a new future, a new society, a new art.

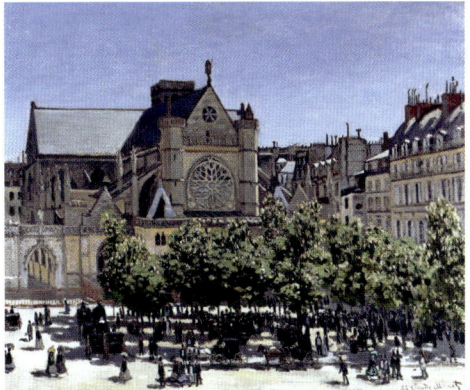

Fig. 3   [p. 86]

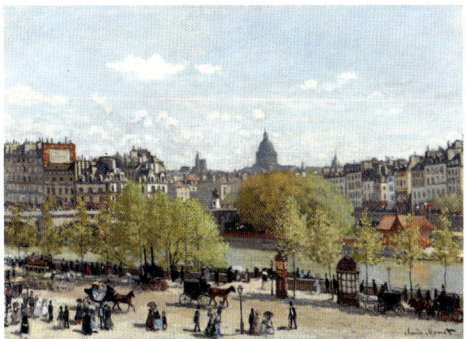

Fig. 4   [pp. 90–91]

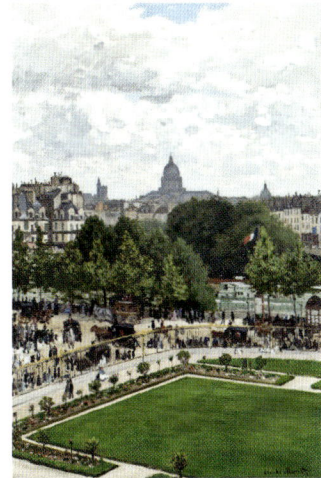

Fig. 5   [p. 89]

Fig. 3
Claude Monet (1840–1926), *Church of Saint-Germain-l'Auxerrois*, 1867
Oil on canvas, 79 × 98 cm, Staatliche Museen zu Berlin, Nationalgalerie

Fig. 4
Claude Monet (1840–1926), *Quai du Louvre*, 1867
Oil on canvas, 65.1 × 92.6 cm, Kunstmuseum Den Haag

Fig. 5
Claude Monet (1840–1926), *Garden of the Princess, Louvre*, 1867
Oil on canvas, 91.8 × 61.9 cm, Allen Memorial Art Museum,
Oberlin College, Oberlin, Ohio. R.T. Miller Jr. Fund

The most significant gesture

There was great symbolism in Monet's activities at the eastern colonnade of the Louvre. While his peers learned their trade inside the museum by diligently copying works in the collection, the young Monet literally turned his back on the old masters to paint modern life on the street. Art historian Linda Nochlin has described Monet's three cityscapes as nothing less than 'the most significant gesture' of an artist in relation to the art world, and describes the works as 'extraordinary... plein-air records of the contemporary city' that questioned once and for all the relationship between the artist and the museum.[5] She continues: '...in their aggressive randomness, visual accuracy and lack of incident or traditional pictorial structure, they asserted a potent visual challenge to that musty museum and all the values it stood for.... From that time on, despite Manet's constant reference to the art of the masters of the past or Renoir's declaration that one learns to paint in museums rather than before nature or Cézanne's numerous copies from the art of tradition, the relation of avant-garde artists toward their cultural heritage, and hence toward the museums as repositories of a viable and transmittable living tradition, becomes a problematic one.'[6]

Between two worlds

Nochlin pointed to these three cityscapes as a turning point in art history a hundred years after they were made, but in 1867 contemporary Parisians also felt that they were on the brink of a historic development: 'We are between two worlds...', wrote the French journalist and art historian Théophile Thoré that year, 'between a world that is ending and a world that is beginning.'[7] This sentiment was palpable in every corner of the Universal Exposition's elliptical palace [fig. 6], where Egyptian mummies and replicas of ancient temples stood cheek by jowl with brand-new inventions such as the typewriter and the hydraulic lift. There was a metres-deep freshwater aquarium: an underwater world that could be visited through specially constructed subterranean caves. Those who wished to ascend skyward could step into 'Le Géant', the photographer Nadar's giant hot-air balloon, and look down over the electrically illuminated festival grounds, where restaurants served cuisines from all over the world.[8] A model of the 'Plongeur', the first motor-driven submarine, inspired visitor Jules Verne to write his science-fiction novel *Twenty Thousand Leagues under the Sea* (1869–70), while Mark Twain described the Universal Exposition in his bestseller, *The Innocents Abroad* (1869), as a 'monstrous establishment' where a visitor would have to spend months to get a good impression of it (Twain himself managed only two hours because of the cacophony).[9]

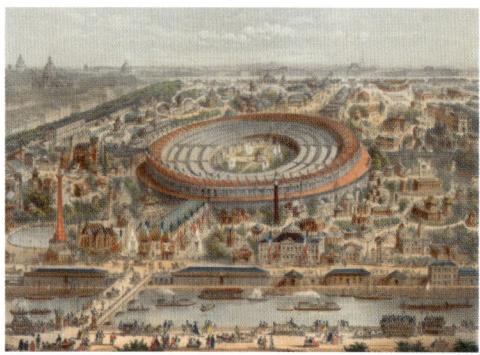

Fig. 6   [p. 103]

Fig. 6
Charles Rivière (1848–1870),
Bird's-eye view of the Universal Exposition in Paris, 1867
Colour lithograph, some parts lacquered, 39.2 × 53 cm, Rijksmuseum, Amsterdam

But nothing was more impressive than the show put on by the host itself. In a sense, France's entry for the Universal Exposition was its own capital, Paris, which had undergone an astonishing transformation in the lead-up to this event. From 1852 onwards, under the leadership of urban planner and city architect Baron Haussmann, Emperor Napoleon III had razed most of the city to the ground in order to recast it as a modern metropolis. The vast rebuilding project was sorely needed. Paris was poor, dirty, dark and dangerous. As its population doubled between 1790 and the 1840s, the medieval city degenerated into a labyrinth of narrow streets and alleyways. Wooden houses posed a fire hazard and without an adequate sewage system or clean drinking water Paris suffered several cholera epidemics that claimed thousands of lives.[10]

Napoleon III, nephew of the famous general and emperor Napoleon Bonaparte, knew only too well how poverty and discontent had (sometimes literally) destroyed many predecessors. The French Revolution of 1789 seemed to have seeped into the DNA of Paris, the city of the guillotine, the barricade, rebellion and resistance. In the nineteenth century, France changed regimes no fewer than six times, often through violent uprisings. As Victor Hugo wrote with pride about his city's radical disposition: 'Athens built the Parthenon, but Paris tore down the Bastille.'[11] This time, however, it was not la peuple but the emperor's architect who was demolishing the city, with the aim of making Paris the most beautiful and powerful city on earth. The pace and scale of this urban renewal were unprecedented. Like a human wrecking ball (though he favoured the term artiste démolisseur), Haussmann cleared away some 20,000 buildings and built 300,000 new homes, planted 80,000 trees and installed 500 kilometres of sewage pipes.[12]

This megalomaniac metamorphosis was far from complete in 1867, but the city did everything it could to make ready the most striking transformations before the opening of the Universal Exposition. The Opéra Garnier – one of the masterpieces of the new Paris – was still under construction, but when the world's public descended upon the city it was sufficiently far advanced to allow the unveiling of its most important component: the spectacular facade.[13] Haussmann's Paris is first and foremost a beautiful spectacle, in which aesthetics are as important as functionality. It is also Napoleon III's greatest legacy. He proudly presented a copy of the street map of Paris, drawn partially by himself, to the king of Prussia at the Universal Exposition.[14] A piquant historical moment, because Prussia would soon demonstrate that the power of the Second Empire was merely a facade...

Three cityscapes

Back to Monet. From the balcony of the Louvre he looked out over a new city. But his three cityscapes do not show only new buildings. In both Quai du Louvre and Garden of the Princess, Louvre, the dome of the Panthéon (1758–90) appears on the horizon. It was one of the historical landmarks that had been spared. After all, Haussmann's Paris was not all about destruction: his street plan also created clear sightlines that allowed old monuments to shine.[15]

In his first Paris cityscapes, Monet also gave a leading role to several old monuments, such as the Church of Saint-Germain-l'Auxerrois directly opposite the Louvre. This was probably the first of the three that he painted.[16] It is the only view that he explicitly mentioned in his letter requesting access to the Louvre's eastern colonnade, precisely because it afforded him a view of the church constructed between the thirteenth and sixteenth centuries.[17] Yet Monet's cityscapes undeniably show Haussmann's hand. In the years prior to 1867 he had made considerable inroads into the area around the Louvre, which for almost four decades had been considered a disgrace to Paris. Within the palace courtyard (where I.M. Pei's glass pyramid now stands), stood a slum that Honoré de Balzac described as dark, dangerous and 'a piece of barbarism'.[18] To connect the Louvre and the Tuileries – until then two separate palaces – all surrounding buildings were demolished and the area between the museum and Saint-Germain-l'Auxerrois was cleared, leaving Monet looking down on a pleasant square with blossoming chestnut trees. Quai du Louvre also shows Haussmann's vision. The street bordering the museum had recently been widened, creating the perfect arena for sunny promenades along the Seine.[19] On the left we see part of the Île de la Cité, the small island in the river where Haussmann worked perhaps most rigorously (and mercilessly), transforming the densely built-up slum into a charming area, mainly by driving out the majority of the island's poor population.[20]

1867: Impressionism's starting shot

Monet's decision to paint life on the street from the temple of classicism can be seen as Impressionism's starting shot, seven years prior to the movement's famous first group exhibition. Today, these three cityscapes may strike us as rather traditional, but Nochlin provides a keen analysis when she speaks of the paintings' 'visual accuracy'. A photograph by Charles Soulier taken from the same vantage point in 1865 shows that, although in Quai du Louvre Monet has bent reality to his will here and there for the sake of the composition, he has given an extremely exacting account of the view, consciously not leaving out such banal features of modern city life as advertising [fig. 7].

The publication in 1867 of Karl Marx's Das Kapital did not come out of the blue. His intensive study of political economy while living in Paris in 1843–45 paved the way for his famous indictment of capitalism. The city's transformation was shaped in part by social changes that Marx witnessed with dismay.[21] Haussmann's Paris may have been built by the proletariat – the thousands of masons, carpenters and other workers drafted into the city – but it was constructed for the bourgeoisie: the new elite who amassed their capital as railway magnates, textile barons or bankers. Everything in the city was geared towards this group. For them, Haussmann designed comfortable apartments to live in, theatres to network in, parks to stroll in, and – very importantly – department stores to shop in. This period saw the advent of mass consumption, and Monet's cityscapes bear witness to this new world.

In *Quai du Louvre*, for example, we see an eye-catching advertisement – a white rectangle with a reddish-brown and yellow frame – painted on a blank wall on the other side of the Seine.[22] Conservative Parisians were horrified by these vulgar corruptions of architecture, but the future Impressionists were clearly fascinated by these public visual expressions of commerce.[23] *Church of Saint-Germain-l'Auxerrois* also appears to depict part of an advertisement. On the right, one of the facades of the narrow side street, the rue des Prêtres Saint-Germain-l'Auxerrois, features a black form that looks suspiciously like a painter's palette.[24] A suspicion that is supported by a contemporary photograph that shows a large advert for Maison Colin, a painting supplies shop that operated at this location [see p. 87].

The advertising industry was still in its infancy at this point. In the decades that followed, Paris would become the mecca of the poster. One of the medium's pioneers was Jules Chéret, who (how could it be otherwise?) launched his career in Paris in 1867.[25] Monet's *Quai du Louvre* illustrates how the expansion of commerce was influencing the city's architecture. On the street we see a newspaper kiosk and what at first glance looks like an advertising column. However, Soulier's aforementioned razor-sharp photo tells us that this is, in fact, a poster-covered public *pissoir*.[26] Monet's recording of this necessary evil on the streetscape once again emphasises the symbolism of his 'significant gesture': not only does he turn away from the Louvre's collection in order to capture a contemporary cityscape, he also exchanges the honour and glory of the old masters for the depiction of a lowly urinal.

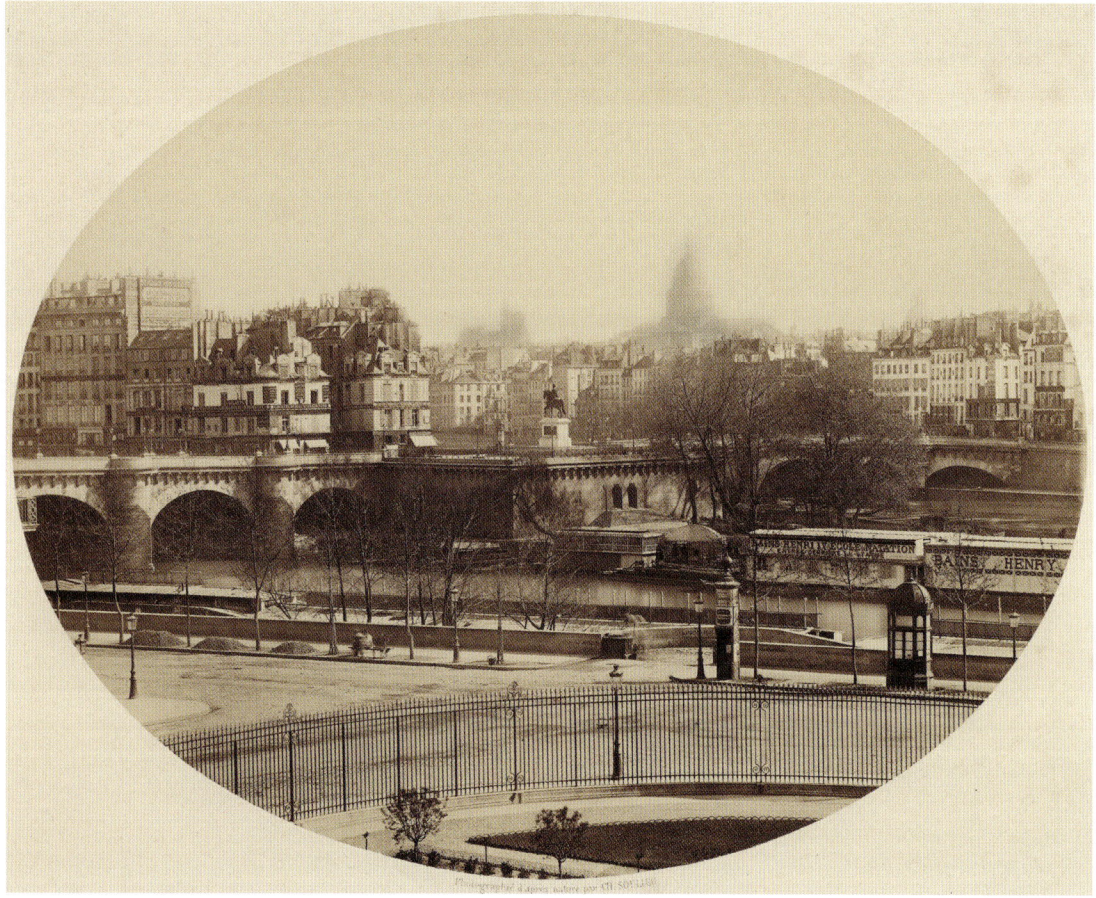

Fig. 7

Fig. 7
Charles Soulier (1840–1875), Pont Neuf, Paris, 1865
Albumen print, 30.8 × 39.7 cm, J. Paul Getty Museum, Los Angeles

Fig. 8
Édouard Manet (1832–1883),
View of the 1867 Exposition Universelle, 1867
Oil on canvas, 108 × 196 cm, Nasjonalmuseet for kunst,
arkitektur og design, The Fine Art Collections, Oslo

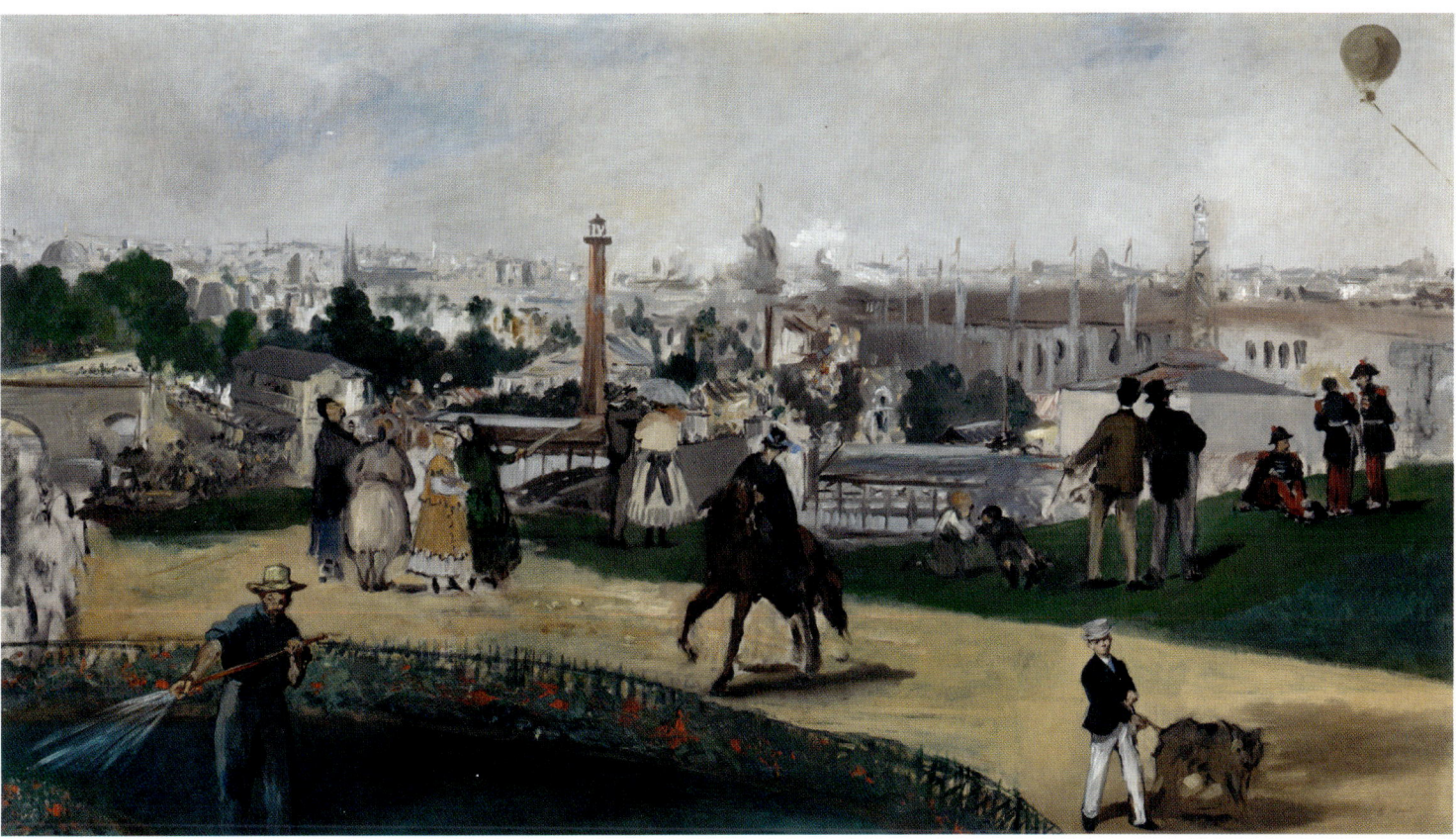

Fig. 8

Painters of modern life

Monet painted his cityscapes in the last months of the life of the writer and poet Charles Baudelaire, whose poem 'The Swan' (1861) is among those that lament the transformation of Paris, especially around the Louvre:

> Paris is changing! But nothing in my melancholy
> Has shifted! New palaces, scaffolding, blocks,
> Old suburbs, all become for me an allegory,
> And my dear memories are heavier than rocks[27]

Baudelaire's death coincided with the birth of Impressionism, but his ideas are strongly linked to this movement. Four years earlier, in his manifesto *The Painter of Modern Life* (1863), he had called on artists to paint contemporary subjects and especially life in the modern city. His text took a stand against the stubborn tradition of classicism and the academy that expected artists to focus on painting historical or biblical scenes. For Baudelaire, this was nonsense; after all, every era has its own specific beauty. To earn a place among the heroes of yesteryear – the Raphaels and Rembrandts in the Louvre – an artist must depict the essence of his own time. No ancient Greek togas or medieval costumes, but suits and crinolines in keeping with the latest fashion! No visions of Arcadia, but truthful renderings of the contemporary city!

Monet would certainly have had Baudelaire in mind when painting Paris, just as Baudelaire himself would have been thinking of Édouard Manet, the *enfant terrible* of realism, when writing his manifesto.[28] Like Monet, the somewhat older Manet attempted his first view of Paris in 1867 when he positioned himself opposite the Universal Exposition and painted a panorama of the festival grounds [fig. 8]. For their cityscapes, both Monet and Manet turned to unconventional means. Monet opted for an atypical portrait-format canvas for *Garden of the Princess, Louvre*, while Manet ignored all the laws of perspective in his *View of the 1867 Exposition Universelle*, compressing the foreground and background in a jarring fashion, making the figures in the foreground seem disconnected from the exhibition grounds in the background.

Manet and other promising young artists were not welcome at the Universal Exposition, which ignored the latest developments in the field of art and instead devoted its major art exhibition to a retrospective survey of the work of Jean-Auguste-Dominique Ingres [fig. 9], whose death in January 1867 represented yet another landmark event: for decades, Ingres had been *the* representative of classicism. Following in the footsteps of painter Gustave Courbet – professional show-off – Manet organised his own solo exhibition directly opposite the entrance to the Universal Exposition.[29] That spring, while Monet turned his back on the Louvre (and thus on the art-world status quo), Manet challenged the academy to a veritable staredown.

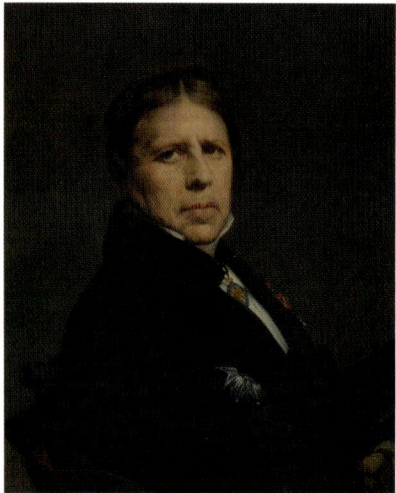

Fig. 9   [p. 108]

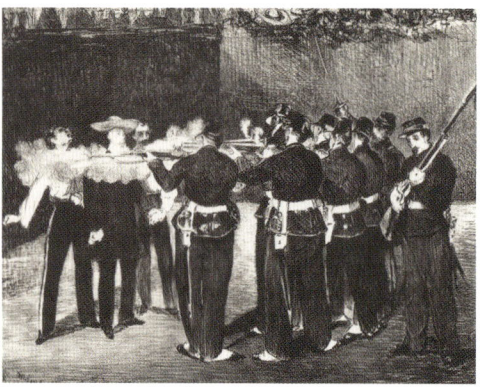

Fig. 10   [pp. 104–105]

Fig. 9
Jean-Auguste-Dominique Ingres (1780–1867),
Self-Portrait, 1864–65

Oil on canvas, 64 × 53 cm, Royal Museum of Fine Arts
(KMSKA), Antwerp

Fig. 10
Édouard Manet (1832–1883),
The Execution of Emperor Maximilian in 1867, 1868

Lithograph on chine collé, 48.2 × 59 cm, Rijksmuseum, Amsterdam.
Purchased with the support of the F.G. Waller-Fonds

Fig. 11
Honoré Daumier (1808–1879), From the series
News of the Day: 'Project for the statue of peace
at the Universal Exposition', 5 January 1867

Page from *Le Charivari*, 41 × 28 cm, Kunstmuseum Den Haag

The death of history painting

For many, Ingres' death symbolised the demise of classicism and thus a turning point in art. When the Universal Exposition closed, it was described by art critics and writers as the 'Death of History Painting'.[30] None of the medals that year was awarded to a history piece. The big winner was genre painting, which the academy viewed sneeringly as low, commercial and superficial. By contrast, critic Théophile Thoré was looking forward eagerly to this change:

> What is dead with M. Ingres, according to one of his eulogists, M. Ronchaud, 'is the last *authority* which has maintained a remnant of rule... it is the glorious *past*.' The past being dead, let us try to console ourselves with the present, and especially, let us hope in the future.[31]

For young artists, that future seemed too far away. Now that their hopes of participating in the Universal Exposition had been dashed, they set their sights on the annual Salon. As the most important podium for living artists, the 1867 edition would be more important than ever now that all eyes were on Paris. It was therefore a great shock when the jury rejected a record number of submissions that year. Among the disappointed were almost all the Impressionists: Monet and his friends and colleagues he had met in Paris from the early 1860s: Frédéric Bazille, Paul Cézanne, Camille Pissaro, Auguste Renoir and Alfred Sisley. Only Edgar Degas and Berthe Morisot succeeded in charming the admissions committee.[32] The narrow-minded jury 'has shown the door to all those who tread the new path,' wrote critic Émile Zola indignantly, while his colleague Jules-Antoine Castagnary complained that 'never in a painter's memory has a jury been more severe. Out of three thousand artists who sent works, two thousand have been refused.'[33] It was Monet's first experience of an official rejection.[34]

Emotions ran high and the Parisian urge for rebellion and revolution again found its way to the surface. It was now time for the painters to mount the barricades. Around 125 of them signed a petition, drafted by Bazille, calling for a new edition of the Salon des refusés, the exhibition of rejected art that had taken place in 1863.[35] Their request was denied. The government wanted to avoid any fuss in that festive year in which all activities were under a magnifying glass. To pacify the artists, Émilien de Nieuwerkerke promised an extra lenient jury for the following year's Salon.[36]

A first Impressionist exhibition

In the manifesto published on the occasion of his solo exhibition, Manet explained his unorthodox decision to organise his own show now that official institutions had closed their doors to him. 'To exhibit is the vital issue, the *sine qua non* for the artist,' wrote Manet, '...To exhibit is to find friends and allies for the struggle.'[37] The venture ended in disillusionment: worse than being subjected to devastating criticism, Manet's exhibition was largely ignored.

The friends and allies Manet spoke of included Monet and his circle, especially Bazille, Degas, Renoir and Sisley. They shared their studios, meals, money (especially the generous Bazille) and worries. But above all, they shared the view that art must break free from the meddlesome academy and from the judgment of an ignorant jury. The time was ripe. Just as the old Paris had been demolished to make way for a modern city, the traditional art world would have to make way for art with a fresh impetus. The 'Impressionists' did not yet officially exist, but in this period the ties between these artists were closer than ever. They could sense the arrival of a new era, in which they were eager to play a leading role.

Spurred by a mix of disappointment, impatience and excitement, and following the example of their friend and mentor, Manet, the young artists decided to organise their own exhibition. In a letter to his mother in April 1867, Bazille wrote:

> It is just too ridiculous, when you know you're not stupid, to expose yourself to these administrative whims, especially when you have no interest at all in medals and prizes.... A dozen talented young people feel the same as I do. We have therefore resolved to rent a large studio each year where we will show as may of our works as we please. We will invite painters whom we like to send pictures. Courbet, Corot, Diaz, Daubigny and many others whom you may not know have promised to send pictures and very much approve of our idea.[38]

But whereas Manet could turn to his wealthy mother to finance his pavilion, the Impressionists lacked the necessary resources for a comparable undertaking. Shortly after his enthusiastic letter, Bazille wrote dejectedly: 'By bleeding ourselves as much as possible, we managed to collect 2,500 francs, which isn't enough. So, we've been forced to give up what we wanted to do. We must return to the bosom of the administration that hasn't nourished us at all and that disowns us.'[39] Had the exhibition taken place, Impressionism would have entered the annals of art history not in 1874 but in 1867.

The swansong

De Nieuwerkerke's decision not to organise a Salon des refusés is understandable. At that moment, the Second Empire had its hands full with negative PR. On the day of the ceremonial presentation of medals at the Universal Exposition, news of the death of Emperor Maximilian of Mexico was spreading through Paris. Ferdinand Maximilian, an Austrian archduke, was little more than a puppet of Napoleon III, installed in Mexico to increase France's grip on the rest of the world, and his execution by the Mexican resistance was a sign that the all-powerful Second Empire may not have been as stable as it appeared. Manet put his finger on the sore spot when, shortly after the news broke, he depicted the execution in several paintings and in a print, distribution of which was soon banned by the government [fig. 10].[40]

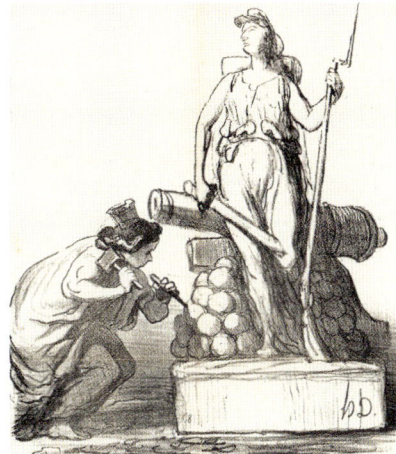

Fig. 11 [p. 98]

Moreover, unrest reigned throughout the world. In a series of biting cartoons [fig. 11], the caricaturist Honoré Daumier criticised the message of the Universal Exposition, which sold itself as a temple of peace while dealing in armaments: Prussia proudly exhibited the Krupp cannon, a ten-ton steel gun capable of demolishing everything in its path. Only three years after the Prussian king received the map of Paris as a gift at the Universal Exposition, these Krupp cannons would surround the French capital, bombing the city's new boulevards, parks and squares for months on end during the Franco-Prussian War of 1870–71. Nadar, whose hot-air balloon, 'Le Géant', had provided so much entertainment in 1867, now used it and his camera to map enemy lines. Monet fled France. Bazille volunteered to join the army and died in the Battle of Beaune-la-Rolande on 28 November 1870. He was Monet's great source of support, godfather of his eldest son – born in 1867 – and the glue within the Impressionist group.

When France capitulated, Paris descended into civil war. The remaining, mostly poor residents felt abandoned and betrayed by their country and opted for self-government, declaring themselves an independent state during the Paris Commune of 1871. Another revolution seized the city. The historic uprising was quickly and ruthlessly suppressed by French government forces and thousands were executed within the space of a single week. Blood flowed through the streets and the Tuileries Palace was set ablaze. The adjacent Louvre remained largely intact, partly thanks to the efforts of artists such as Courbet.

Monet did not yet know all this when he stood on the balcony of the Louvre in 1867. He looked out over a glorious city and a promising future. The time for Monet and the Impressionists seemed within reach. Were they wrong? No, there would merely be a delay of a few years. In 1867, Bazille had no doubts: 'With these people and Monet, the strongest of all, we are certain to succeed. You will see that everyone will be talking of us.'[41]

1. Edmond and Jules de Goncourt, *Dagboek* (Amsterdam, 2014), p. 167. English translation by Gerard Forde.

2. François Ducuing (ed.), *L'exposition universelle de 1867 illustrée* (Paris, 5 September 1867).

3. The Universal Exposition opened on 1 April 1867 and Monet requested permission to paint from the balcony of the Louvre on 27 April 1867. It is not known exactly when he painted the three cityscapes, but based on the works themselves and Monet's letters it is assumed he completed them during the spring and summer of 1867. For more information on the three cityscapes, see Joel Isaacson, 'Monet's Views of Paris', *Bulletin of the Allen Memorial Art Museum* 24 (Autumn 1966), pp. 5–6.

4. Letter from Claude Monet to Émilien de Nieuwerkerke, Paris, 27 April 1867, National Archives, Paris.

5. Linda Nochlin, 'Museums and Radicals: A History of Emergencies', *Art in America* (August 1971), pp. 32–33.

6. Nochlin 1971 (note 5), p. 33.

7. Théophile Thoré, *Exposition universelle de 1867* II (Paris, 1867), p. 285, as quoted in Patricia Mainardi, *Art and Politics of the Second Empire: The Universal Expositions of 1855 and 1867* (New Haven, CT & London, 1987), p. 151.

8. Ducuing 1867 (note 2), p. 76, 100.

9. Mark Twain, *The Innocents Abroad* (Hartford, CT, 1869), chapter 13.

10. David H. Pinkney, *Napoleon III and the Rebuilding of Paris* (Princeton, NJ, 1972), p. 4.

11. Quoted in Priscilla Parkhurst Ferguson, *Paris as Revolution: Writing the Nineteenth-Century City* (Berkeley, CA, 1994), p. 70.

12. Information from the Musée Carnavalet – Histoire de Paris.

13. Pinkney 1972 (note 10), p. 85.

14. Pinkney 1972 (note 10), p. 26.

15. James H. Rubin, *Impressionism and the Modern Landscape: Productivity, Technology and Urbanization from Manet to Van Gogh* (Berkeley, Los Angeles & London, 2008), p. 30.

16. *Church of Saint-Germain-l'Auxerrois* is dated 1866, but this is believed to be incorrect. See Isaacson 1966 (note 3), pp. 8–9.

17. Letter from Claude Monet to Émilien de Nieuwerkerke, Paris, 27 April 1867, National Archives, Paris.

18. Honoré de Balzac, *La cousine bette* (1846) in *Oeuvres complètes de Honoré de Balzac* (Paris 1912–14), quoted in Pinkney 1972 (note 10), p. 11.

19. Rubin 2008 (note 15), p. 28.

20. Pinkney 1972 (note 10), pp. 87–88.

21. Ruth E. Iskin, *The Poster: Art, Advertising, Design, and Collecting, 1860s–1900s* (Hanover, NH, 2014), p. 6.

22. The wording in the advert is legible in Soulier's photo. In 1865, it was an advert for a dentist.

23. In the same period, Auguste Renoir depicted this advert in his painting *The Pont des Arts, Paris*, 1867–68, Norton Simon Museum, Pasadena.

24. Many thanks to Mayken Jonkman for pointing out this detail.

25. Iskin 2014 (note 21), p. 6.

26. The cylindrical billboard columns, based on the urinals and better known in France as Morris columns, were introduced into the cityscape in 1868, the year after Monet's views of Paris.

27. Charles Baudelaire, 'Le cygne', from 'Tableaux parisiens', part of *Les fleurs du mal*, 1861.

28. Baudelaire does not refer to Manet in *The Painter of Modern Life*. The only artist he refers to is Constantin Guys.

29. Mainardi 1987 (note 7), p. 134.

30. Patricia Mainardi, *The End of the Salon: Art and the State in the Early Third Republic* (Cambridge, 1993), p. 154.

31. Quoted in Mainardi 1987 (note 7), p. 151.

32. Mainardi 1987 (note 7), p. 137.

33. Letter from Émile Zola to Antony Valabrègue, 4 April 1867; Jules-Antoine Castagnary, 'Salon de 1867', *La Liberté* (1 April 1867), p. 2.

34. 'Claude Monet: A Summary Chronology, 1840-1872', in George T.M. Shackelford (ed.), *Monet: The Early Years*, exh. cat. Fort Worth & San Francisco (Kimbell Art Museum & Fine Arts Museums of San Francisco), 2017, p. 110.

35. In addition to Bazille, Monet, Manet, Pissarro, Renoir and Sisley, other signatories included Marie Bracquemond, Charles-François Daubigny, Narcisse Virgilio Diaz, Antoine Guillemet and Johan Jongkind.

36. Mainardi 1987 (note 7), p. 187.

37. Mainardi 1987 (note 7), p. 141.

38. Letter from Frédéric Bazille to his mother, undated [April 1867], Musée Fabre, Montpellier.

39. Letter from Frédéric Bazille to his mother, undated [May 1867], Musée Fabre, Montpellier, as quoted in Mainardi 1987 (note 7), pp. 137–138.

40. For an extensive analysis of Manet's various versions of *The Execution of Emperor Maximilian* (1868), see John Elderfield, *Manet and the Execution of Maximilian*, exh. cat. New York (Museum of Modern Art), 2007.

41. Letter from Frédéric Bazille to his mother, April 1867, Musée Fabre, Montpellier. As quoted in Mainardi 1987 (note 7), p. 137.

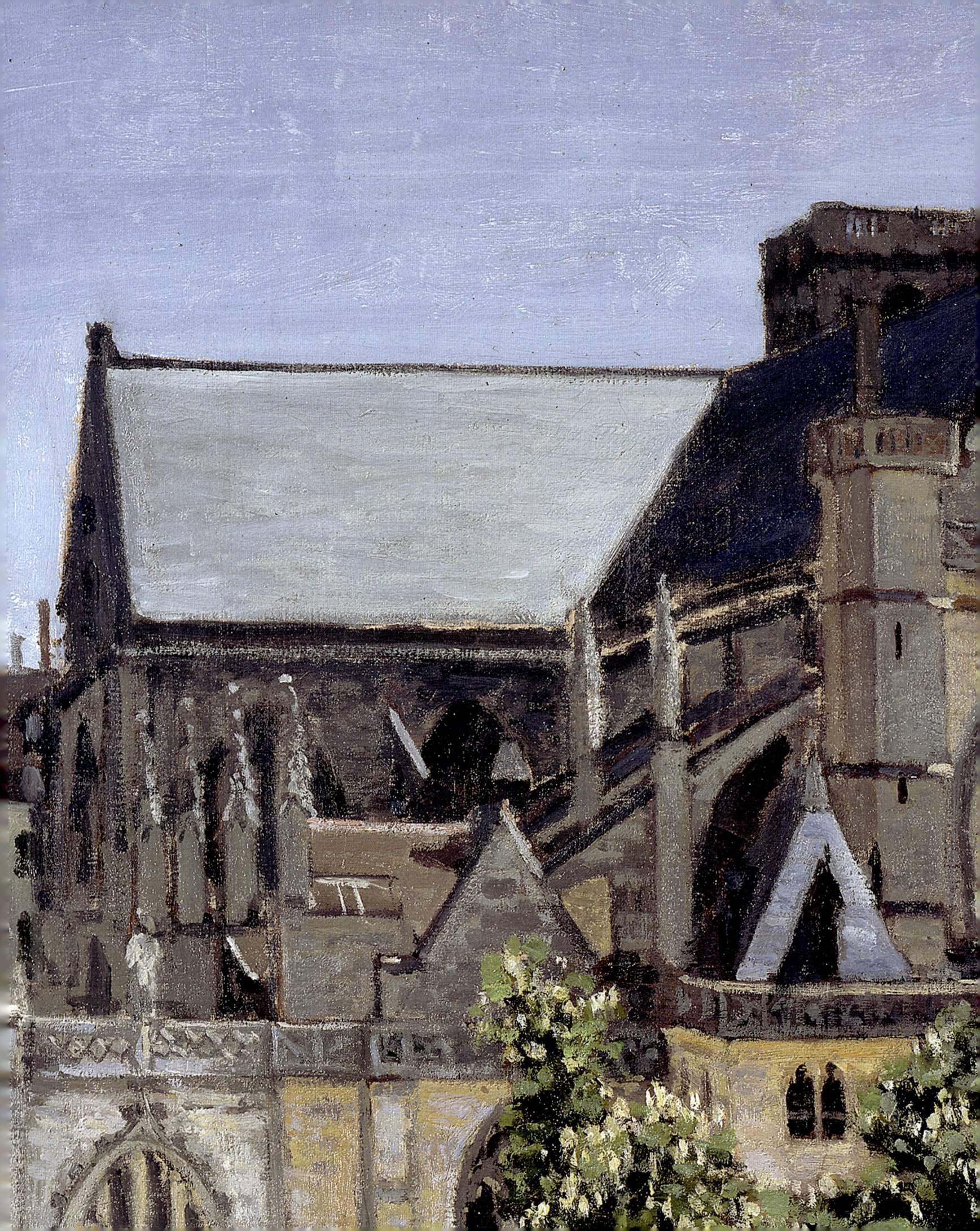

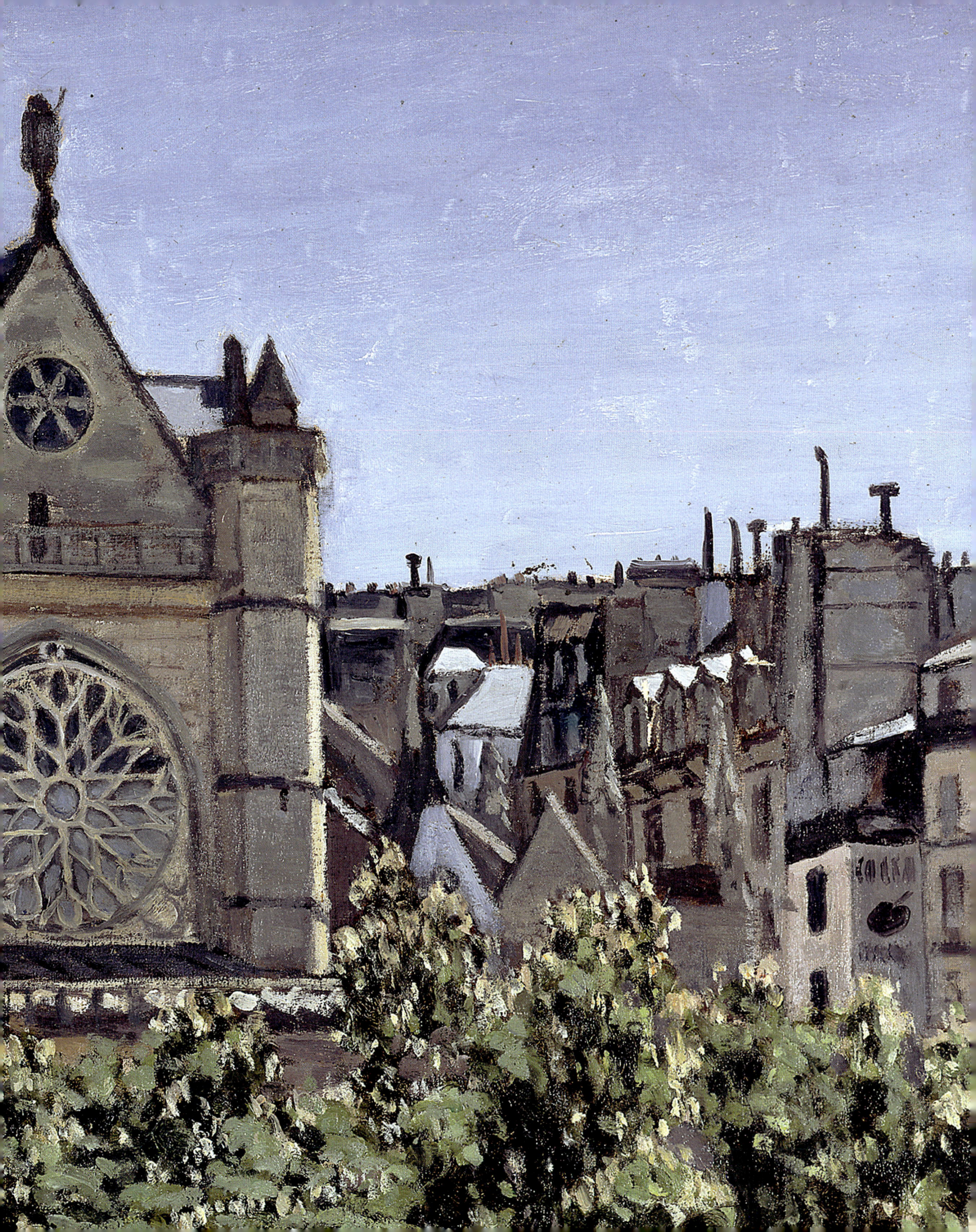

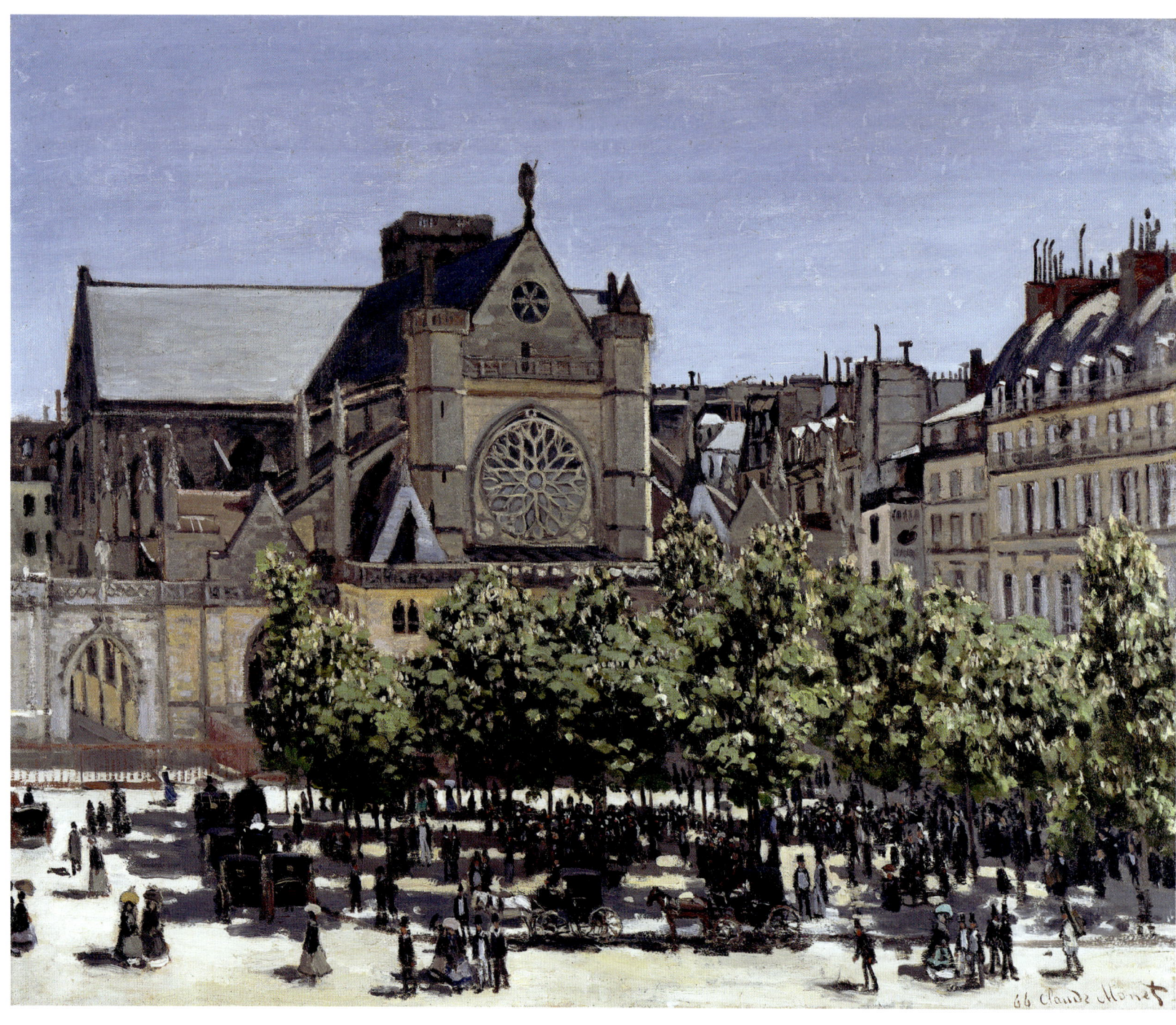

Claude Monet (1840–1926), *Church of Saint-Germain-l'Auxerrois*, 1867
Oil on canvas, 79 × 98 cm, Staatliche Museen zu Berlin, Nationalgalerie

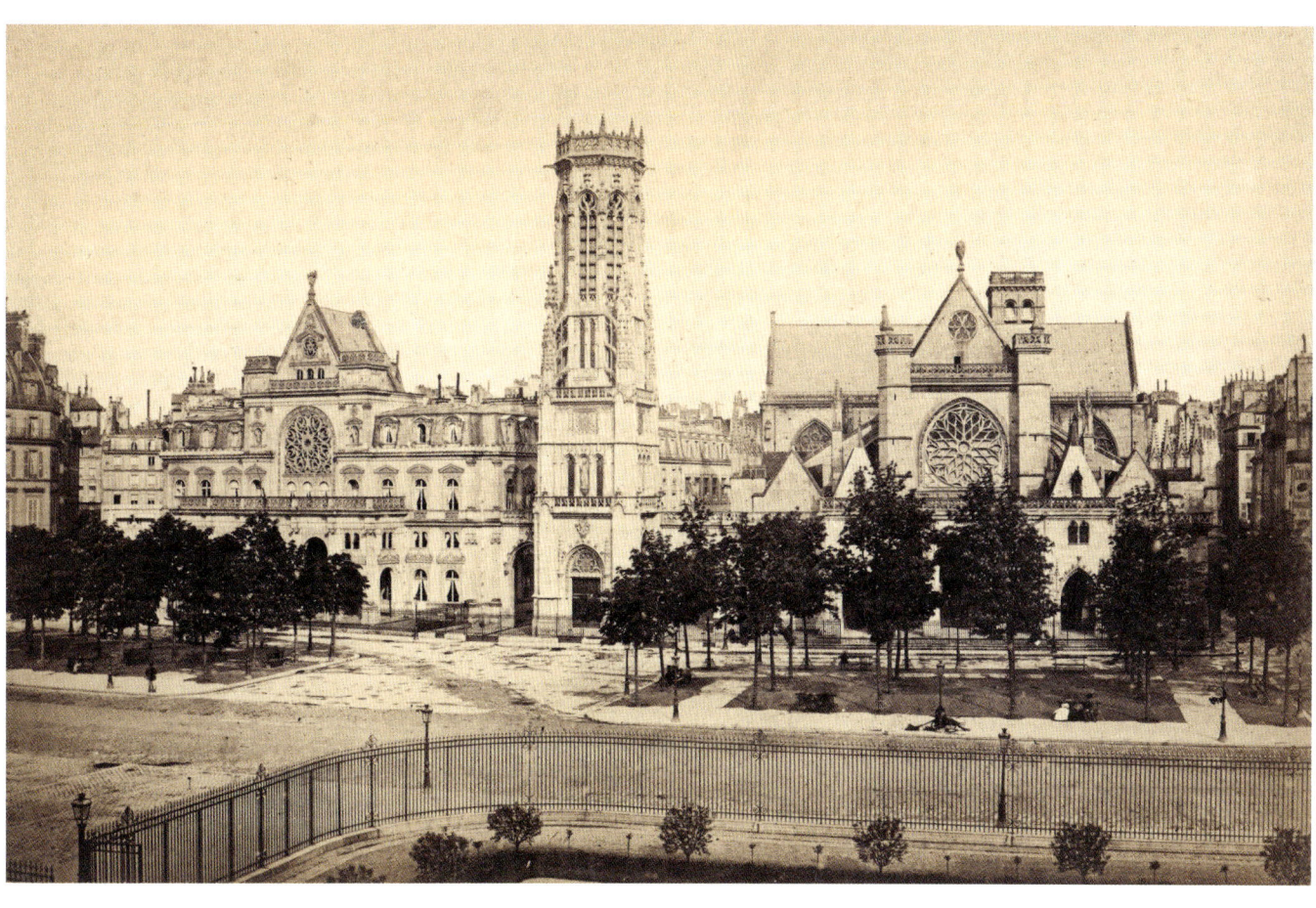

Anonymous, View of the Church Saint-Germain-l'Auxerrois, with the fence of the Garden of the Princess on the foreground, undated

Cabinet photo, 10.2 × 16.5 cm, Kunstmuseum Den Haag

Claude Monet (1840–1926), *Garden of the Princess, Louvre*, 1867
Oil on canvas, 91.8 × 61.9 cm, Allen Memorial Art Museum, Oberlin College, Oberlin, Ohio. R.T. Miller Jr. Fund

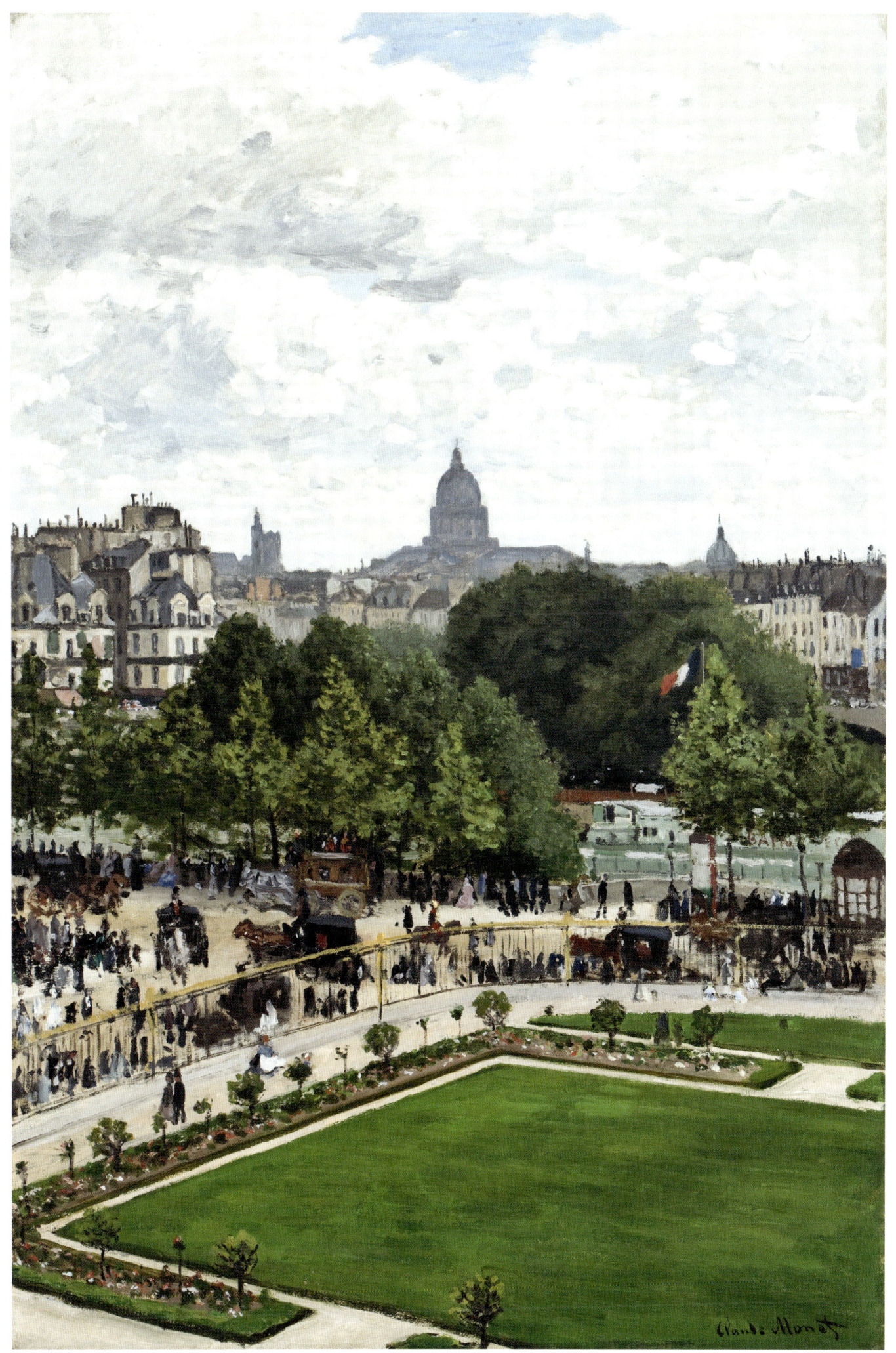

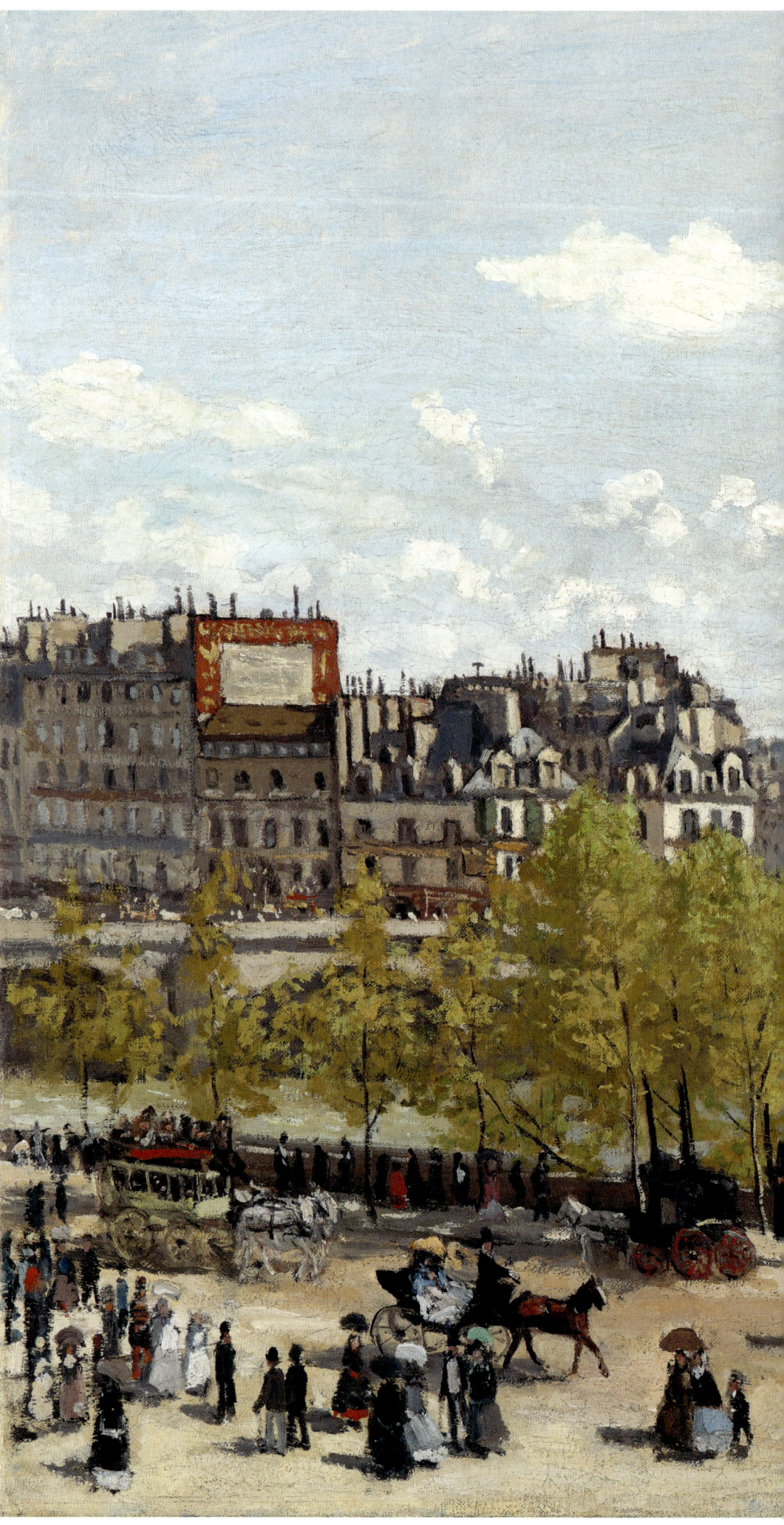

Claude Monet (1840–1926), *Quai du Louvre*, 1867
Oil on canvas, 65.1 × 92.6 cm, Kunstmuseum Den Haag

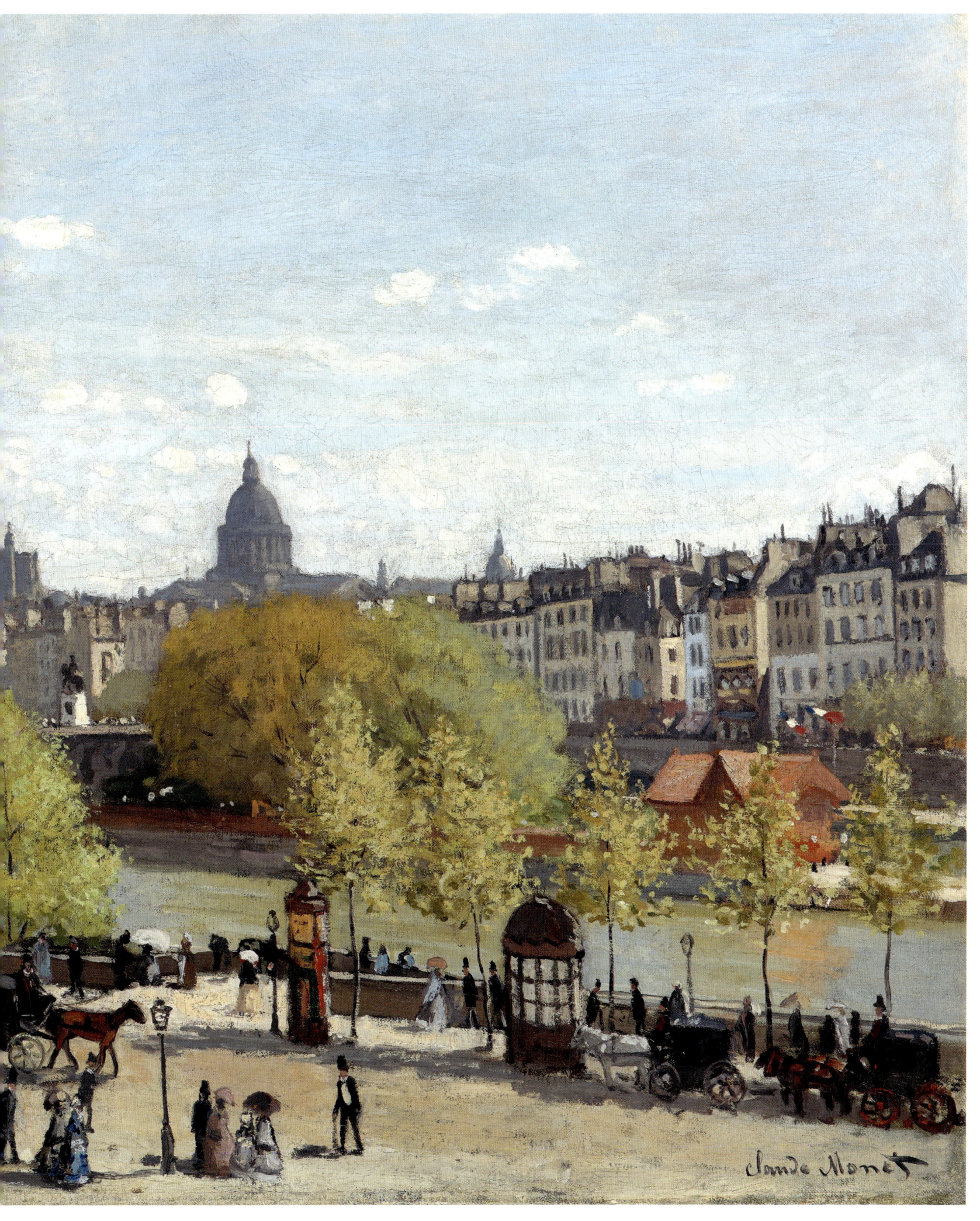

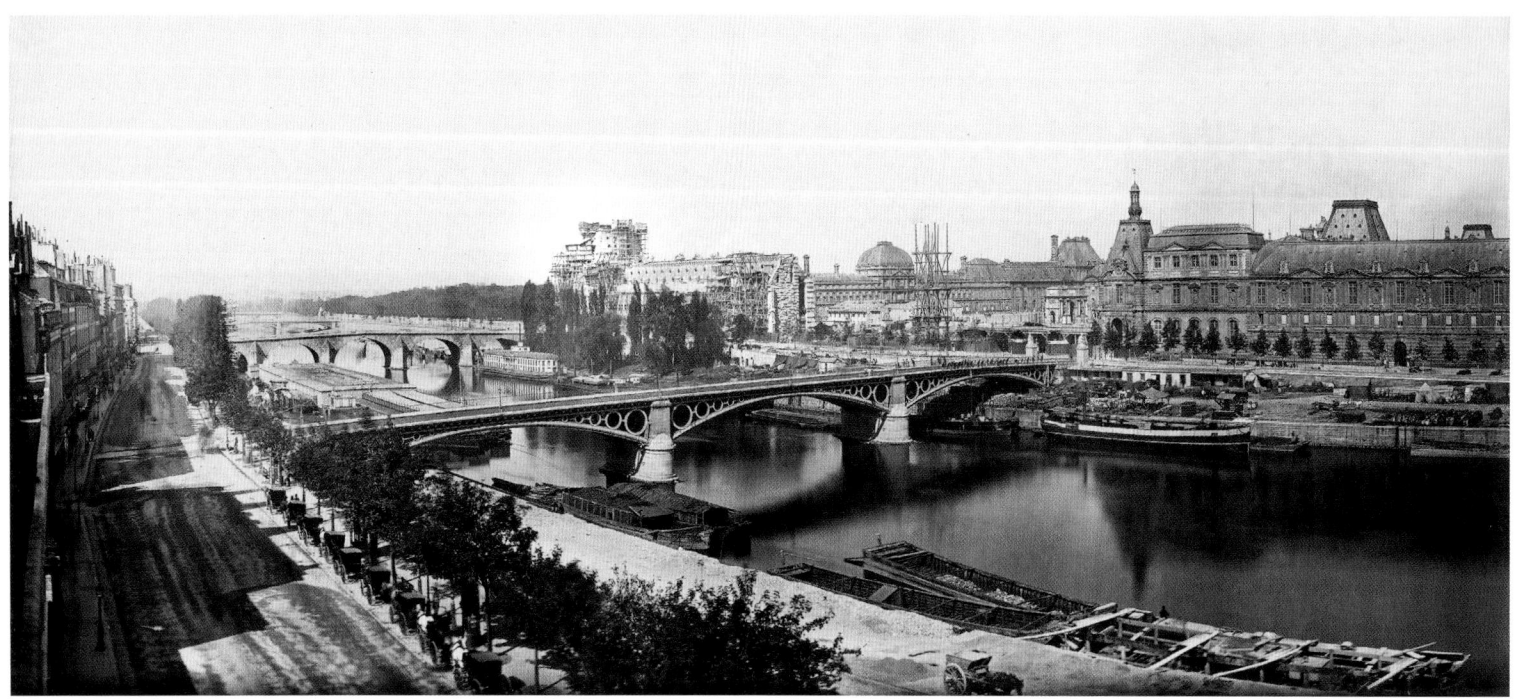

Adolphe Braun (1812–1877), Construction work on the expansion of the Louvre, seen from the Left Bank of the Seine, 1866–67
Albumen print, 19.1 × 41.6 cm, Staatsgalerie Stuttgart, Graphische Sammlung

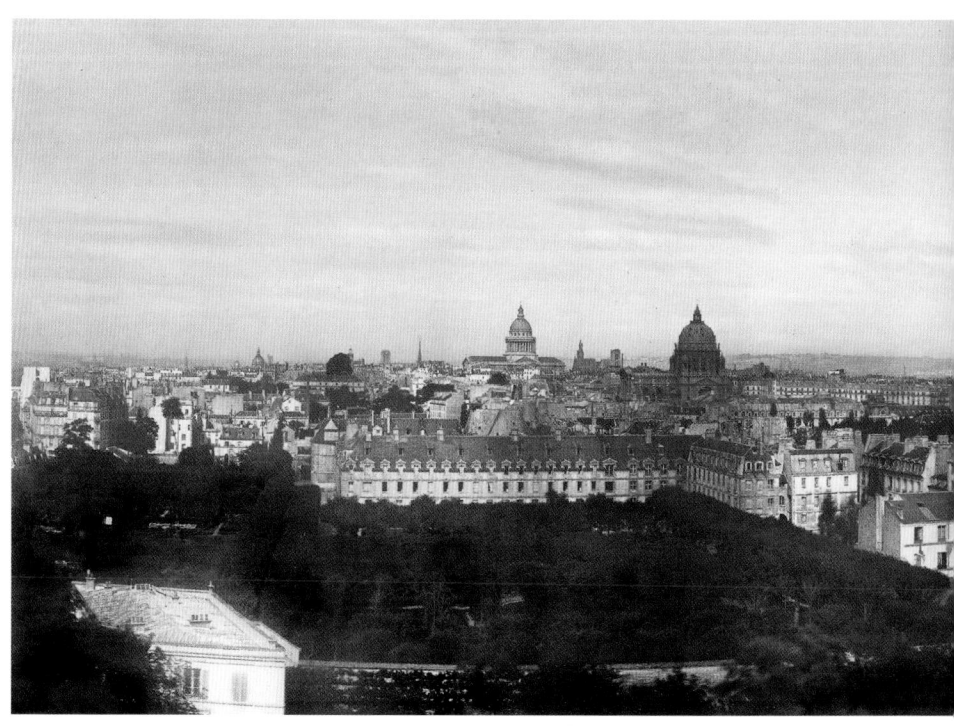

Adolphe Braun (1812–1877), View of the domes of the Sorbonne Church and the Panthéon, 1866–67
Albumen print, 20.4 × 44.4 cm, Staatsgalerie Stuttgart, Graphische Sammlung

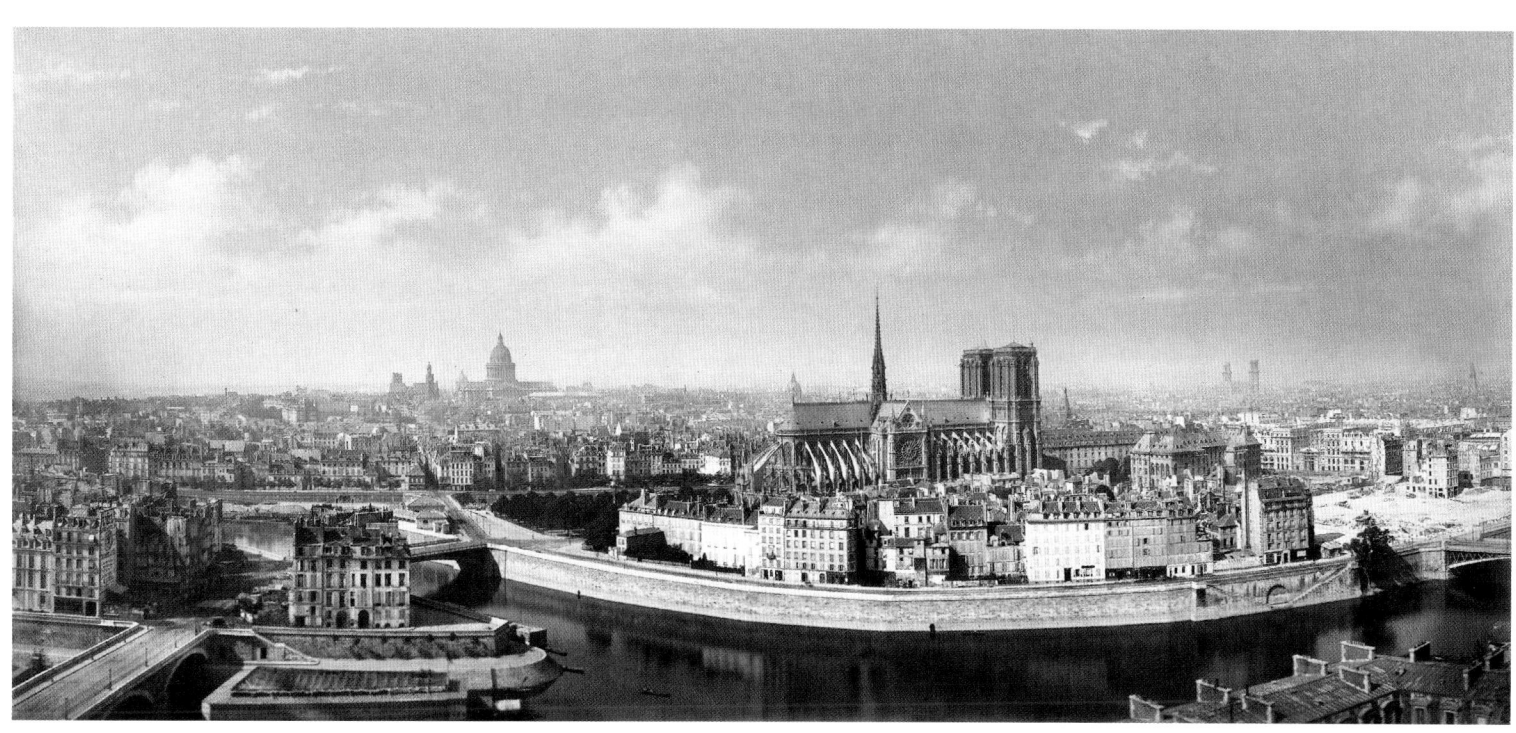

Adolphe Braun (1812–1877), The Île de la Cité, seen from the Right Bank of the Seine, 1867

Albumen print, 19 × 41.1 cm, Staatsgalerie Stuttgart, Graphische Sammlung

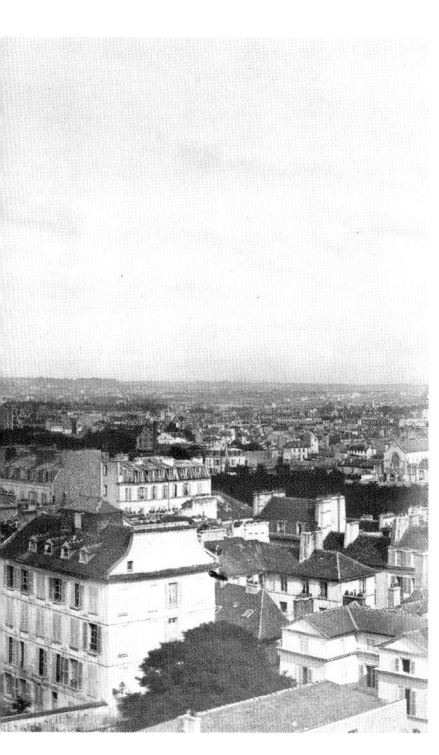

CLAUDE MONET (1840–1926)

The Pont de l'Europe. Gare Saint-Lazare, 1877

In January 1877, Claude Monet moved into a studio at 17 rue Moncey.[1] His new workplace was within walking distance of Gare Saint-Lazare, the railway station from which he regularly commuted from his studio in busy Paris to his home in Argenteuil, about 15 kilometres outside the city.[2]

Saint-Lazare was the busiest station in Paris, located in the new heart of the city.[3] The modernisation and expansion of the station in the 1860s included the construction of the impressive Pont de l'Europe, the cast-iron bridge that cuts Monet's composition in half.[4] The bridge had several branches leading towards the place de l'Europe and was an important connection point in the new neighbourhood. The railways were seen as a symbol of progress and development in that period, allowing the inhabitants of Paris to travel more rapidly to all kinds of destinations outside the city. The railways also facilitated trade: the trains transported a wide variety of products from industrial areas or the countryside to the city.[5]

Initially, Monet made only a few quick sketches of the station, but soon he was given official permission to paint in the area.

Between January and March 1877, he made a total of 12 paintings of the station building and the surrounding tracks. Monet was clearly fascinated by the industrial landscape and the special atmospheric effects it evoked. The locomotives enveloped the entire station in a thick cloud of steam. Monet did not shy away from giving reality a helping hand, often instructing the train crew to create the best possible conditions for his paintings. They slowed the trains down for him or loaded them with coal to generate extra steam.[6] Thanks to this manipulation, Monet bent unpredictable phenomena such as steam to his will, creating the perfect formula for a series of extraordinary cityscapes of Paris.

A year before Monet, in 1876, Gustave Caillebotte also painted this area in his painting, also entitled *The Pont de l'Europe*. Caillebotte focused his attention on the bridge, while Monet's works focus mainly on the train station. Monet exhibited half of his series of views of Gare Saint-Lazare at the third Impressionist exhibition in 1877, which was largely organised and financed by Caillebotte.[7]

[VERA MERKS]

1   Charles F. Stuckey, *Claude Monet 1840–1926* (London, 1995), p. 203.
2   Caroline Shields, 'Geographies of Impressionism in the Age of Industry: An Introduction', in Caroline Shields (ed.), *Impressionism in the Age of Industry* (New York, 2019), p. 24.
3   Shields 2019 (note 2), p. 23.
4   Shields 2019 (note 2), p. 26.
5   Caroline Shields, 'Exhibited Works', in Shields 2019 (note 2), p. 120.
6   Stuckey 1995 (note 1), p. 203.
7   James H. Rubin, 'Industry and Labour at the Impressionist Exhibitions', in Shields 2019 (note 2), p. 74.

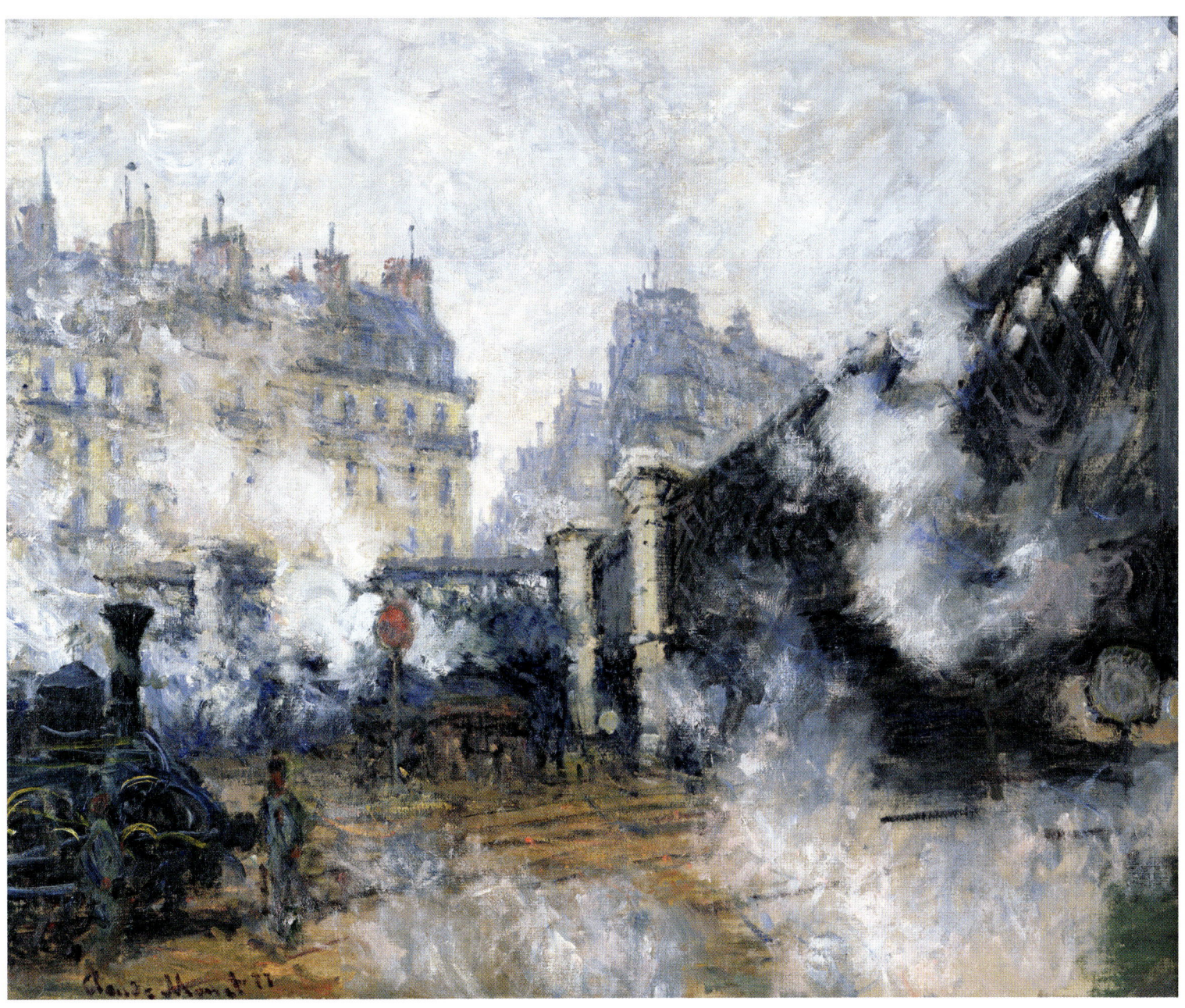

Claude Monet (1840–1926), *The Pont de l'Europe. Gare Saint-Lazare*, 1877
Oil on canvas, 65 × 81 cm, Gift of Eugène and Victorine Donop de Monchy, 1940, Musée Marmottan Monet, Paris

Norbert Goeneutte (1854–1894), *The Pont de l'Europe at Night*, 1887

Oil on canvas, 46 × 37.5 cm, Private collection

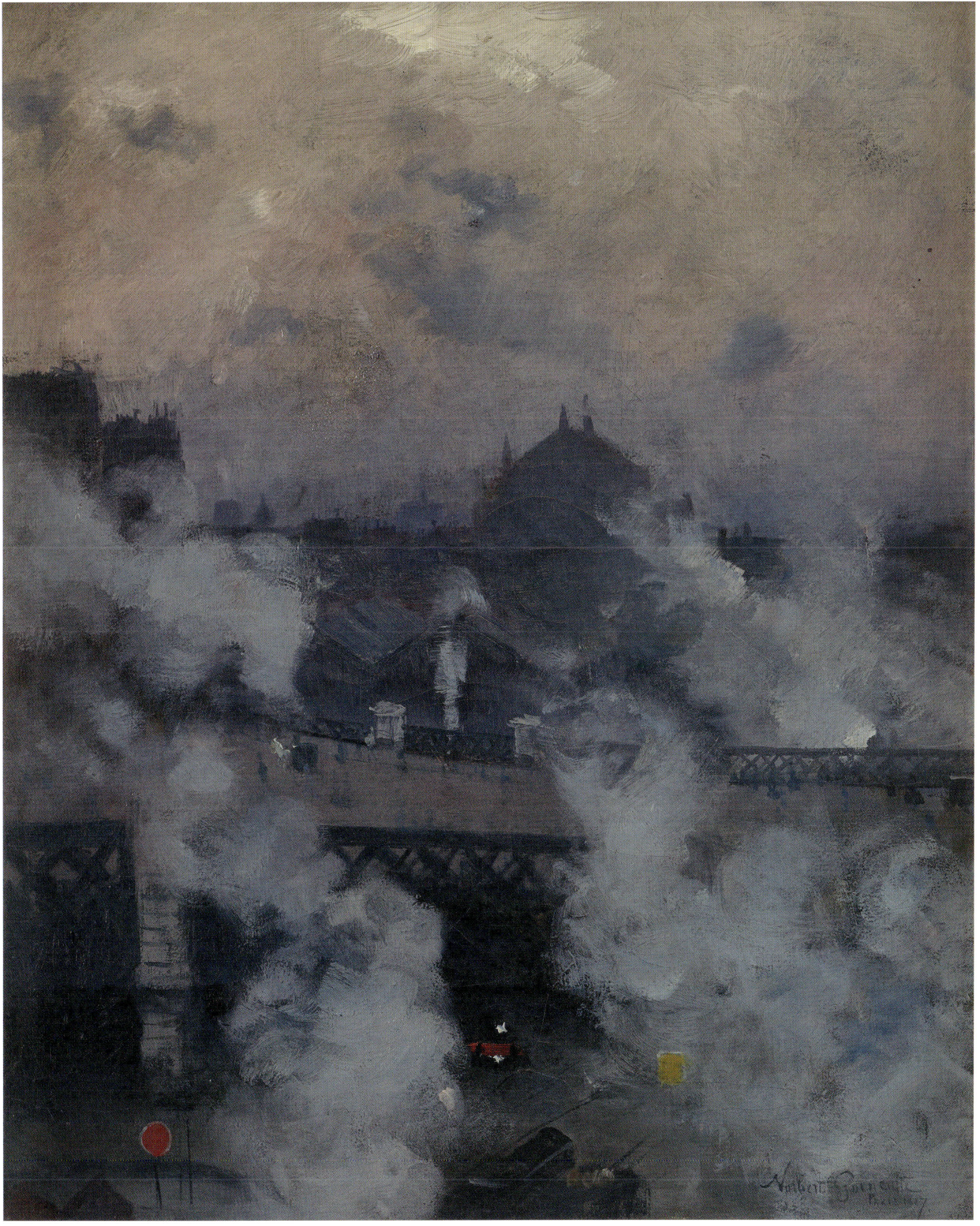

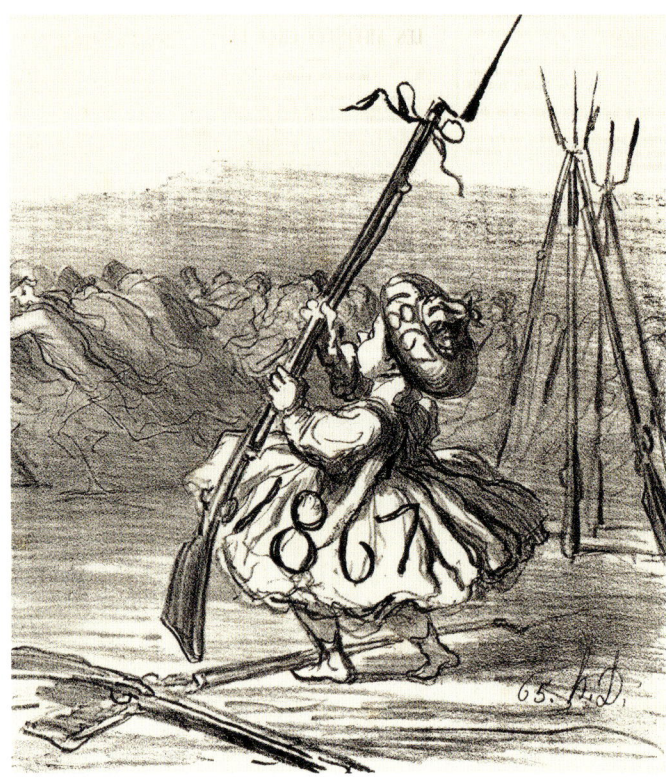

Honoré Daumier (1808–1879), From the series
News of the Day, no. 242: 'New Year's gifts for 1867', 1866
Page from *Le Charivari*, 41 × 28 cm, Kunstmuseum Den Haag

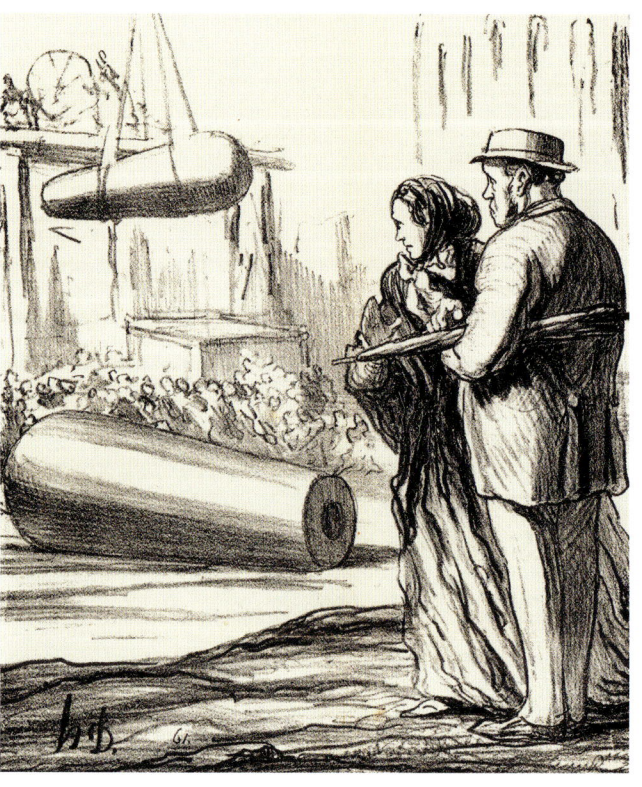

Honoré Daumier (1808–1879), From the series *News of the Day*:
'Moving the exhibition. The bourgeois (humming mechanically):
"The people are brothers to us"', 1867
Page from *Le Charivari*, 41 × 28 cm, Kunstmuseum Den Haag

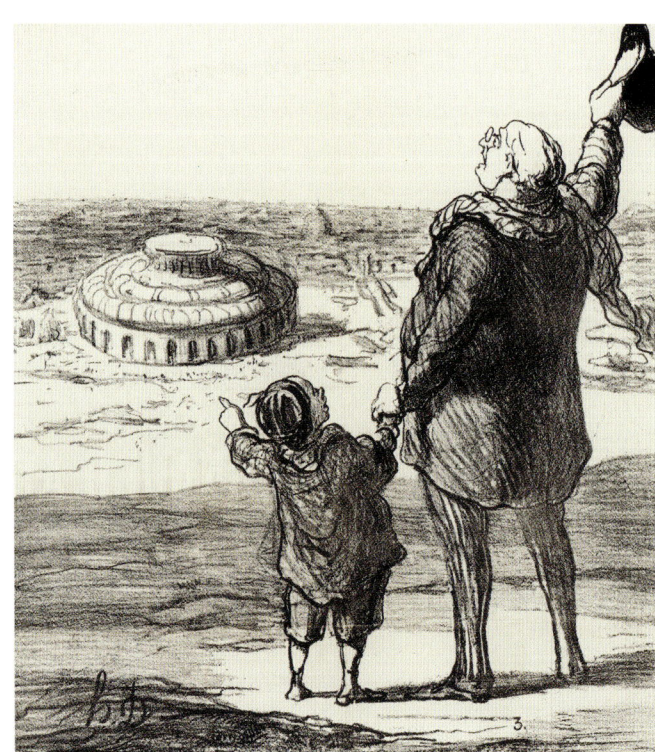

Honoré Daumier (1808–1879), From the series *Universal Expositions*:
'Oh my son, what a wonderful scene! You see here the exhibition hall of
the temple of peace! – Yes, papa, and the military academy too!', 1867
Page from *Le Charivari*, 40 × 28 cm, Kunstmuseum Den Haag

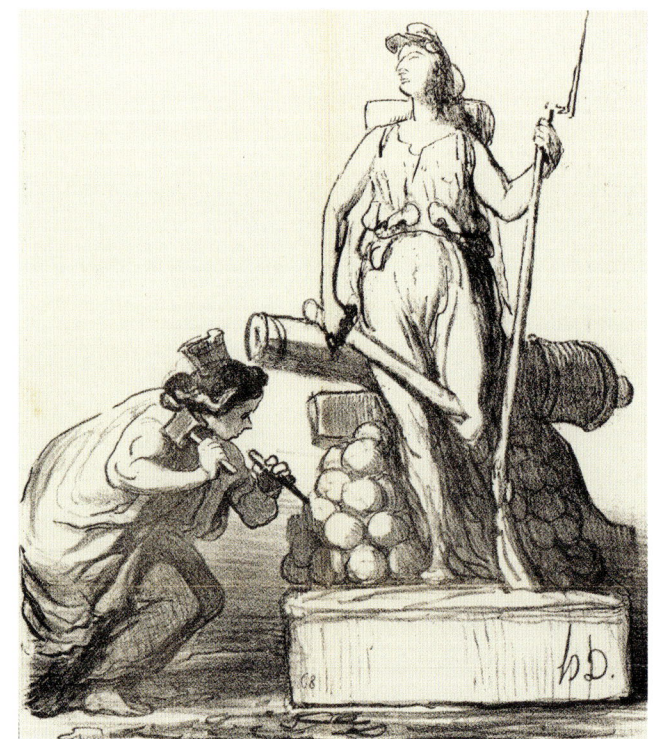

Honoré Daumier (1808–1879), From the series *News of the Day*: 'Project
for the statue of peace at the Universal Exposition', 5 January 1867
Page from *Le Charivari*, 41 × 28 cm, Kunstmuseum Den Haag

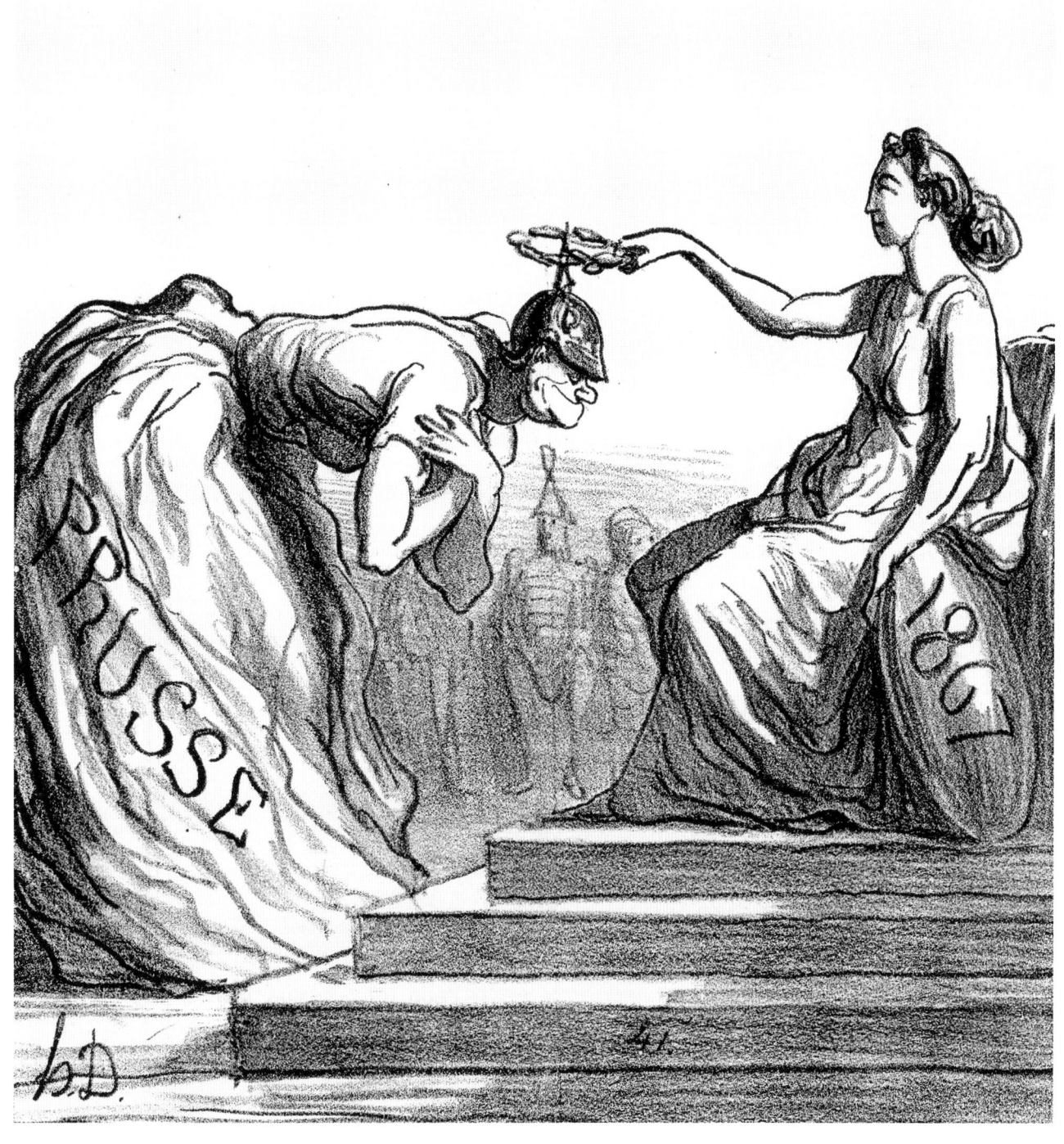

Honoré Daumier (1808–1879), From the series *News of the Day*: 'First Prize for Growth: Prussia', 1867
Page from *Le Charivari*, 40 × 28 cm, Kunstmuseum Den Haag

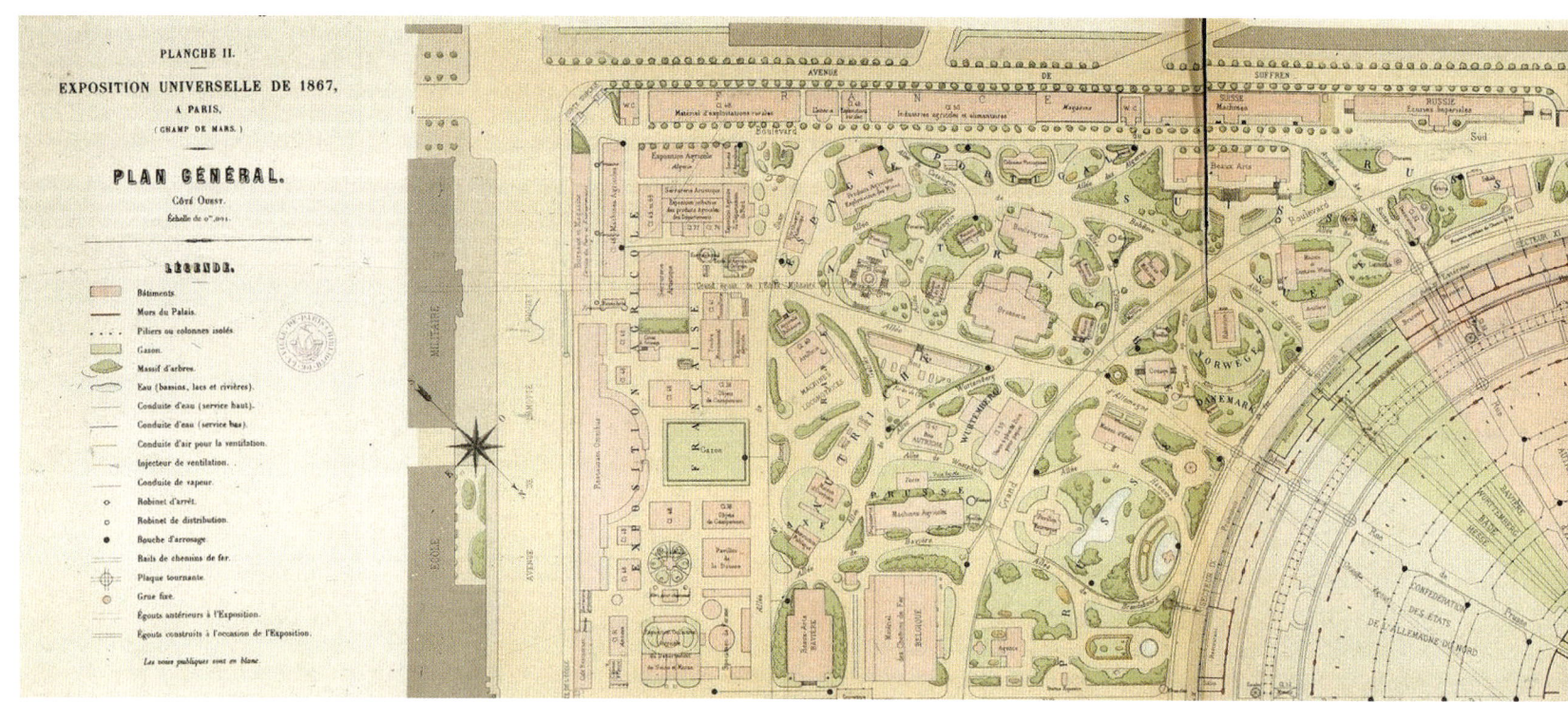

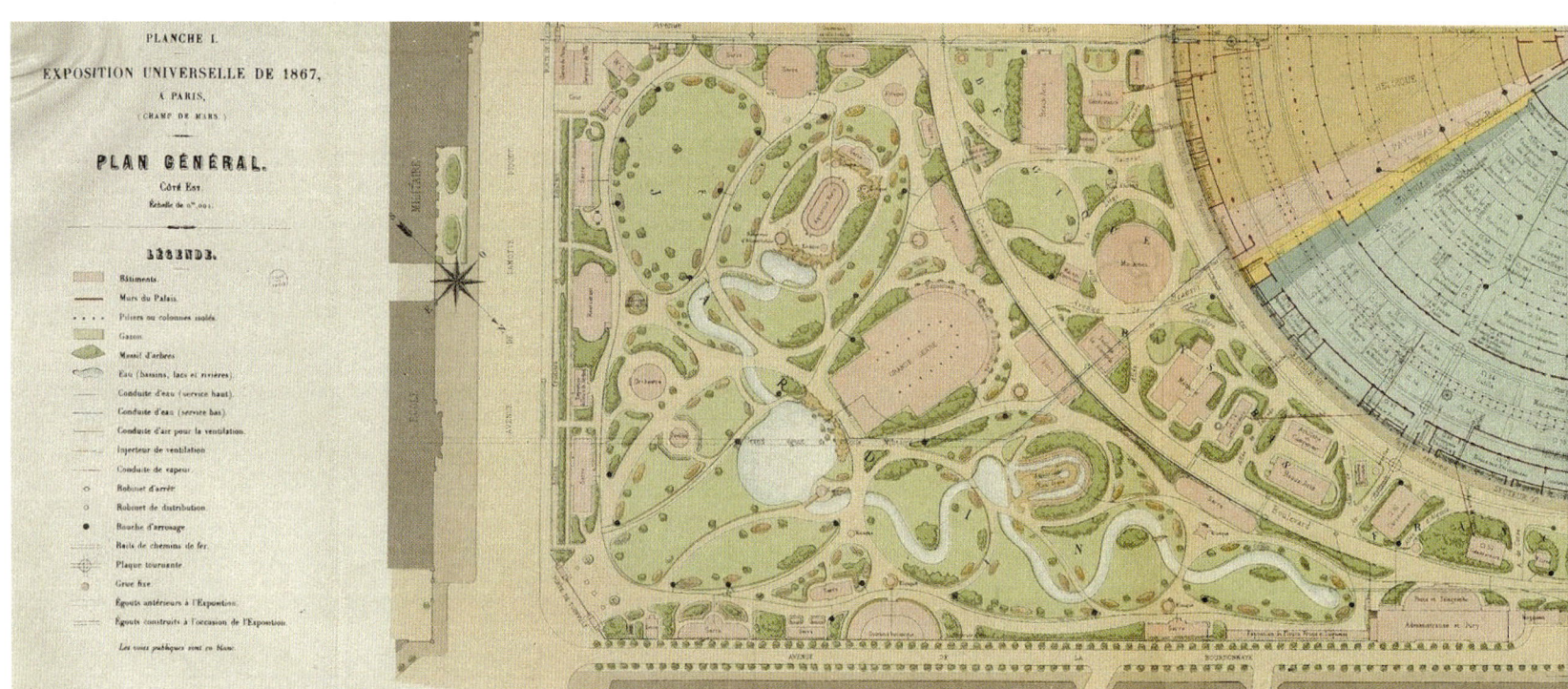

Anonymous, Map of the Universal Exposition, 1868   Lithograph, each part 27 × 136 cm, Musée Carnavalet – Histoire de Paris

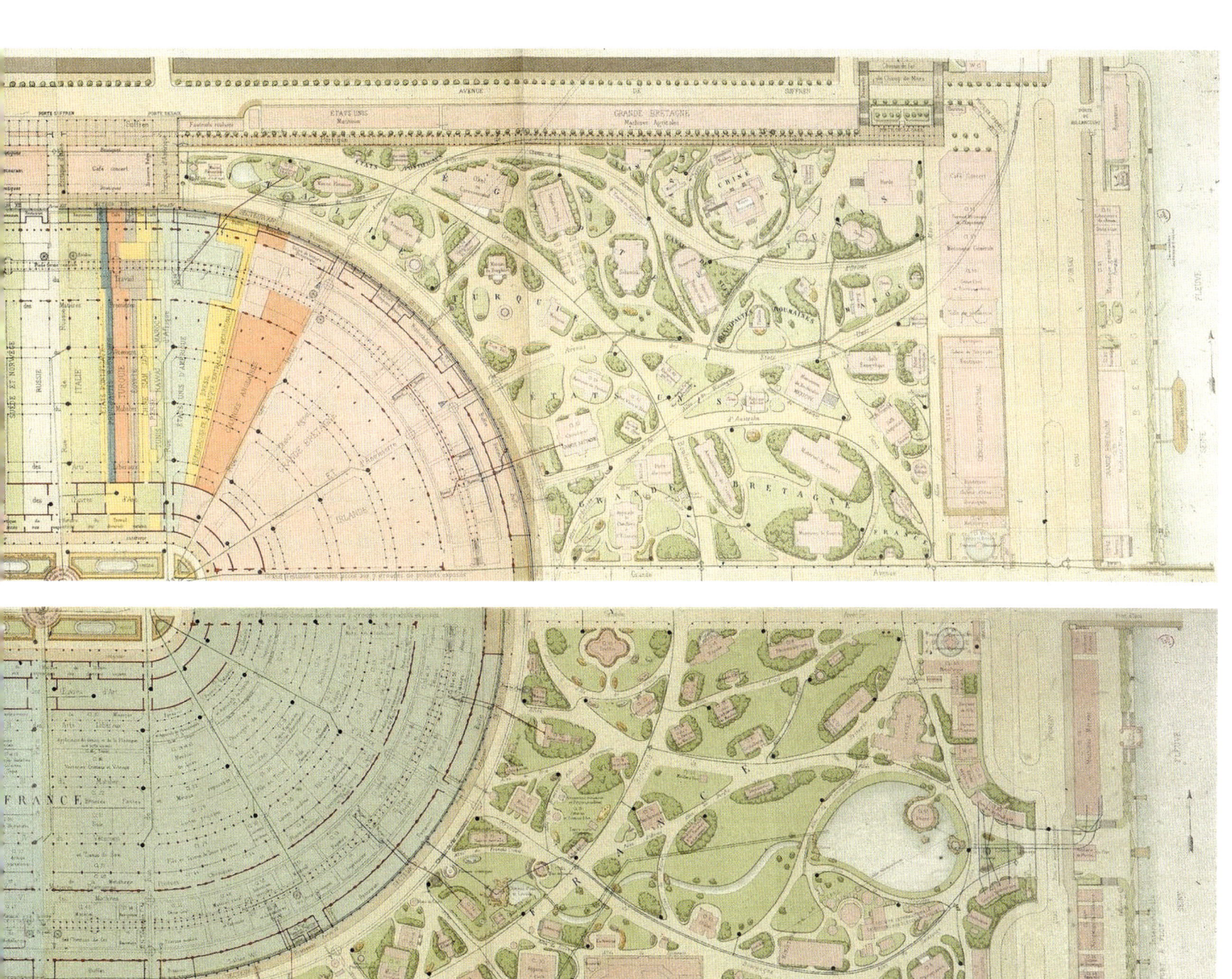

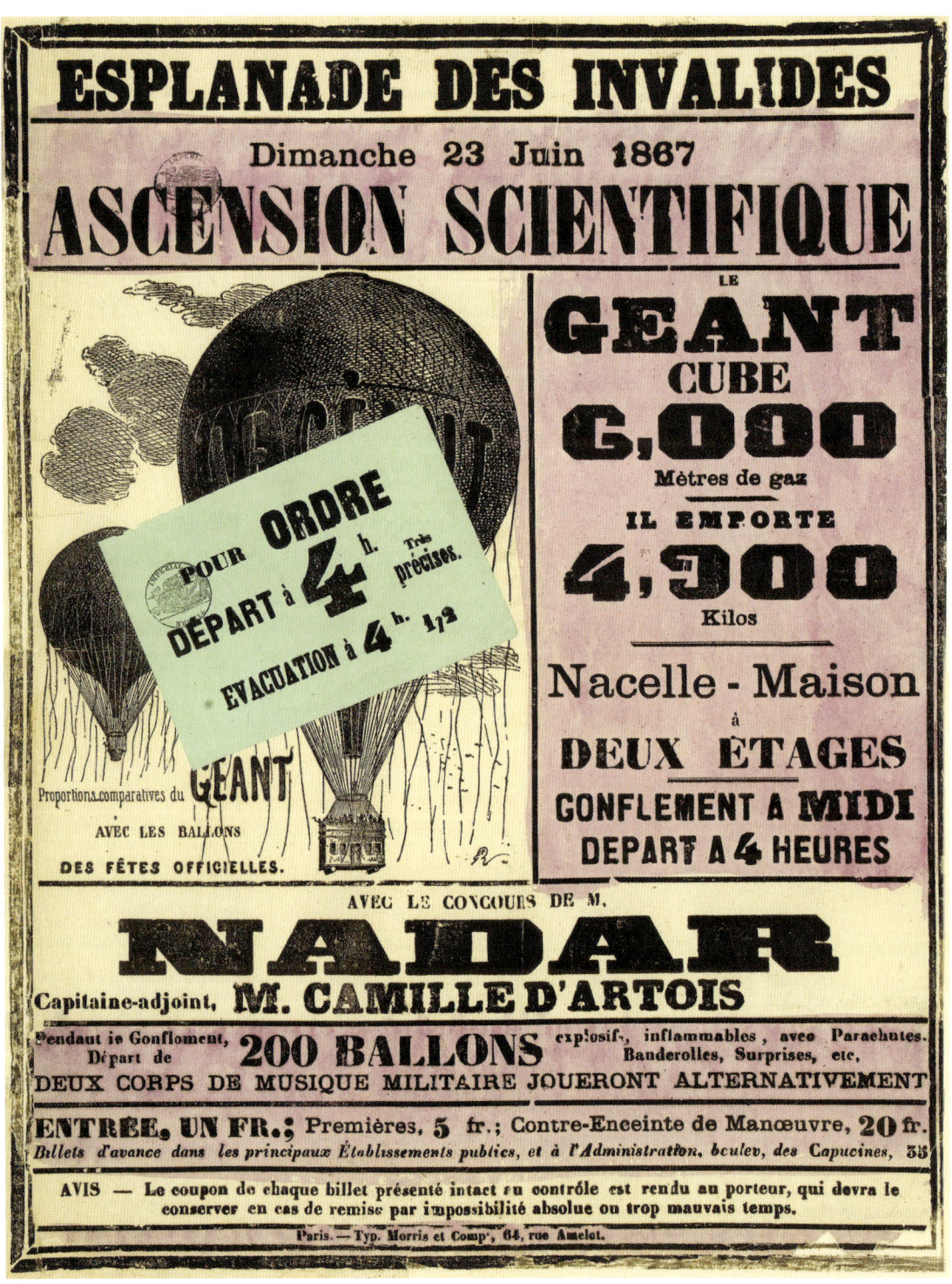

E.R. (monogram), Poster for the 'scientific' ascent of Nadar's hot-air balloon
'Le Géant' (The Giant) from the Esplanade des Invalides, 1867

Poster, 58.5 × 41.5 cm, Musée Carnavalet – Histoire de Paris

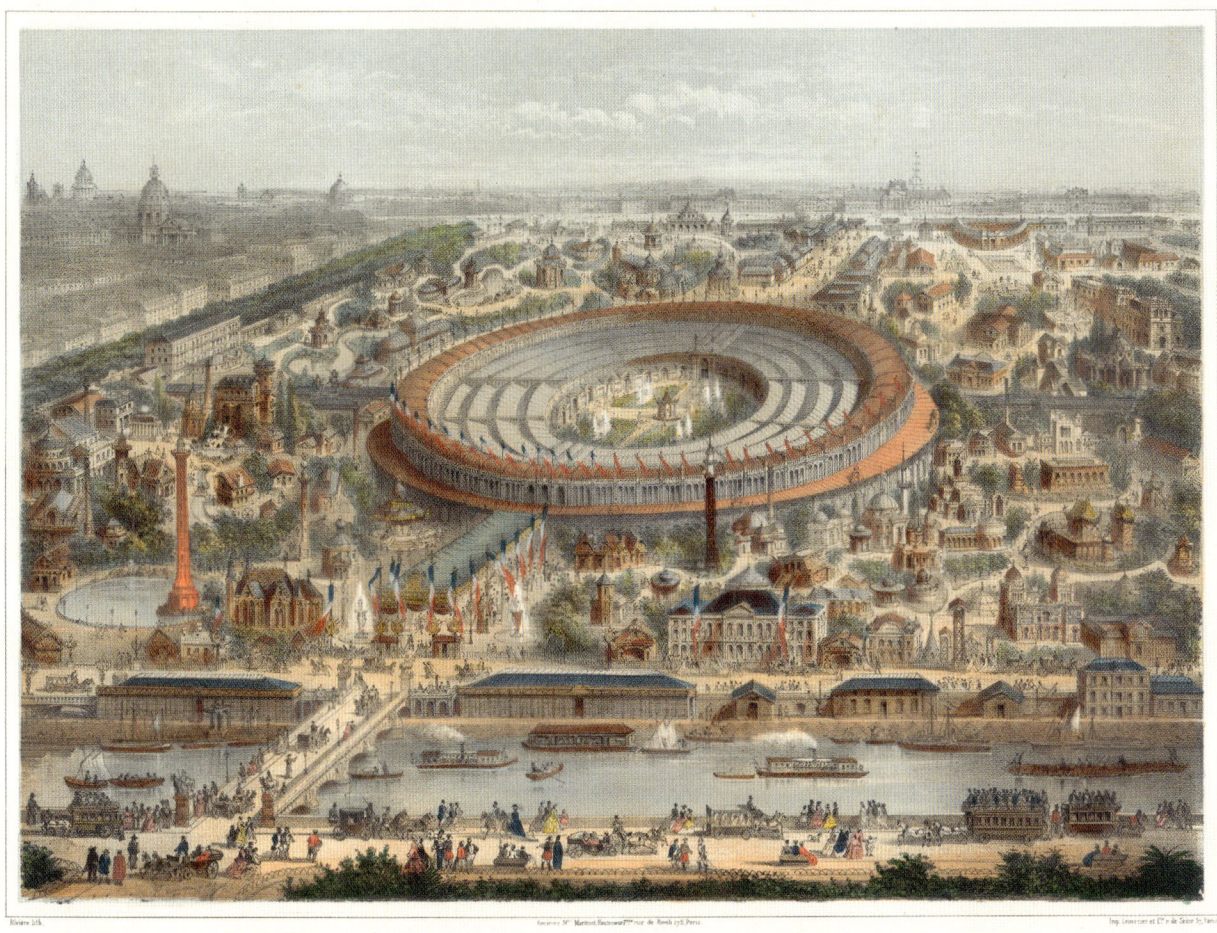

EXPOSITION UNIVERSELLE.
1867

Charles Rivière (1848–1870), Bird's-eye view of the Universal Exposition in Paris, 1867

Colour lithograph, some parts lacquered, 39.2 × 53 cm, Rijksmuseum, Amsterdam

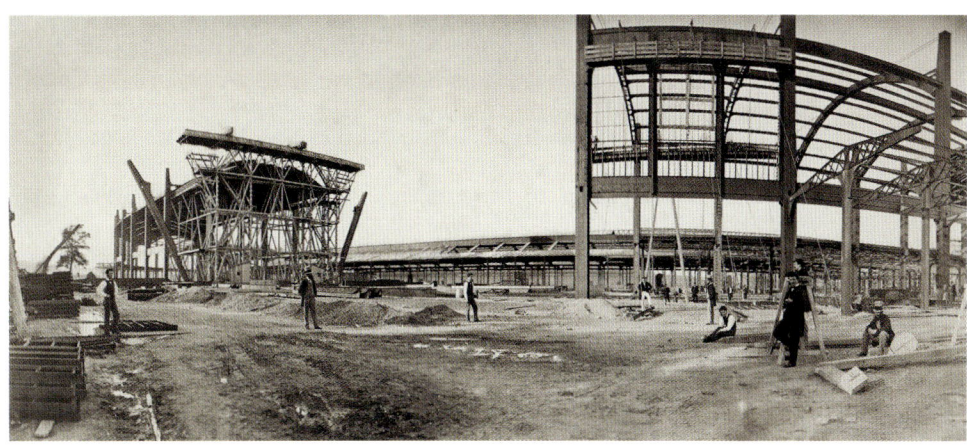

Pierre Petit (1831–1909), Construction of the World's Fair of 1867, 1867

Salt print, 20.5 × 48 cm, Bibliothèque nationale de France, Paris

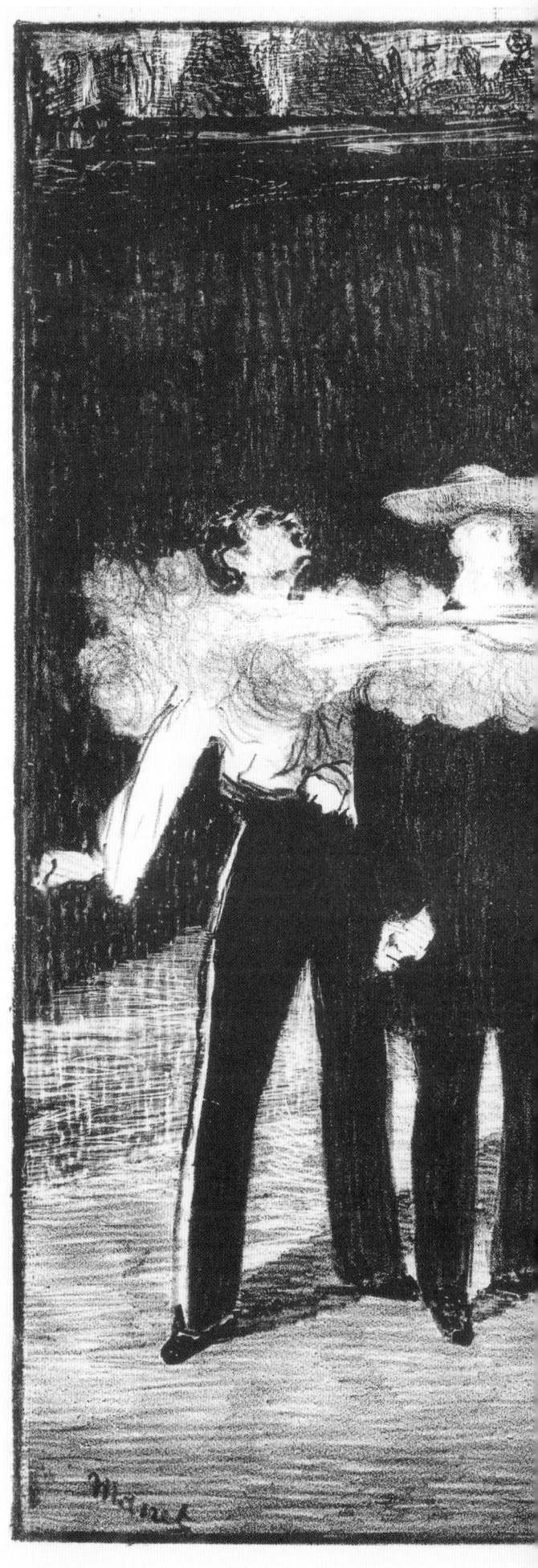

Édouard Manet (1832–1883), *The Execution of Emperor Maximilian in 1867*, 1868
Lithograph on chine collé, 48.2 × 59 cm, Rijksmuseum, Amsterdam.
Purchased with the support of the F.G. Waller-Fonds

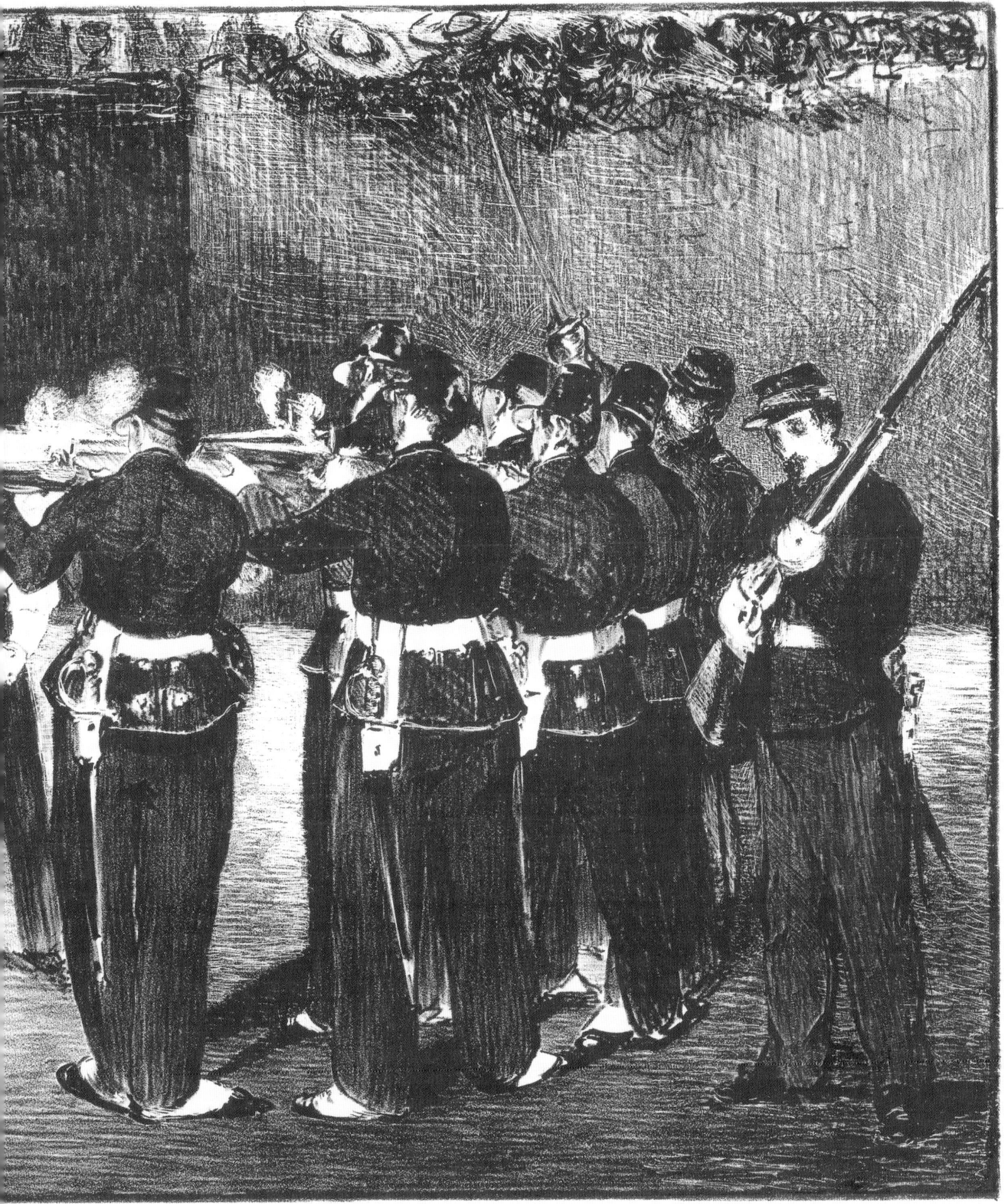

ÉDOUARD MANET (1832–1883)

Portrait of Théodore Duret, 1868

The author, journalist and art critic Théodore Duret was a good friend of Édouard Manet. In his younger years he travelled the world doing business for his father's cognac dealership. His first book on art, *Les peintres français en 1867* [French Painters in 1867], examined the state of the French art world during the year of the Universal Exposition. Although Duret was mildly critical of the shortcomings in Manet's canvases – too hastily painted and sloppily finished – he wrote admiringly of the young artist's originality. Later, Duret would become one of the most important supporters of the Impressionists.

Manet portrayed Duret a year after his debut as a writer in a rather unconventional way: a full-length pose but on a very small canvas. The young critic – he is 30 years old here – has a dandyish appearance. His left hand is gloved; with his right he holds,

in a relaxed fashion, a walking cane. In the foreground is an upholstered stool with a tray, on which Manet has placed a water carafe, a spoon and a drinking glass with a bright yellow lemon on top of it. According to Duret, Manet added the still life last. It may be a reference to the art of the seventeenth-century Spanish painter Diego Velázquez. The friendship between Manet and Duret began in Spain, where they both admired the Spanish masters in the Prado after meeting in a restaurant.

During the Franco-Prussian War, Manet gave his paintings to Duret for safekeeping, including such famous canvases as *Olympia* and *Le Déjeuner sur l'herbe*, both from 1863. 'In the event of my death,' the painter wrote to his friend, 'you can take your choice of *Moonlight* or *The Reader*, or if you prefer you can ask for the *Boy with the Soap Bubbles*'.[1]

In addition to writing about art, Duret was also active politically. In 1868, he founded the republican newspaper *La tribune*. The Second Empire did not appreciate criticism, and Duret's editorship brought him censorship and lawsuits. As a moderate republican, he condemned the excessive violence on both sides during the Commune in 1871 and advocated for peaceful cooperation. He narrowly escaped death during the chaotic Bloody Week, when the government army led him to an alleyway to be executed on the spot. At the last moment, one of the soldiers recognised him and removed him from the line.

[FROUKE VAN DIJKE]

1   Juliet Wilson-Bareau (ed.),
    *Manet by Himself: Correspondence
    & Conversation, Paintings,
    Pastels, Prints & Drawings*
    (London, 1995), p. 56.

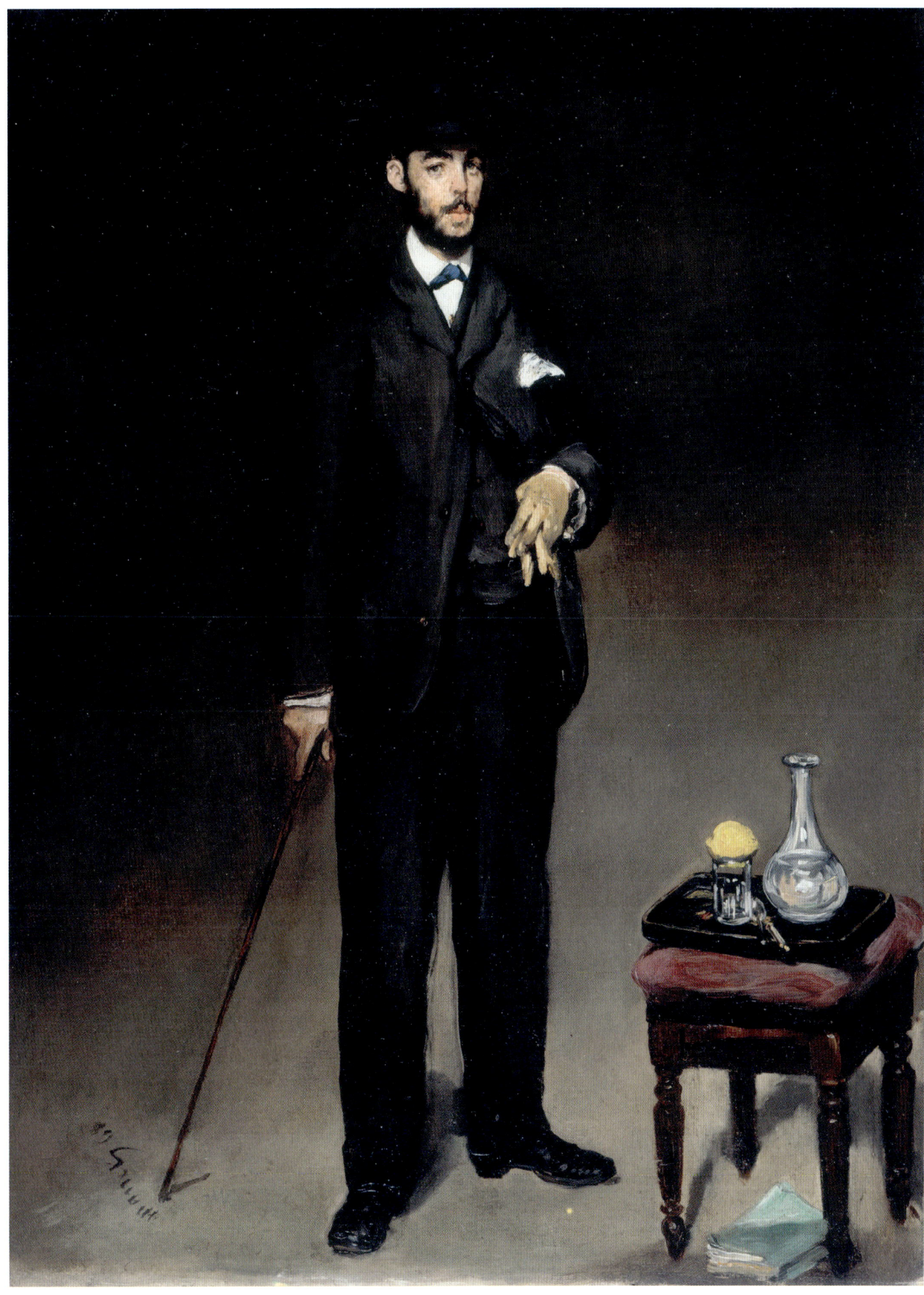

Édouard Manet (1832–1883), *Portrait of Théodore Duret*, 1868

Oil on canvas, 46.5 × 35.5 cm, Petit Palais, Musée des Beaux-Arts de la Ville de Paris

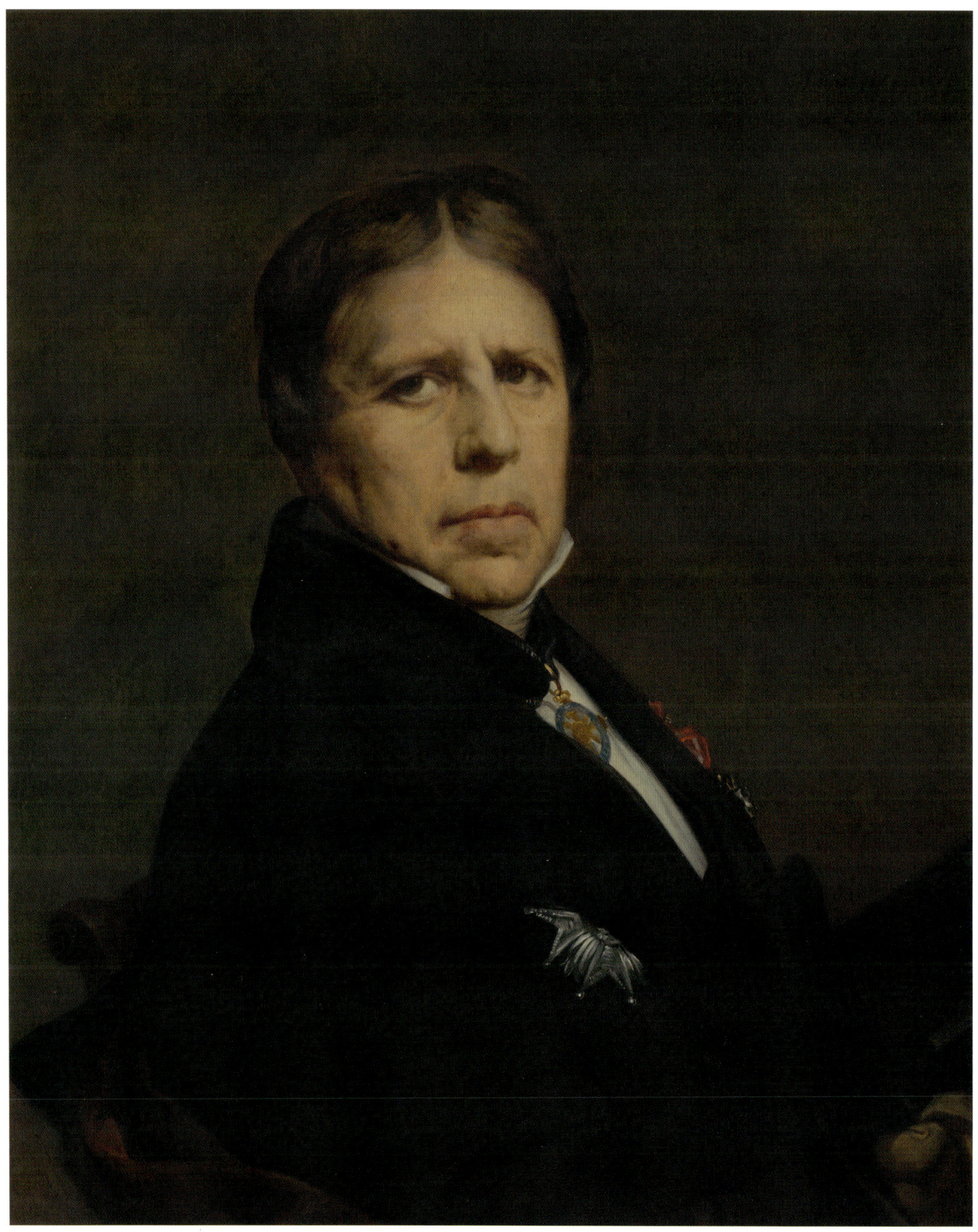

Jean-Auguste-Dominique Ingres (1780–1867), *Self-Portrait*, 1864–65
Oil on canvas, 64 × 53 cm, Royal Museum of Fine Arts (KMSKA), Antwerp

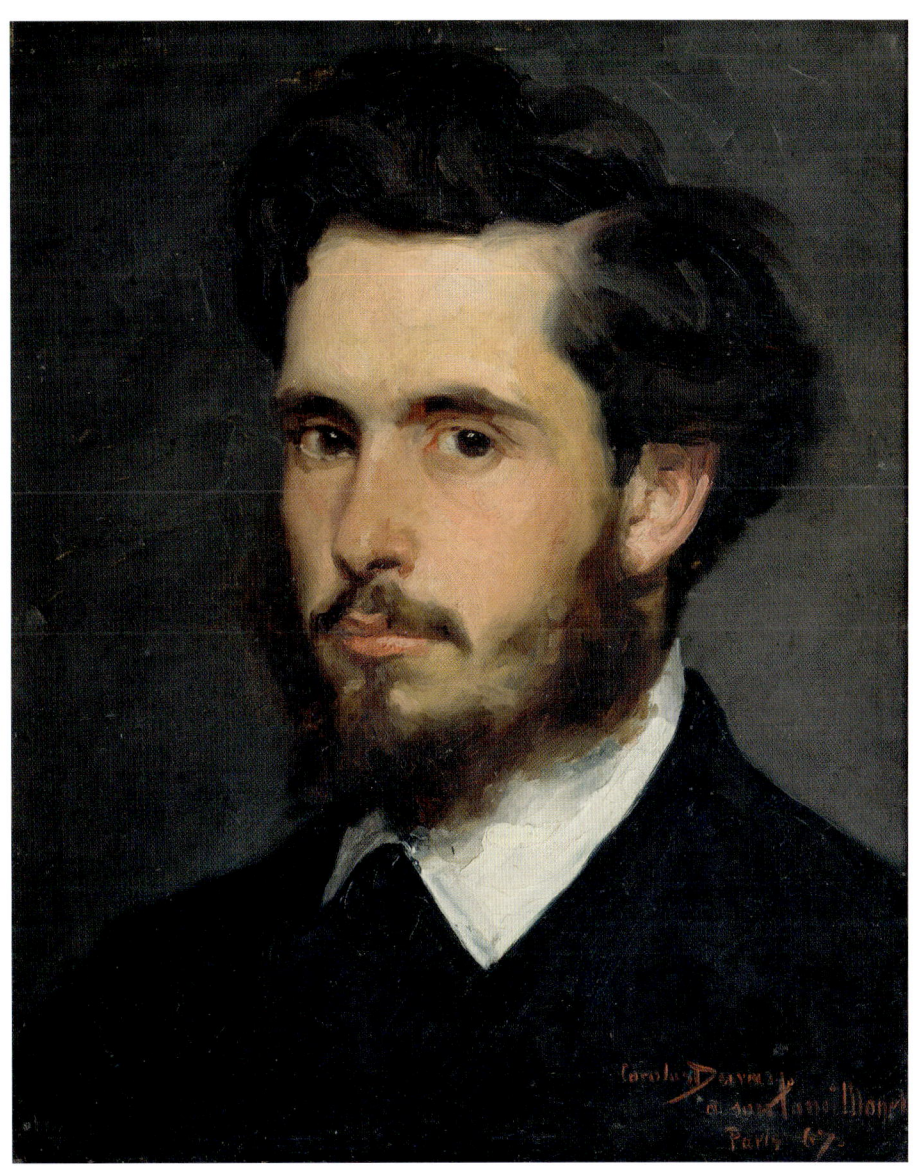

Charles-Émile Auguste Durand, known as Carolus-Duran (1837–1917), *Portrait of Claude Monet*, 1867

Oil on canvas, 46 × 38 cm, Musée Marmottan Monet, Paris, Michel Monet bequest, 1966

Gilbert Alexandre de Séverac (1834–1897), *Portrait of Claude Monet*, 1865
Oil on canvas, 40 × 32 cm, Musée Marmottan Monet, Paris, Michel Monet bequest, 1966

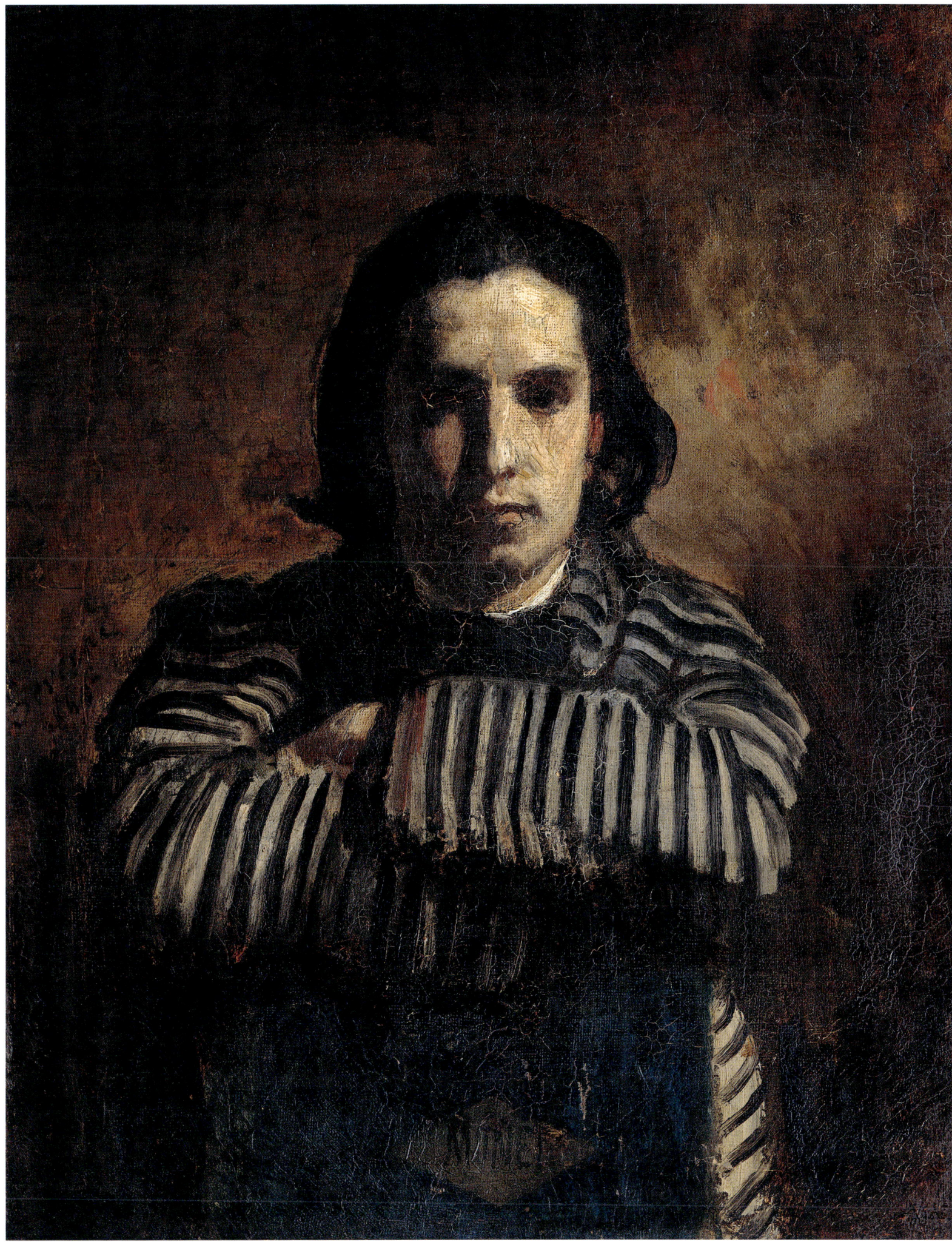

FRÉDÉRIC BAZILLE (1841–1870)

Bazille's Studio, 1870

When Frédéric Bazille moved from Montpellier in the South of France to Paris in 1862, he asked his parents for financial help to set up a studio. Between 1863 and 1870, he had six in succession. The interior views he made of three of them are indirect self-portraits, manifestos of how he envisioned the life of a painter, and 'totems' for a new generation of artists.[1] Bazille shared several of these studios with friends, thus allowing them to benefit from his parents' generosity: in 1864 he and Claude Monet set up a studio on rue de Furstemberg and in 1867 he shared his studio on rue Visconti with Auguste Renoir and sometimes with Monet and Alfred Sisley.[2] The artists and visiting friends worked from life with female models, posed for each other or painted still lifes.

In January 1868, Bazille moved to 9 rue La Condamine, in the heart of the rapidly changing working-class district of Les Batignolles, not far from Édouard Manet's studio and Café Guerbois, frequented by the realist avant-garde and the future Impressionists.[3] This was the largest of his studios, which he shared for a time with Renoir, who was always short of money.

In the winter of 1869–70, Bazille painted his studio for the last time. His earlier studio pictures were devoid of figures, but here he depicted himself – standing at the centre – in the company of friends. Edmond Maître plays the piano, Manet and possibly Zacharie Astruc examine a framed work by Bazille on an easel, and Renoir, standing on the stairs, talks to a seated man beneath, perhaps Monet or Sisley. The interior is sparsely furnished without items typical of studios of the period. A 'Voltaire' armchair, an upright piano (Bazille liked to play) and the paintings of Bazille and Renoir are these young men's only possessions.

The work is neither a group portrait nor a genre scene, but a studio portrait in which Bazille shows that a 'modern' studio is not only a place for working and exhibiting, but also a social space that can spawn an art collective. In its depiction of Bazille's friends and his and their paintings, this work has a biographical and retrospective character.[4] It is a portrait of a new generation of artists and the so-called 'new painting'.[5] The Batignolles group (a name coined by Edmond Duranty) or the 'actualists' (as Émile Zola called them) came to public attention with the exhibition of Henri Fantin-Latour's canvas *A Studio in Les Batignolles* (Musée d'Orsay, Paris) at the 1870 Salon. The work, dating from the winter of 1869–70, features Astruc, Bazille, Manet, Monet and Renoir.

As these two paintings show, Manet was a mentor to the new generation. In a letter to his father, Bazille wrote that his likeness in the painting was the work of Manet, an intervention that attests to Manet's great affection for Bazille (he owned a portrait of Bazille by Renoir).[6]

In Bazille's studio portrait, works that had been rejected by the Salon are not only framed, but also prominently displayed on the wall. Bazille and his friends clearly wanted to break away from established art standards, and in 1867 had plans for an independent exhibition. Had it happened, it would have been the forerunner of the exhibition that the Anonymous Association of Painters, Sculptors and Engravers organised in the spring of 1874 in the studio of photographer Nadar, making it, in essence, the first Impressionist exhibition.

In April 1870, Bazille moved to a studio on rue des Beaux-Arts and returned to Montpellier the following month. In August of that year, he enlisted to fight in the Franco-Prussian War. He died on 28 November at the Battle of Beaune-la-Rolande.

[PAUL PERRIN]

1   See Kimberly A. Jones, 'Practice and Process in the Work of Frédéric Bazille', in Michel Hilaire and Paul Perrin (eds.), *Frédéric Bazille and the Birth of Impressionism* (Paris, 2016), pp. 164–168.

2   Frédéric Bazille, *Studio on Rue de Furstenberg*, 1865, Musée Fabre, Montpellier; Frédéric Bazille, *Studio on Rue Visconti*, 1867, Virginia Museum of Fine Arts, Richmond.

3   As rue de la Paix was known from December 1868. Letter from Bazille to his father, 20 November 1867, quoted in Hilaire and Perrin 2016 (note 1), pp. 136–137.

4   On the left wall at the top, Bazille's *Fisherman with a Net* (1868, Rau Collection for Unicef), rejected at the 1869 Salon; on the easel, *View of the Village* (1868, Musée Fabre), shown at the 1869 Salon; on the back wall, Renoir's large painting of two female figures, rejected at the 1867 Salon (and now partially destroyed) and Bazille's unfinished *La Toilette* (1870, Musée Fabre); and on the right wall, Bazille's *Terrace at Méric* (1866–67, Geneva, Association des amis du Petit Palais), rejected at the 1867 Salon.

5   The term is borrowed from Louis-Edmond Duranty, *La nouvelle peinture* (Paris, 1876).

6   Letter from Bazille to his father, 1 January 1870, Musée d'Orsay, Paris. Auguste Renoir, *Frédéric Bazille*, 1867, Musée d'Orsay, Paris.

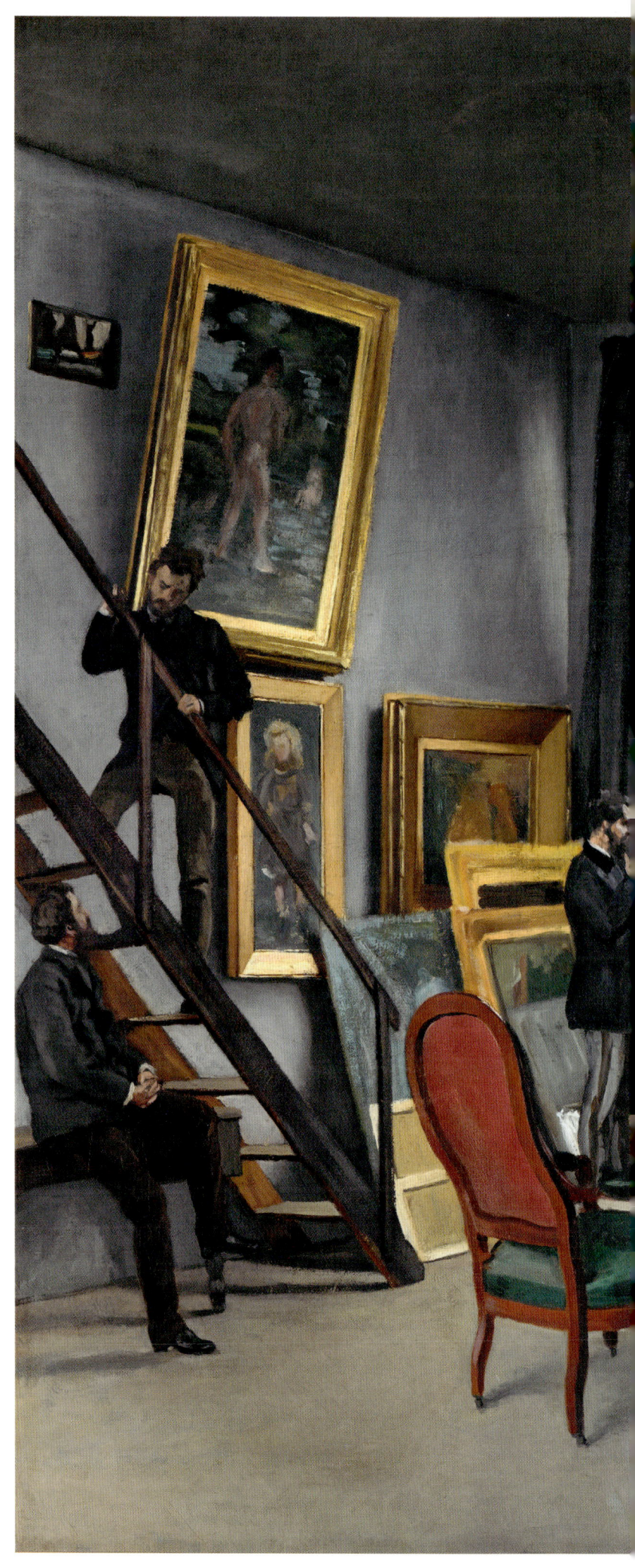

Frédéric Bazille (1841–1870), *Bazille's Studio*
(also known as *The Studio on the Rue La Condamine*), 1870
Oil on canvas, 98 cm × 128 cm, Musée d'Orsay, Paris. Accepted by the State
as a bequest from Marc Bazille to the Musées nationaux in 1924

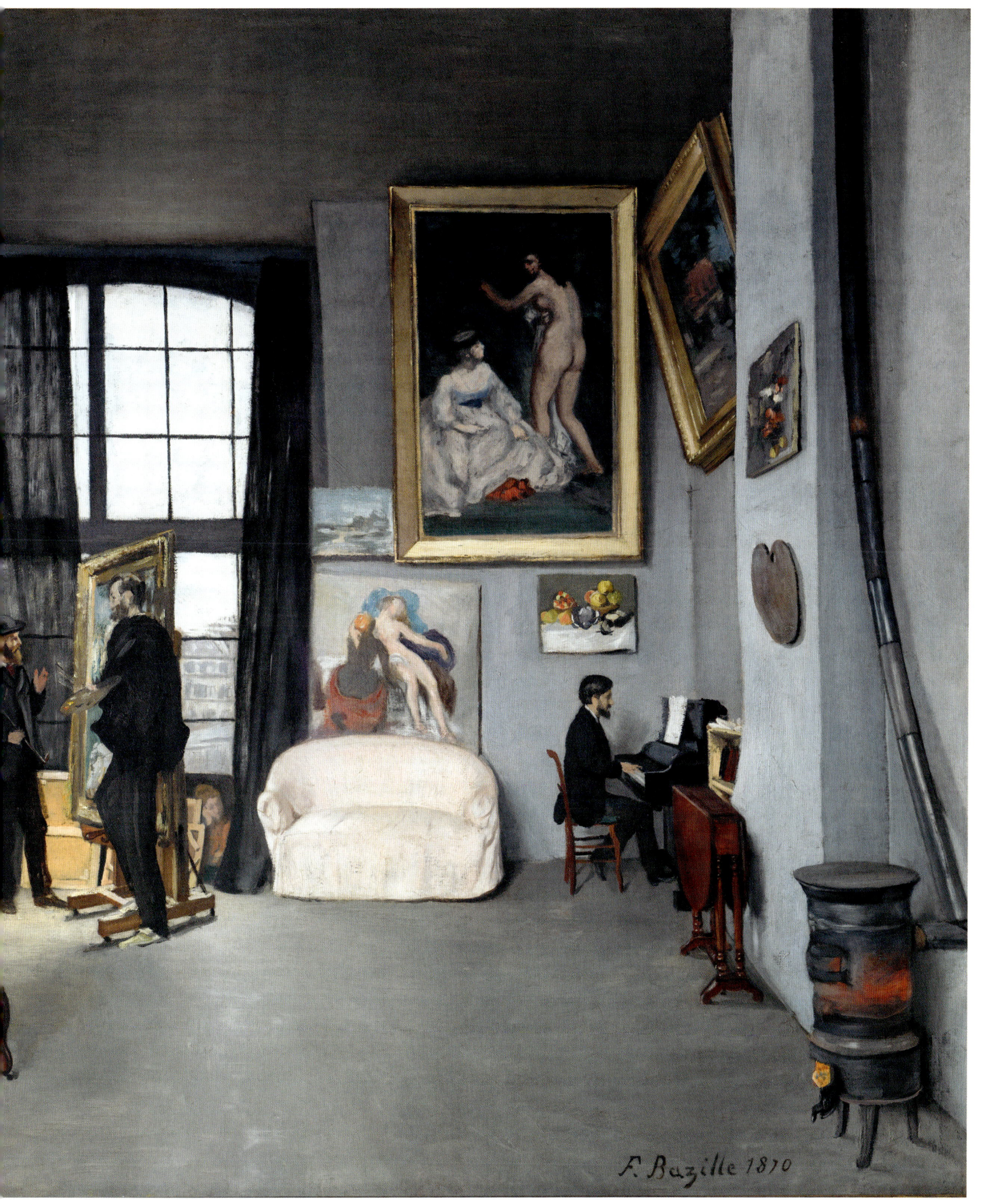

F. Bazille 1870

Mardi

F B

Ma chère mère

La dernière lettre de papa
m'a rendu bien malheureux,
plus même, que vous ne pouvez vous
le figurer, j'ai passé quelques tristes
journées. Maintenant c'est fini
les idées de mariage ont reçu en moi
une rude coup. Il est probable qu'elles
mettront du temps à se relever.
Peut-être vaut-il mieux que je
sois complètement libre pour
travailler à mon aise et comme je
veux. C'est ce que je fais en ce
moment plus que jamais.

Voici que j'ai une autre mauvaise
nouvelle à vous annoncer.

Mes tableaux sont refusés à
l'exposition. Ne vous affligez pas
trop de cela, cela n'a rien de
décourageant, au contraire. Je
partage ce tort avec tout ce qu'il
y avait de bon au salon de cette
année. On signe en ce moment
une pétition pour demander une
exposition des refusés, cette pétition
est appuyée par tous les peintres
de Paris qui ont quelque valeur.
Cependant elle n'aboutira pas.

Dans tous les cas le désagrément
qui m'arrive cette année ne se renouvellera
plus, car je n'enverrai plus rien devant
le jury. Il est par trop ridicule, quand
on sait n'être pas une bête, de s'exposer
à ces caprices d'administration, surtout
quand on ne tient aucunement
aux médailles et aux distributions de
prix.

Letter from Frédéric Bazille to his mother, April 1867
Musée Fabre de Montpellier Méditerranée Métropole

ce que je vous dis là une douzaine
de jeunes gens de talent le pensent
comme moi. nous avons donc résolu
de louer chaque année un grand
atelier où nous exposerons nos œuvres
en aussi grand nombre que nous le
voudrons. nous inviterons les peintres
qui nous plaisent à nous envoyer des
tableaux. Courbet, Corot, Diaz,
Daubigny et beaucoup d'autres que vous
ne connaissez peut-être pas, nous ont
promis d'envoyer des tableaux, et
approuvent beaucoup notre idée.
Avec ces gens là et Monet qui est
plus fort qu'eux tous, nous sommes
surs de réussir. vous verrez qu'on
parlera de nous. Si par hazard l'exposition
des refusés était accordée nous ne ferions
rien cette année, et notre cercle ne commencerait
que l'année prochaine. J'en serais bien aise
pour ma part. J'aurais le temps de faire
à Montpellier deux ou trois tableaux

importants. Ne vous effrayez pas,
je vous assure que je suis fort
raisonnable, nous avons certainement
raison; ce n'est rien moins qu'une
révolte de collégiens. Je fais en ce moment
un tableau de deux femmes de grandeur
naturelle qui arrangent des fleurs
je le finirai à l'époque des pivoines.
Je voudrais fort qu'il fut fini si notre
exposition particulière commence cette
année. J'y enverrais aussi un portrait que
je fais de Monet.

Ne craignez rien pour les Marsignan,
j'ai tout arrangé.

Donnez moi beaucoup de détails
sur ce que vous comptez faire ce printemps.
Je ne vous conseille vraiment pas de venir
cette fois-ci — Il y a déjà une cohue
énorme le moment n'est pas bon pour
voir Paris. Vous ne sauriez où loger, je
crois même si papa vient, qu'il fera bien
de venir prendre mon lit.
Je vous embrasse bien ainsi que les cousines
faites mes amitiés aux Gachon — F. Bazille

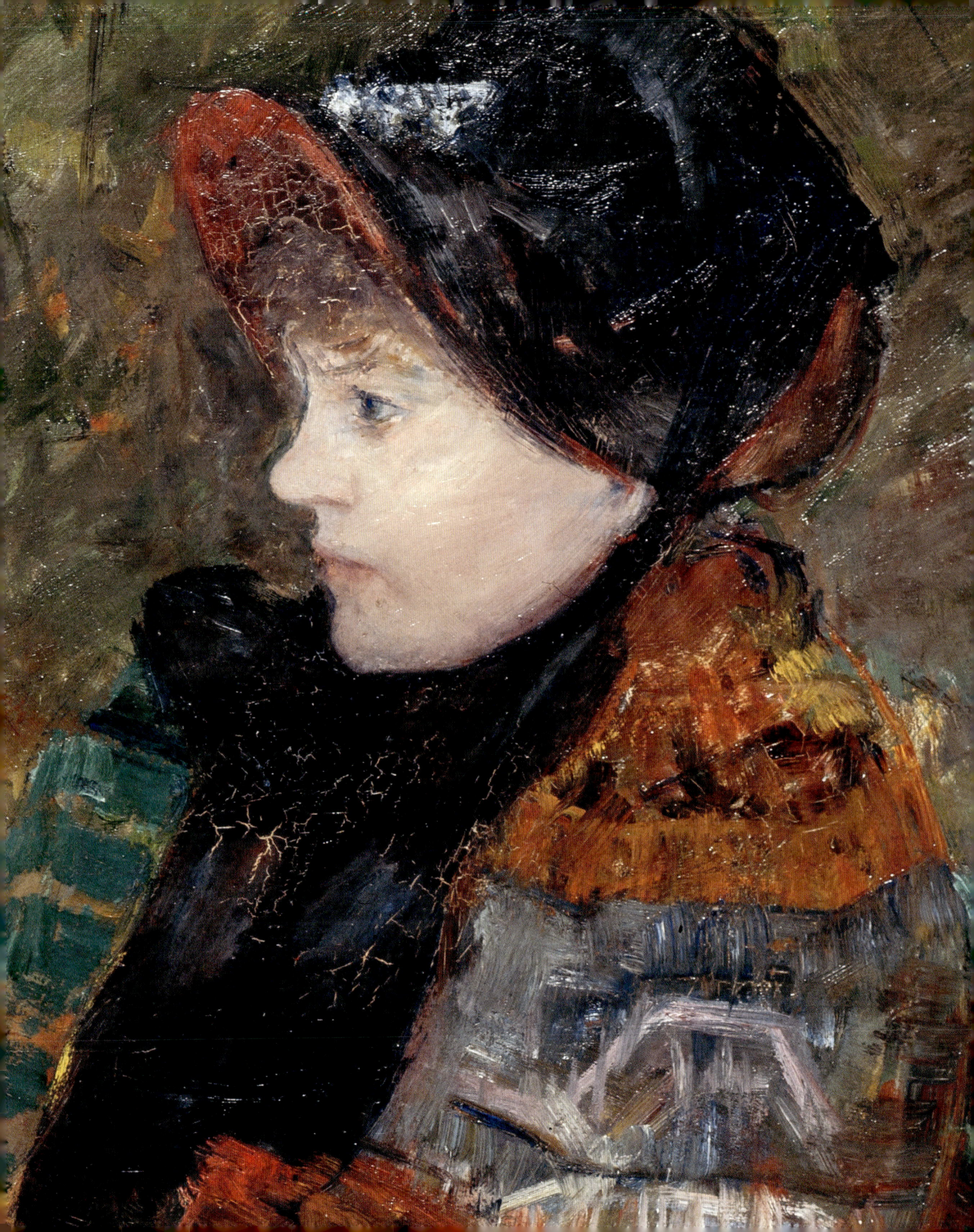

THE
PARISIENNE

Frouke van Dijke

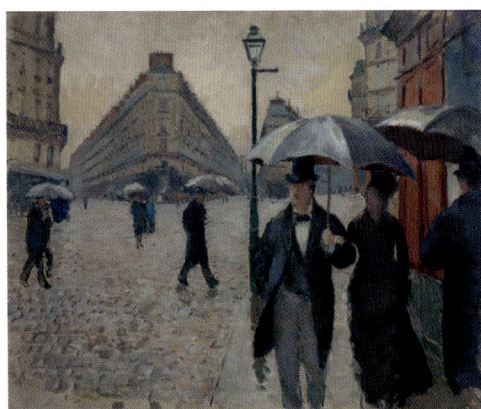

Fig. 1   [pp. 134–135]

Fig. 1
Gustave Caillebotte (1848–1894),
Paris Street. Rainy Day, 1877
Oil on canvas, 54 × 65 cm, Musée Marmottan
Monet, Paris, Michel Monet bequest, 1966

Fig. 2
Claude Monet (1840–1926), *Camille*, 1866
Oil on canvas, 231 × 151 cm, Kunsthalle Bremen

A city is more than a collection of streets and buildings. The Impressionists were less interested in an accurate topographical representation of Paris than in portraying its energy. Even before artists such as Claude Monet and Auguste Renoir painted their first cityscapes, they attempted to capture the essence of modern Paris through the figure who best embodied this metropolis: the Parisienne, a figure who represented flair, independence, beauty, superiority and good taste. In the nineteenth century, she appeared frequently in magazines and advertising posters. The young Impressionists, in particular, made grateful use of this character. Through the figure piece – a genre more highly regarded than the cityscape within the academy – they attempted to reconcile the Salon jury's conservative preferences with their own ambition to paint contemporary Paris. The Parisienne embodied modernity and was thus the face of the city. But how did Haussmann's reforms affect her life? There was clearly more than just a gap between rich and poor in Paris: experiences of the city also differed greatly for men and women.

A contemporary allegory

In his travel book *The Innocents Abroad* (1869), the American author Mark Twain reported on his visit to Paris, where he was constantly irritated by the local guide who happily showed him all the city's attractions, as long as they were shops for shirts, gloves or boots. The low point was Twain's intended visit to the Louvre, which he reached after closing time because his carriage kept stopping to take in silk shops forced upon him by his guide.[1] Twain was in Paris at the time of the Universal Exposition of 1867, in which France presented itself as a world leader in all aspects of life, including industry. In reality, in this latter sphere it lagged far behind competitors such as England and what is now Germany. But France *did* lead the way in the production of fashion and perfume. In a short time, the number of couturiers and department stores in Paris doubled. Alongside construction, these luxury industries were one of the most important pillars of the French economy. And these export products required strong advertising campaigns. The advent of the poster not only radically changed the streetscape of Paris, but also confirmed the idea that an attractive lady could sell anything. Soap, eau de cologne or throat lozenges: the modern woman promoted it all. This commerce contributed to the birth of the Parisienne as an ideal image and (status) symbol of the city.

Woman as allegory is not a new phenomenon. A stroll through Paris is a journey past theatres, bridges and palaces decorated with female figures. These statues symbolise abstract concepts such as prosperity, chastity, peace and justice. In her book *Monuments and Maidens: The Allegory of the Female Form* (1985), Marina Warner identifies the feminine form as the most dominant emblem of Paris. She points not only to the greater number of female symbols in the City of Light, but also to an important difference in representations of male and female figures on monuments or decorations: the woman is given a much more idealised – and therefore anonymous – appearance than the man. In an era dominated by the male gaze, the woman was depicted as either desirable or neutral.[2] Her figure was thus considered ideally suited to the representation of the most varied ideas. But where allegories such as Lady Justice wore timeless robes, the modern symbol of Paris dressed according to the latest fashion.

When the Parisienne emerged as the icon of the city, there was a broader connection between fashion and the construction of identity. The nineteenth century saw the rise of nationalism, a sentiment accompanied throughout Europe by the search for (and thus the creation of) a unique 'nature'. Fashion, and local and national costume in particular, played an essential role in this.[3] Paris also used fashion to create an image. However, the Parisian's choice of clothing was characterised not by tradition and convention but was instead in constant flux. The latest trends spread like wildfire via fashion magazines, and consumers were seduced by the newest fad. Fashion journalist Emmeline Raymond, one of the few female contributors to the 1867 *Paris guide*, characterised the total surrender to these trends as a 'voluntary serfdom' from which no woman could escape.[4] Fashion was Paris; Paris was fashion.

Fashion and modern Paris

The preoccupation with fashion can easily be dismissed as a superficial pastime but nothing could be further from the truth. In the Paris of the Impressionists, fashion represented progress, just as much as the light bulb, the steam train and photography. The poet Charles Baudelaire embraced its ephemeral nature as the preeminent sign of modern life and regarded commercial fashion prints as the most characteristic expression of the aesthetic and moral temperament of his time.[5] He wrote: 'If a fashion or the cut of a garment has been slightly modified, if bows and curls have been supplanted by cockades, if *bavolets* have been enlarged and *chignons* have dropped a fraction towards the nape of the neck, if waists have been raised and skirts have become fuller, be very sure that his eagle eye will already have spotted it from however great a distance.'[6] The keen eye in question belonged to the artist, who, according to Baudelaire, must be fully aware of the latest fashions in order to depict his own era accurately.

The Impressionists did not look down on fashion or commerce. Their cityscapes, populated by Parisiennes and dandies, are sometimes mockingly dismissed by critics as inflated shop advertisements. Edmond Lepelletier, for example, pointed to the fashionably dressed figures in Gustave Caillebotte's painting *Paris Street. Rainy Day* (1877) [fig. 1], for which Caillebotte also made a preparatory sketch, 'sheltered under an umbrella that seems freshly taken from the racks of [the department stores] Au Louvre and Bon Marché'.[7] Mary Cassatt, Claude Monet and Berthe Morisot sought inspiration by leafing through fashion magazines such as *La mode illustrée* and *Petit courrier des dames*. A year before the 1867 Salon at which the Impressionists' submissions were rejected en masse, Monet celebrated a great success there with his monumental figure painting *Camille* [fig. 2]. It depicts his future wife, Camille Doncieux, dressed in a black and green striped dress and a fur-trimmed jacket. Not only does the satin dress correspond to the latest cut prescribed by the fashion magazines, but Doncieux's pose also corresponds to that of the figures in these popular prints.

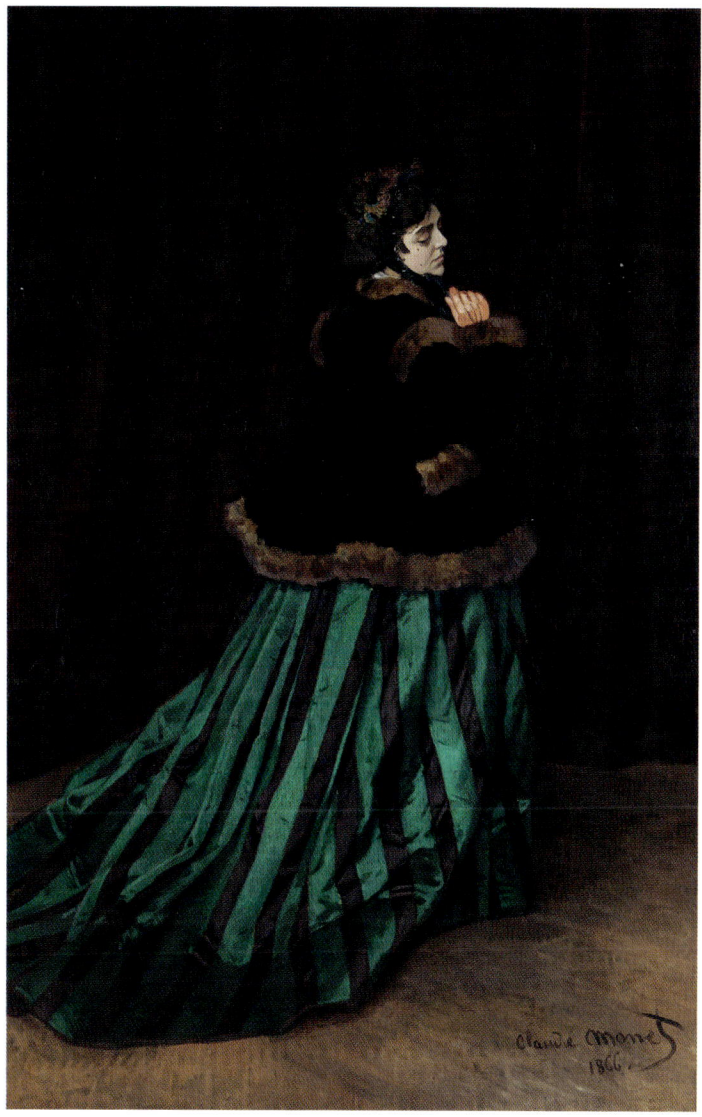

Fig. 2

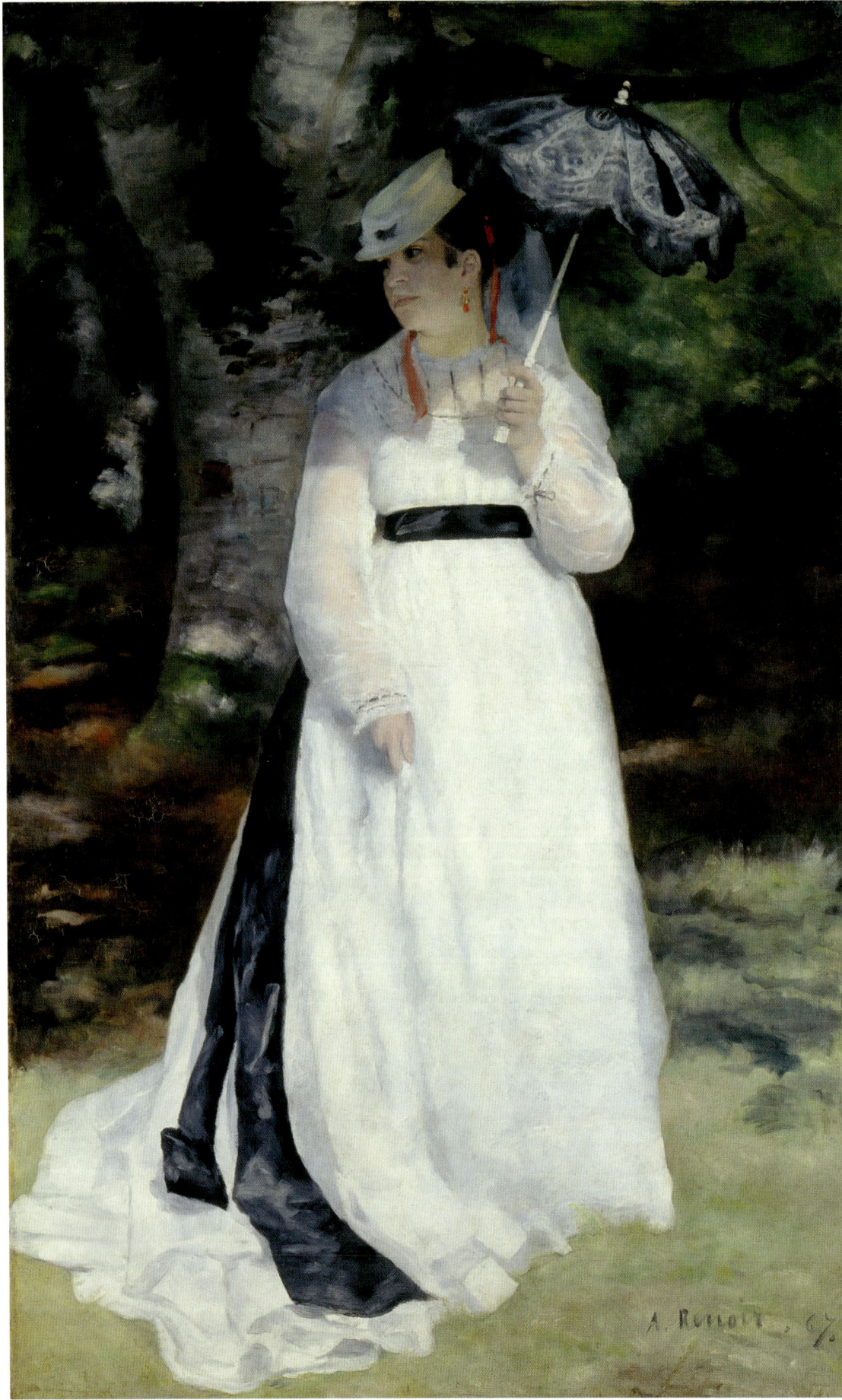

Fig. 3

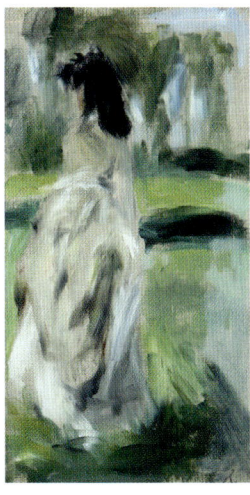 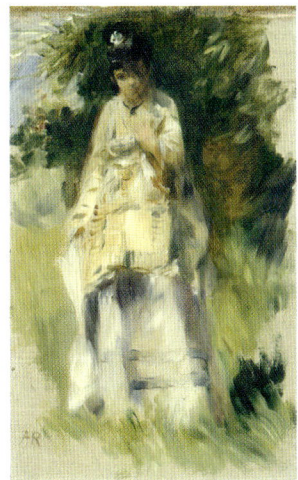 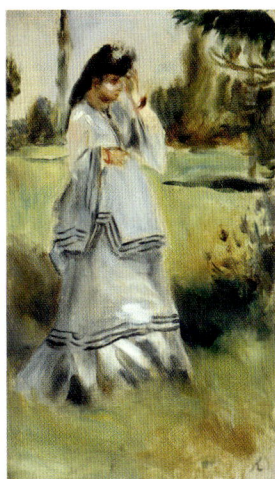

Fig. 4   [p. 148]   Fig. 5   [p. 143]   Fig. 6   [p. 142]

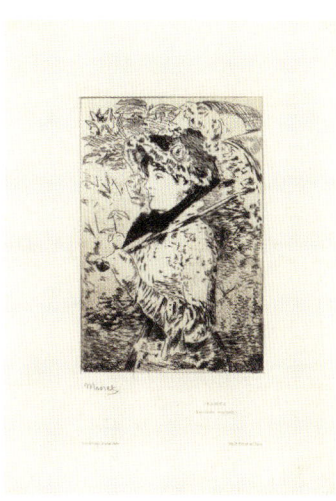

Fig. 7   [p. 138]

In *Camille*, Monet painted Paris without showing the slightest glimpse of the city. The presence of a well-dressed lady automatically transported any environment to the French capital. According to the writer Émile Zola, Monet even depicted the life of the metropolis in his landscapes through fashion: 'He loves our women, from their parasols, their gloves and their muslins to their false hair and rice powder, everything that makes them the daughters of their civilisation…. Like a true Parisian he carries Paris into the country…'[8]

Monet's Salon success inspired his good friend Renoir to do the same. His painting *Lise. The Woman with the Umbrella* (1867) depicts his lover, Lise Tréhot [figs. 3–6]. Critics also interpreted her image as a portrait of Paris, despite the background, which betrays nothing of an urban environment. Here, Paris resides in the white muslin of Tréhot's summer dress, in her airy transparent sleeves and stylish accessories. In each case, Monet and Renoir have not painted a portrait of their partner. Both women serve as types, as stand-ins for the Parisienne. In 1881, Édouard Manet went a step further with his work *Jeanne (Spring)*, a portrait of the successful actress Anne Darlaud, better known as Jeanne Demarsy [fig. 7].[9] Manet carefully painted the floral pattern of her blouse, the creases in her glove, the bonnet decorated with roses and ruffles, and the delicate lace of her parasol. We see her face in profile, like a figure depicted on a coin. 'She is not a woman,' wrote Maurice du Seigneur. 'She is a bouquet, truly a visible perfume.'[10] Manet painted a contemporary icon, a universal representation of the Parisienne and thus of the city, who, thanks to her fashionable spring attire, also embodies spring.

Fig. 3
Auguste Renoir (1841–1919),
Lise. The Woman with the Umbrella, 1867
Oil on canvas, 184 × 115.6 cm, Museum Folkwang, Essen

Fig. 4
Auguste Renoir (1841–1919),
Young Woman Seen From Behind (Lise Tréhot), 1866
Oil on canvas, 24 × 12.8 cm, JK Art Foundation

Fig. 5
Auguste Renoir (1841–1919),
Woman Standing by a Tree, 1866
Oil on canvas, 25.2 × 15.9 cm, National Gallery of Art, Washington, Ailsa Mellon Bruce Collection

Fig. 6
Auguste Renoir (1841–1919), *Woman in a Park*, 1866
Oil on canvas, 26.1 × 16.1 cm, National Gallery of Art, Washington, Ailsa Mellon Bruce Collection

Fig. 7
Édouard Manet (1832–1882), *Jeanne (Spring)*, 1882
(print after painting from 1881)
Etching and aquatint, 28 × 20.5 cm, Kunstmuseum Den Haag

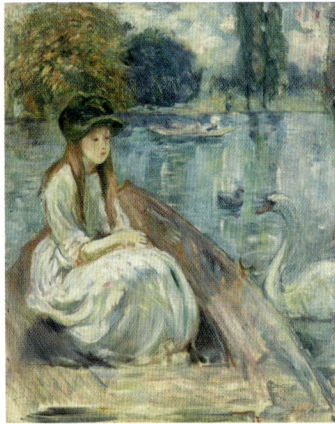

Fig. 8   [p. 42]

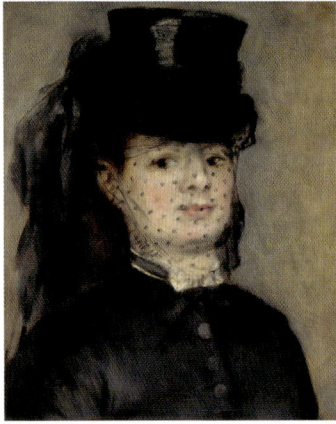

Fig. 9   [p. 133]

Fig. 8
Berthe Morisot (1841–1895),
Jeanne Fourmanoir on the Lake, 1892
Oil on canvas, 61 × 50.5 cm, FAMM Museum,
Mougins, The Levett Collection

Fig. 9
Auguste Renoir (1841–1919), *Madame Darras*, c. 1868
Oil on canvas, 48 × 40 cm, Musée d'Orsay, Paris. Accepted
by the State as a donation from Baroness Eva Gebhard-
Gourgaud to the Musée du Jeu de Paume in 1965

Fig. 10
Honoré Daumier (1808–1879), From the series
The Bluestockings, no. 27: 'It's odd... I only get
good ideas when in the Bois de Boulogne,
horseback riding with Mr. Edouard!.../ What ideas
could come to my wife when she rides with Mr.
Edouard?... it intrigues me... it makes me angry
to see that she has made herself an Amazon...
I would much prefer she'd ride the path of virtue!'
Page from *Le Charivari*, 12 May 1844, 34 × 26 cm,
Kunstmuseum Den Haag

Fig. 11
Edgar Degas (1834–1917),
At the Louvre - Museum of Antiquities, c. 1867
Etching, aquatint and drypoint, ink on Japanese paper,
35.6 × 26.8 cm, Kunstmuseum Den Haag

Safe streets

In many cases, Manet, Monet and Renoir portrayed the Parisienne as a cult figure and less as a woman of flesh and blood. But what about those artists who were Parisiennes themselves, the female Impressionists such as Mary Cassatt, Berthe Morisot, Marie Bracquemond and Eva Gonzalès? Critics explicitly linked Morisot's work at the first Impressionist exhibition with creations by the English-born, Paris-based couturier Charles Frederick Worth and with fashion prints.[11] While fashion magazines mainly inspired Monet and Renoir to copy poses and garments, Morisot showed more interest in the depiction of the modern woman. Fashion prints were first and foremost a showcase for the industry, but were also unique early representations of the middle-class woman engaged in everyday activities, illustrating the Parisienne during a walk in the park or boarding a train.[12] Morisot and Cassatt did the same. They show us the new woman and the life that modern Paris had to offer her.

In the 1867 *Paris guide*, the writer George Sand gives a vivid account of how Haussmann had improved her experience of Paris:

> Mourn the old Paris, if you will. My intellectual faculties have never allowed me to fathom its detours, even though, like so many others, I was raised there. Today, when the grand boulevards, too straight for the artist's eye but eminently safe, enable us to walk for long stretches, hands in our pockets, without getting lost and without constantly having to ask the errand boy or the affable grocer the way...[13]

Sand was not exactly the typical Parisienne. The habit of walking through the streets with one's hands in one's pockets was at that time the preserve of men – women's dresses did not have pockets – but Sand frequently wore trousers and other men's clothing. Nonetheless, here she describes a genuine benefit that women derived from Haussmann's rational street plan: they could now walk more independently through the city without risking their good reputation by asking directions from a stranger, no matter how friendly he might be.

Sand singles out the city park as an inclusive oasis, as one of the few fully public spaces where the presence of a respectable lady was accepted. Previously, her place had been largely indoors, but in the modern city she could spread her wings further. It is no coincidence that the Bois de Boulogne is a recurring subject in the works of Cassatt and Morisot [fig. 8], who portrayed their friends and family members enjoying carriage rides and boat trips there. The park was also one of the few places where a woman could ride a horse without a chaperone.[14] The horsewoman – *amazone* in French – was a very special kind of Parisienne. Her black riding costume was sober and functional. An early version of women's sportswear, its cut, colour and materials were inspired by men's clothing. In his study for a monumental equestrian portrait of Henriette Darras in the Bois de Boulogne, Renoir has depicted this Parisienne in *amazone* costume [fig. 9]. Her top hat – traditionally a man's accessory – is combined with an elegant veil, rendering her an androgynous figure, with a mix of feminine and masculine qualities and therefore independent and free-spirited.[15] This reputation was the subject of ridicule from, among others, Honoré Daumier, who caricatured the *amazone* as a female philanderer in a series of cartoons that mocked feminism [fig. 10].

Museums, theatres and department stores also increased female mobility. In these semi-public places, women emerged as consumers and thus as active participants in society. The Parisienne was not only a mascot of the fashion industry but also a member of a lucrative new target group. This led to changes in the streetscape, such as the introduction of shop windows and the advertising column. In the past, it was the mainly the *pissoirs* – public toilets exclusively for men – that were covered with posters. In 1868, the printer and entrepreneur Gabriel Morris introduced the advertising column, based on the urinals' cylindrical form, as a more hygienic and gender-neutral alternative.

The Impressionists also mobilised women as consumers. In an open letter addressed 'To women', Degas' friend Georges Rivière addresses women directly as potential customers of Impressionism. He did not mince his words: 'Admit that a husband is a ferocious tyrant... a despot who abuses the right that an arbitrary law has conferred upon him to thwart your tastes and force you to adopt his own.'[16] Rivière characterises the bourgeois man as well educated but with poor taste, partly formed in the dusty galleries of the Louvre, who needed a push from his wife. 'Because you alone have taste,' Rivière flatters her in this charm offensive, 'you alone are without prejudice, and it is to you alone to whom all painters should address themselves.'[17] Degas sincerely considered women to be experts in aesthetics, partly because of the amount of time they were able to devote to matters such as fashion and interior design: 'Think of a treatise on ornament for women or by women,' he noted to himself, 'based on their manner of observing, of combining, of sensing their fashionable outfits etc. On a daily basis they compare, more than men, a thousand visible things with each other.'[18]

It was Degas who convinced Cassatt and Morisot to join the Impressionists. Their participation demanded courage. As bourgeois women, they were expected to take an interest in art, but it was an altogether different matter to pursue a career in that world, let alone among a rebellious group of avant-gardists. Cassatt posed like a typical Parisienne for Degas, leaning elegantly on her parasol in the Louvre's Etruscan gallery [fig. 11]. Both she and Morisot frequently inhabited the dual role of creative artist and passive model for the Impressionists. In one of her many theatre scenes – a passion she shared with Degas – Cassatt reflects on the interplay between looking and being looked at, subtly demonstrating her feminine vision of Paris. In her painting *In the Loge* (c. 1878) [fig. 12], a lady peers intently through her opera glasses. A man in the background does the same, but he clearly directs his gaze at the woman instead of at the stage. Or is this voyeur looking at us? We are the viewer, but we also feel secretly watched. In this way, Cassatt gives us a glimpse into the daily reality of the Parisienne.

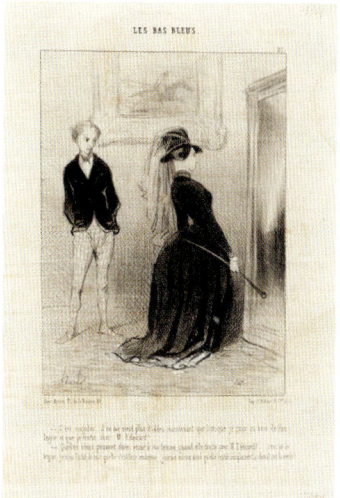

Fig. 10

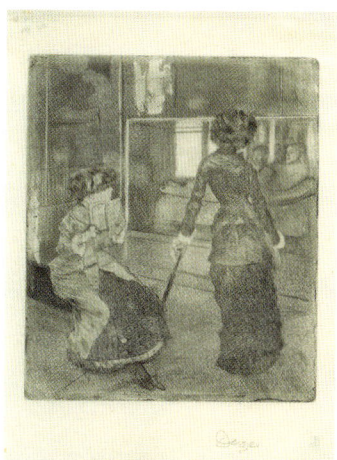

Fig. 11 [p. 132]

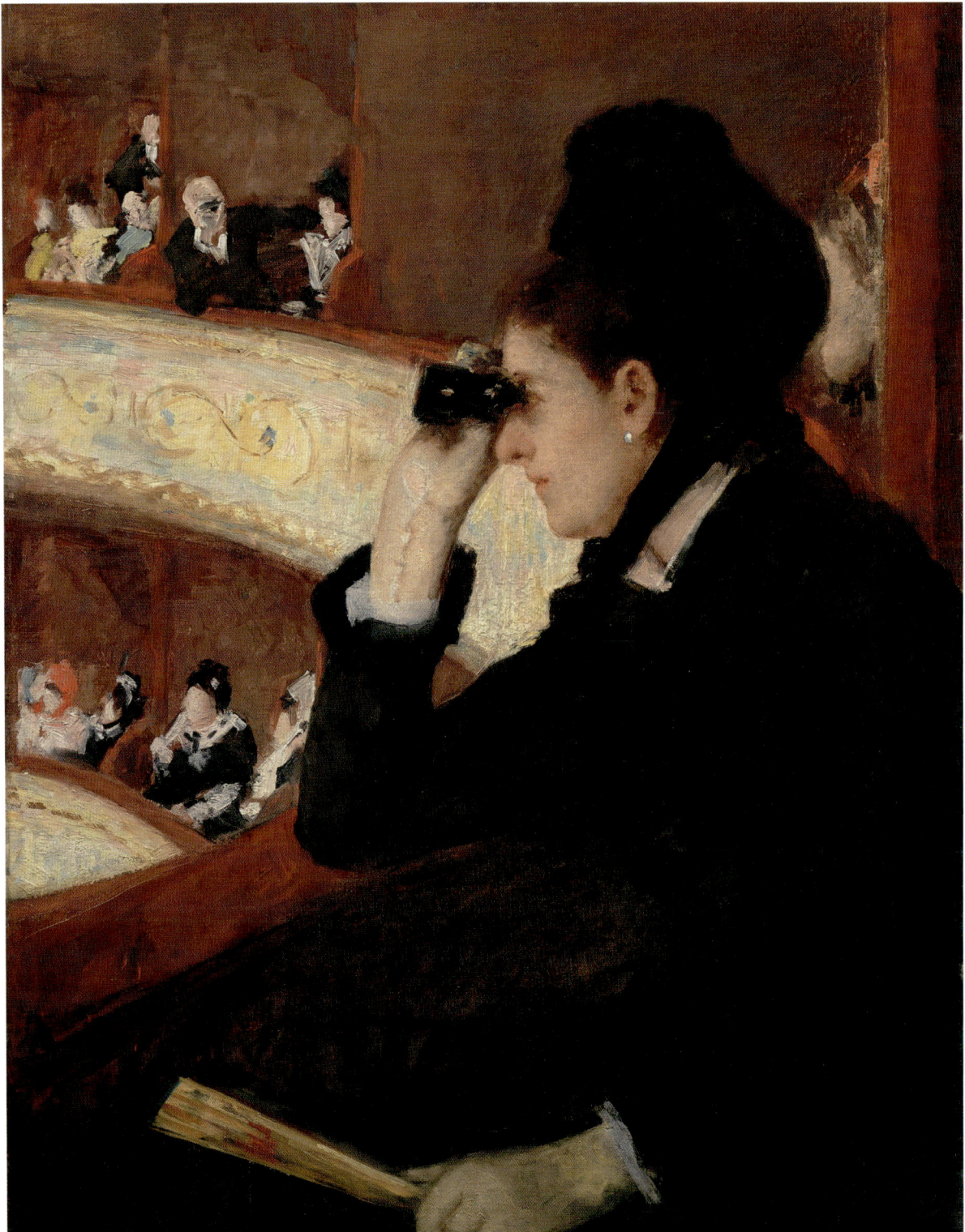

Fig. 12

Fig. 12
Mary Cassatt (1844–1926), *In the Loge*, c. 1878

Oil on canvas, 81.3 × 66 cm, Museum of Fine Arts, Boston.
The Hayden Collection – Charles Henry Hayden Fund

Fig. 13
Berthe Morisot (1841–1895), *View of Paris from the Trocadéro*, 1871–73

Oil on canvas, 46.1 × 81.5 cm, Santa Barbara Museum of Art, Santa Barbara

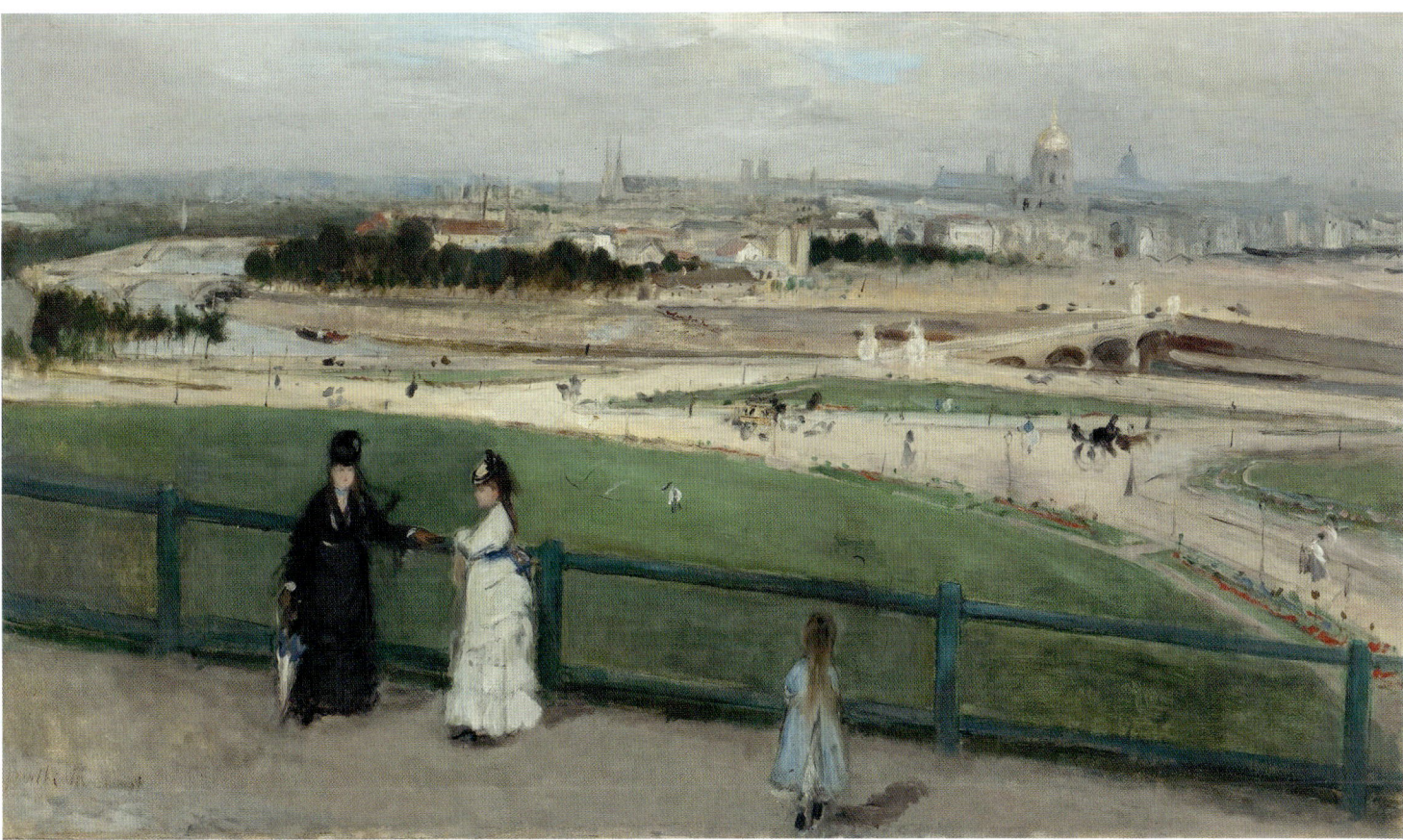

Fig. 13

The new Paris expanded the arena available to women. The work of the Impressionists shows her freedoms, but also her limitations. There was no bar-hopping and no night-time walks through the city for Cassatt and Morisot. Painting a café scene – a typical theme within Impressionism – was forbidden territory for them. The work of the women artists remained close to home, depicting family portraits, still lifes, interiors or a nearby park. This notwithstanding, three years before the first Impressionist exhibition, Morisot painted a magnificent panorama of the city. *View of Paris from the Trocadéro* (1871–73) offers an expansive view of the site where the Universal Exposition had been held in 1867 [fig. 13]. Two Parisiennes and a girl look out over a city that offers them some new opportunities but is not yet quite their playground.

The invisible half

Capitalism discovered women as customers and offered them a hand in their search for more breathing space and greater participation. Nevertheless, they remained second-class citizens. In many aspects, women's rights had even been curtailed: newly acquired freedoms after the French Revolution were taken away from them just as quickly at the beginning of the nineteenth century. The birth of the Parisienne as a paragon of modernity coincided with a heated debate about *la femme nouvelle*, the emancipated woman.[19] Spurred by the growing anger about the discrimination against women in education, marriage and the labour market, in 1866 Victoire Léodile Béra founded one of the

first feminist organisations in France. Under the pseudonym André Léo, she emphasised the importance of progress through education, and combated sexist prejudices, such as women's notional physical and mental inferiority to men.[20] In 1871, Julie-Victoire Daubié became the first French woman to obtain a university degree. In her publication *La femme pauvre au XIXe siècle* [The Poor Woman in the Nineteenth Century] (1866), she came to the defence of the women who had thus far been neglected in this story: those from the working classes.[21]

In Paris in particular, their situation was deplorable. In 1872, women made up approximately 30 per cent of the workforce. As a minority, they were especially vulnerable: paid considerably less, they were thus excluded and distrusted by their male colleagues who feared that these cheap workers would undercut them in the labour market.[22] They laundered and ironed clothes, lit the streetlamps in the evening and swept the streets clean, or made matches and candles in poorly ventilated factories. The ballerinas in Degas' paintings and drawings, known as street rats, were undernourished adolescents who tried to dance their way to a better life, often without success [fig. 14].

Young women from the provinces moved to the capital to work as maids in wealthy neighbourhoods. The diarists Edmond and Jules de Goncourt had a sinister, yet realistic, prediction for one such new arrival with whom they shared the omnibus one day, observing that she was 'ready to slip into the limp routine of a Parisian streetwalker'.[23] Léo and Daubié denounced this

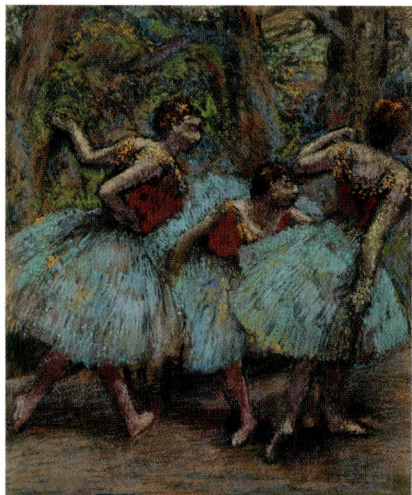

Fig. 14   [p. 157]

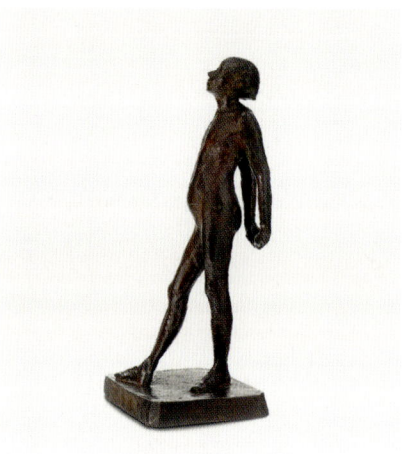

Fig. 15   [p. 159]

injustice, pointing out to their readers that the average working woman could not live on her wages. 'A new social force – industry – accepts women only to crush them,' writes Léo, 'civil and economic laws condemn them to poverty, and poverty forces them into shame.'[24]

The clothing sector was another important employer. 'In Paris, half the female population lives from fashion, the other half lives for it,' writes Raymond in her previously cited account of the importance of this industry.[25] The women who earned a living from fashion lived in Paris, but were not considered Parisiennes. They served as saleswomen in chic department stores, made hats in millinery factories or toiled as seamstresses in one of the many airless sweatshops – a term coined in this period – to keep up with the growing demand for ready-to-wear clothing. They figure rarely or not at all in the works of Caillebotte, Cassatt, Monet and Morisot. Degas' oeuvre is an exception, featuring not only well-dressed ladies but also the women who dressed them and the washerwomen who kept their wardrobes presentable. In addition to enchanting ballerinas on the stage of the Opéra Garnier, Degas' etchings depict burnt-out sex workers in the brothels of Paris, the world in which many less-talented dancers became entangled. Remarkably enough, Degas mainly painted female workers while his impressions of the elite predominantly feature men.

Class and ready-to-wear fashion

In addition to creating a growing workforce that could barely afford a decent existence in Paris, the mass production of ready-to-wear clothing had another effect on class society. In 1877, the art critic Charles Blanc noted that it was increasingly difficult to distinguish 'respectable' ladies and women of easy virtue from their attire.[26] Formerly, a woman's social status had been readily

Fig. 14
Edgar Degas (1834–1917),
Three Dancers (Blue Skirts, Red Bodices), c. 1903
Pastel on paper on cardboard, 94 × 81 cm, Fondation Beyeler,
Riehen/Basel, Beyeler Collection

Fig. 15
Edgar Degas (1834–1917),
Nude Study for the Little Dancer, c. 1878
Bronze, 72 × 34 × 26 cm, Kunstmuseum Den Haag

Fig. 16
Edgar Degas (1834–1917),
Study of a Ballet Dancer 'dégagée en quatrième ouverte', 1885
Black chalk on paper, 32.9 × 23.1 cm, Collection Museum Boijmans
Van Beuningen, Rotterdam. Loan Foundation Museum Boijmans
Van Beuningen, 1940 (former Koenigs Collection)

Fig. 17
Edgar Degas (1834–1917), *Dancer with Double Bass*, 1885–87
Black chalk on paper, 31.1 × 24.3 cm, Collection Museum Boijmans
Van Beuningen, Rotterdam, Vitale Bloch bequest, 1976

Fig. 18
Édouard Manet (1832–1883),
Woman with a Fan (Portrait of Jeanne Duval), 1862
Oil on canvas, 90 × 113 cm, Szépművészeti Múzeum/Museum
of Fine Arts, Budapest

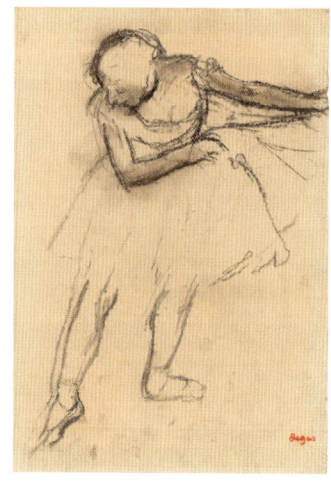

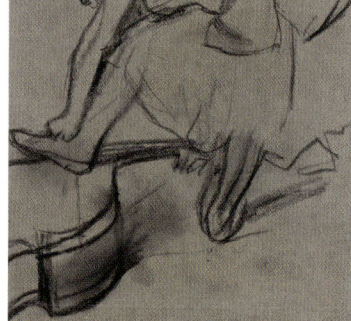

Fig. 16   [p. 160] 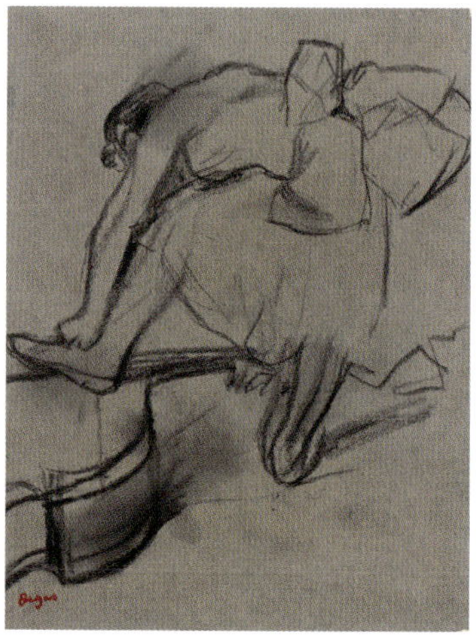   Fig. 17   [p. 161]

apparent from her clothing, but the rise of ready-to-wear fashions blurred this distinction. In this way, the fashion industry in Paris contributed not only to the exploitation of the working classes, but also to their upward mobility. In their reviews of Monet's painting *Camille* and Renoir's depiction of Lise Tréhot, several critics seemed fully aware that these 'Parisiennes' did not come from the class they purported to represent. Caricatures made the comparison with a fancy-dress party, a masquerade in borrowed luxury.[27] And indeed, Tréhot earned her money in Paris as a simple seamstress, while Renoir depicted her as one of her wealthy clients.

In this respect, one last portrait of a Parisienne deserves our attention here. In the year of Baudelaire's passionate argument about fashion and modernity, his good friend Manet painted a lady in a crinoline so large that it does not fit in the picture frame [fig. 18]. Lying on a divan, she almost drowns in her enormous white dress, decorated with subtle blue stripes. Her crinoline's excessive diameter seems to be a nod to Baudelaire's desire for more fashion in art. The lady is Jeanne Duval, known principally as Baudelaire's long-term lover and a great source of inspiration for his famous collection of poems *The Flowers of Evil* (1857). As a French-Haitian, she had left the former colony for Paris, where she probably worked as an actress. Duval's dark complexion has often been praised, but also sexualised and discussed in racist terms. She is the antithesis of the nineteenth-century Parisienne, a character celebrated as a paragon of civilisation and therefore of superiority over other cultures. But with her fashionable dress, jewellery and fan, Manet portrays Duval as a woman of the world, a woman of Paris.

1 Mark Twain, *The Innocents Abroad* (Hartford, CT, 1869), chapter 13.
2 Marina Warner, *Monuments and Maidens: The Allegory of the Female Form* (London, 1985), pp. 52–53.
3 Ruth E. Iskin, *Modern Women and Parisian Consumer Culture in Impressionist Painting* (Cambridge, 2007), p. 194.
4 Emmeline Raymond, 'La mode et la parisienne', in *Paris guide par les principaux écrivains et artistes de la France*, vol. 2 (Paris, 1867), p. 923.
5 Iskin 2007 (note 3), p. 200.
6 Charles Baudelaire, *The Painter of Modern Life and Other Essays*, edited and translated by Jonathan Mayne (London, 1964), p. 11.
7 Edmond Lepelletier, 'Les impressionnistes', *Le radical* (8 April 1877). Quoted in Iskin 2007 (note 3), p. 117.
8 Émile Zola, 'Les actualistes: mon salon IV', *L'événement illustré* (24 May 1868). Quoted in Iskin 2007 (note 3), p. 203.
9 Manet also made an etching based on this painting.
10 Maurice du Seigneur, 'L'art et les artistes au salon de 1882', *L'artiste* (1 June 1882). Quoted in Helen Burnham, 'Changing Silhouettes', in Gloria Groom (ed.), *Impressionism, Fashion & Modernity*, exh. cat. New York & Chicago (The Metropolitan Museum of Art & Art Institute of Chicago), 2012, p. 256.
11 Iskin 2007 (note 3), p. 210.
12 Iskin 2007 (note 3), p. 66.
13 George Sand, 'La rêverie à Paris' in *Paris guide* 1867 (note 4), pp. 1196–1197.
14 Albert Boime, *Art and the French Commune: Imagining Paris after War and Revolution* (Princeton, NJ, 1995), p. 98.
15 Patricia Mainardi, *Art and Politics of the Second Empire: The Universal Expositions of 1855 and 1867* (New Haven, CT & London, 1987), p. 147.
16 Georges Rivière, 'Aux femmes', *L'impressionniste, journal d'art* (21 April 1877).
17 Rivière 1877 (note 16).
18 Degas quoted in Gloria Groom, 'Edgar Degas: The Millinery Shop', in Groom 2012 (note 10), p. 221.
19 Iskin 2007 (note 3), p. 24.
20 André Léo, *La femme et les mœurs: liberté ou monarchie* (Paris, 1869).
21 Julie-Victoire Daubié, *La femme pauvre au XIXe siècle* (Paris, 1866).
22 Iskin 2007 (note 3), p. 46.
23 Edmond and Jules de Goncourt, *Pages from the Goncourt Journal*, edited, translated and introduced by Robert Baldick (London, 1984), p. 151. Entry for 1 April 1869.
24 Léo 1869 (note 20), p. 29.
25 Raymond 1867 (note 4), p. 923.
26 Nancy Forgione, 'Everyday Life in Motion: The Art of Walking in Late-Nineteenth-Century Paris', *The Art Bulletin*, vol. 87, no. 4 (December 2005), p. 674.
27 Groom 2012 (note 10), p. 42.

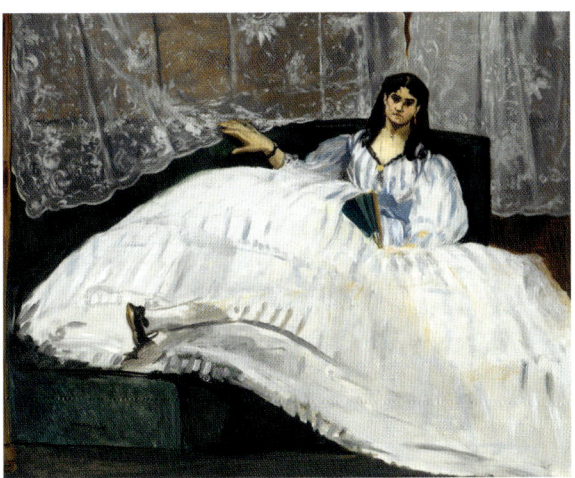

Fig. 18 [p. 151]

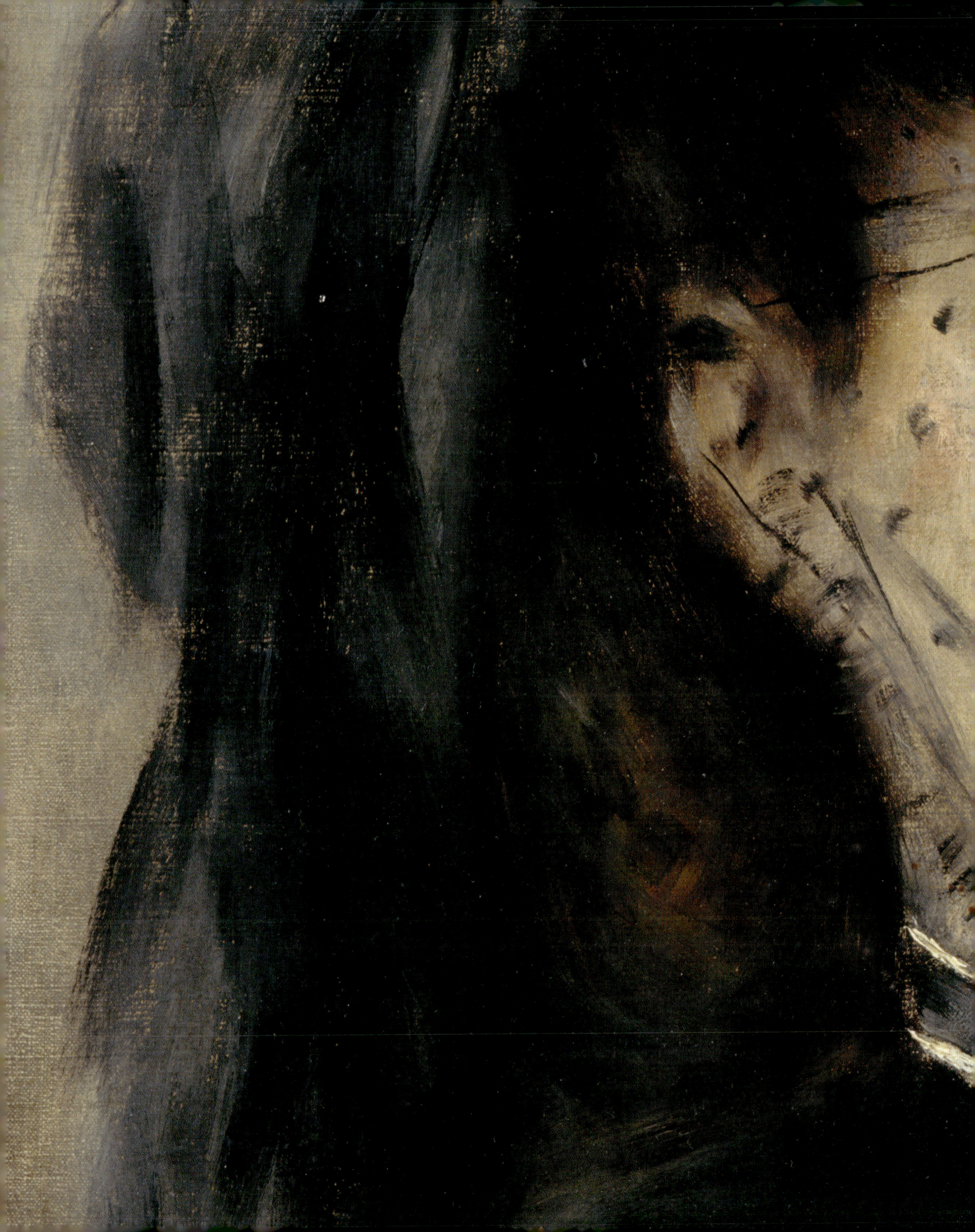

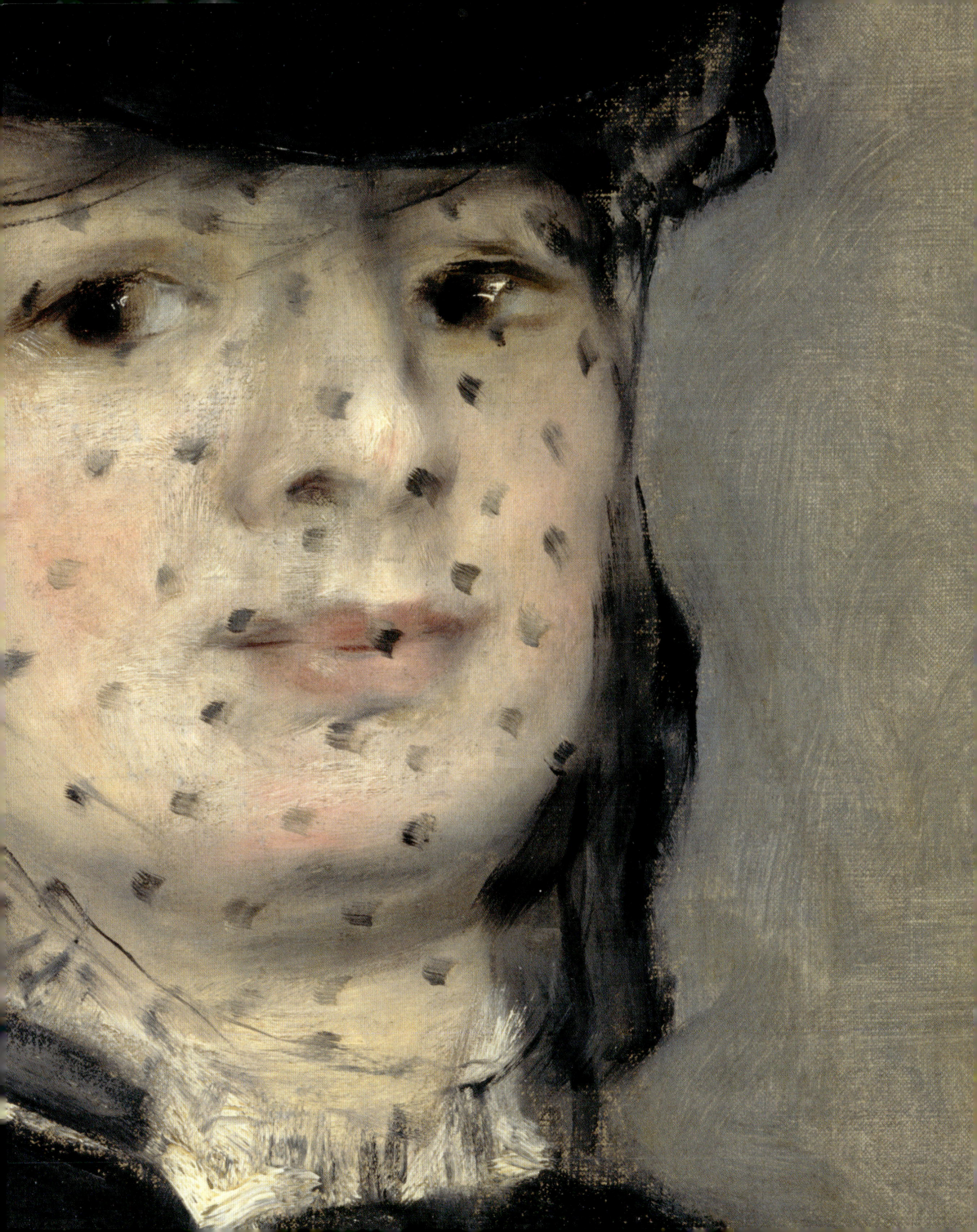

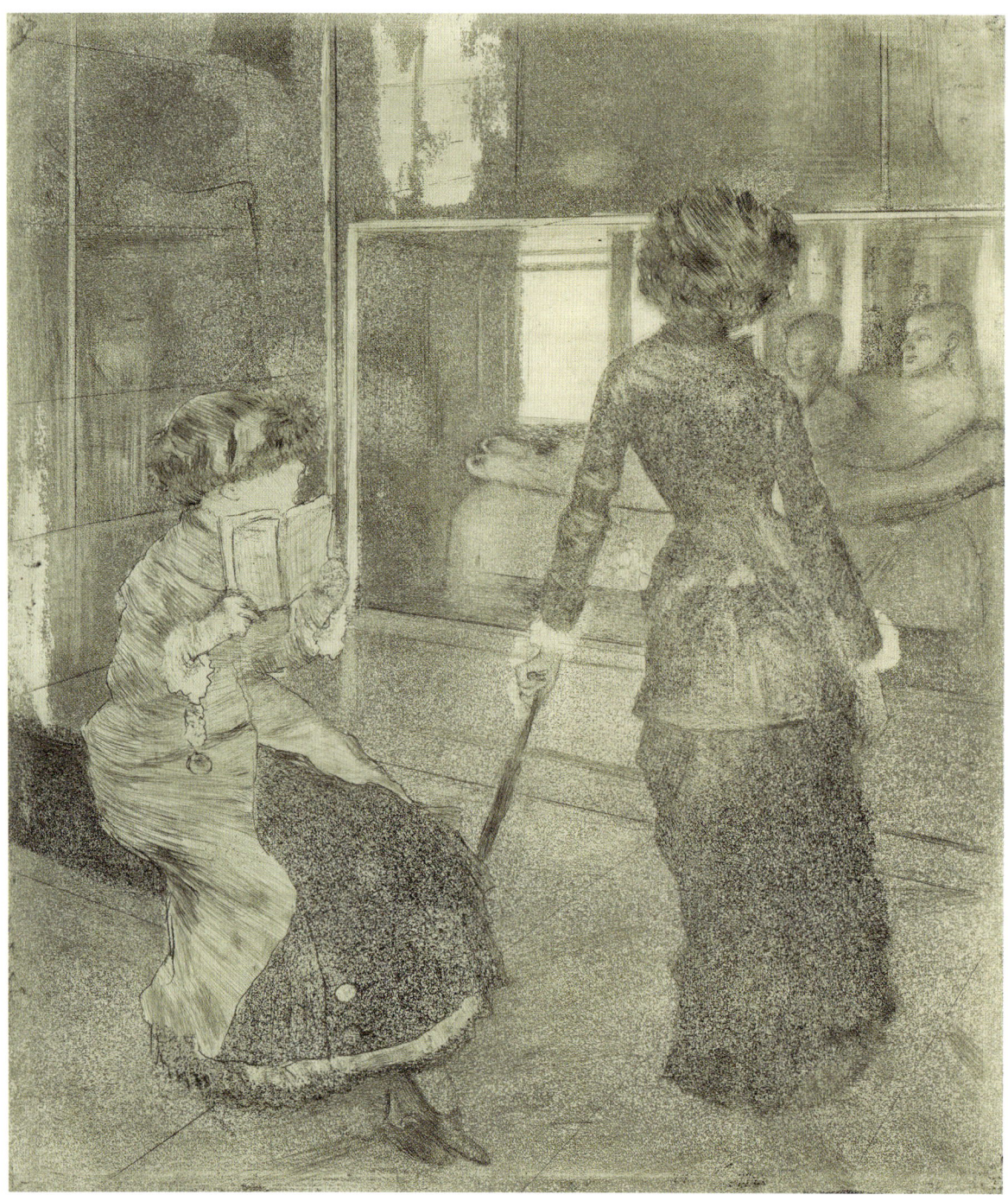

Edgar Degas (1834–1917), *At the Louvre – Museum of Antiquities*, c. 1867
Etching, aquatint and drypoint, ink on Japanese paper, 35.6 × 26.8 cm, Kunstmuseum Den Haag

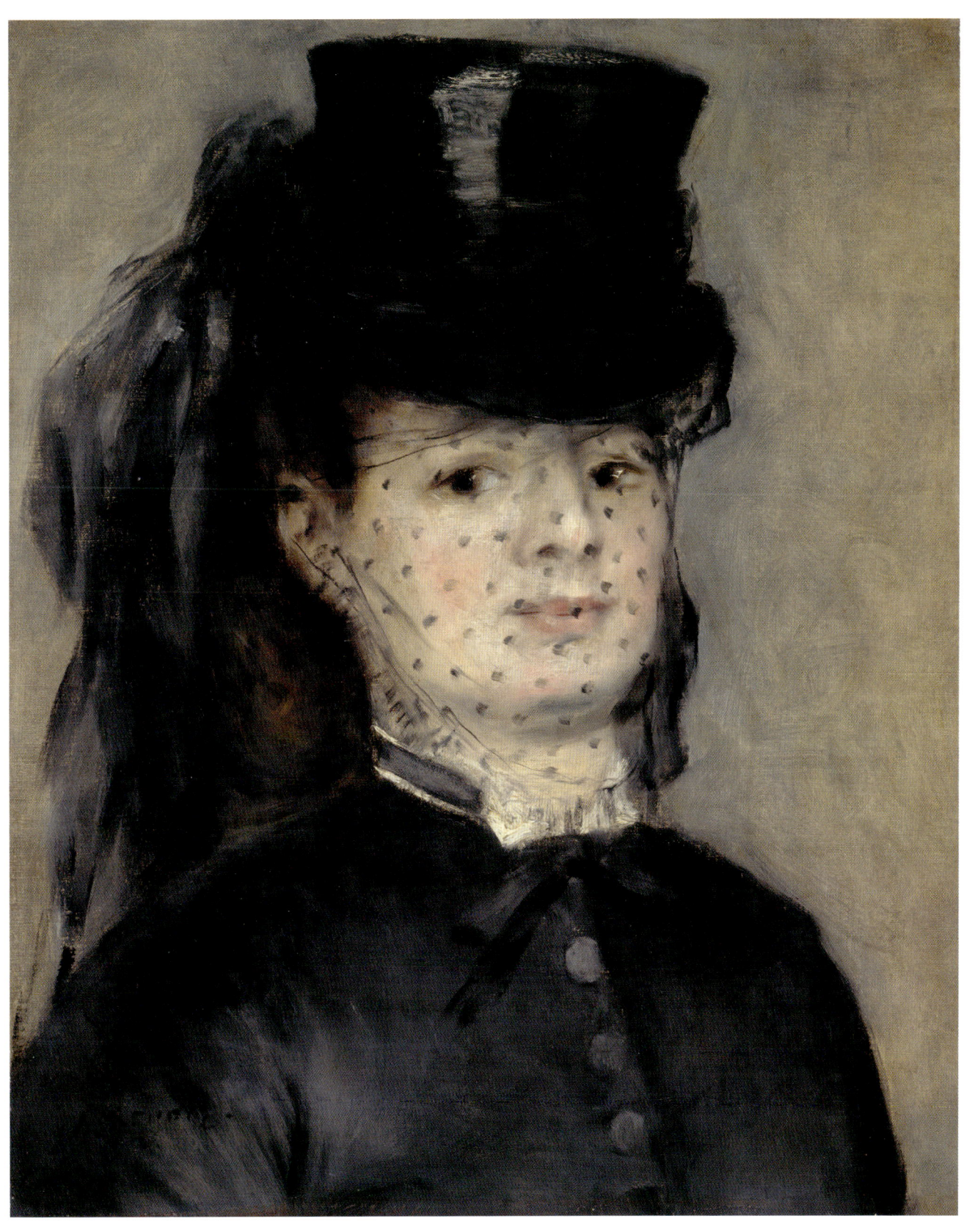

Auguste Renoir (1841–1919), *Madame Darras*, c. 1868

Oil on canvas, 48 × 40 cm, Musée d'Orsay, Paris. Accepted by the State as a donation from Baroness Eva Gebhard-Gourgaud to the Musée du Jeu de Paume in 1965

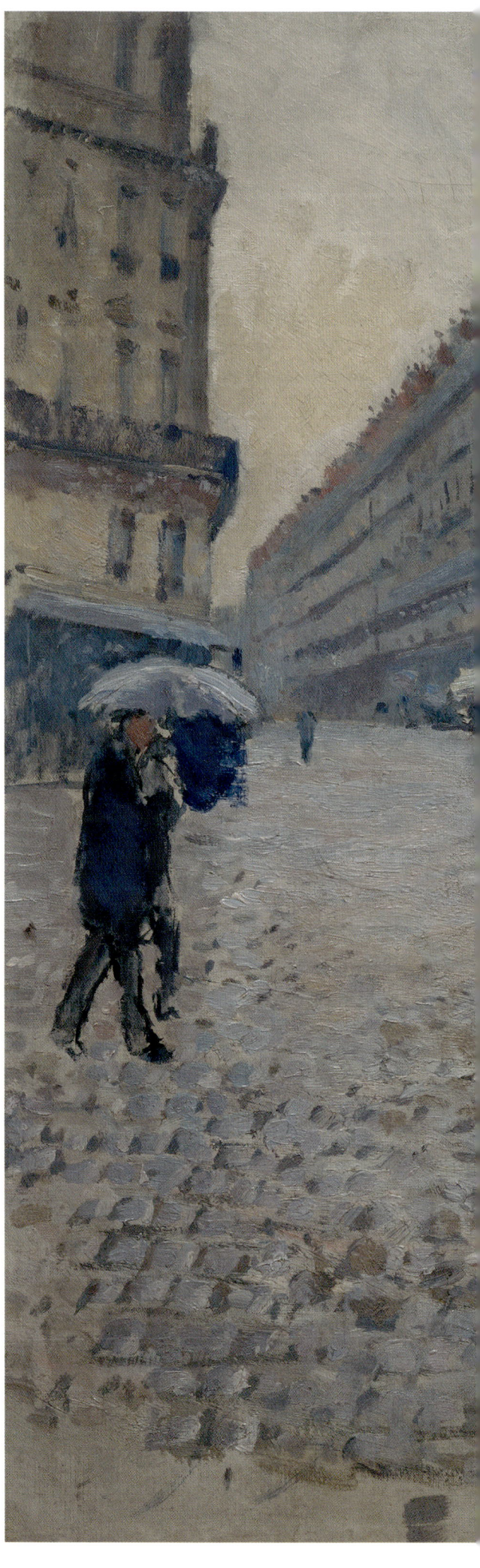

Gustave Caillebotte (1848–1894), *Paris Street. Rainy Day*, 1877
Oil on canvas, 54 × 65 cm, Musée Marmottan Monet, Paris, Michel Monet bequest, 1966

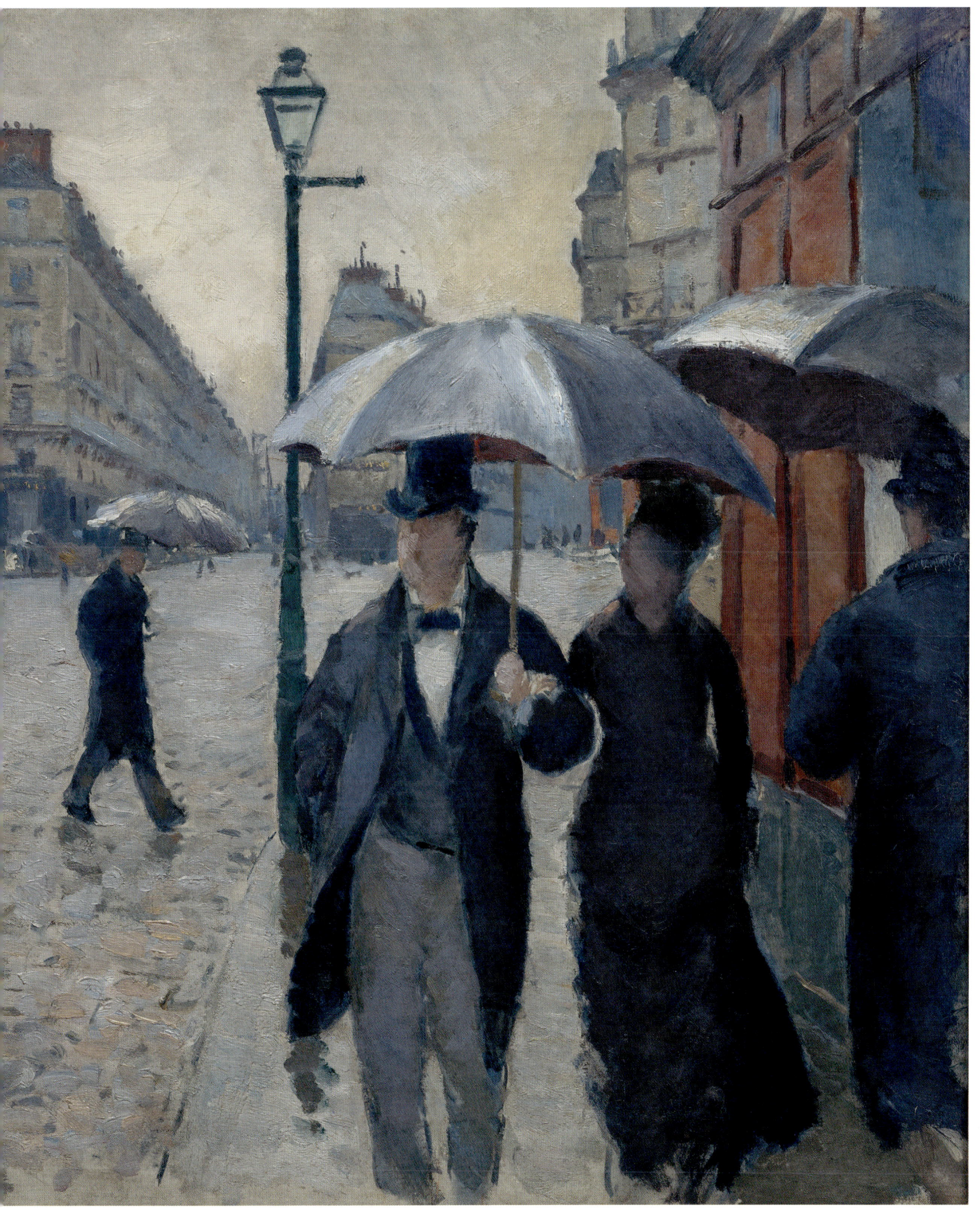

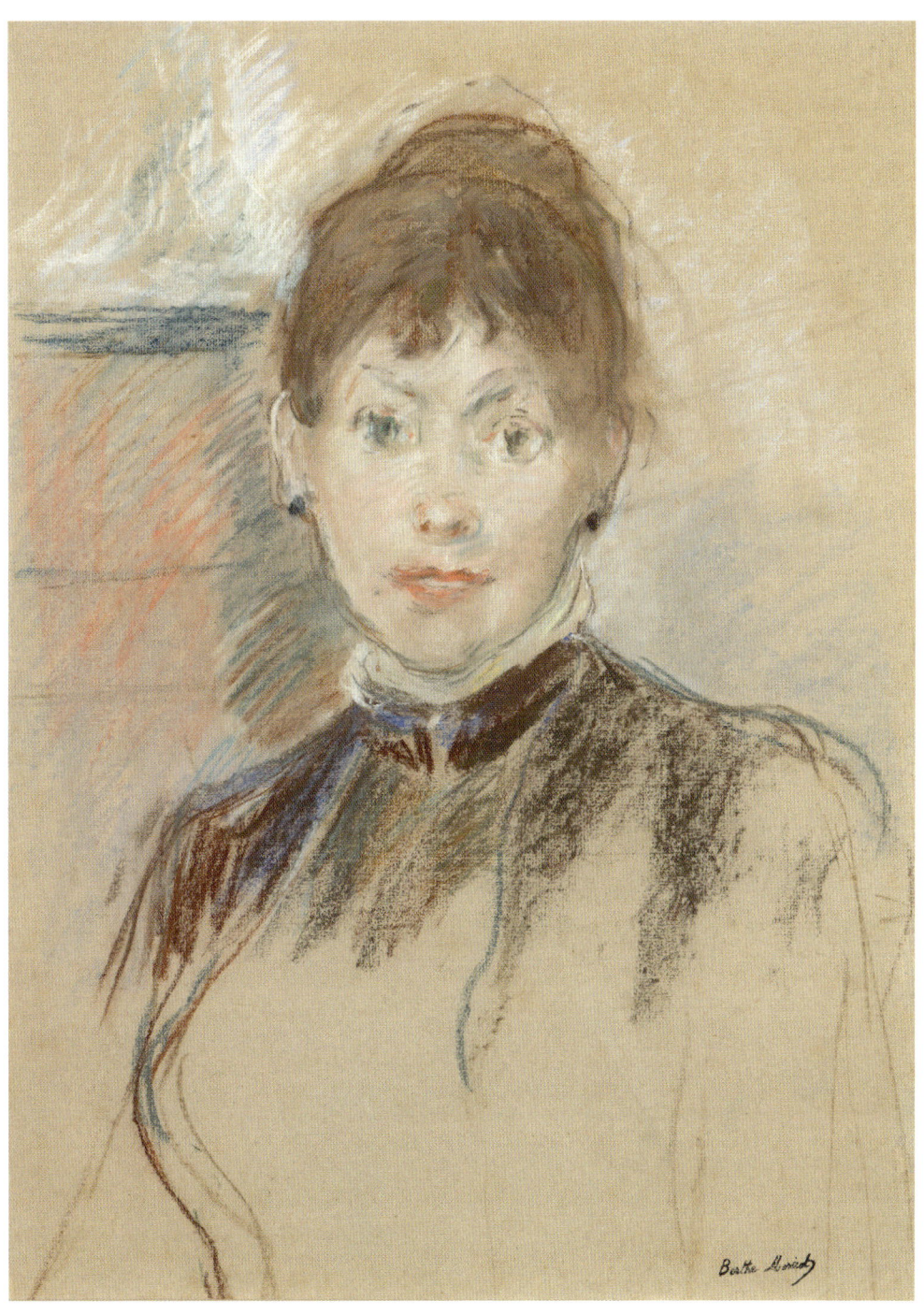

Berthe Morisot (1841–1895), *L'Anglaise (The Englishwoman)*, 1884
Pastel on paper, 53 × 38 cm, Private collection

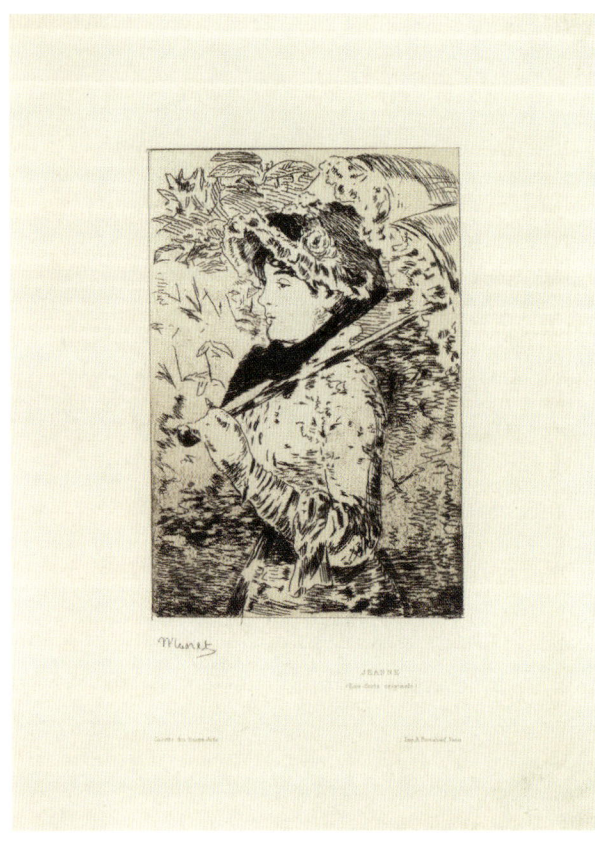

Édouard Manet (1832–1883), *Jeanne (Spring)*, 1882
(print after painting from 1881)
Etching and aquatint, 28 × 20.5 cm, Kunstmuseum Den Haag

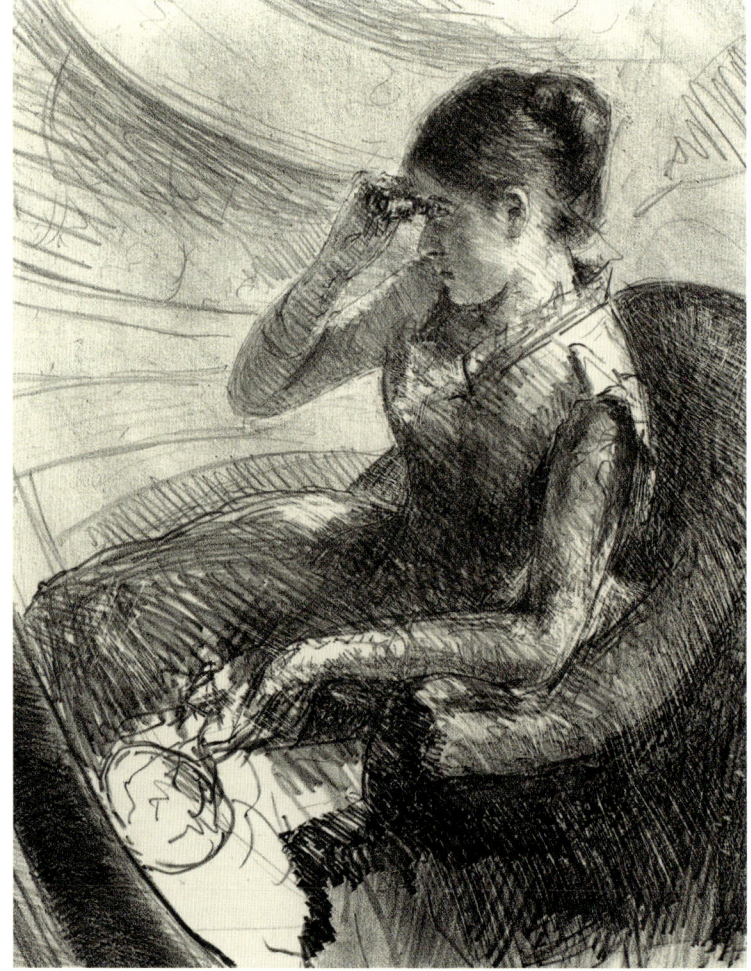

Mary Cassatt (1844–1926), *Woman Seated in a Loge (At the Theatre)*, c. 1880
Lithograph on paper, 45 cm × 31.5 cm, Van Gogh Museum, Amsterdam. Purchased with support
from the VriendenLoterij, the Mondrian Fund, the Rembrandt Association (thanks in part to the
Maljers-de Jongh Fund, The Liesbeth van Dorp Fund, the Marijke Laarhoven Fund and the Claude
Monet Fund) and the members of the Yellow House Circle

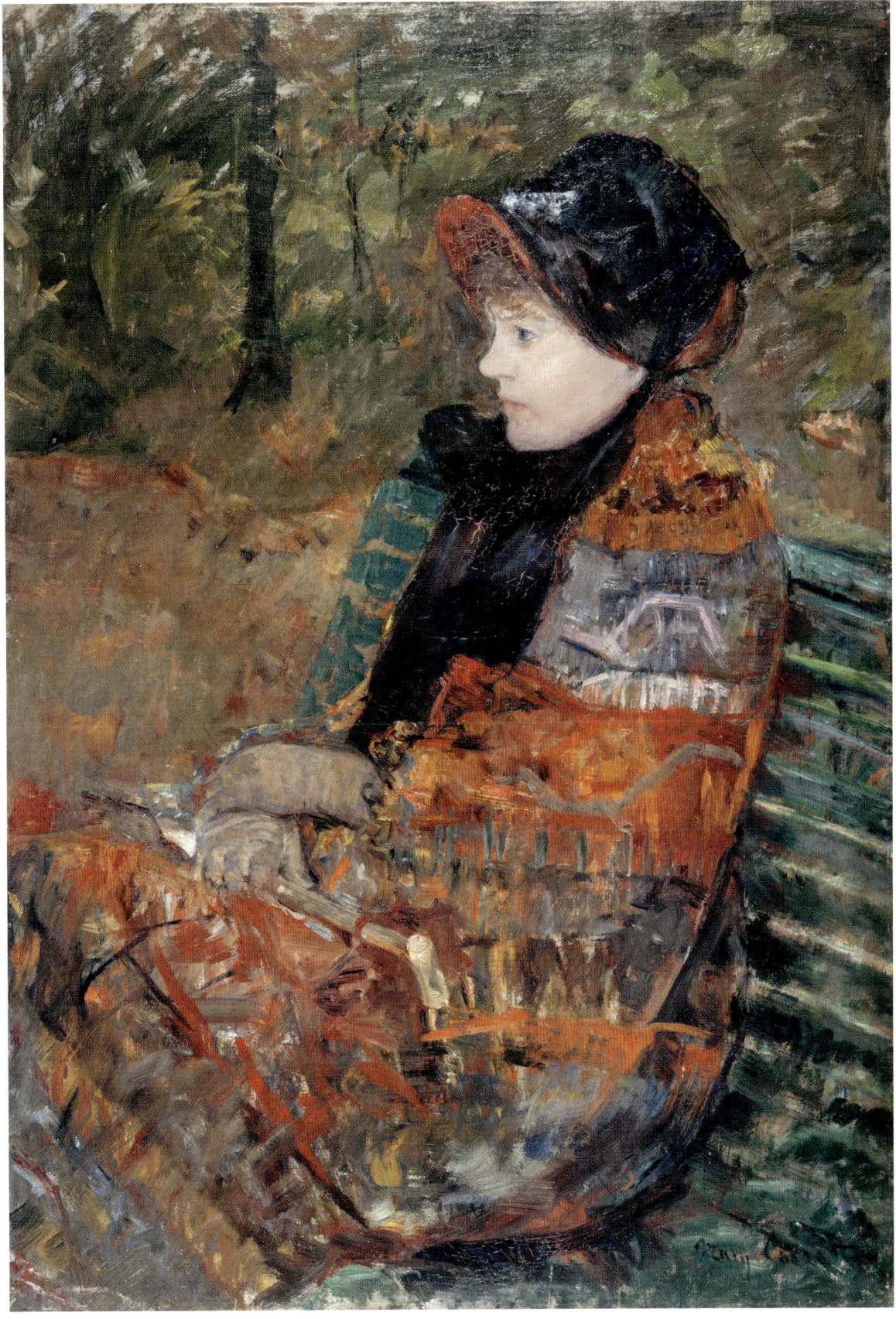

Mary Cassatt (1844–1926), *Autumn, Portrait of Lydia Cassatt*, 1880
Oil on canvas, 92.5 × 65.5 cm, Petit Palais, Musée des Beaux-Arts de la Ville de Paris

Auguste Renoir (1841–1919), *At the Café*, c. 1877
Oil on canvas, 36 × 27.5 cm, Kröller-Müller Museum, Otterlo

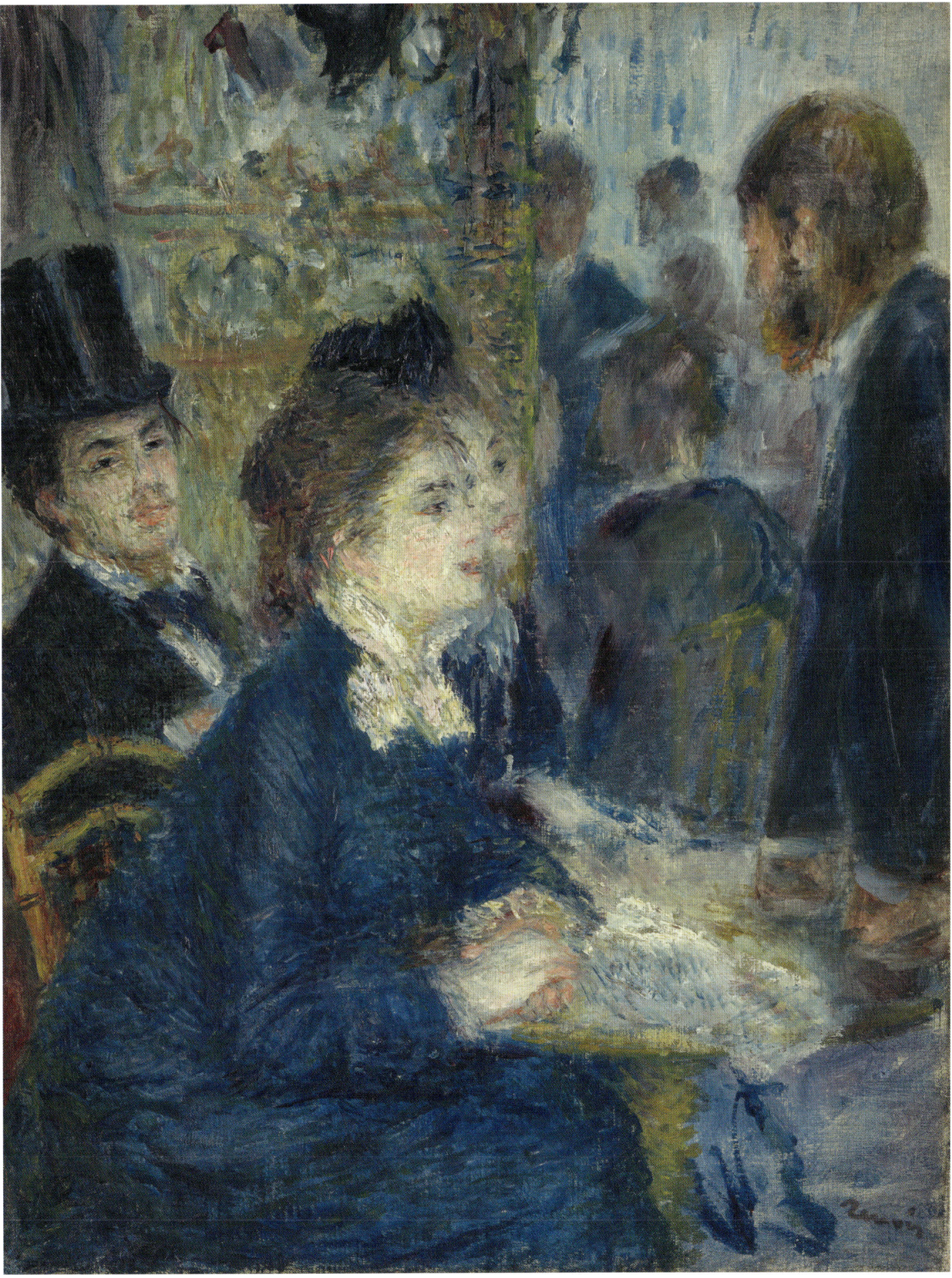

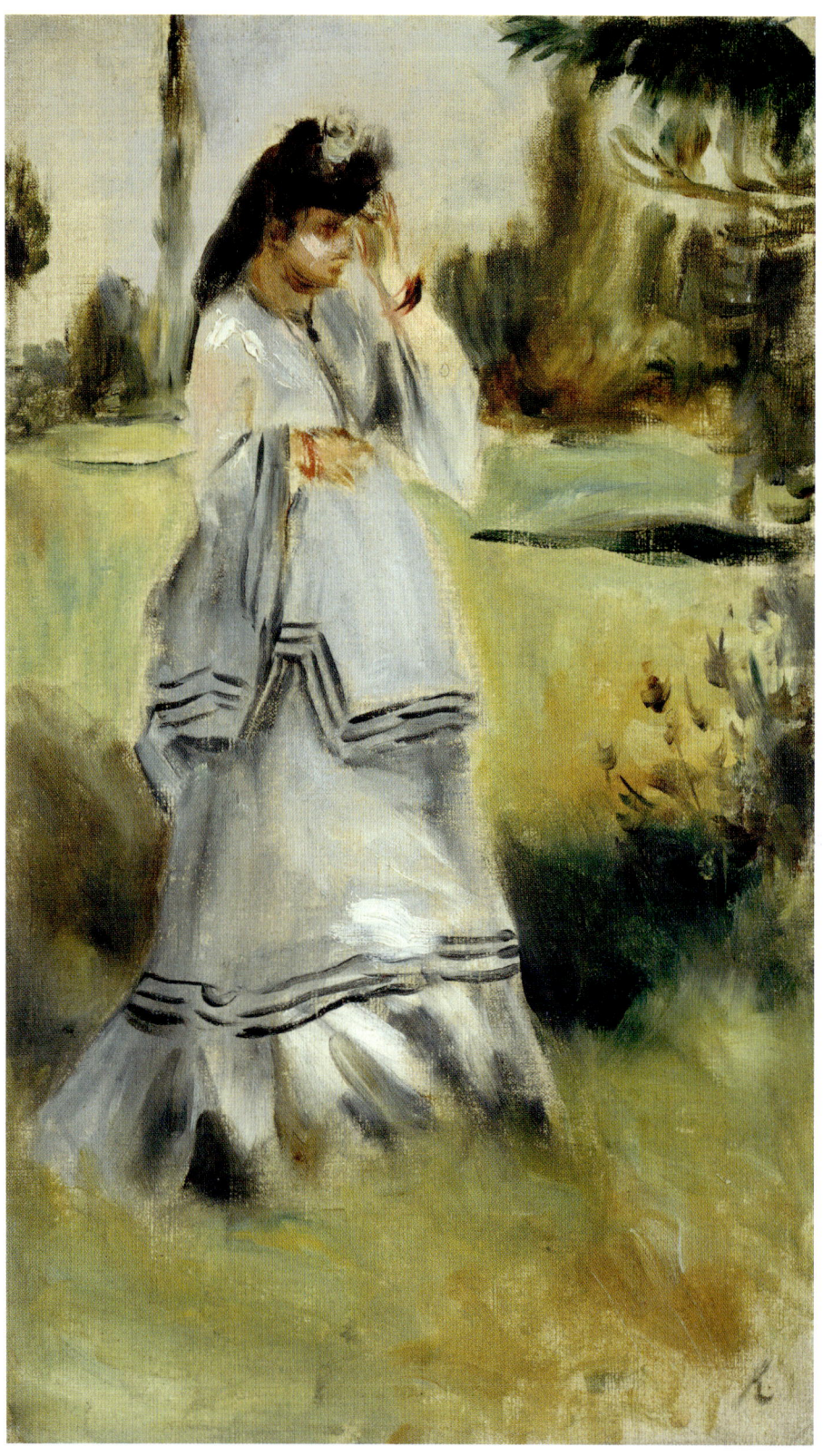

Auguste Renoir (1841–1919), *Woman in a Park*, 1866
Oil on canvas, 26.1 × 16.1 cm, National Gallery of Art, Washington, Ailsa Mellon Bruce Collection

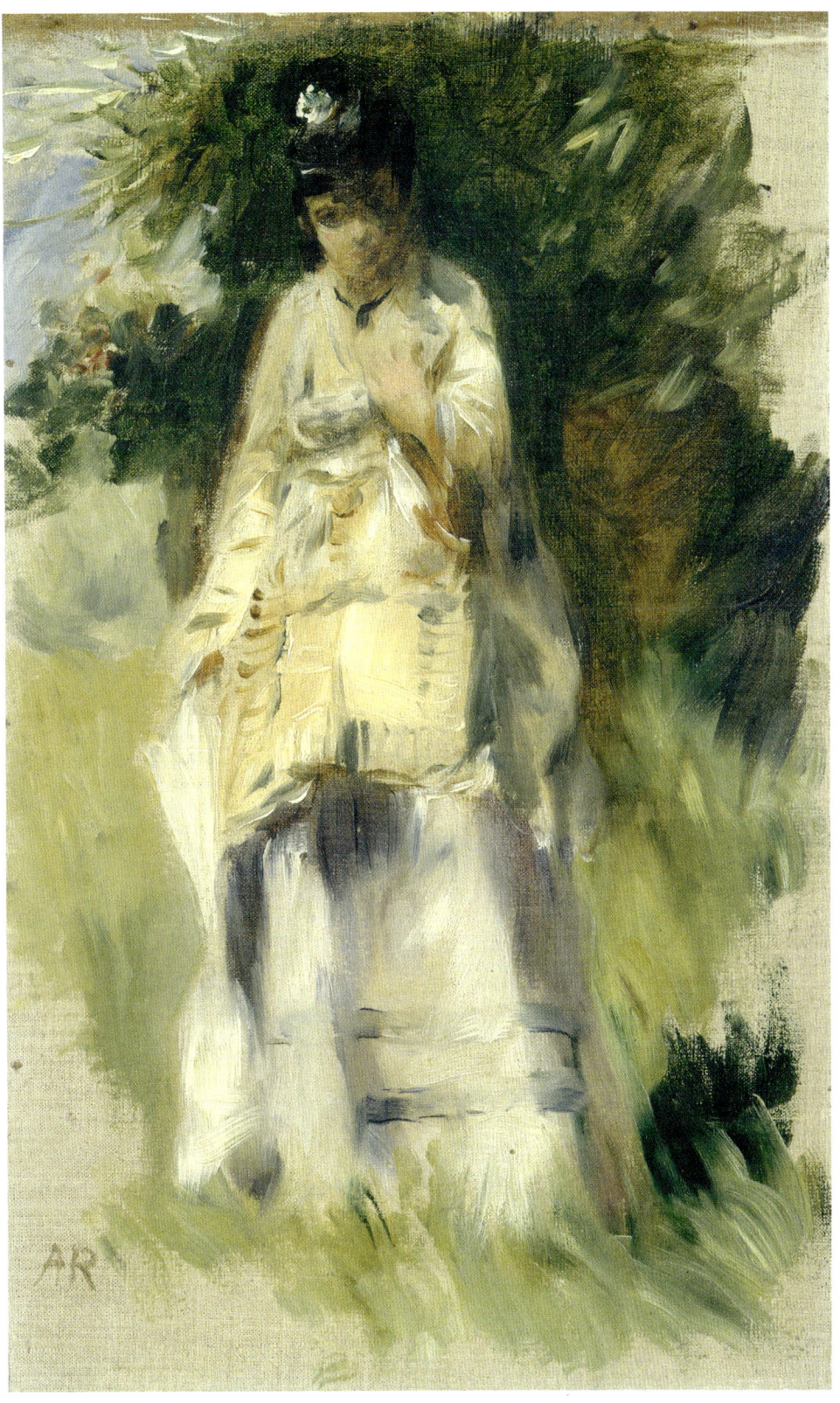

Auguste Renoir (1841–1919), *Woman Standing by a Tree*, 1866
Oil on canvas, 25.2 × 15.9 cm, National Gallery of Art, Washington, Ailsa Mellon Bruce Collection

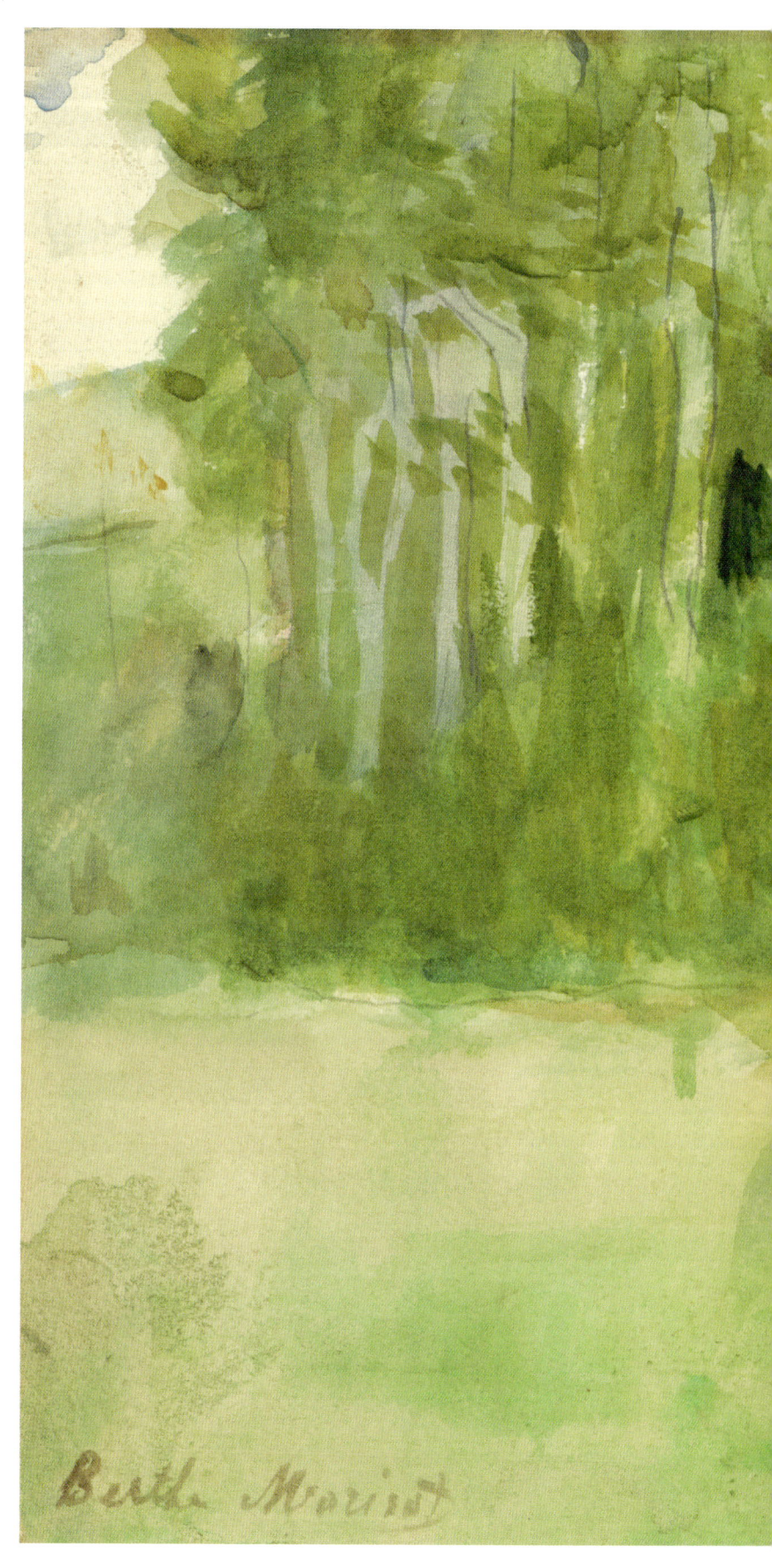

Berthe Morisot (1841–1895), *Walk in the Woods*, 1876
Pencil and watercolour on paper, 17.5 cm × 24.1 cm, Van Gogh Museum,
Amsterdam. Purchased with support from the VriendenLoterij

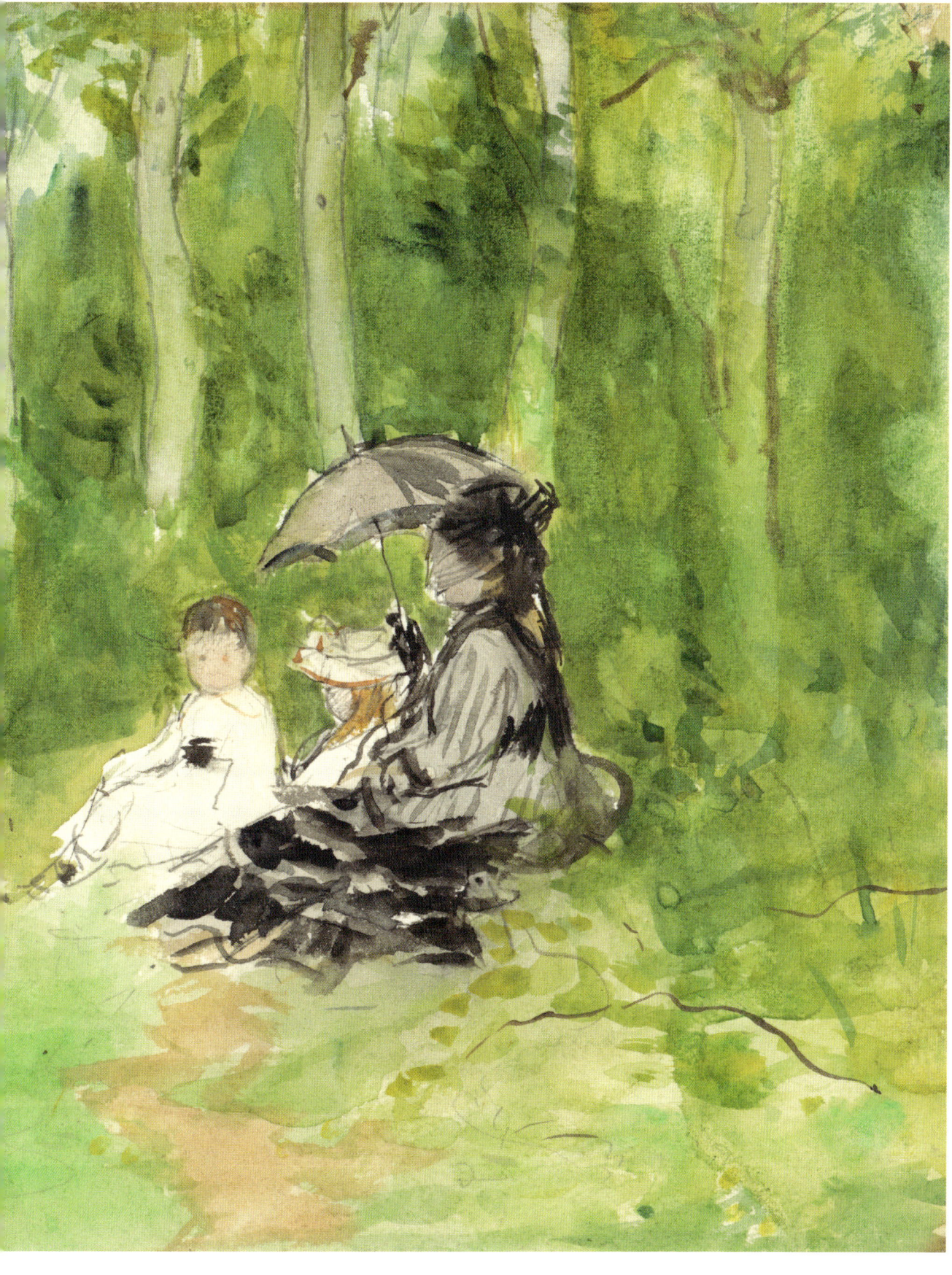

MARY CASSATT (1844–1926)

Susan Seated in a Garden, c. 1882–83

In 1877, Edgar Degas invited fellow painter Mary Cassatt to join the Impressionists. The timing was perfect. Having suffered her first rejection at the Salon that year, Cassatt seized the opportunity for independent success with both hands. As an outsider – not only a woman, but also American – she had won her place in the Parisian avant-garde.

Cassatt was born into a wealthy family in Allegheny City, which was annexed by Pittsburgh in the early twentieth century. Her father made his fortune as a stockbroker and her mother came from a wealthy banking family. Cassatt's life revolved around art and travel. Even so, her unconventional ambition to pursue a professional career as an artist came as a surprise. Dissatisfied with her training at the Pennsylvania Academy of the Fine Arts, in 1866 she convinced her father to allow her to continue her studies in Europe. Chaperoned by her mother, she travelled to Paris, where she studied privately with several painters. When, after more than ten years, the determined Cassatt refused to return to America, the rest of her family joined her in the French capital.

Cassatt almost exclusively painted women, mostly from her own circle. She depicted them indoors, in gardens or in the Bois de Boulogne. In this way, her work offers a unique glimpse into women's social lives and the intimacy that exists between mothers, children and sisters. The painting *Susan Seated in a Garden* features a girl against a background of sketchily painted flowers. She seems sunk in thought, unaware of the viewer. The painting is exemplary of Cassatt's favoured motif: spontaneous and unposed images of women. The sitter was a cousin of Cassatt's housekeeper, Mathilde Valet, who must have enjoyed a warm bond with Cassatt because she owned several works by the artist. This painting was created after a difficult period. Cassatt's sister Lydia had died in 1882, leading to a lull in Cassatt's boundless urge to paint.

Cassatt's depictions of women's lives culminated in a monumental mural commissioned for the Chicago World's Fair in 1893. The triptych *Modern Woman* shows the independent woman in pursuit of knowledge, art and fame. In this respect, the work – which, sadly, has been lost – reflected Cassatt's vision of life. She would eventually play an important role for the Impressionists, not only as an artist, but also as a trusted advisor to collectors. These included Louisine Waldron Elder, Cassat's friend and an outspoken feminist, who emerged as one of the most important collectors of artists such as Degas, Manet and Monet following her marriage to the sugar magnate Henry Osborne Havermeyer.

[FROUKE VAN DIJKE]

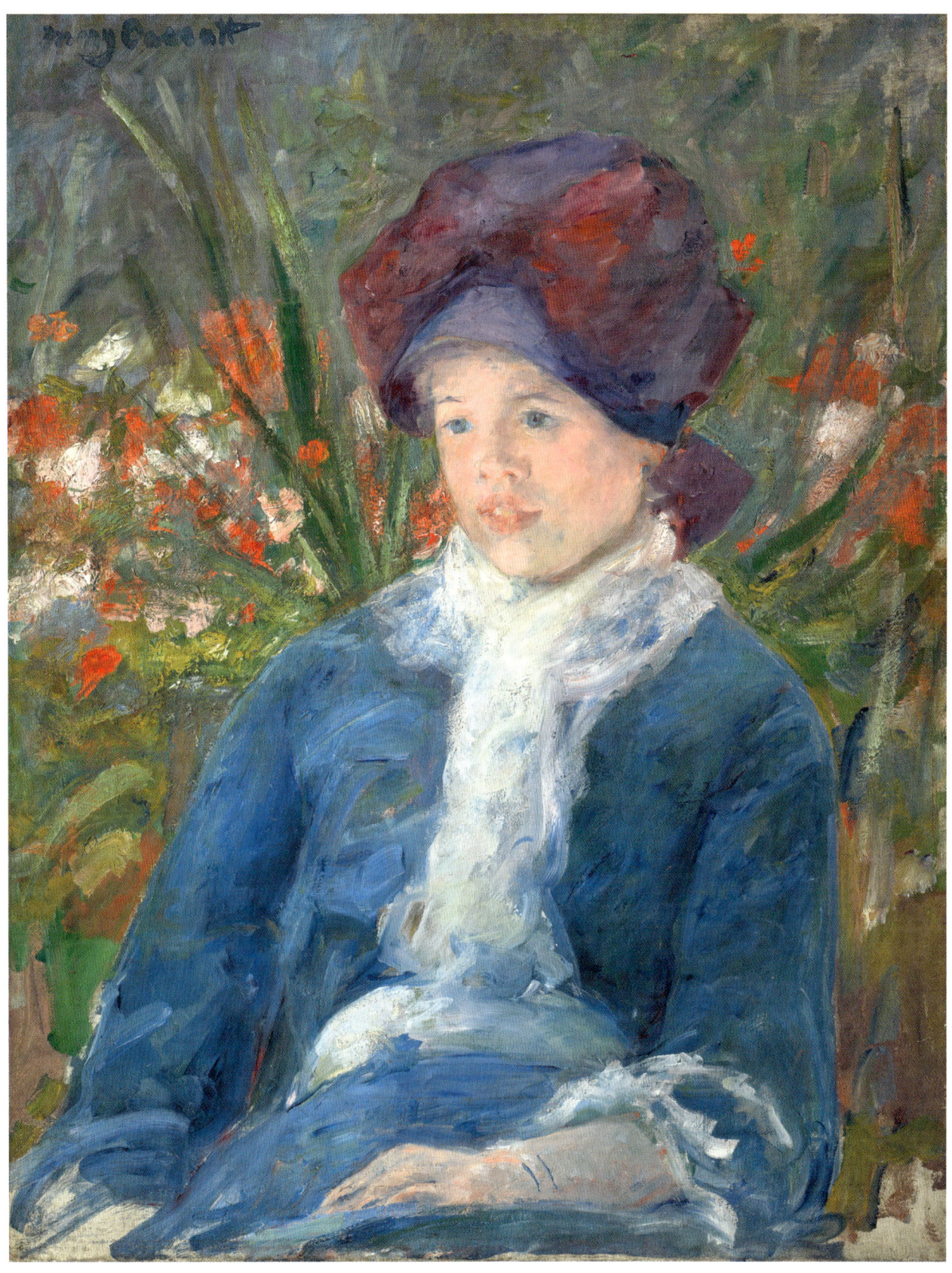

Mary Cassatt (1844–1926), *Susan Seated in a Garden*, c. 1882–83
Oil on canvas, 65.1 × 50.7 cm, FAMM Museum, Mougins, The Levett Collection

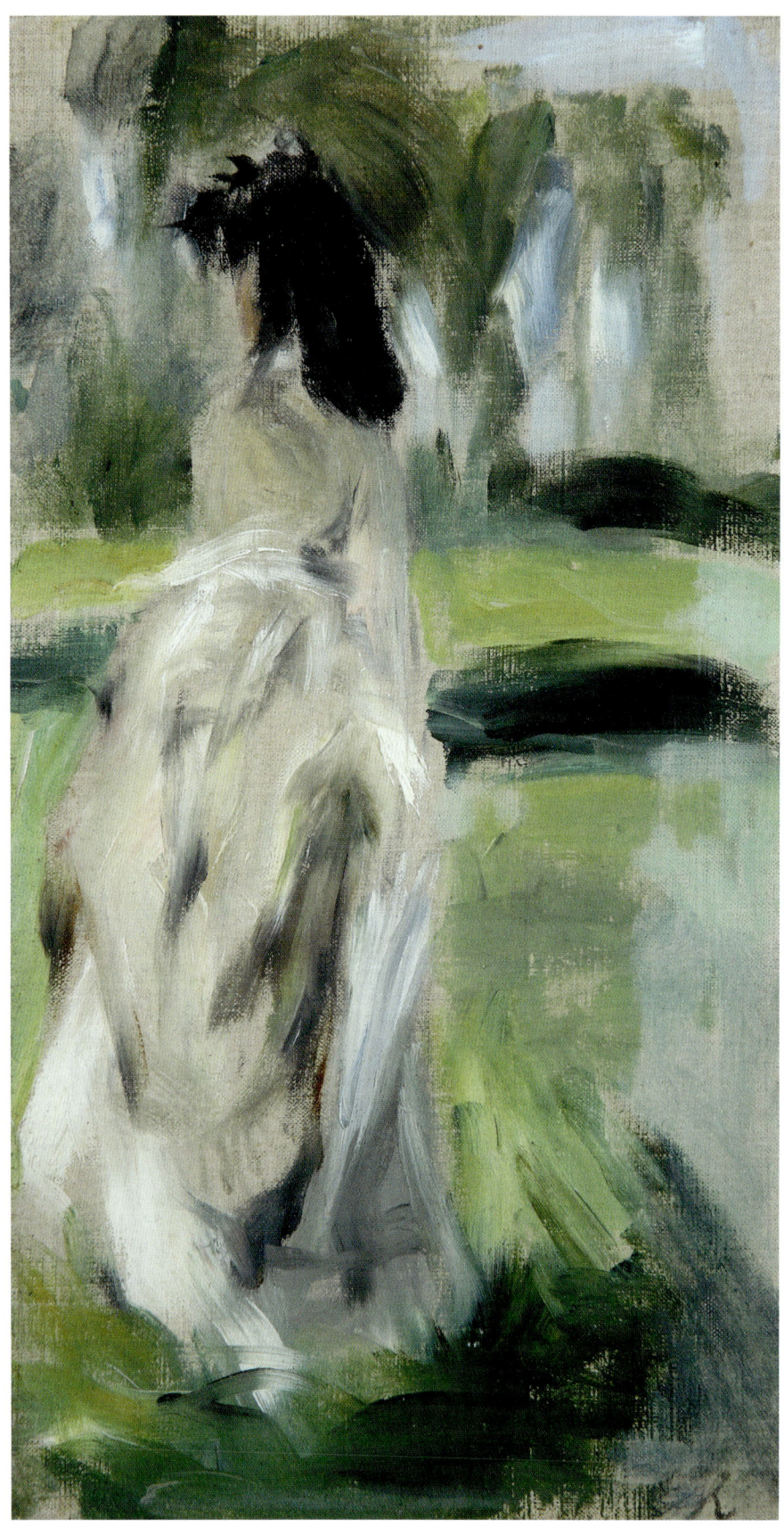

Auguste Renoir (1841–1919), *Young Woman Seen From Behind (Lise Tréhot),* 1866
Oil on canvas, 24 × 12.8 cm, JK Art Foundation

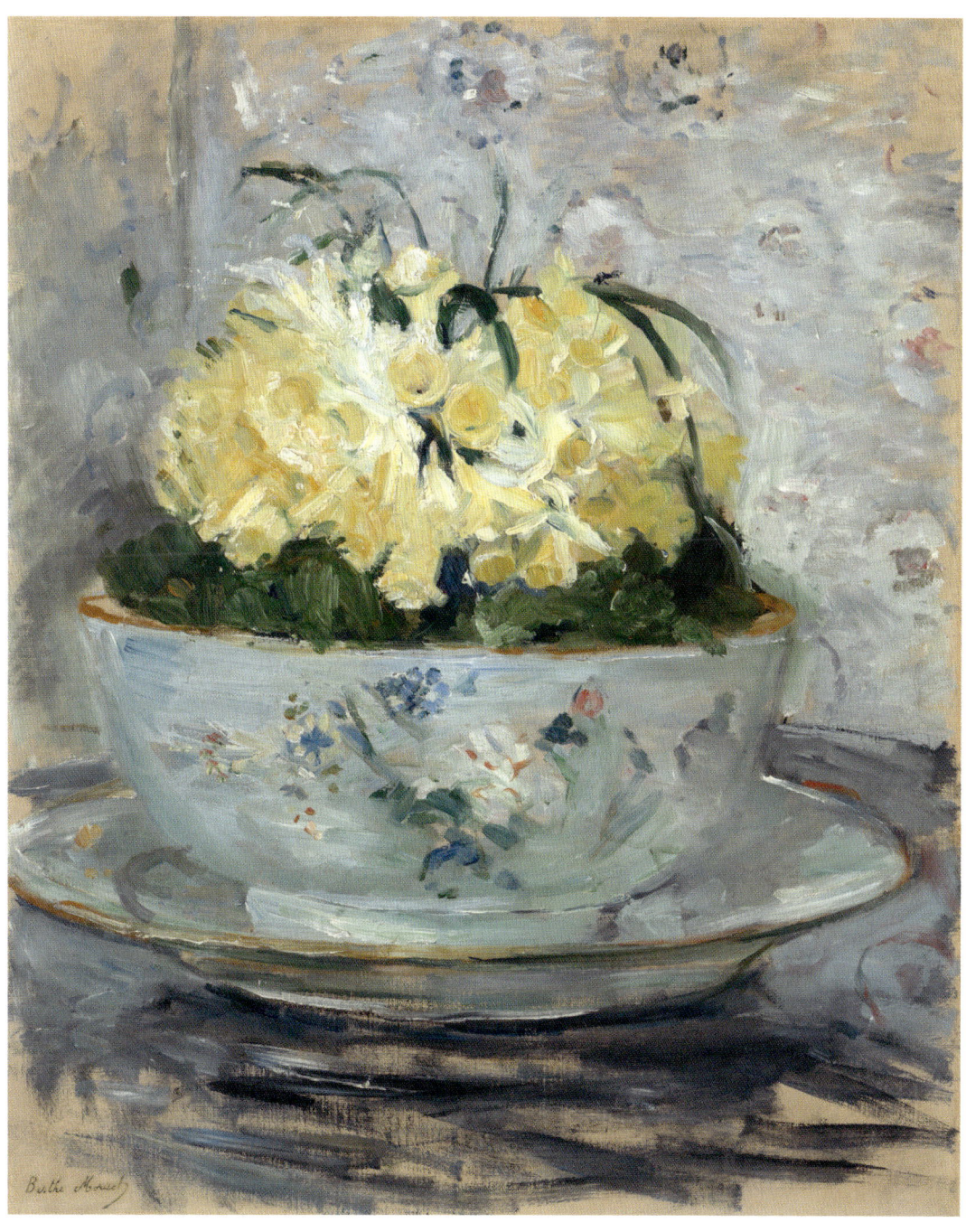

Berthe Morisot (1841–1895), *Daffodils*, 1884
Oil on canvas, 47 × 37 cm, Private collection

ÉDOUARD MANET (1832–1883)

Woman with a Fan (Portrait of Jeanne Duval), 1862

Charles Baudelaire, one of the greatest French poets spanning the artistic period from Romanticism to Symbolism, first met Jeanne Duval, an actress of mixed French and Haitian heritage, in 1842. Baudelaire wrote about her in his poem 'Sed non satiata':

> Singular deity, brown as the nights,
> Scented with the perfume of Havana and musk,
> Work of some obeah, Faust of the savanna,
> Witch with ebony flanks, child of the black midnight[1]

Their romance lasted around ten years, but Baudelaire continued to support Duval, including after she became partially paralysed in 1859. He produced several small drawings of her, which are now held in the Louvre.[2]

Manet painted his 'Black Venus' in 1862, at the height of his powers. After his death, Manet's widow revealed the identity of the model in the painting. The composition is unconventional yet masterly. The canvas is dominated by the enormous white crinoline, whose lyrical magnificence in myriad shades of white almost comes to life itself. Her right hand rests on the curved back of the couch, forming a counterpoint to the foot peeking out beneath the dress. The unusual placement of her foot might be a reference to her tragic illness. The lace curtain surrounds Jeanne Duval as though she were seated in a proscenium box.

When Simon Meller, curator at the Szépművészeti Múzeum in Budapest, purchased the painting from a private collector in 1916, he highlighted the tradition of colourism in classical Spanish painting, which Manet had studied both in Spain and in Louis Philippe's Spanish Gallery in Paris. One of the first documents that reveals the changes to Manet's aesthetics, themes and style, the painting is still tied to tradition by the influence of Velázquez and the use of black and white. The almost casual brushwork, regarded by some early commentators as sketchy and unfinished rather than innovative, demonstrates Manet's shift towards impressionism, similar to his painting *Music in the Tuileries Gardens*.

A recent restoration amplified the loose brushstrokes that characterise Manet's style after his 'Spanish period' and revealed more about the pentimento (changes made by the painter himself) at the model's braceleted right hand, resting on the edge of the couch. The pentimento, visible before cleaning, was left unchanged afterwards. Infrared examination provided no additional information to what can be seen with the naked eye. The artist painted the hand quickly and spontaneously, in a manner reminiscent of Velázquez. The hand is roughly painted, with the form reflecting the dynamism of the movement. During restoration, no pencil underdrawing was found, so the painter must have worked spontaneously, applying the motifs in almost a single flourish, resulting in the brilliantly fresh effect.

The previously cited poem appears, along with others about Jeanne Duval, in Baudelaire's renowned *Les Fleurs du Mal* from 1857. Ten years earlier – and thus fifteen years before Manet's painting was created – the great French writer had already described her as follows in his novella *La Fanfarlo*:

> She liked material that made some sound, long skirts, crackling, spangled, ornamented with tin jewelry, that had to be raised high by a vigorous knee, and tumbler's blouses. She danced, not with earrings, but with huge pendants that I would call almost chandeliers ... Her heavy, thick hair tumbled forward on both sides just tickling her breast and obscuring her eyes, so that she constantly had to disturb it by pushing it back.[3]

[JUDIT GESKÓ]

1 Charles Baudelaire, *Les Fleurs du Mal illustrées par la peinture symboliste et décadente* (Paris: Diane de Selliers Éditeur, 2005), p. 95. English translation: William Aggeler, *The Flowers of Evil* (Fresno: Academy Library Guild, 1954).

2 Denise Murrell, *Posing Modernity: The Black Model from Manet and Matisse to Today* (New Haven and London: Yale University Press, 2018), p. 29.

3 Charles Baudelaire, *La Fanfarlo, Bulletin de la Société des gens de lettres* (1847), pp. 10–11. English translation: *Paris Spleen and La Fanfarlo*, trans. Raymond N. Mackenzie (Indianapolis: Hackett, 2008), pp. 125–126.

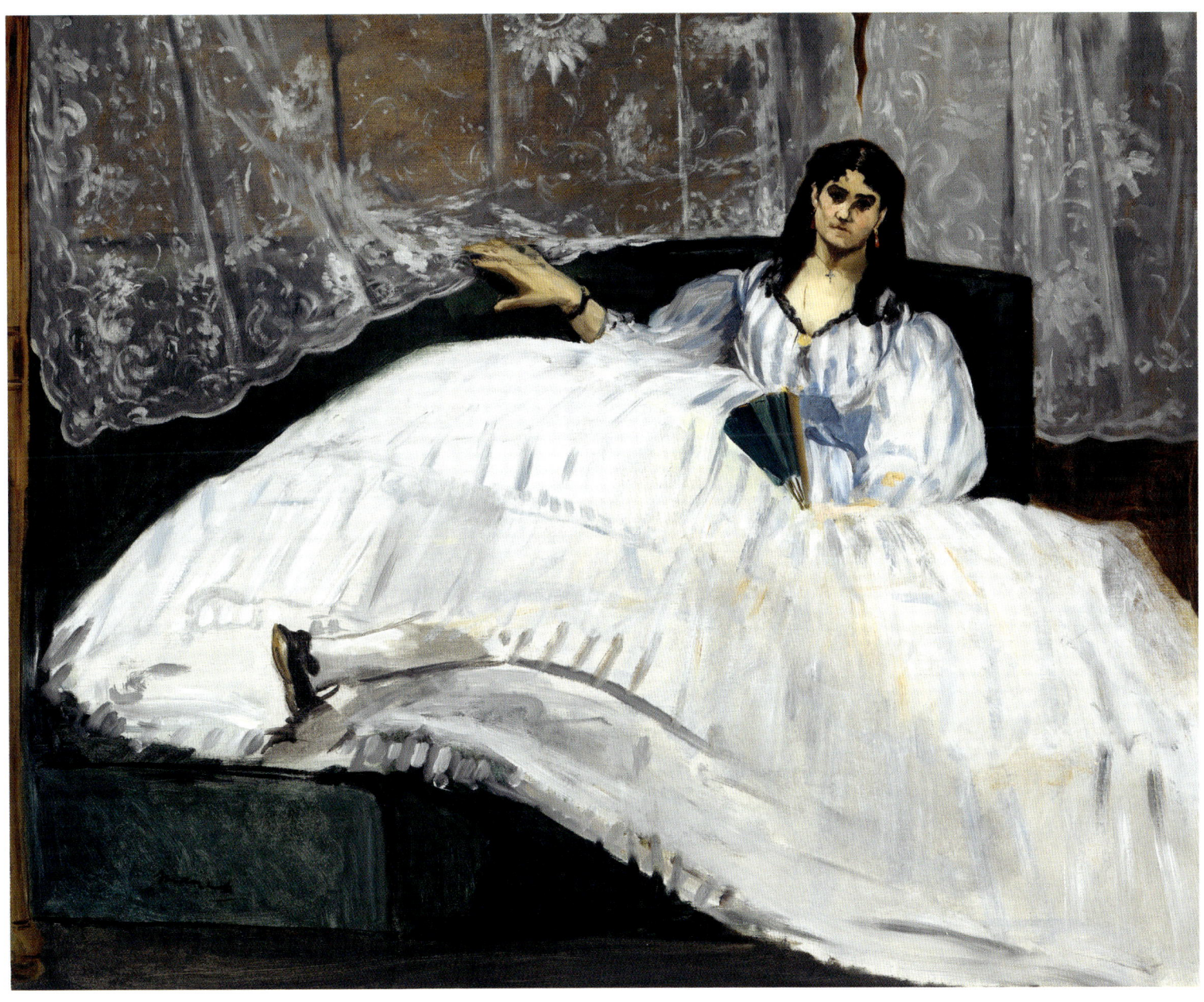

Édouard Manet (1832–1883), *Woman with a Fan (Portrait of Jeanne Duval)*, 1862
Oil on canvas, 90 × 113 cm, Szépművészeti Múzeum/Museum of Fine Arts, Budapest

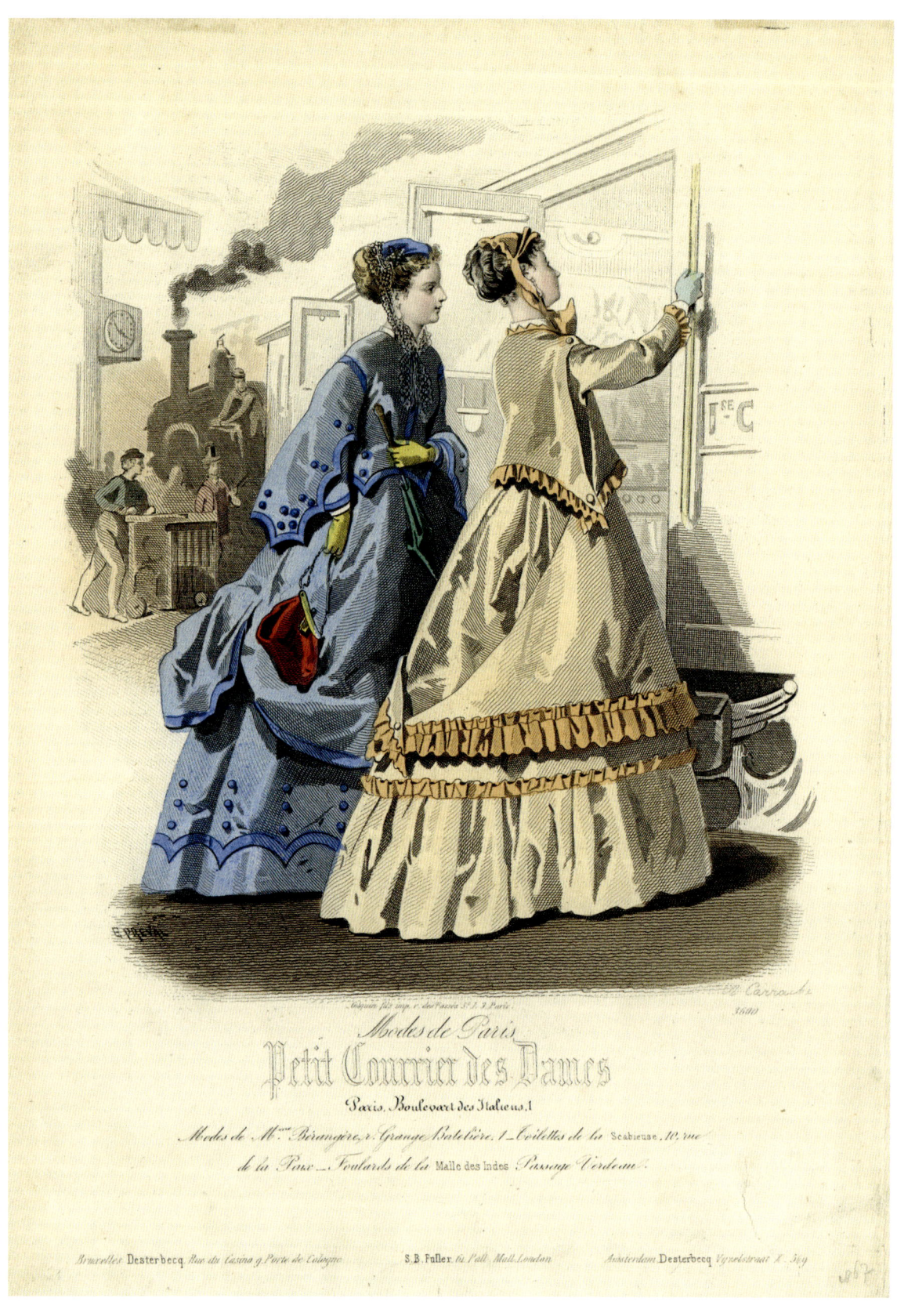

Modes de Paris, Fashion print from *Petit Courrier des Dames*, 1867
Engraving, 29 × 20 cm, Kunstmuseum Den Haag

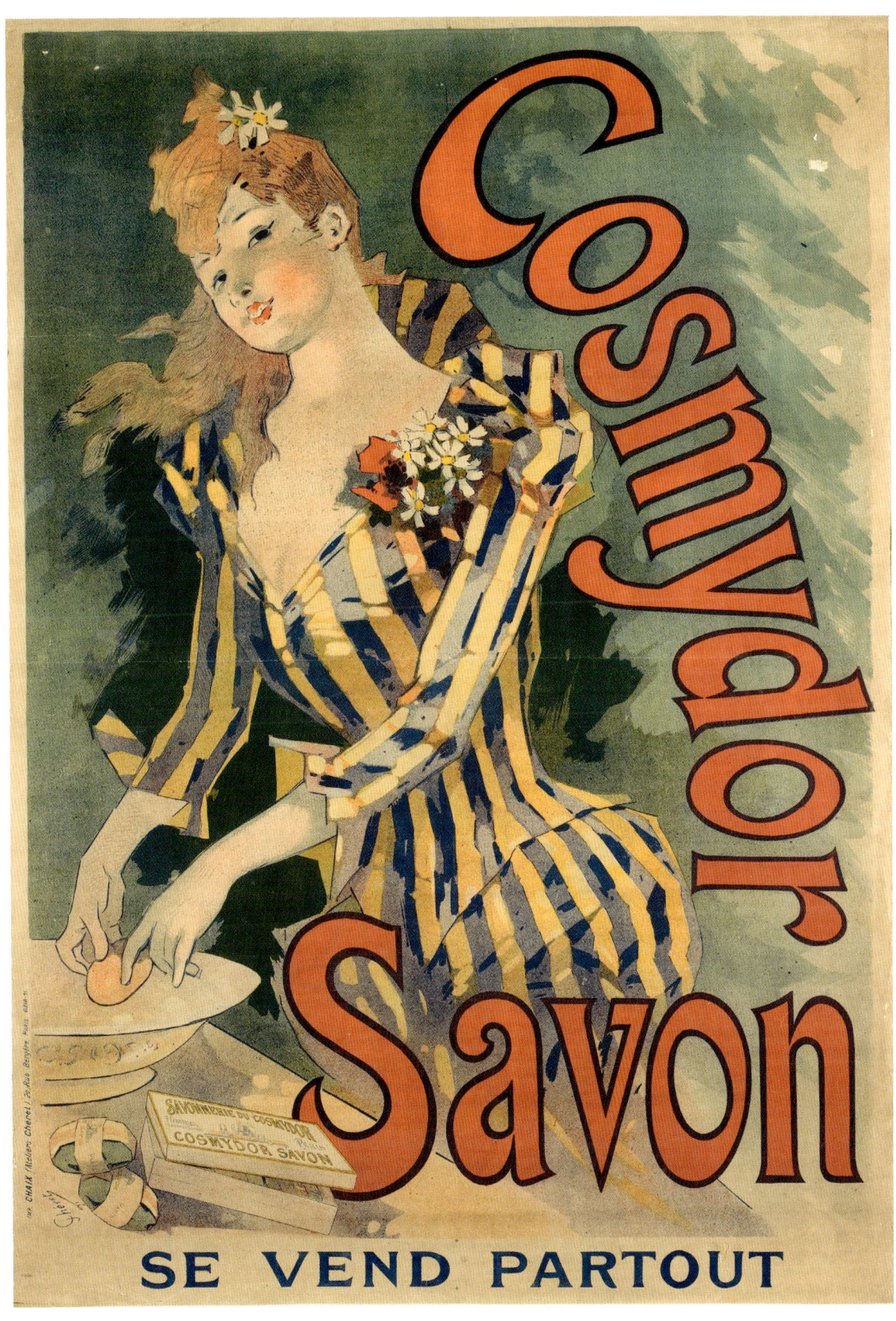

Jules Chéret (1836–1832), Advertisement poster for soap ('Cosmydor Savon is sold everywhere'), undated

Lithograph, 123 x 88 cm, Kunstmuseum Den Haag

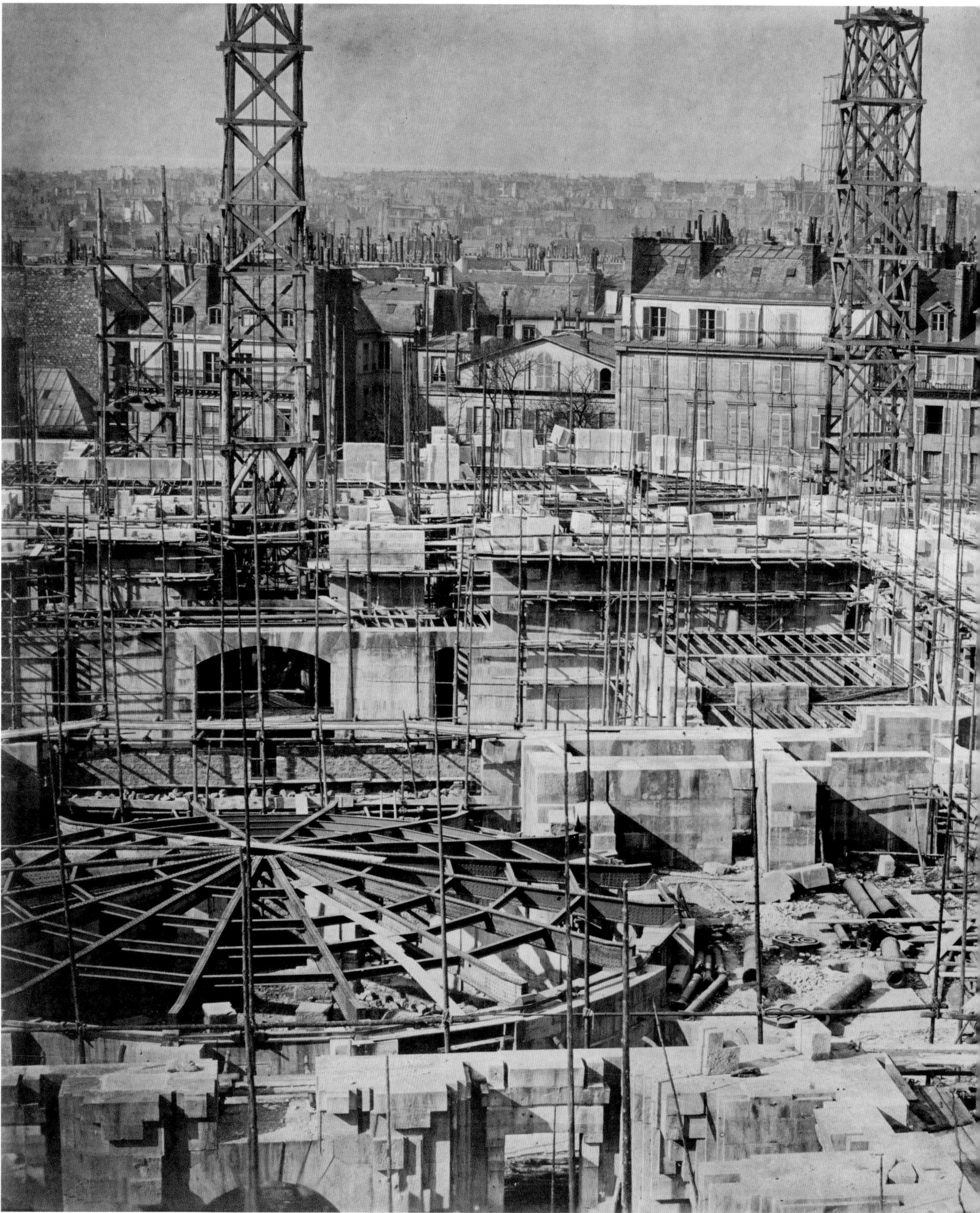

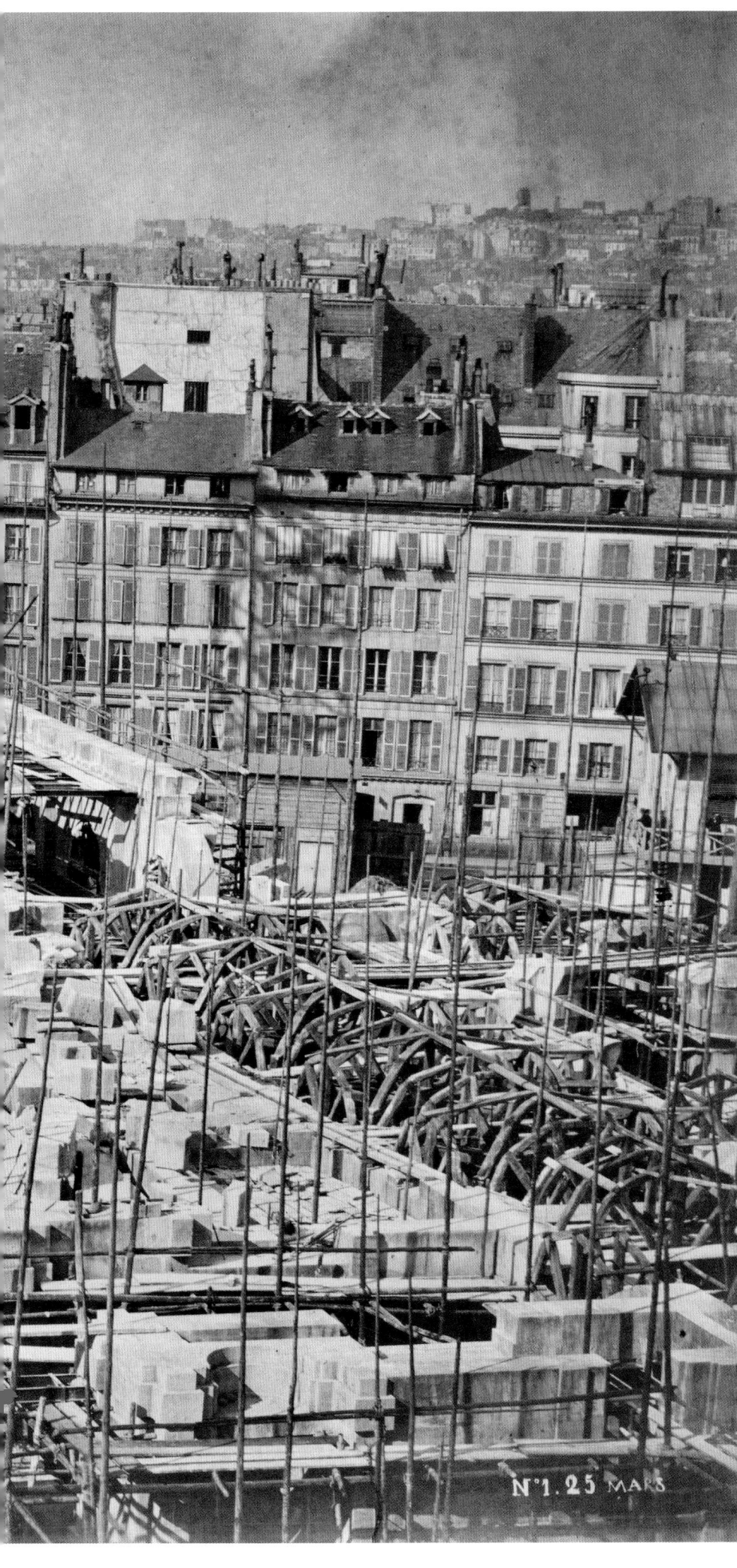

N°1. 25 MARS

Louis-Émile Durendelle (1839–1917) (Delmaet & Durandelle),
Building site of the Opéra Garnier, side wall, c. 1867

Albumen print, 27.7 × 38.9 cm, Bibliothèque nationale de France

Edgar Degas (1834–1917), *Three Dancers (Blue Skirts, Red Bodices)*, c. 1903
Pastel on paper on cardboard, 94 × 81 cm, Fondation Beyeler, Riehen/Basel, Beyeler Collection

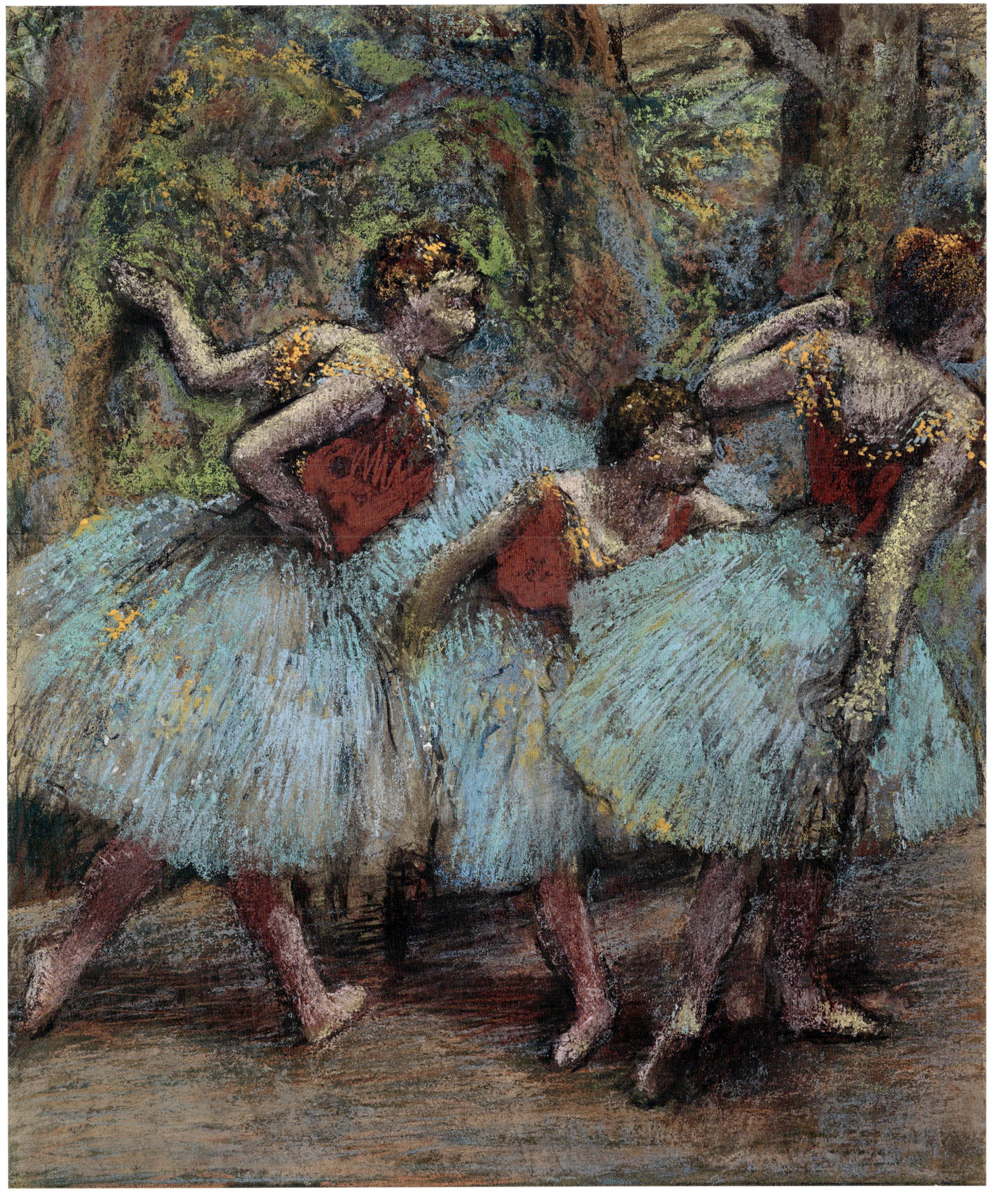

EDGAR DEGAS (1834–1917)

Nude Study for the Little Dancer, c. 1878

In the summer of 1867, a special unveiling took place in the 9th arrondissement of the French capital. For seven years, wooden scaffolding had hidden the construction of one of the city's new monuments, the Opéra Garnier. The Universal Exposition that year provided an ideal opportunity to show off the work in progress. The building was far from finished, but its impressive facade was ready to be seen. With its marble and gold elements, architect Charles Garnier, a remarkably young talent for such a prestigious assignment, had created a veritable palace for the arts. The Opéra was the jewel in the crown of the new Paris, reinforcing the city's position as an artistic centre.

Life in and around the Opéra Garnier was an important theme in the work of Edgar Degas. He drew and painted young ballerinas on stage, in the wings and in ballet classes, but also during unguarded moments of boredom. For Degas, the appeal of ballet resided in the depiction of movement.

In addition to making pastels and paintings, he turned to the medium of sculpture. In 1881, at the sixth independent Impressionist exhibition, he exhibited *The Little Fourteen-Year-Old Dancer*, a wax sculpture dressed in a real tutu.

The Little Fourteen-Year-Old Dancer is the only sculpture that Degas exhibited during his lifetime. After his death, 150 small wax, clay and plaster sculptures were discovered in his studio, which had served as study materials. One of these objects is *Nude Study for the Little Dancer*, which was cast posthumously in bronze. It is now known that the model for this work was the young ballerina Marie van Goethem. Together with her two sisters, she was one of the so-called *petits rats*, street urchins from poor areas of Paris who tried to build a better life via the Opéra. However, the registered addresses of the Van Goethem family reveal a downward spiral, moving to increasingly poorer accommodation.

Marie van Goethem's circumstances were typical of those of the average young dancer in Paris, many of whom fell prey to exploitation, violence, coerced sex work and crime. In their joint diary, the brothers Edmond and Jules de Goncourt describe this reality with a chilling anecdote: 'Today, at dinner with the princess, [the author Théophile] Gautier told a horrible story about an unfortunate dancer who had refused a ballet. He had taken her to her dressing room, where he had seized her head and threatened to smash her four front teeth against the marble mantlepiece. He told that story and even repeated it again; he couldn't get enough of it. He thought it was the correct way to make a woman do something she didn't want to do.'[1]

[FROUKE VAN DIJKE]

1   Edmond and Jules de Goncourt, *Dagboek* (Amsterdam, 2014), p. 207. Entry for 31 March 1869. English translation by Gerard Forde.

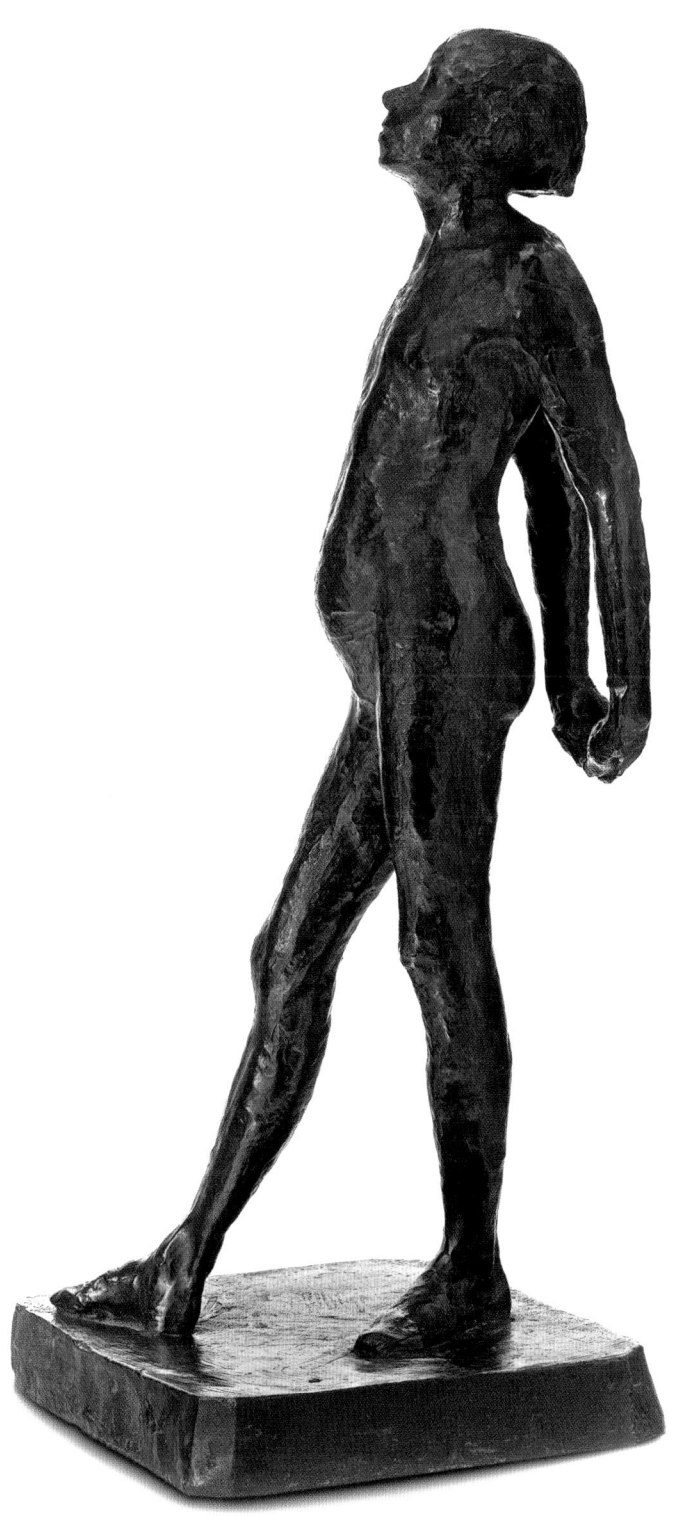

Edgar Degas (1834–1917), *Nude Study for the Little Dancer*, c. 1878
Bronze, 72 × 34 × 26 cm, Kunstmuseum Den Haag

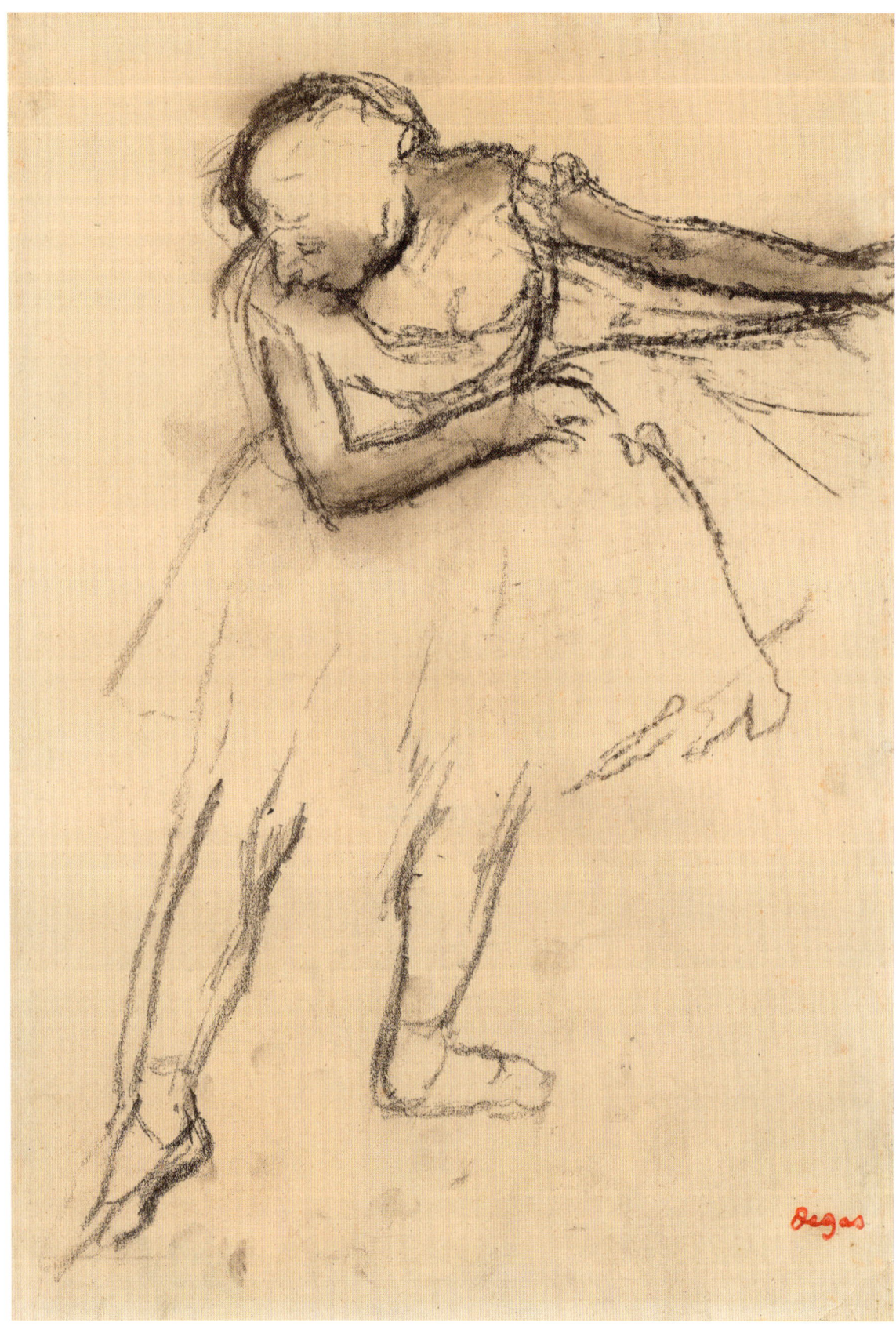

Edgar Degas (1834–1917), *Study of a Ballet Dancer 'dégagée en quatrième ouverte'*, 1885

Black chalk on paper, 32.9 × 23.1 cm, Collection Museum Boijmans Van Beuningen, Rotterdam.
Loan Foundation Museum Boijmans Van Beuningen, 1940 (former Koenigs Collection)

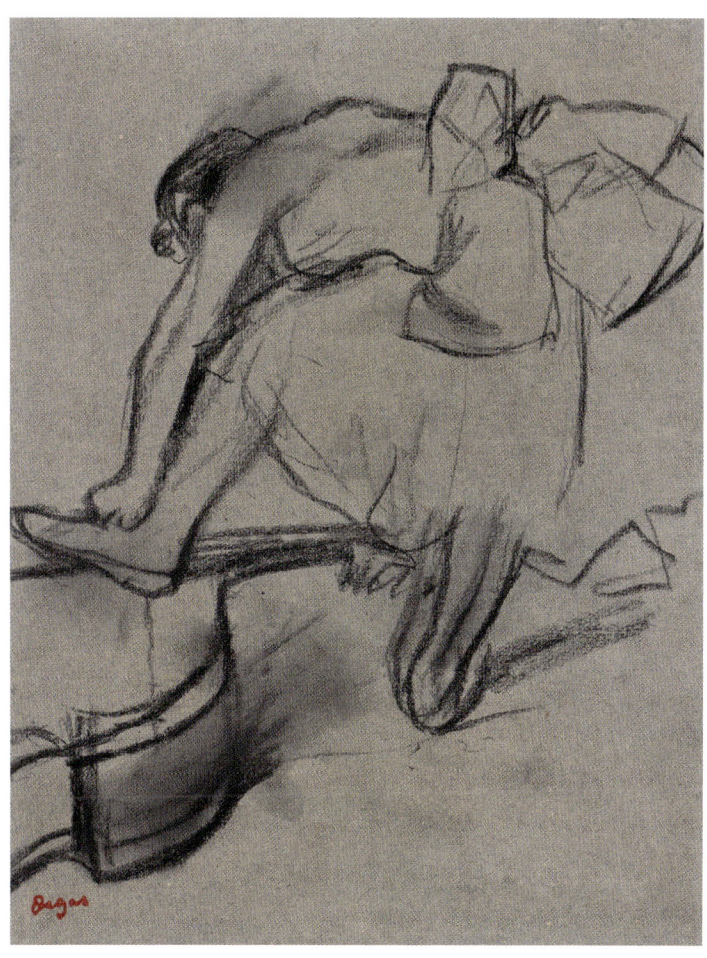

Edgar Degas (1834–1917), *Dancer with Double Bass*, 1885–87

Black chalk on paper, 31.1 × 24.3 cm, Collection Museum Boijmans
Van Beuningen, Rotterdam, Vitale Bloch bequest, 1976

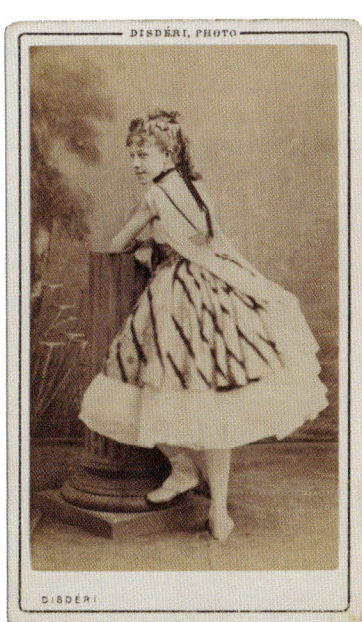

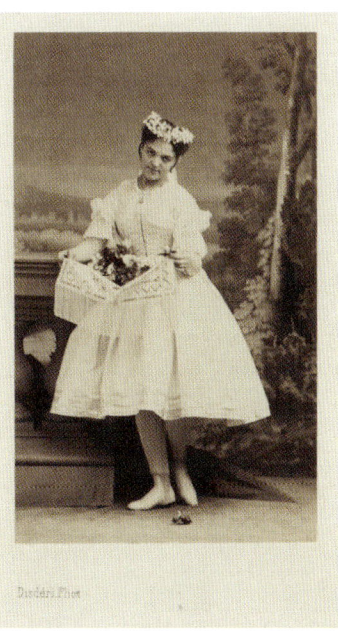

André Adolphe-Eugène Disdéri
(1819–1889), Marie Monchanin, c. 1870

Carte de visite, 9 × 5.5 cm, Kunstmuseum Den Haag

André Adolphe-Eugène Disdéri
(1819–1889), Marie Sanlaville, Paris, c. 1865

Carte de visite, 9 × 5.5 cm, Kunstmuseum Den Haag

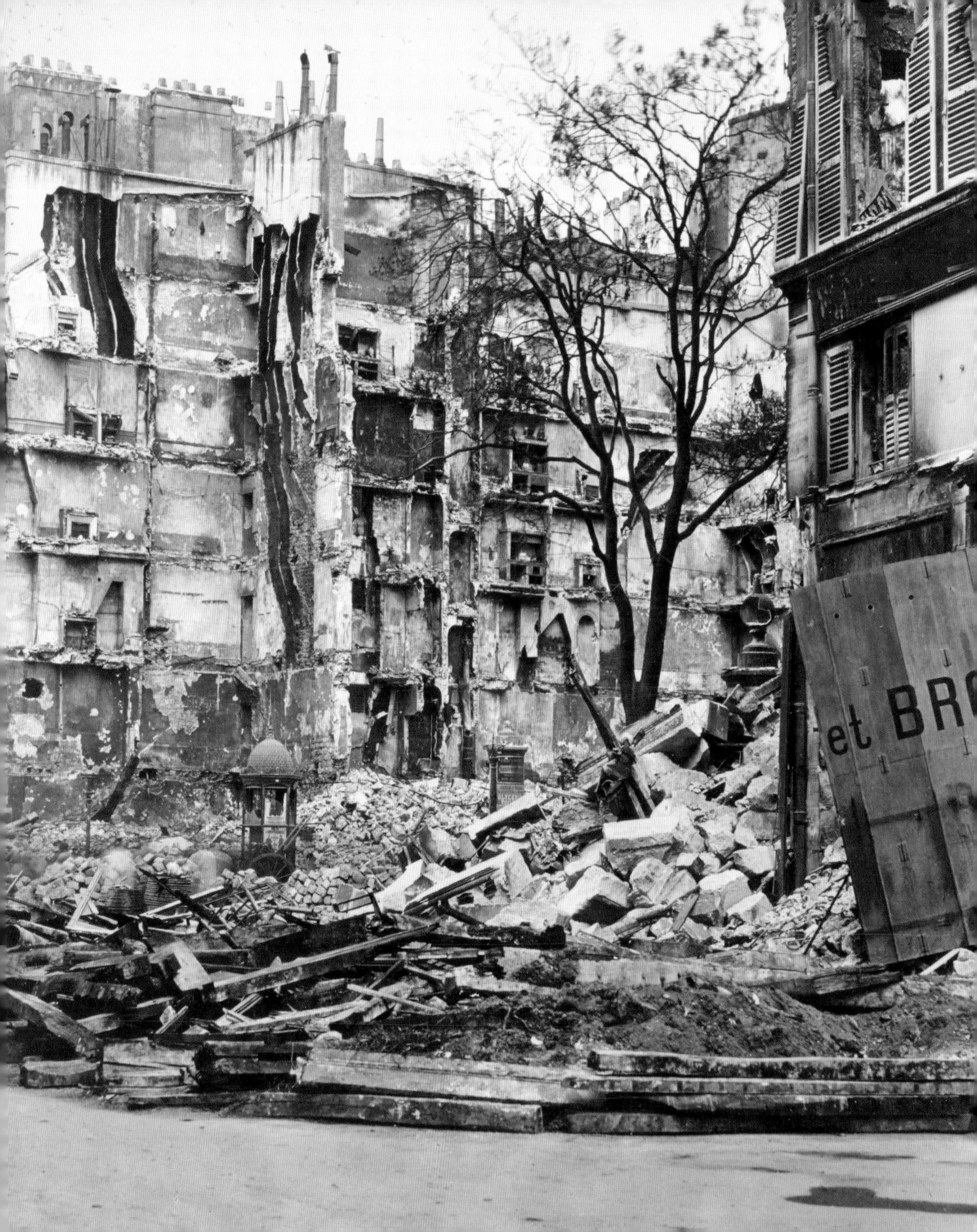

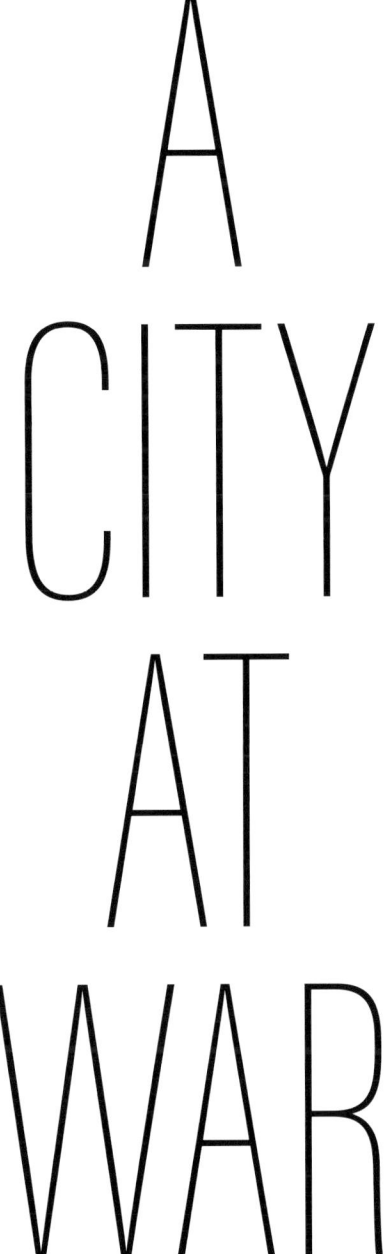

A CITY AT WAR

Frouke van Dijke

On the eve of his reign, Napoleon III made a promise: 'The empire is peace'.[1] Eighteen years later, these words formed the cynical caption of a cartoon by Honoré Daumier, who had drawn a city in ruins, with buildings on fire and the dead lying in the streets [fig. 1]. It was 1870 and Paris was at war. The Franco-Prussian War erupted after years of tension in Europe. What is now Germany had historically comprised two dozen kingdoms, principalities and duchies that were now preparing for unification, with Prussia taking the lead. The birth of a new major power on its border caused tempers to flare in France. After a series of conflicts, Napoleon III declared war on 19 July 1870. But the Second Empire was not nearly as well prepared as Prussia, which was armed to the teeth. After a battle of only six weeks, Napoleon III was forced to surrender.

The hastily formed Government of National Defence then re-sisted Prussia's advance with its remaining forces. A four-month siege of Paris finally forced the country to its knees. To complete the humiliation, the new German Empire was proclaimed in the Hall of Mirrors at Versailles. France accepted the painful defeat, but Paris refused to bow its head. The capital declared itself an independent state – the Commune – precipitating a short but bloody civil war. The Impressionists returned to a badly damaged city, but their paintings betray nothing of the trauma that had shaped Paris. Their sunny cityscapes met the need for forward-looking optimism, reconciliation and forgetting.

The Siege of Paris

With the declaration of war, Frédéric Bazille, the original Impressionist, enlisted in the army. His friends thought he was crazy and begged him to change his mind, but Bazille stood his ground and joined the Zouaves, a notorious unit trained in the French colony of Algeria. 'Trois fois merde,' (a slang phrase meaning 'good luck') a worried Auguste Renoir wished his com-rade.[2] Bazille himself had no fear. 'I'm sure I will not be killed,' he said shortly before his death, 'I have too much left to do in my life.'[3] On 28 November 1870, two bullets struck him in the arm and stomach during the Battle of Beaune-la-Rolande. He died eight days before his 29th birthday.[4]

His fellow artists thus lost a great talent and a good friend – Bazille was godfather to Claude Monet's son – and the driving force behind the unrealised plan to organise an inde-pendent Impressionist exhibition as early as 1867. They were therefore all too aware of the fleeting nature of life when the Prussian army surrounded the capital a few weeks later. Most of the Impressionists fled. When war broke out, Monet was honeymooning in Normandy. In Le Havre, he saw thousands of refugees fighting for a place on the boat to England. Shortly afterwards, he and his family also made the crossing. Camille Pissarro did the same. His Danish passport (he was born in the Danish West Indies) exempted him from military service, but his leftist ideals prevented him from taking up arms in the name of the French emperor. Paul Cézanne and Alfred Sisley also fled Paris. Gustave Caillebotte and Auguste Renoir did respond to the call-up for military service, but saw little action at the front.[5]

Edgar Degas, Édouard Manet and Berthe Morisot were still in Paris when Prussia installed its heavy Krupp guns in front of the city walls. Both men reported to the artillery of the National Guard, the citizen militia tasked with defending the capital. 'I think we poor Parisians are going to be caught up in a terrible drama – death and destruction, looting and carnage,' Manet correctly predicted shortly before the Siege of Paris.[6] Morisot refused to leave her family behind. Their home was transformed into a base for soldiers, including Morisot's brother Tiburce. The family experienced anxious times: Morisot herself contracted a severe case of pneumonia and Tiburce was captured by the Prussians.[7] Most of their friends and acquaintances had long since left the city. Fearing violence, the middle classes fled the capital en masse. Meanwhile, Paris was inundated with poor refugees from the surrounding areas, seeking shelter in the city.

Those left behind were mostly workers. But the longer the Siege of Paris lasted, the less class distinctions mattered. The supply of food and information was completely cut off for every-one, and Haussmann's newly built streets and boulevards were bombarded day in and day out. The writer Edmond de Goncourt, who had also decided to stay, wrote in his diary about the stray grenades and the wounded, but above all about the hunger. He describes the long queues at the soup kitchens, which now served anything deemed edible: cats, dogs, rats, as well as the kangaroos and camels from the zoo in the Bois de Boulogne, shot in desperation. At a butcher's shop on boulevard Haussmann, de Goncourt saw the skinned trunk of the elephant Pollux – once entertainment, now dinner. 'In the streets of Paris, death passes death, the undertaker's waggon drives past the hearse,' de Goncourt wrote bitterly on New Year's Eve 1870.[8]

The misery would continue for another month until the armistice was signed on 28 January 1871. In the meantime, some 40,000 people, including 25,000 soldiers, had died of hunger, smallpox or violence. The surrender forced France to pay repa-rations and to cede territory, constituting a serious loss of face. But Paris also felt abandoned by its own government. Those who remained, mostly the working class – looked down upon for decades – had fought with all their might for a city that they were now being asked to hand back to the bourgeoisie, who had largely waited out the war in safety elsewhere. Their homecoming would also mean a return to the old order and thus to the power relations in which the worker found himself at the bottom of the ladder. When the army of the Third Republic, the new government of France, returned to Paris to confiscate a group of cannons sta-tioned in Montmartre, all hell broke loose. The city turned against its own government and declared independence. On 26 March 1871, it proclaimed the Paris Commune.

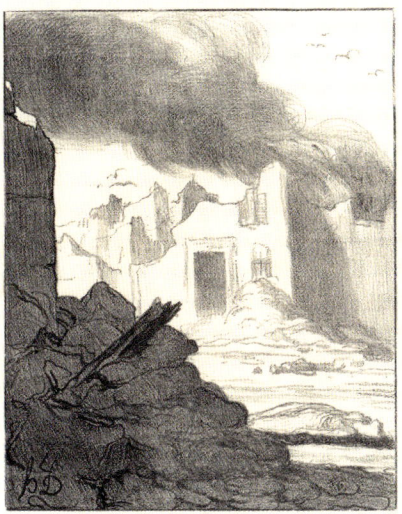

Fig. 1 [p. 184]

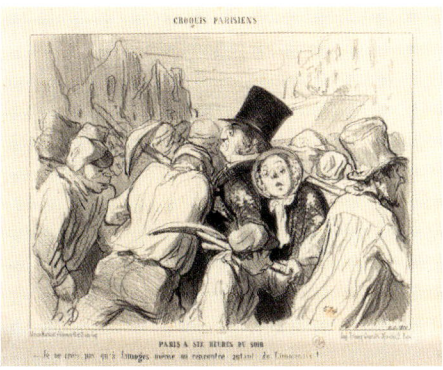

Fig. 2

Fig. 1
Honoré Daumier (1808–1879), From the series
News of the Day, no. 232: 'The empire is peace', 1870
Lithograph, 32.1 × 24.4 cm, Kunstmuseum Den Haag

Fig. 2
Honoré Daumier (1808–1879), 'Paris at six o'clock
in the evening – I believe that in Limoges itself we
won't meet so many Limousins!', January 1853
Lithograph, 26.5 × 35.8 cm, Musée Carnavalet – Histoire de Paris

Radical freedom and equality

The Commune was born out of frustration with the French defeat and the trauma of the Siege of Paris, but above all out of the systemic oppression of the working class. Writing in his diary during the siege, de Goncourt bitterly expressed the contrast between rich and poor: 'The wounded soldier has become fashionable. He is now a useful object, a sort of lightning conductor. He defends your house against the invasion of the suburban populations.'[9] De Goncourt heard the rumour that a bourgeois gentleman had fitted out his home in Paris as a field hospital for this reason. When not a single wounded man showed up, he purchased one from the hospital – for no less than 3,000 francs. Even the Prussian invasion did not quell the ever-present fear of an invasion of the poor.[10]

Fear of the 'lower' classes was deeply rooted. Migrant workers in Paris did the jobs that others could not or would not do, but were often mocked and distrusted. 'I doubt you'll find so many Limousins in Limoges itself!' exclaims a bourgeois couple in a cartoon by Daumier as they push their way through a crowd of construction workers during the evening rush hour [fig. 2]. The couple were referring to the migrant workers from the department of Creuse, which supplied Paris with tens of thousands of workers each year. The masons from this area, who formed a close-knit group in the city, were considered foreign by the Parisians because of their provincial dialect and customs.[11] On their construction sites, discontent over low wages, unsafe working conditions and housing shortages was growing, as was support for Marxist ideals.

Napoleon III certainly had this group in mind during the preparations for the urban renewal of Paris. Unemployment was an acknowledged source of discontent, and the large-scale transformation of the city would create plenty of jobs. But with the new street plan, the emperor also kept in mind the risk of rebellion. Poor neighbourhoods were wiped off the map or isolated to prevent the rapid spread of riots. The straight, broad boulevards would not only benefit everyday traffic logistics, but also the efficient movement of the army.[12] In this way Napoleon III hoped to quickly suppress any possible insurgencies and to easily remove barricades. But unrest about inequality continued to smoulder, also in the new Paris, and the Franco-Prussian war was adding fuel to the fire.

The government of the Paris Commune demanded radical changes. Its supporters wanted the separation of the Church and State, more power for the citizen over elected officials, education for girls and fair wages. In doing so, the Communards were taking serious steps towards a new revolutionary social order. 'At the moment, Paris and France are in the hands of the crowd, which has given us a government entirely of its own making. How will it last? There is no knowing. The unlikely rules,' wrote de Goncourt in disbelief.[13] As a well-to-do bourgeois, he was not reassured. The inhabitants of the suburbs were once again conquering Paris's city centre. There was partying on the streets and in the halls of the Tuileries Palace. But France could not take this popular uprising lying down. Both parties were holding their breath. In April, 700 women marched from Paris to Versailles, where the national government had withdrawn. They advocated a peaceful solution, but on 21 May the government's army invaded the city and within a week had brutally suppressed the Commune. The citizen's army was no match for professionally trained troops, who were also full of frustration after the defeat at the hands of the Prussians. Although the actual numbers are still subject to speculation, it is estimated that around 15,000 Parisians were executed during the so-called 'Bloody Week' [fig. 3].

Restoring order

As they retreated, members of the Commune set fire to parts of Paris to slow down the advance of the government army, or, from a purely anarchist perspective: if Paris is no longer ours, then it belongs to no one! Among the buildings that went up in flames were the City Hall and the Palace of Justice. The Tuileries Palace burned for three days. As the court martial later determined, the main culprits of this vandalism were the *pétroleuses*: women who had turned Paris into a sea of fire with bottles of petrol or paraffin. One of those convicted was Louise Michel, a feminist Communard known as the 'red virgin' because of her socialist fanaticism [fig. 4]. 'Concerning the fire in Paris, yes, I participated in it,' Michel declared combatively during her interrogation in court, 'I wanted to erect a barrier of flames against the invaders from Versailles.'[14] Michel escaped the firing squad, but was sent with many others to the French penal colony of New Caledonia in the South Pacific.

After Bloody Week, de Goncourt saw a group of arrested Communards along the railway line, frozen, drenched to the skin and disillusioned. Their new society had gone up in smoke. De Goncourt was surprised by the diversity of the women among the detainees, who had fought not only a class struggle but also a feminist battle: 'I noticed housewives, working girls and prostitutes, one of whom was wearing the uniform of a National Guard... Not one of these women showed the apathetic resignation of the men. There was anger and scorn on their faces, and many of them had a gleam of madness in their eyes.'[15] In reality, both the number of the *pétroleuses* and their contribution within the Commune was much smaller than the government sought to make out. Their role was deliberately exaggerated to instil fear of the rebellious woman in society. The new Third Republic used the revolt as a spectre of barbarism enabling them to tighten the reins on all fronts. The revolt legitimised the excessive violence with which it was suppressed in the name of peace, as de Goncourt coldly observed:

> There has been neither compromise nor conciliation. The solution has been brutal, imposed by sheer force of arms.... The bleeding has been done thoroughly, and a bleeding like that, by killing the rebellious part of a population, postpones the next revolution by a whole conscription. The old society has twenty years of peace before it, if the powers that be dare what they are free to dare at the moment.[16]

The government made a clean sweep. What France needed now was order, which justified the witch hunt against all those who might have had anything to do with the rebels.

In 1871, the Impressionists returned to a city that, in parts, was damaged beyond recognition. The artistic climate too had changed considerably. The need for unity demanded more than ever heroic images of national pride. The academy's conservative principles, which had seemed to be slowly weakening before the war, were again high on the agenda.[17] With acceptance within the official Salon seemingly more distant than ever for the young avant-garde, in 1874 the Impressionists organised their own independent exhibition. The responses varied widely. The first

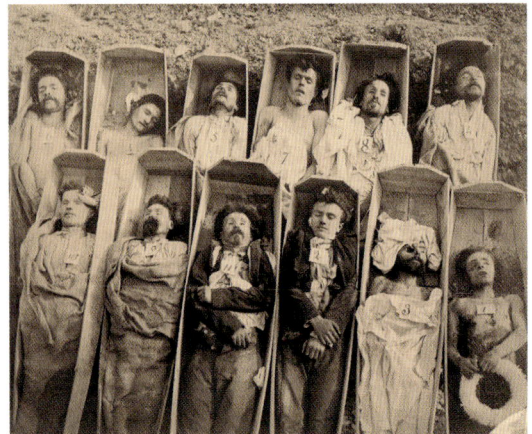

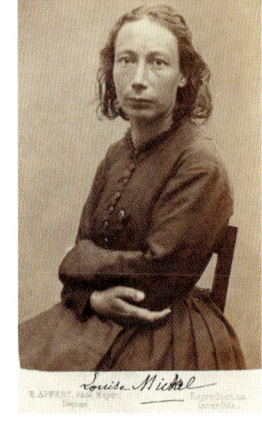

Fig. 3   [p. 182]   Fig. 4   [p. 182]

Impressionist exhibition was praised, thoroughly denounced or completely ignored. What is striking is the characterisation of the participating artists as radicals. In 1874, the Commune was still fresh in the memory and the Impressionist exhibition had the whiff of revolution.

The first Impressionist exhibition

For decades, specific painters or art movements had been associated with certain regimes or sections of the population. For example, classicist artists represented the academy, but in a broader sense also the monarchists and other members of the old elite. The bourgeoisie mainly bought genre paintings – representations of everyday life – which made this art form representative of the republican middle classes. Art criticism was therefore often a subtle form of social criticism.[18] Impressionism was considered to be genre painting. Because the Commune was an uprising of radical republicans, this label also stuck to Degas, Monet, Morisot and Renoir.

The first Impressionist exhibition took place at a politically charged time. France was in recovery, which required conformity. The organisation of an independent exhibition, without interference from official bodies, was in itself a political act of resistance. Every anti-academic initiative was seen as a radical republican initiative.[19] The exhibition's democratic set-up reinforced this feeling. There was no jury and there were no medals to be won. The proceeds were divided equally among all participating artists, and the display was non-hierarchical: the works were simply hung alphabetically, with the starting letter chosen blindly.[20]

Then there was the location. The exhibition was held at 35 boulevard des Capucines in the empty studio of Nadar, who was famous both for his photographs and his balloon flights throughout Europe. During the siege of Paris, Nadar had shown his patriotic side by smuggling letters and politicians in and out of the city in his hot-air balloon and had mapped out the enemy lines from the air [fig. 5]. But he was also known as a left-wing progressive with close connections to the Communards, some of whom he was said to have hidden in his house after the uprising.[21]

The avant-garde were, by definition, suspect. They too moved predominantly in left-wing circles. The treasurer of the first Impressionist exhibition, for example, the sculptor Auguste Ottin, was a member of the Commune at the time of the uprising.[22] A much more problematic contact of the Impressionists was the painter Gustave Courbet. Although not an Impressionist, like Manet he was closely connected to the group through friendship and artistic ideals, and had never hidden his moderately anarchist ideas. It therefore came as no surprise that he was at the forefront when the revolution broke out. Courbet was the artistic face of the Commune, designated as the scapegoat for the destruction of the column at place Vendôme. This monument, a bronze triumphal column crowned with a statue of Napoleon, had been pulled down by the Communards as a symbol of imperial power amid loud cheers [fig. 6]. After Bloody Week, Courbet was held responsible for the column's destruction and fled to Switzerland to avoid having to pay the high cost of its reconstruction.[23]

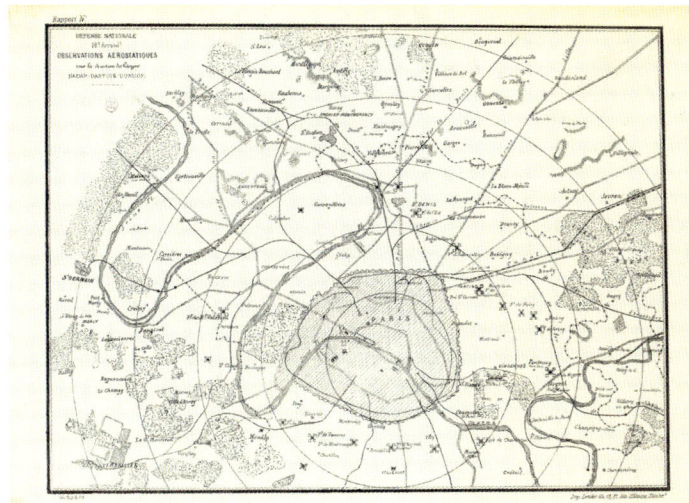

Fig. 5 [p. 193]

Fig. 3
André-Adolphe-Eugène Disdéri (1819–1889), Presentation of twelve corpses of members of the Commune, arranged in coffins, 1871
Albumen print, 21 × 28.3 cm, Musée Carnavalet – Histoire de Paris

Fig. 4
Ernest Charles Appert (1831–1890), Portrait of Louise Michel in the prison of Versailles, after her arrest, 1871
Albumen print, 9.2 × 5.7 cm, Musée Carnavalet – Histoire de Paris

Fig. 5
Nadar (1820–1910), National Defense, 18th District, Aerostatic Observations under the direction of Citizens Nadar-Dartois-Duruof, c. 1870
Lithograph, 31.9 × 45.1 cm, Musée Carnavalet – Histoire de Paris

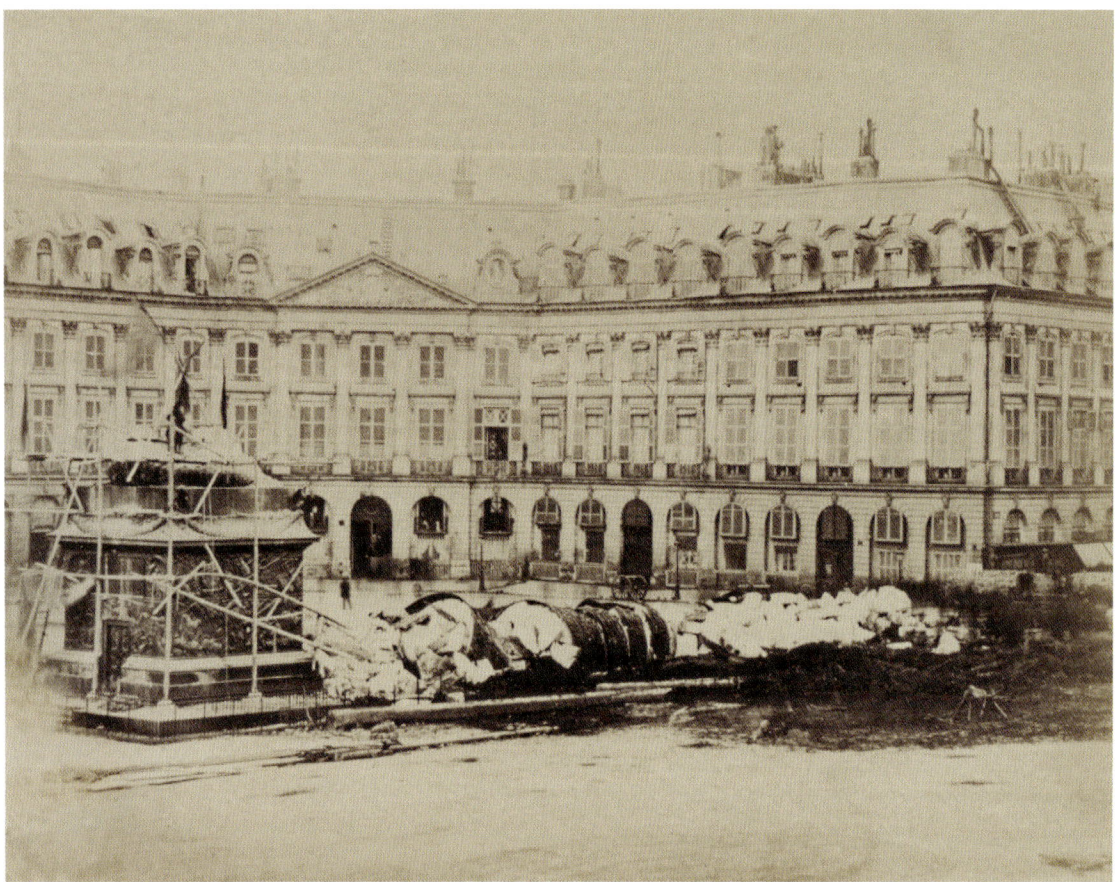

Fig. 6

The Impressionists' artworks shocked the public in many ways: through their modern themes, everyday scenes and painting style that was loose, colourful and therefore anti-academic. But in addition, it was the association with an extreme left-wing ideology that made critics describe the first Impressionist exhibition as an 'exposition des révoltés'.[24]

Art and the Commune

In reality, the average Impressionist was nowhere to be seen during the great Paris uprising. As the Communards clashed with the government's army, Monet was painting the charming waterfront houses in the Dutch city of Zaandam, more than 500 kilometres away. The exiled Pissarro – an anarchist and therefore ideologically in favour of the revolution – was eager to help Paris, but the tragic death of his newborn child made him stay with his family in England. Before the uprising, Morisot went to stay with her sister in the safety of Cherbourg. Meanwhile, her brother assisted in the negotiations between the national government and the Communards.[25] The family's sympathies did not lie with the rebels: during Bloody Week, notable figures in the Third Republic dined at the Morisot house.

Morisot had to defend herself several times in the well-to-do circles she moved in because of her contacts with the 'pro-rebel' Impressionists. The artist Pierre Puvis de Chavannes wrote to her in early June: 'Tiburce met up with two Communards, Manet and Degas, at the time when they were all being shot! Even now they still condemn the forceful means of repression. I think they are mad, and you?'[26] In fact there was no unified political affinity among the Impressionists. Renoir was a pronounced right-wing conservative and therefore a fierce opponent of the Commune. Degas seems to have had some sympathy for the Communards despite sharing Renoir's political conservatism. This great diversity of political ideals would cause friction within the group for years to come. Renoir withdrew from later independent Impressionist exhibitions because of Armand Guillaumin and Pissarro's left-wing views; he also made antisemitic statements about Pissarro.[27]

As a convinced Republican, Manet – not officially an Impressionist – seems to have fostered the most sympathy for the Communards, although he condemned the excessive violence on both sides, depicting the grimness of both the Franco-Prussian War and Bloody Week in a series of impressive prints [figs. 7–8].

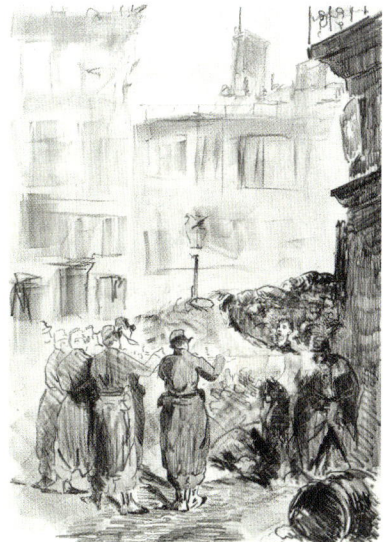

Fig. 7 [p. 189]

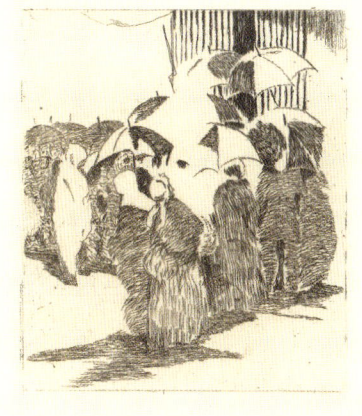

Fig. 8 [p. 188]

Manet shows the queues at the butcher's shops, the corpses in the streets and the execution of Communards by the government army in graphic terms. He followed the aftermath of the war closely. In a sketchbook he drew a scene of the court martial against Marshal Bazaine, the commander-in-chief of the army during the Franco-Prussian war, who was sentenced to death for high treason after the war [fig. 9]. Manet's critical observations more than once led to government censorship. For example, an injunction was brought against the distribution of his print *Punch* [fig. 10] in the republican magazine *Le temps*. At first glance, the figure depicted appears to be nothing more than a jocular clown, but observant viewers would have noticed a striking resemblance to the then president, Patrice de MacMahon, who ordered the mass executions of the rebels during the Commune.

The resurrection of Paris

The depiction of French soldiers killing their own countrymen was daring and something that Manet's Impressionist friends shied away from. But Manet too seemed to become more cautious in his politically tinted images, perhaps because of the intensity with which the Third Republic hunted down sympathisers of the Commune in the ensuing years. It is therefore not possible to say with certainty whether the amputee in the foreground of Manet's cityscape *The Rue Mosnier with Flags* (1878) [fig. 12] is a subtle critical note on the exuberance with which France celebrated in 1878. That year, the country once again organised a Universal Exposition, 11 years after the previous one. At the inauguration ceremony, future president of France Jules Grévy announced that 'France has restored itself.... The Exposition is now opened, and all the world may admire the marvellous vitality, the astonishing resources of that France, formerly so humiliated and crushed, now thrusting ahead to the admiration of all.'[28]

France was back on top: that was the image that the Third Republic wanted to promote. A national holiday on 30 June was intended to further emphasise national unity. Paris hung out the

Fig. 6
Anonymous, The destruction of the Vendôme column during the Commune, 1871
Photo, 10.7 × 14 cm, Kunstmuseum Den Haag

Fig. 7
Édouard Manet (1832–1883), *The Barricade (Execution by Firing Squad of Commune Supporters)*, 1871, posthumous edition 1884
Lithograph on paper, 49.2 × 36.8 cm, Loan from the Rijksmuseum, Amsterdam

Fig. 8
Édouard Manet (1832–1883), *Queue in Front of the Butcher's Shop*, 1870–71, edition 1905
Etching, 23.5 × 15.9 cm, Rijksmuseum, Amsterdam

Fig. 9
Édouard Manet (1832–1883), *The Court Martial of Bazaine*, 1873
Pencil on paper, 18.5 × 23.8 cm, Collection Museum Boijmans Van Beuningen, Rotterdam. Loan Foundation Museum Boijmans Van Beuningen, 1940 (former Koenigs Collection)

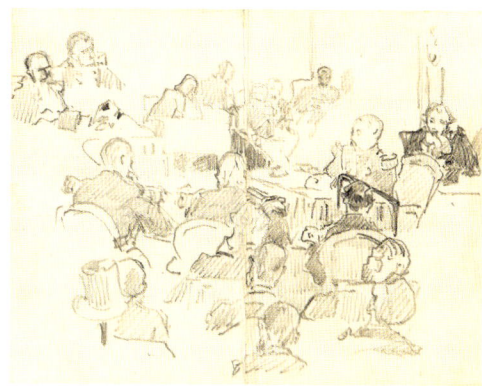

Fig. 9 [p. 188]

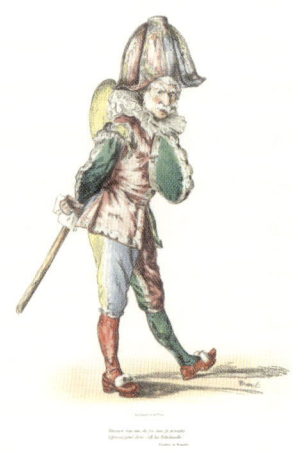

Fig. 10   [p. 177]

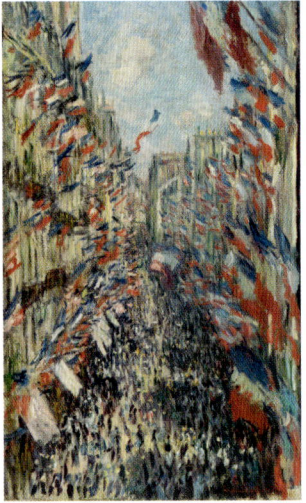

Fig. 11   [p. 195]

Fig. 10
Édouard Manet (1832–1883), *Punch*, 1874–76
Lithograph in seven colours, 43 × 31.5 cm,
Rijksmuseum, Amsterdam. Purchased with the
support of the F.G. Waller-Fonds, 1939

Fig. 11
Claude Monet (1840–1926), *La Rue Montorgueil,
in Paris. Celebration of 30 June 1878*, 1878
Oil on canvas, 81 × 50 cm, Musée d'Orsay, Paris.
Accepted by the State as a donation in payment
of inheritance taxes for the Musées nationaux in 1982

Fig. 12
Édouard Manet (1832–1883),
The Rue Mosnier with Flags, 1878
Oil on canvas, 65.4 × 80 cm, J. Paul Getty Museum

flags. Monet observed this spectacle in rue Montorgueil, in a working-class neighbourhood where fierce fighting had taken place during the Commune [fig. 11]. With loose brushstrokes, he brings to life a sea of fluttering flags. We see the crowded street from above, trapped between two walls of flickering red, white and blue. Monet painted the festivities on exactly the same day as Manet, who captured rue Mosnier at street level. Here too, the call to raise the flag had been heeded. In the foreground, Manet places a stocky man in a blue coat. Supported by his crutches, he moves through Paris on one leg. France today is peaceful and cheerful, Manet seems to want to tell us, but at what cost?

The contrast between the two paintings is emblematic of the way the Impressionists depicted postwar Paris. In 1872, only a year after the bloody suppression of the Commune, Renoir returned to the 1st arrondissement, where, as a young man, he had painted his first Parisian cityscapes with Monet. Under a clear blue sky, he depicted the Pont Neuf as a bustling hub of industry and prosperity. The sun is shining, and the national flag is fluttering in the wind. The painting's message is clear: everything is in order. Shortly after the uprising's bloody dénouement, de Goncourt described how the bourgeoisie returned to Paris and swept aside the brief interruption of its power: 'There are tricolours in every window and on every carriage. The cellar ventilators of all the houses have been blocked up again. Across the paving stones, which are being replaced, the people of Paris, dressed in their travelling clothes, are swarming in to take possession of their city once more. All is well.'[29]

This sentiment was also reflected in the city's architecture. The column on the place Vendôme was rebuilt and Paris erected new memorials to compensate for the loss of old monuments. In 1875, construction began on the Sacré-Coeur Basilica, an immaculate white edifice in memory of the victims of the Franco-Prussian war. In an early example of disaster tourism, travel guides led people around the remaining ruins, which themselves were the subject of debate: should they be cleared away or preserved as a warning? In his painting *The Tuileries*, Monet seems to express his preference for the first option. In this cityscape, he focuses his gaze exclusively on the flowering garden of the burnt-out palace. The relatively unscathed Pavillon de Flore glistens in the sun, but Monet has left the ruins of the rest of the building completely out of the picture [see p. 197]. Twelve years later, in 1883, Paris finally demolished the remains of the Tuileries Palace. Reconstruction through demolition: it was a formula that the city knew all too well.

Impressionism was not a political movement. The opinions of its members differed too greatly for that. But neither was their art neutral. With their depictions of modern Paris – sunny and radiant – they fulfilled the widely shared need among the bourgeoisie to treat the war as a bad dream. Perhaps this desire was also inherent to Paris, a city with a rich history of revolutions. 'Paris wants to live; it wants it imperiously,' George Sand wrote in 1867. 'The day after the fighting it needs to party: people cut each other's throats and embrace each other with the same ease and the same good faith.'[30]

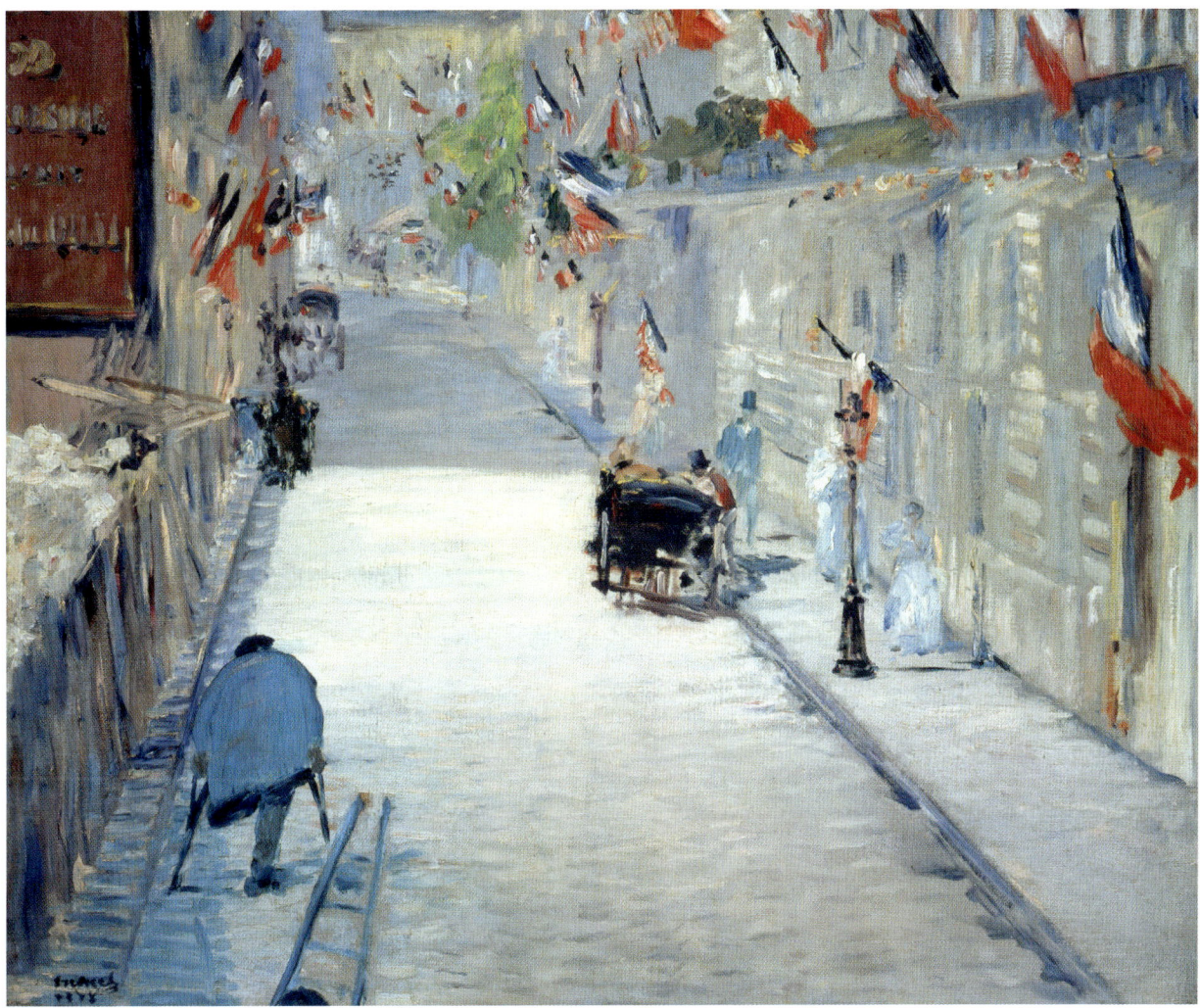

Fig. 12

1 Speech given by Napoleon III in Bordeaux, 9 October 1852. Quoted in James Harvey Robinson, *Readings in European History*, vol. 2 (New York, 1906), pp. 563–564.

2 Michel Hilaire, 'Frédéric Bazille: Heavenly Long Vacations', in Michel Hilaire and Paul Perrin (eds.), *Frédéric Bazille and the Birth of Impressionism*, exh. cat. Montpellier (Musée Fabre, 2016), p. 42.

3 Hilaire 2016 (note 2), p. 19.

4 Hilaire 2016 (note 2), p. 19.

5 Albert Boime, *Art and the French Commune: Imagining Paris after War and Revolution* (Princeton, NJ, 1995), p. 51.

6 Juliet Wilson-Bareau (ed.), *Manet by Himself: Correspondence & Conversation: Paintings, Pastels, Prints & Drawings* (London, 1995), p. 55.

7 Sylvie Patry (ed.), *Berthe Morisot: Woman Impressionist* (New York, 2018), p. 194.

8 Edmond and Jules de Goncourt, *Pages from the Goncourt Journal*, edited, translated and introduced by Robert Baldick (London, 1984), p. 179.

9 Edmond and Jules de Goncourt, *The Journal of the De Goncourts*, edited and introduced by Julius West (London, 1900), p. 137.

10 De Goncourt 1900 (note 9), p. 137.

11 Esther da Costa Meyer, *Dividing Paris: Urban Renewal and Social Inequality, 1852–1870* (Princeton, NJ, 2022), p. 7, 281. See also David H. Pinkney, 'Migrations to Paris During the Second Empire', *The Journal of Modern History*, vol. 25, no. 1 (March 1953), p. 3.

12 Da Costa Meyer 2022 (note 11), p. 100. See also: David H. Pinkney, *Napoleon III and the Rebuilding of Paris*, (Princeton, NJ, 1972), p. 36.

13 De Goncourt 1900 (note 9), p. 176.

14 *La Gazette des tribunaux*, 17 December 1871, p. 862.

15 De Goncourt 1984 (note 8), p. 191.

16 De Goncourt 1984 (note 8), p. 194.

17 Patricia Mainardi, *The End of the Salon: Art and the State in the Early Third Republic* (Cambridge, 1994), p. 37.

18 Patricia Mainardi, *Art and Politics of the Second Empire: The Universal Expositions of 1855 and 1867* (New Haven, CT & London, 1987), p. 72.

19 James H. Rubin, *Impressionism and the Modern Landscape: Productivity, Technology and Urbanization from Manet to Van Gogh* (Berkeley, Los Angeles and London, 2008), p. 177.

20 Rubin 2008 (note 19), p. 177.

21 Boime 1995 (note 5), p. 37.

22 Rubin 2008 (note 19), p. 178.

23 Priscilla Parkhurst Ferguson, *Paris as Revolution: Writing the Nineteenth-Century City* (Berkeley, CA, 1994), p. 176.

24 Émile Cardon, 'Avant le salon: l'exposition des révoltés', *La presse*, 29 April 1874. See also Rubin 2008 (note 19), p. 8.

25 Denis Rouart, *Correspondance de Berthe Morisot avec sa famille et ses amis Manet, Puvis de Chavannes, Degas, Monet, Renoir et Mallarmé* (Paris, 1950), pp. 56–57.

26 Letter from Pierre Puvis de Chavannes to Berthe Morisot, 5 June 1871, in Rouart 1950 (note 25), p. 58.

27 Rubin 2008 (note 19), p. 183.

28 Boime 1995 (note 5), p. 132.

29 De Goncourt 1984 (note 8), p. 194.

30 George Sand, 'La rêverie à Paris', in *Paris guide par les principaux écrivains et artistes de la France*, vol. 2 (Paris, 1867), p. 1198.

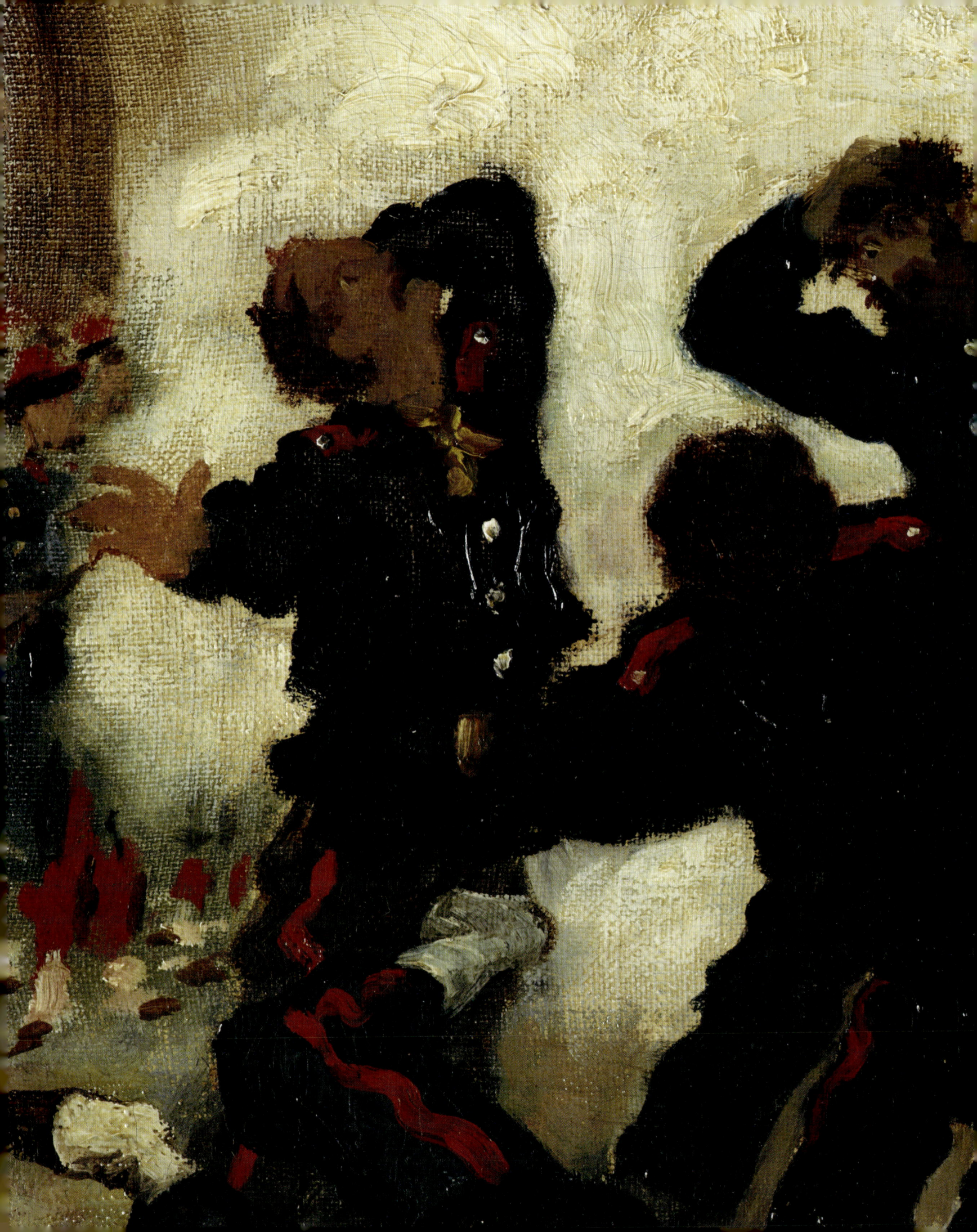

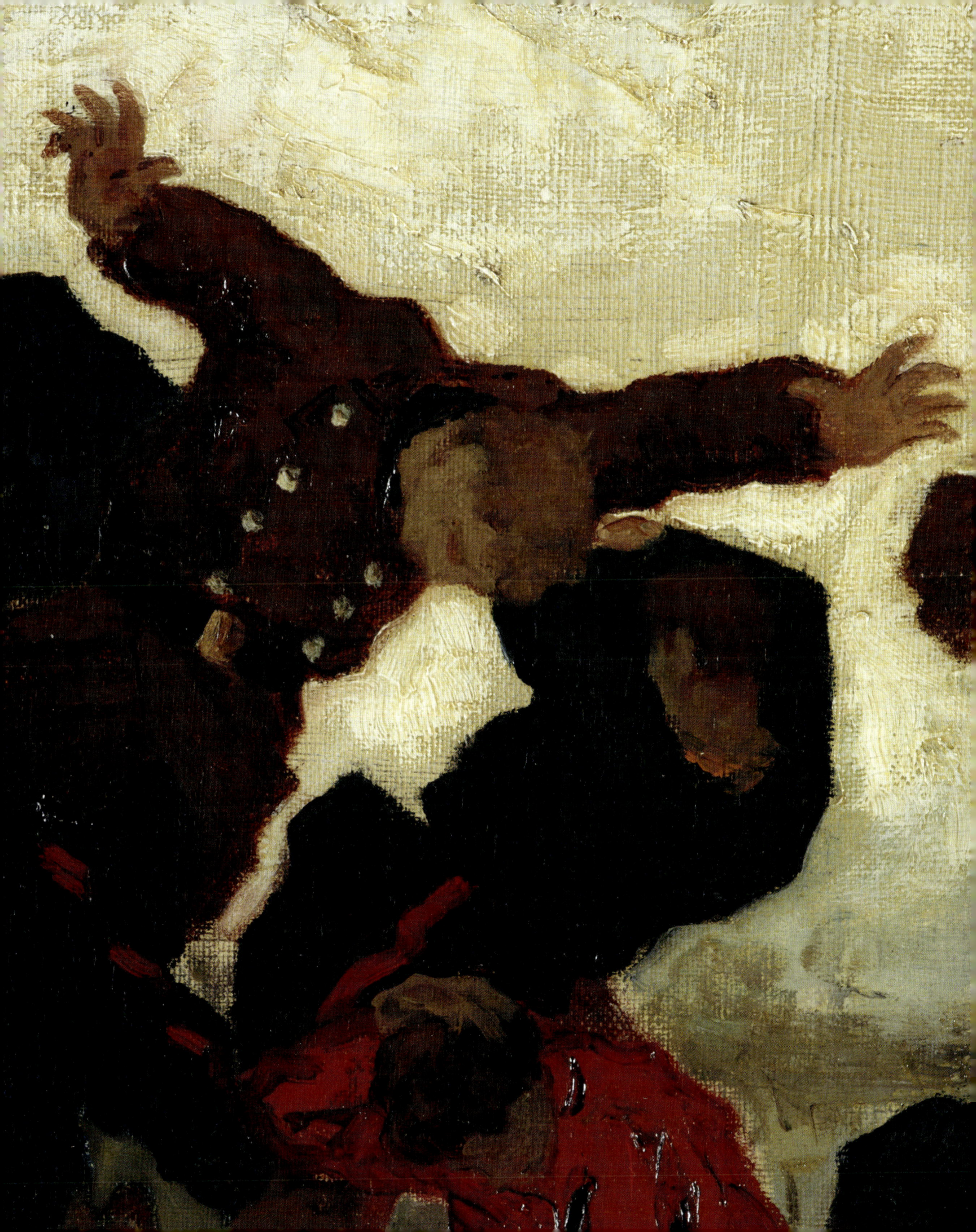

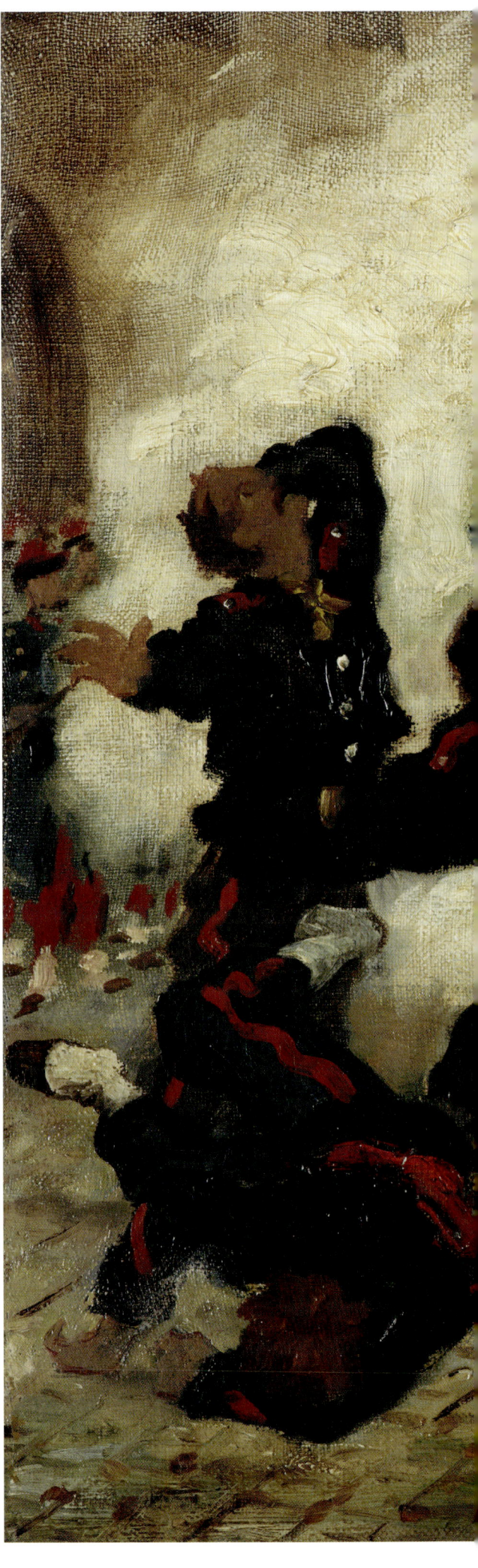

174

Édouard Manet (1832–1882), *The Explosion*, 1871
Oil on canvas, 37.5 × 45.5 cm, Museum Folkwang, Essen

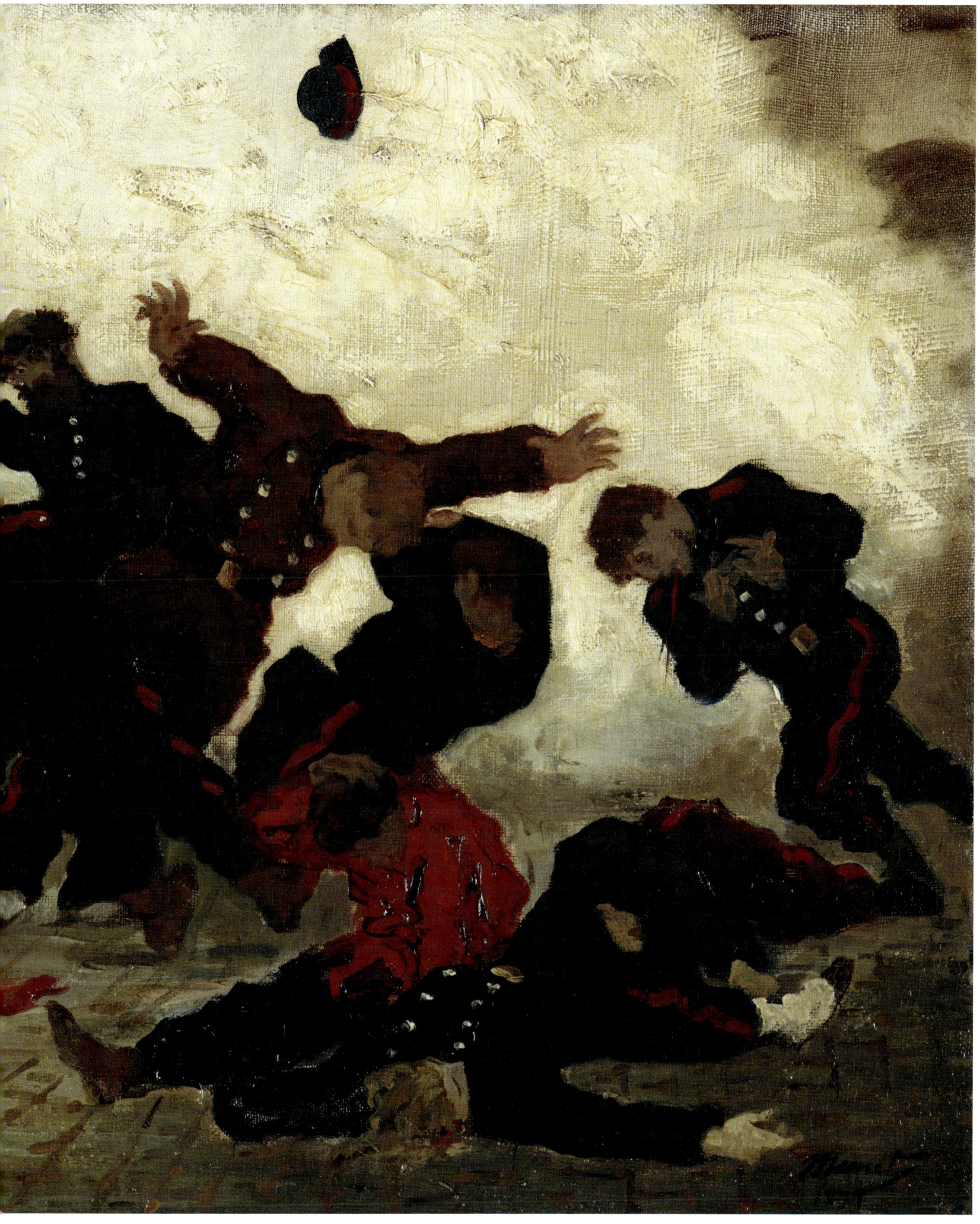

176

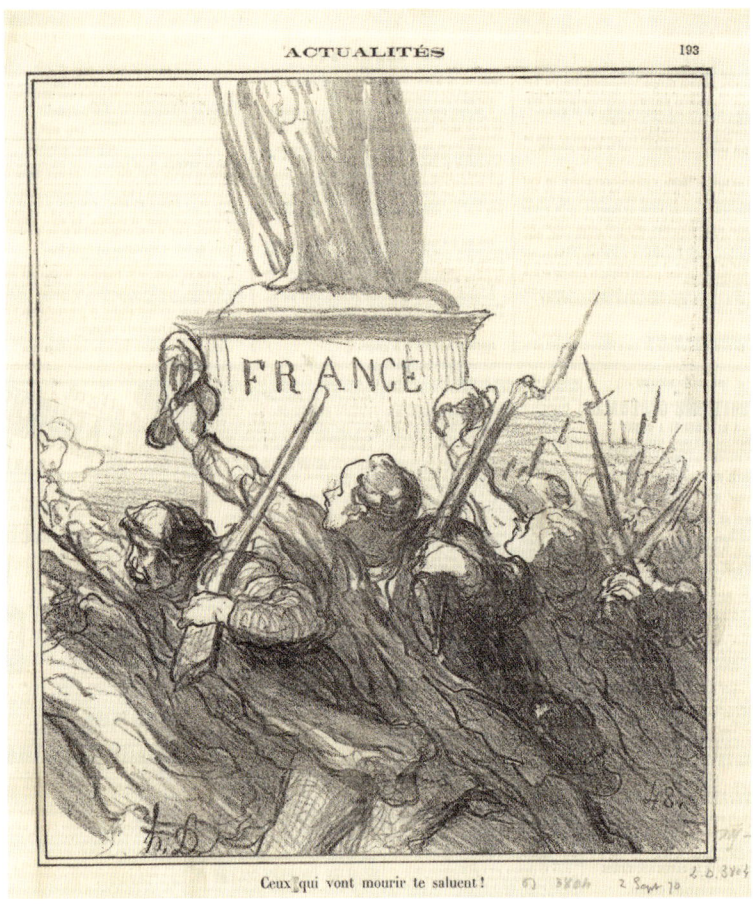

Honoré Daumier (1808–1879), From the series *News of the Day*,
no. 193: 'Those who are about to die salute you!', 1870

Lithograph, 29 × 27 cm, Kunstmuseum Den Haag

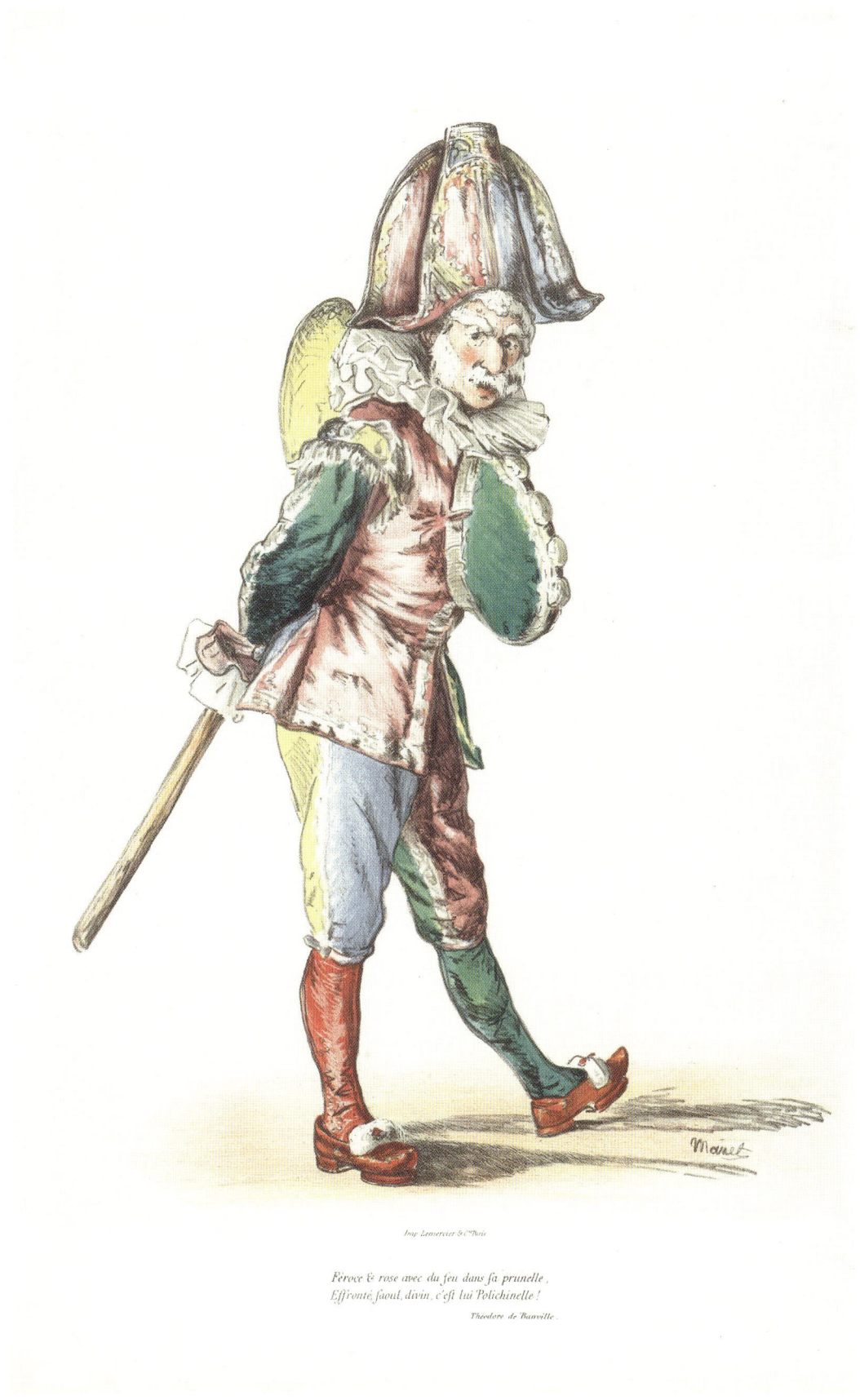

Imp. Lemercier & Cie Paris

Féroce & rose avec du feu dans sa prunelle,
Effronté, saoul, divin, c'est lui Polichinelle !

Théodore de Banville.

Édouard Manet (1832–1882), *Punch,* 1874–76

Lithograph in seven colours, 43 × 31.5 cm, Rijksmuseum, Amsterdam. Purchased with the support of the F.G. Waller-Fonds, 1939

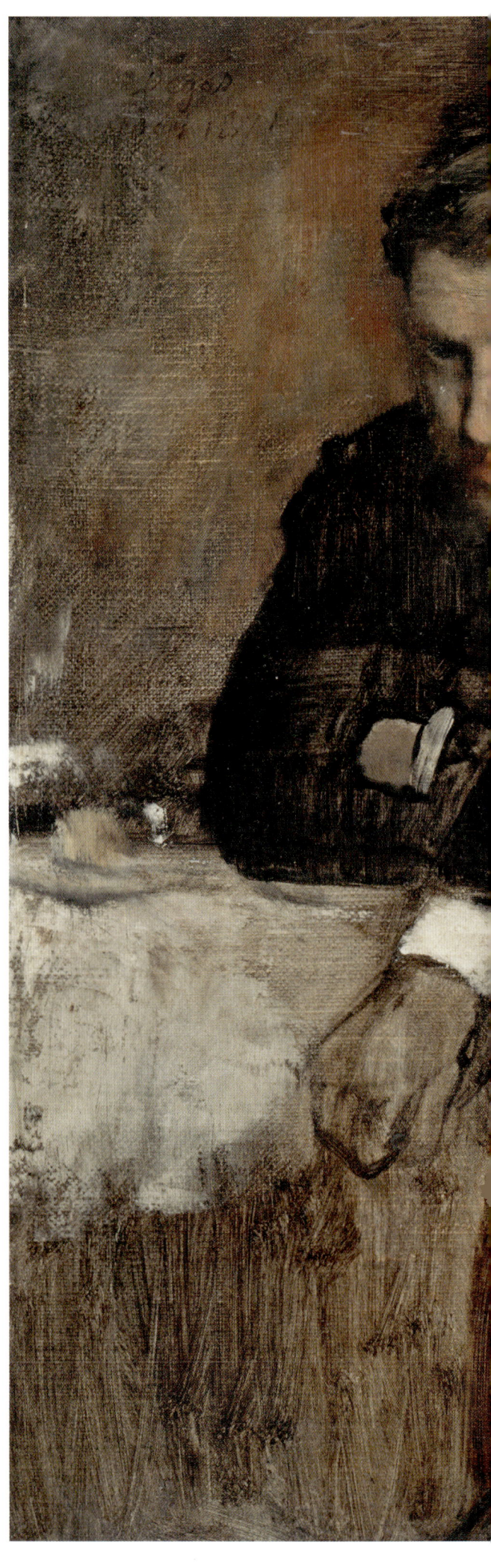

Edgar Degas (1834–1917), *Jeantaud, Linet, Lainé*, 1871

Oil on canvas, 38 × 46 cm, Musée d'Orsay, Paris. Bequest of Mme Jeantaud
to the Musées nationaux for the Musée du Louvre, 1929

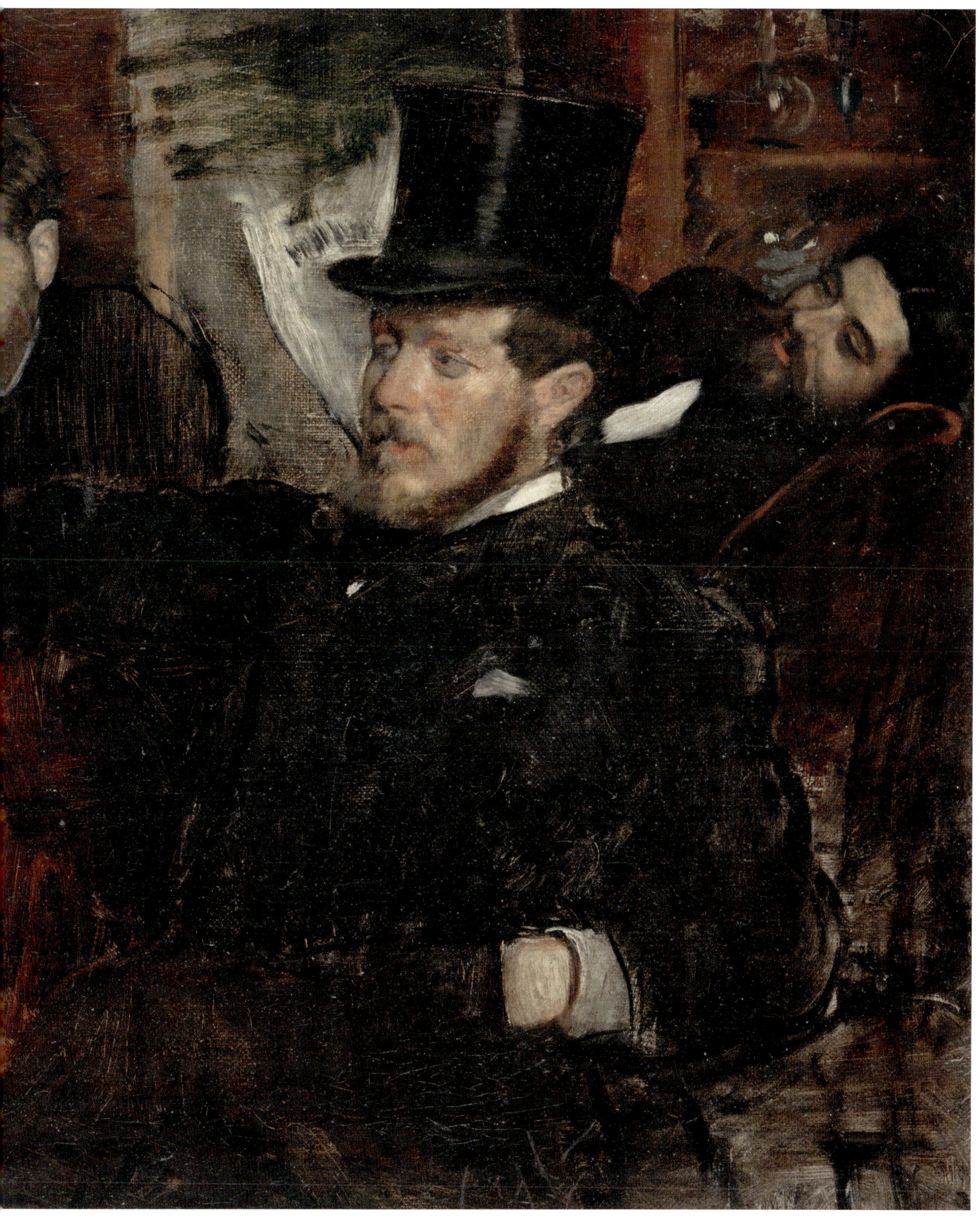

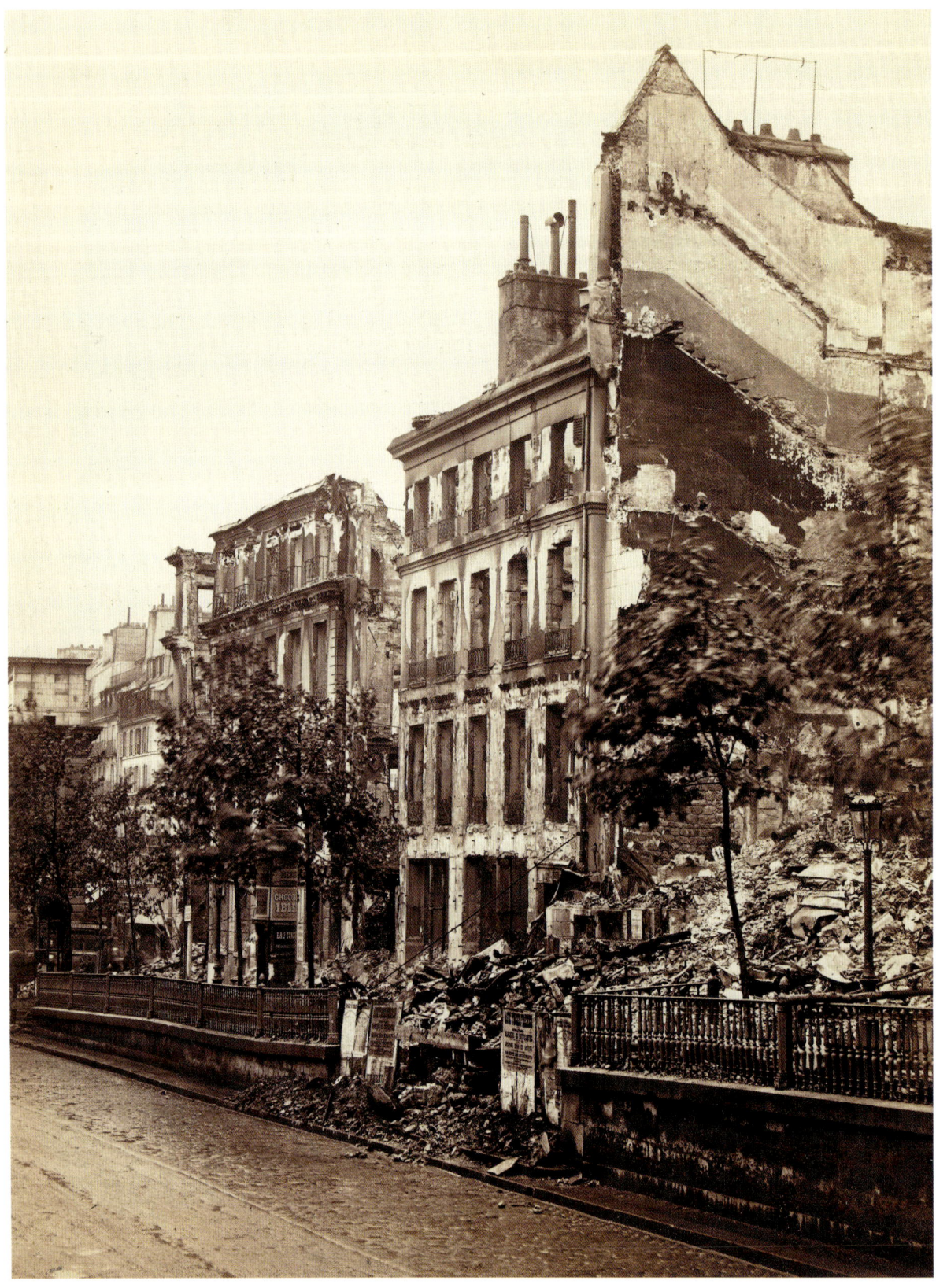

Anonymous, Ruined buildings at rue Royale, Paris, 1871
Albumen print, 25.2 × 19.4 cm, Loan from the Rijksmuseum, Amsterdam

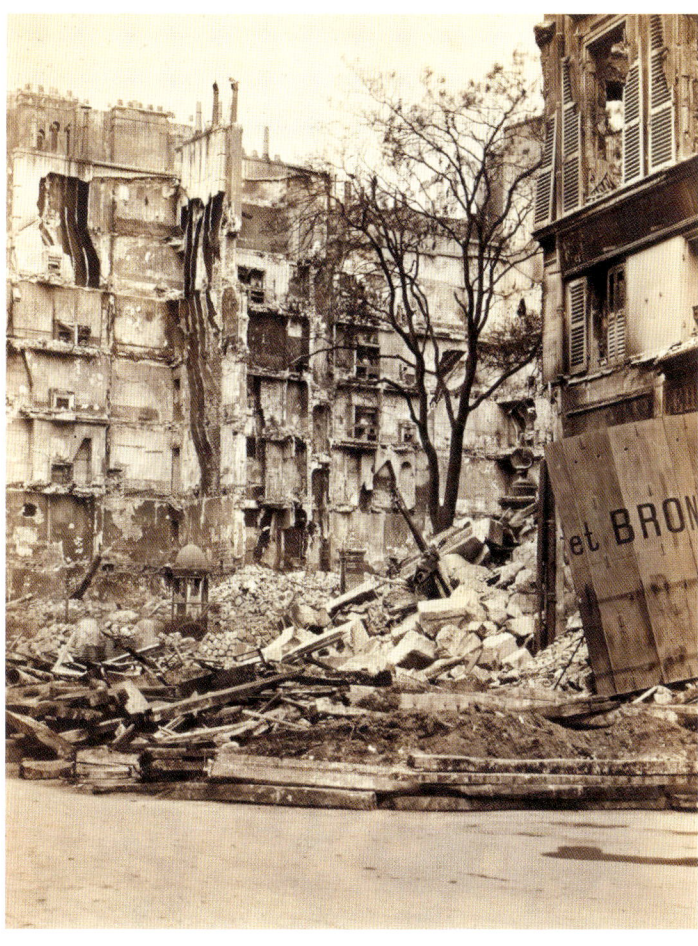

Anonymous, Ruined buildings at rue Royale, Paris, 1871
Albumen print, 25.2 × 19.4 cm, Loan from the Rijksmuseum, Amsterdam

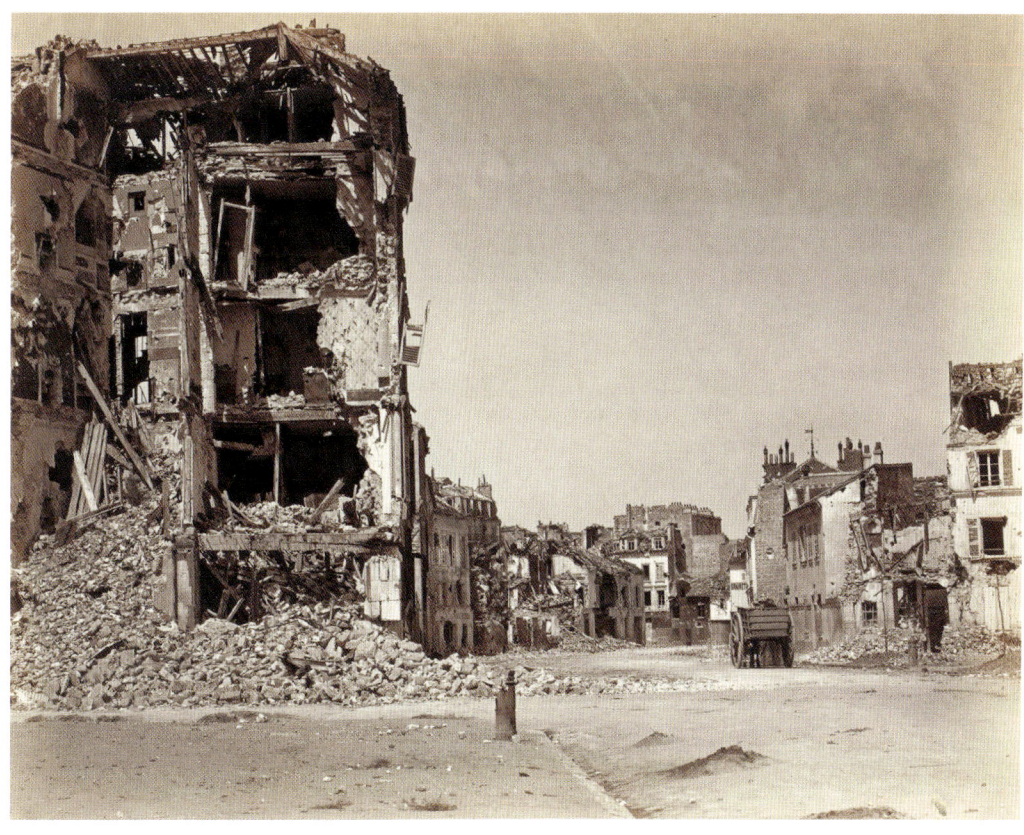

Charles Soulier (1840–1875), View of Avenue du Roule, Neuilly, with ruins of buildings on either side, 1871
Albumen print, 19.6 × 25.4 cm, Loan from the Rijksmuseum, Amsterdam

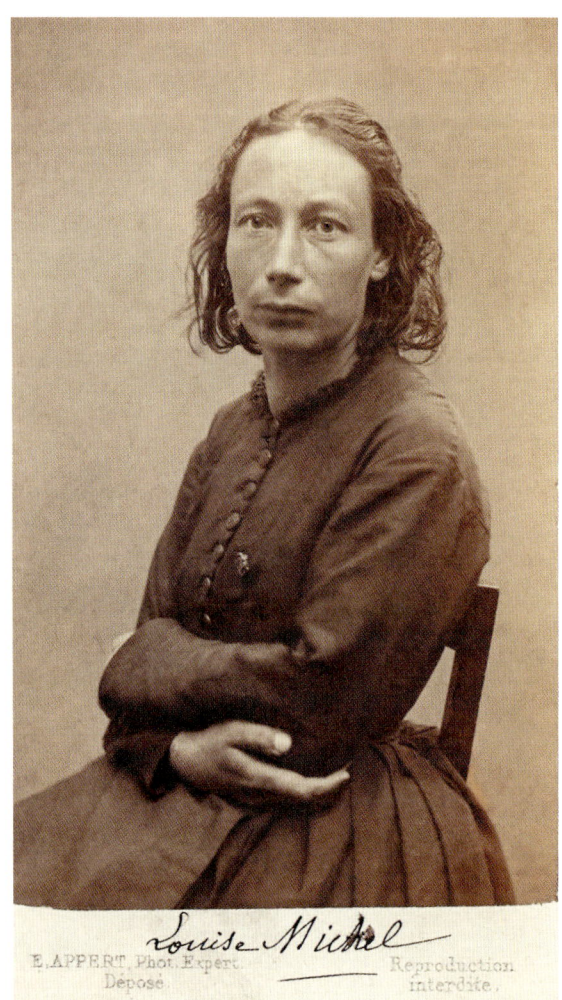

Ernest Charles Appert (1831–1890), Portrait of Louise
Michel in the prison of Versailles, after her arrest, 1871
Albumen print, 9.2 × 5.7 cm, Musée Carnavalet – Histoire de Paris

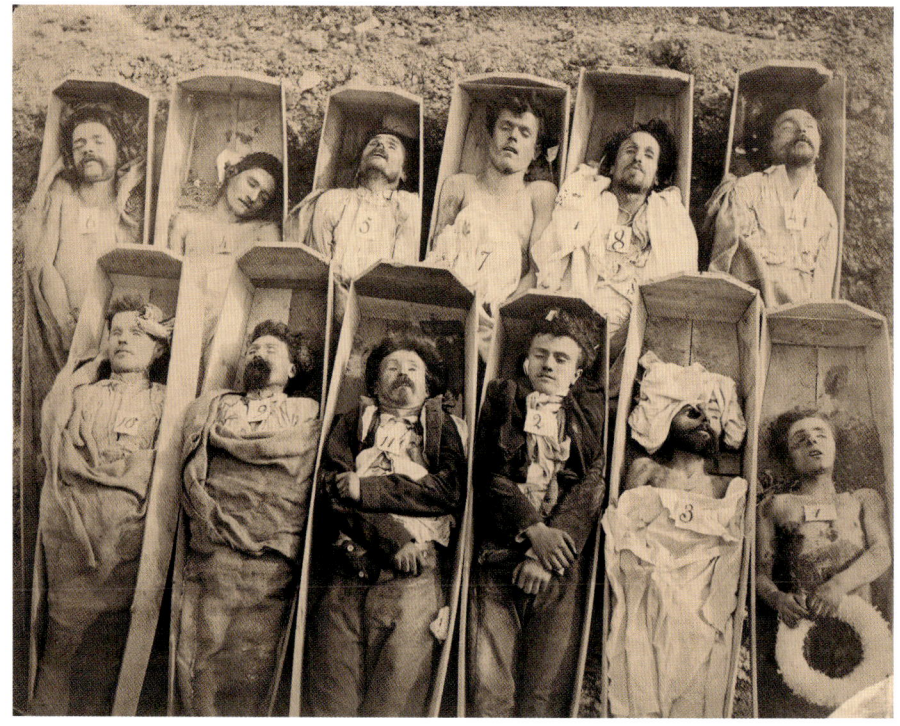

André-Adolphe-Eugène Disdéri (1819–1889), Presentation of twelve
corpses of members of the Commune, arranged in coffins, 1871
Albumen print, 21 × 28.3 cm, Musée Carnavalet – Histoire de Paris

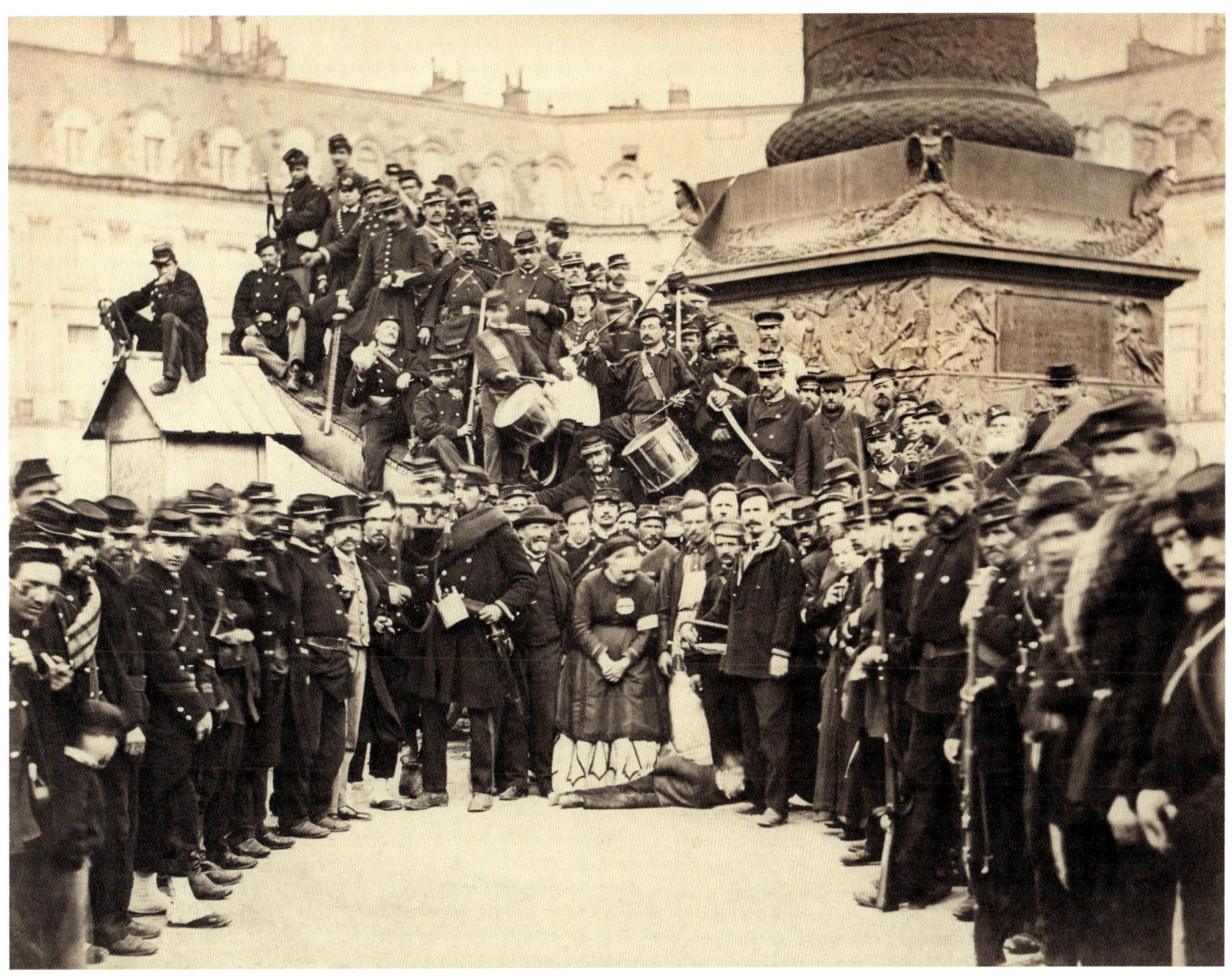

Attributed to Auguste Bruno Braquehais (1923–1875), Communards at the foot of the column at the Place Vendôme, 1871

Albumen print, 16 × 21.2 cm, Musée Carnavalet – Histoire de Paris

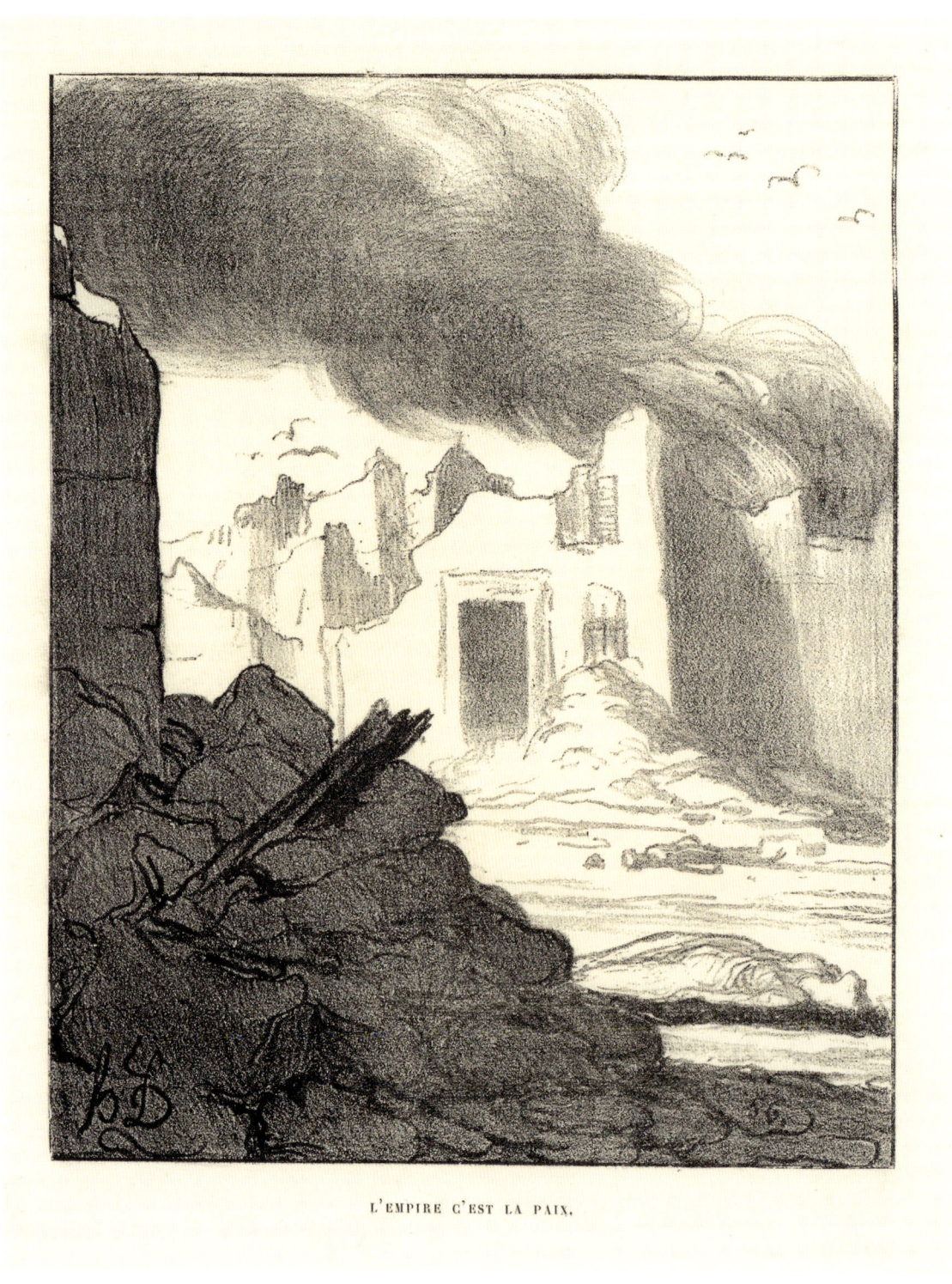

L'EMPIRE C'EST LA PAIX.

Honoré Daumier (1808–1879), From the series *News of the Day*, no. 232: 'The empire is peace', 1870
Lithograph, 32.1 × 24.4 cm, Kunstmuseum Den Haag

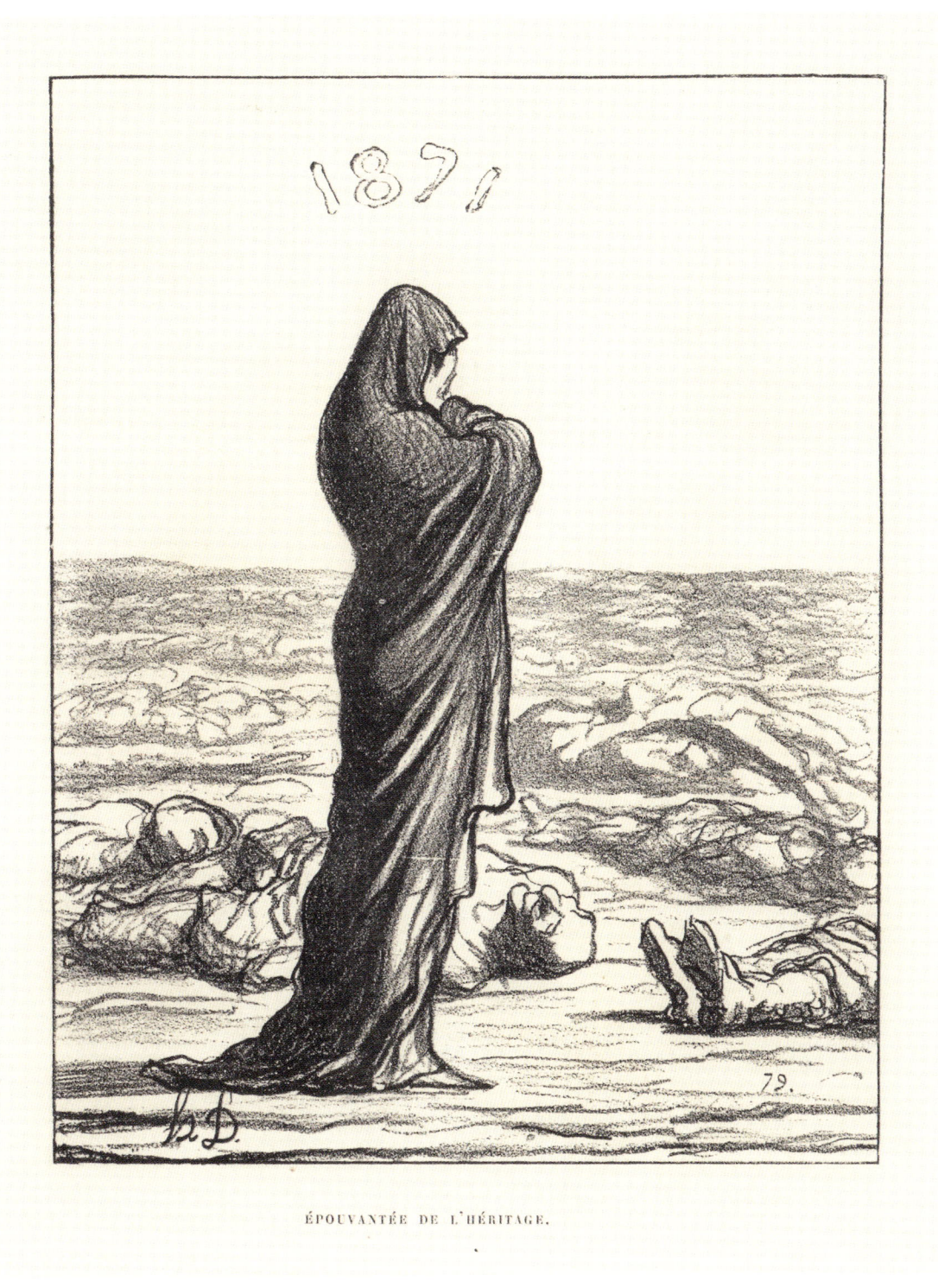

ÉPOUVANTÉE DE L'HÉRITAGE.

Honoré Daumier (1808–1879), From the series *News of the Day*, no. 280: 'Fear of Inheritance', 1871
Lithograph, 31.8 × 24.6 cm, Kunstmuseum Den Haag

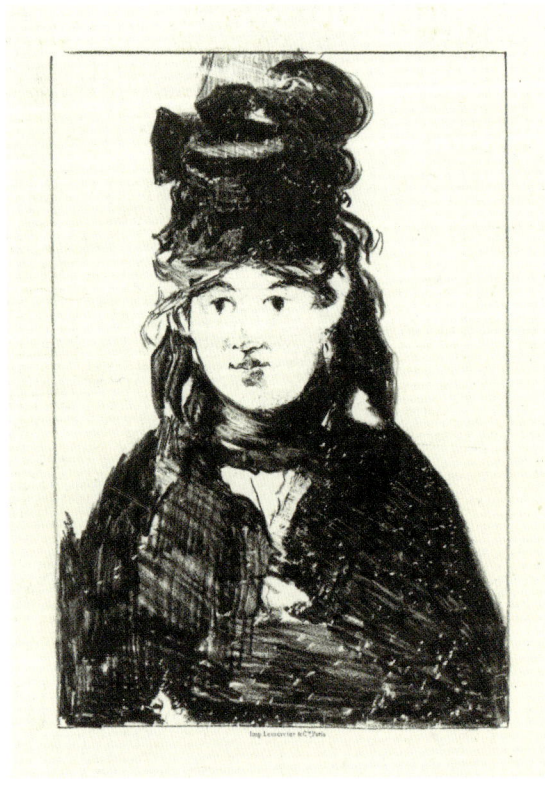

Édouard Manet (1832–1883), *Berthe Morisot in Black*, 1872

Lithograph on paper, 44.9 cm × 30.5 cm, Van Gogh Museum,
Amsterdam (Vincent van Gogh Foundation)

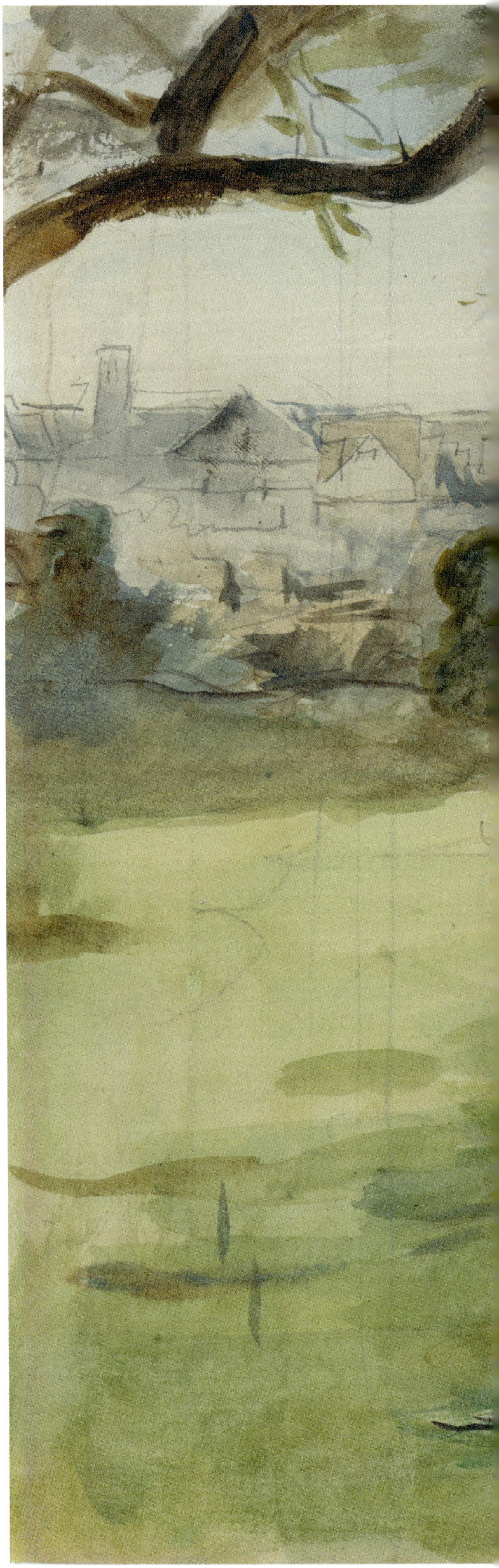

Berthe Morisot (1841–1895), *Woman and Child Sitting in a Meadow*, 1871

Watercolour, 19.5 × 24 cm, Private collection

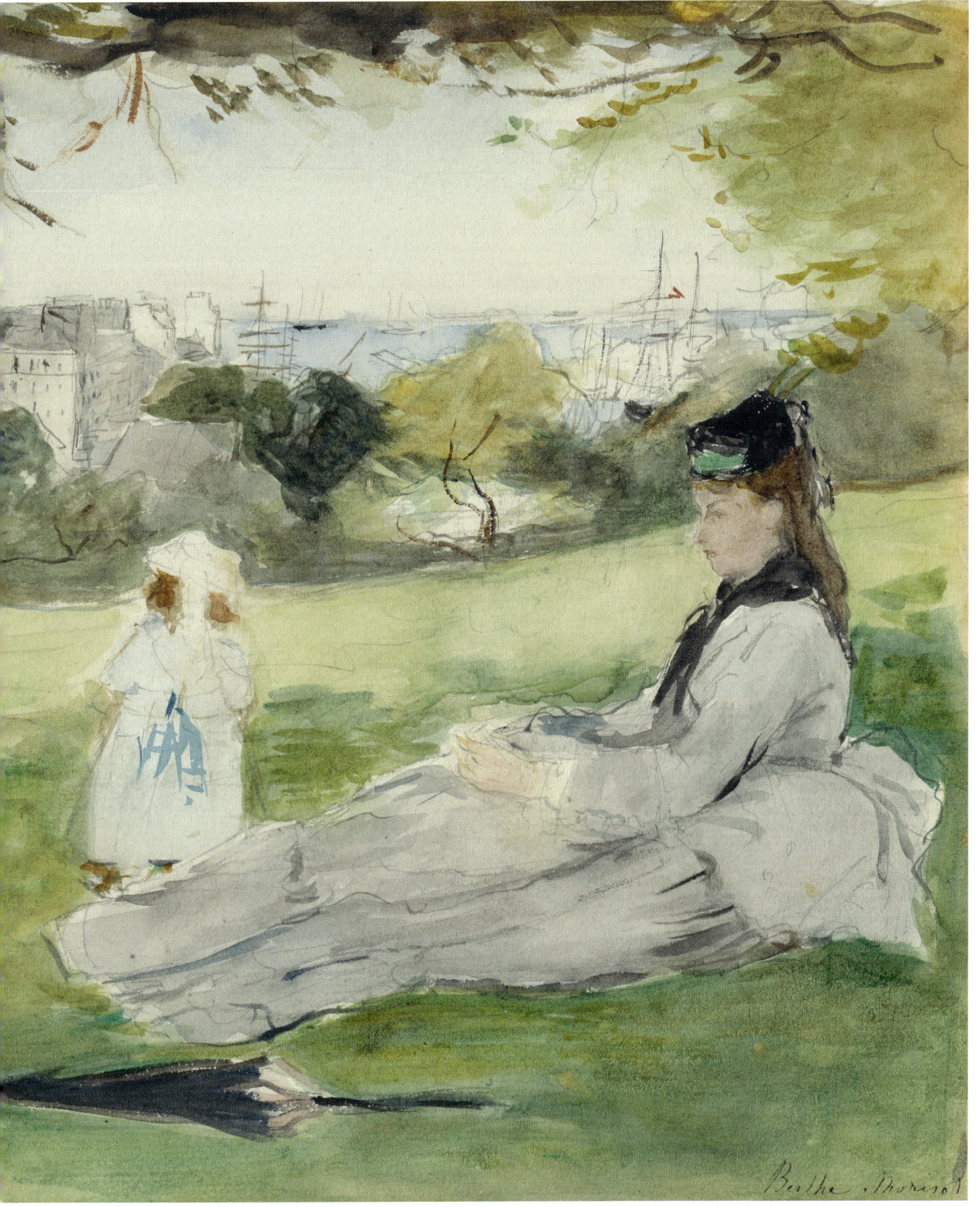

Berthe Morisot

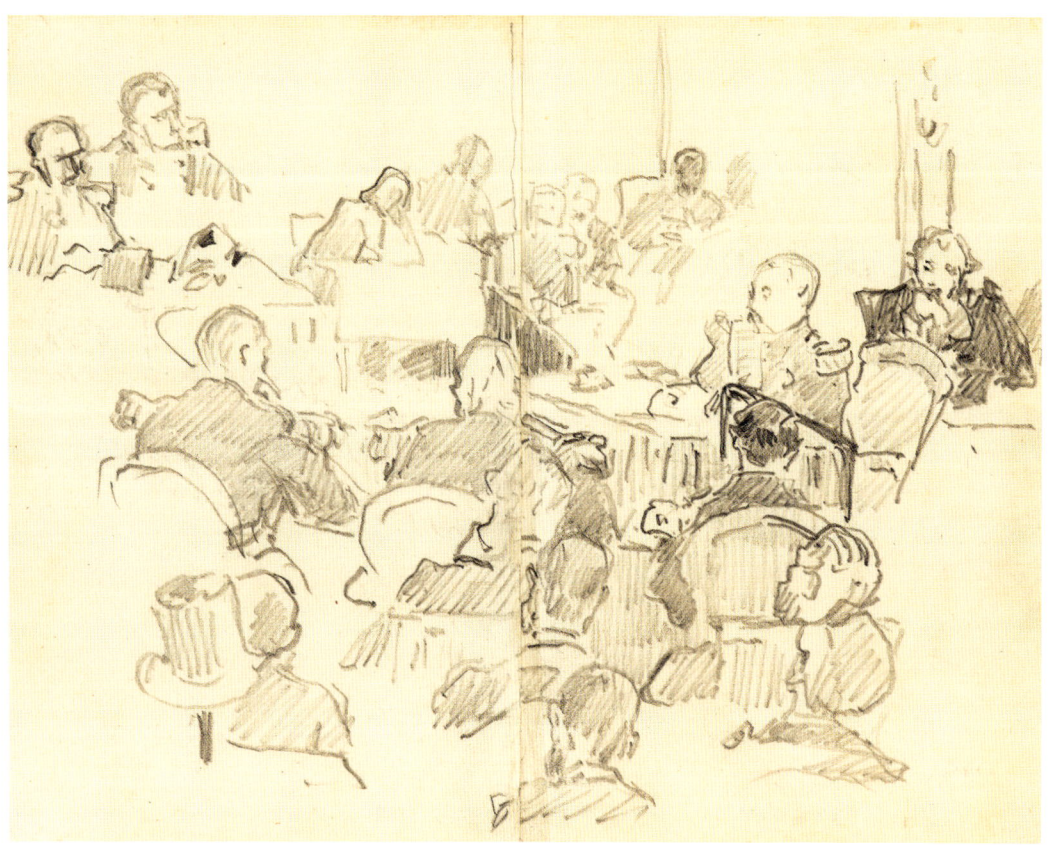

Édouard Manet (1832–1883), *The Court Martial of Bazaine*, 1873

Pencil on paper, 18.5 × 23.8 cm, Collection Museum Boijmans Van Beuningen, Rotterdam.
Loan Foundation Museum Boijmans Van Beuningen, 1940 (former Koenigs Collection)

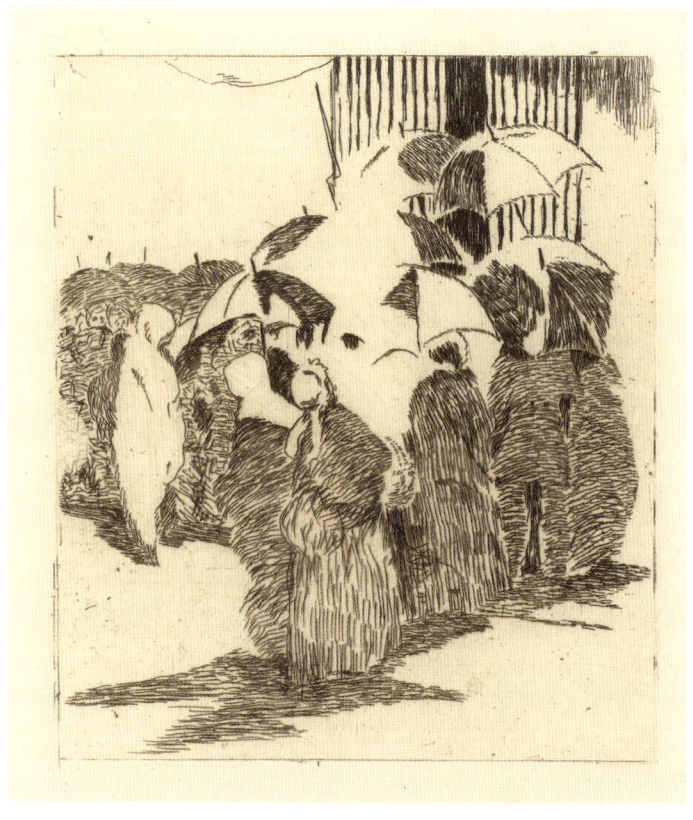

Édouard Manet (1832–1882), *Queue in Front of
the Butcher's Shop*, 1870–71, edition 1905

Etching, 23.5 × 15.9 cm, Rijksmuseum, Amsterdam

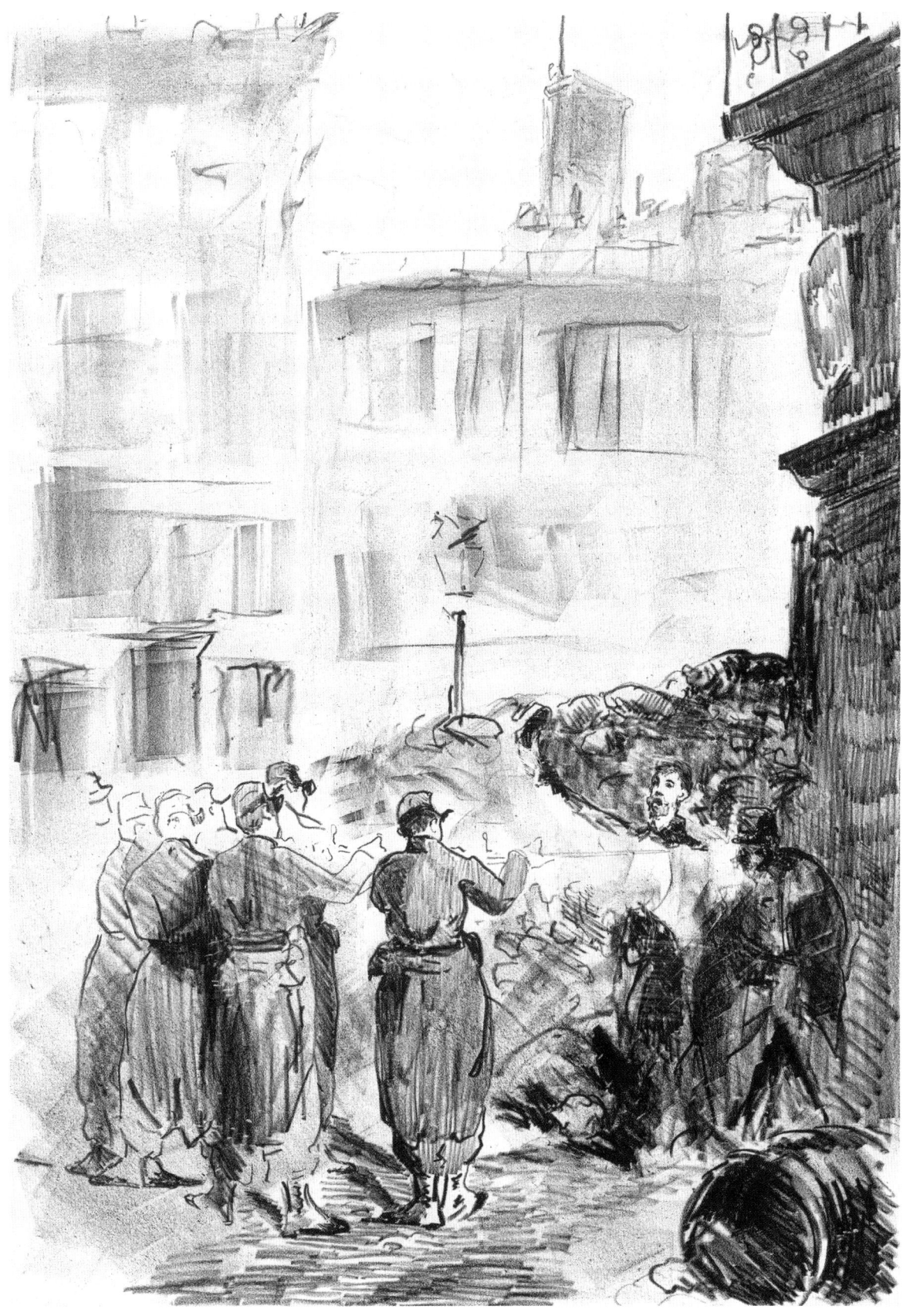

Édouard Manet (1832–1882), *The Barricade (Execution by Firing Squad of Commune Supporters)*, 1871, posthumous edition 1884
Lithograph on paper, 49.2 × 36.8 cm, Loan from the Rijksmuseum, Amsterdam

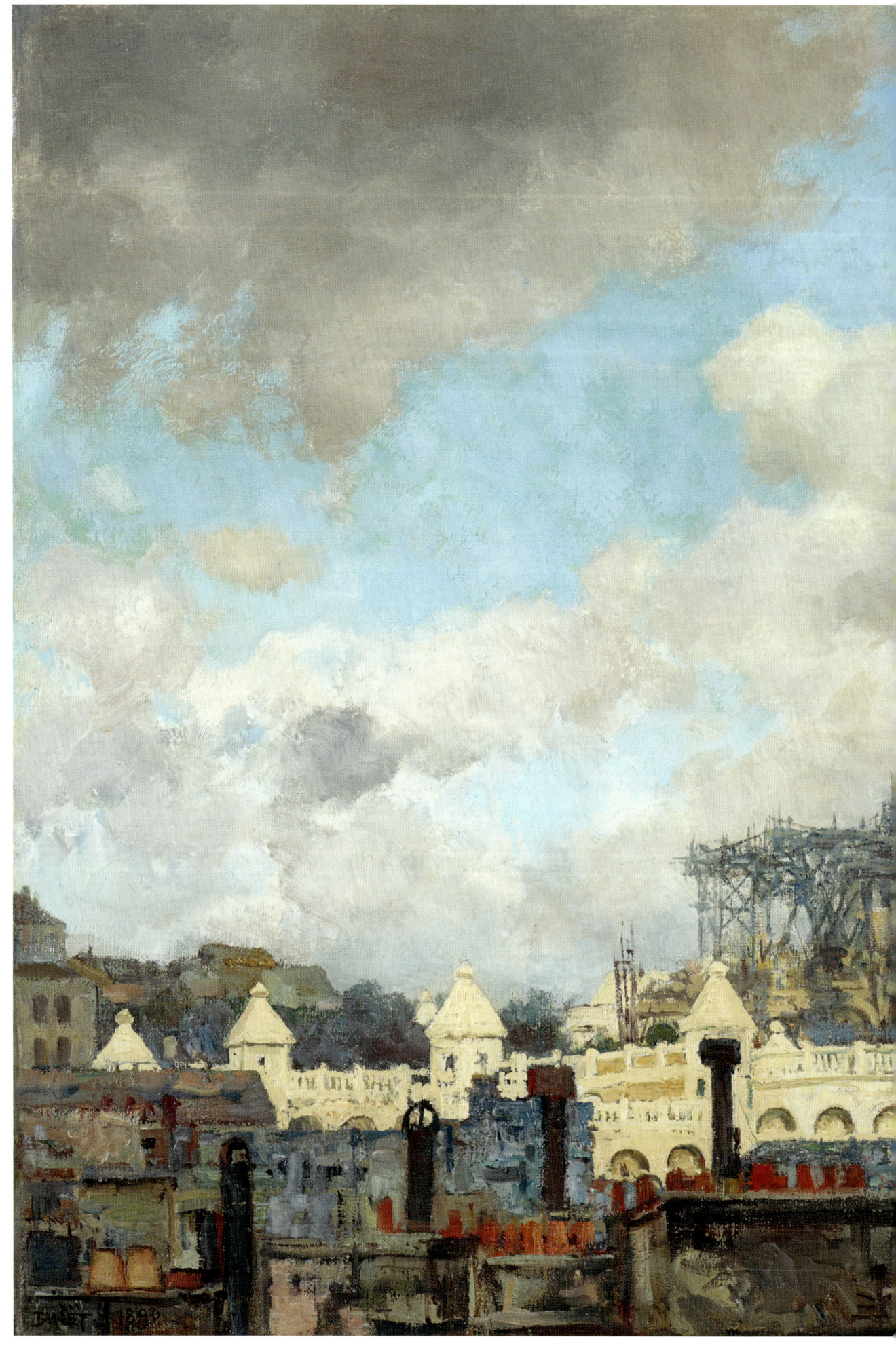

Arthur Briët (1867–1939), *The Sacré Coeur in Montmartre under Construction*, 1890   Oil on canvas, 40 × 65 cm, Kunstmuseum Den Haag

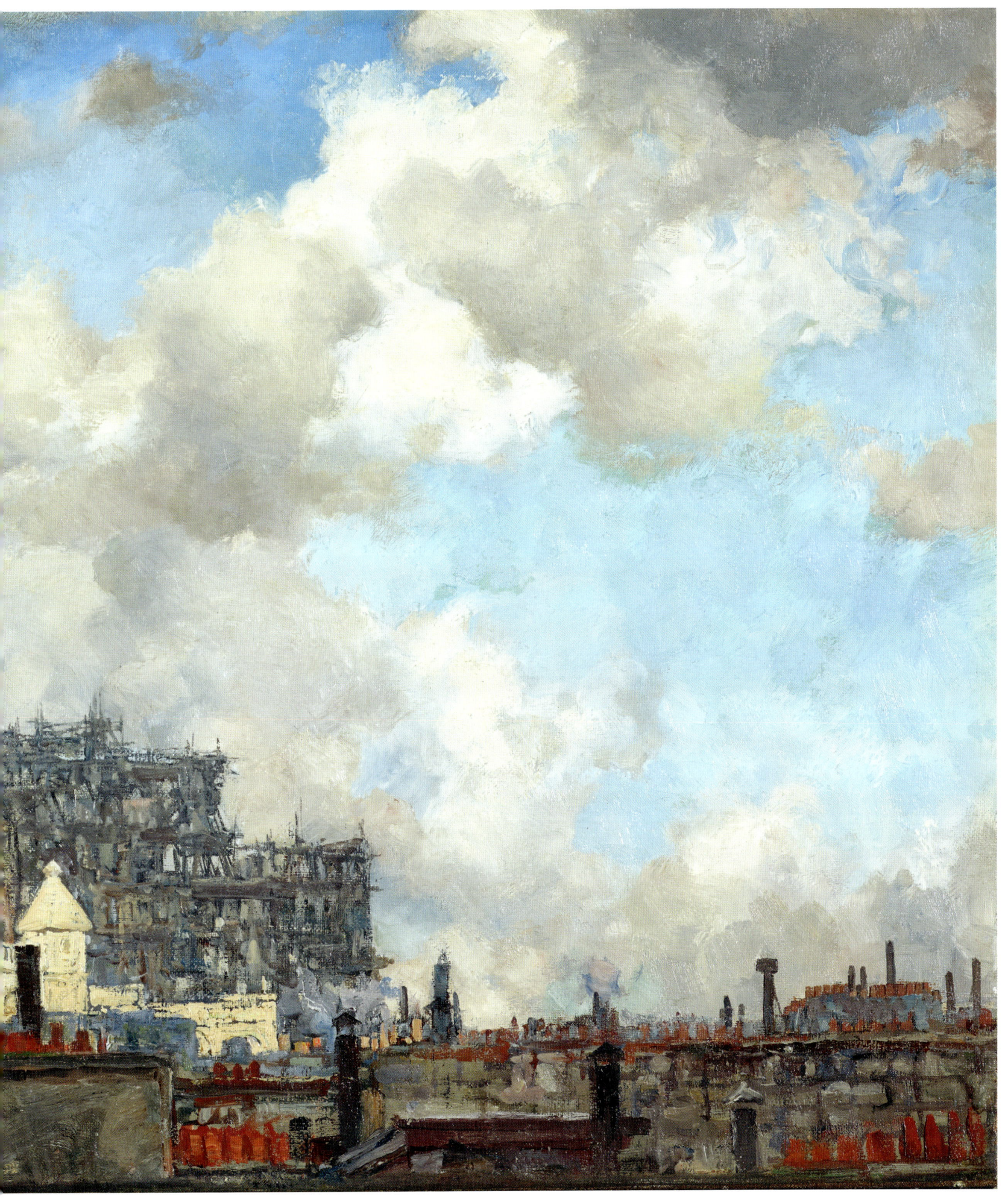

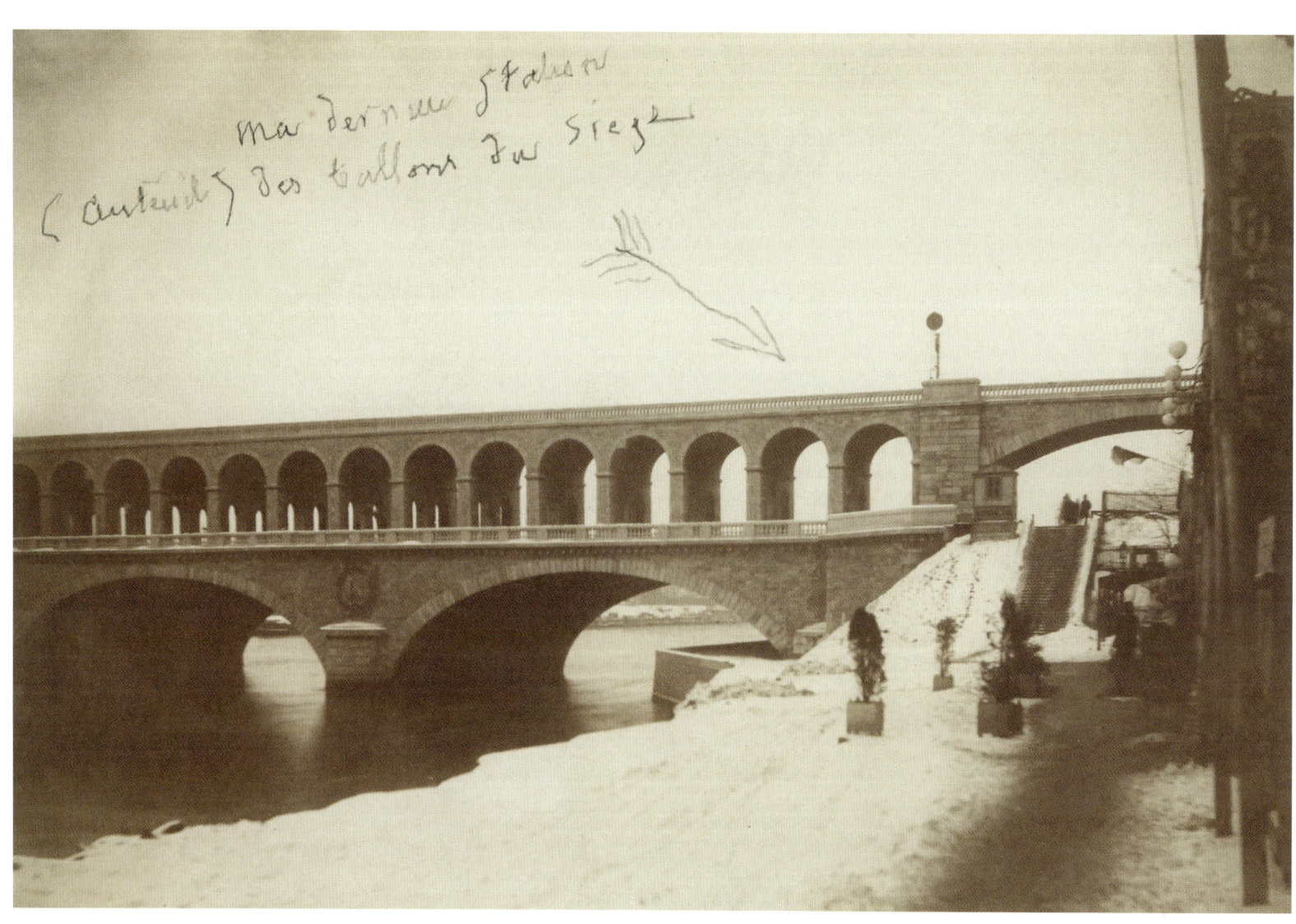

Nadar (1820–1910), 'The last station (Auteuil) of the Paris siege balloons', 1870

Photo (unknown technique), 17.8 × 25.4 cm, Bibliothèque nationale de France

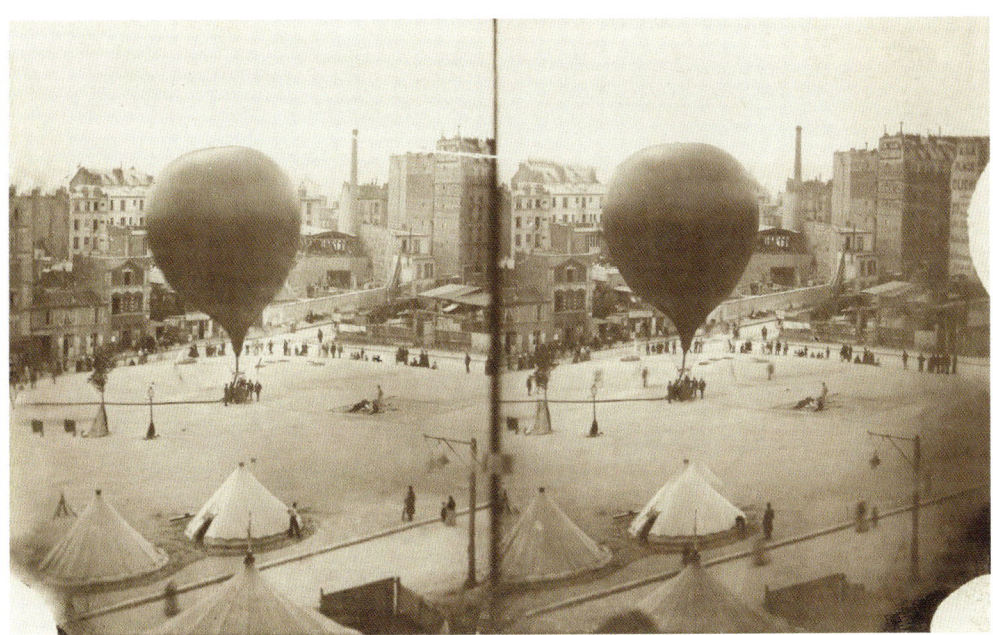

Nadar (1820–1910), Place St Pierre in Montmartre during the siege of Paris in 1870
(with observation balloon 'Le Neptune'). Military aeronautical observations by Nadar, 1870
Stereophoto, 10.9 × 17.7 cm, Bibliothèque nationale de France

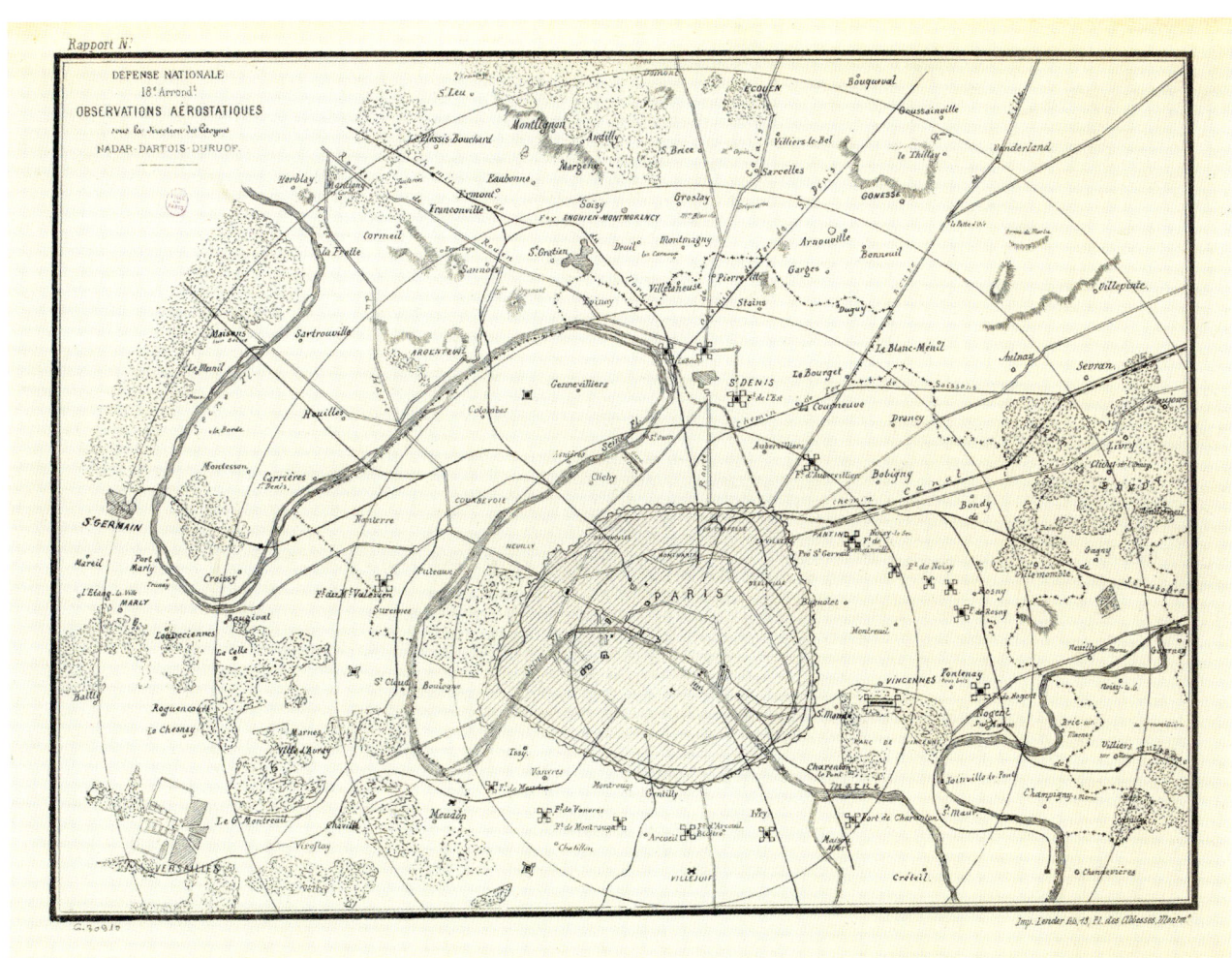

Nadar (1820–1910), National Defense, 18th District, Aerostatic Observations under the direction of Citizens Nadar-Dartois-Duruof, c. 1870
Lithograph, 31.9 × 45.1 cm, Musée Carnavalet – Histoire de Paris

Claude Monet (1840–1926), *La Rue Montorgueil, in Paris. Celebration of 30 June 1878*, 1878

Oil on canvas, 81 × 50 cm, Musée d'Orsay, Paris. Accepted by the State as a donation in payment of inheritance taxes for the Musées nationaux in 1982

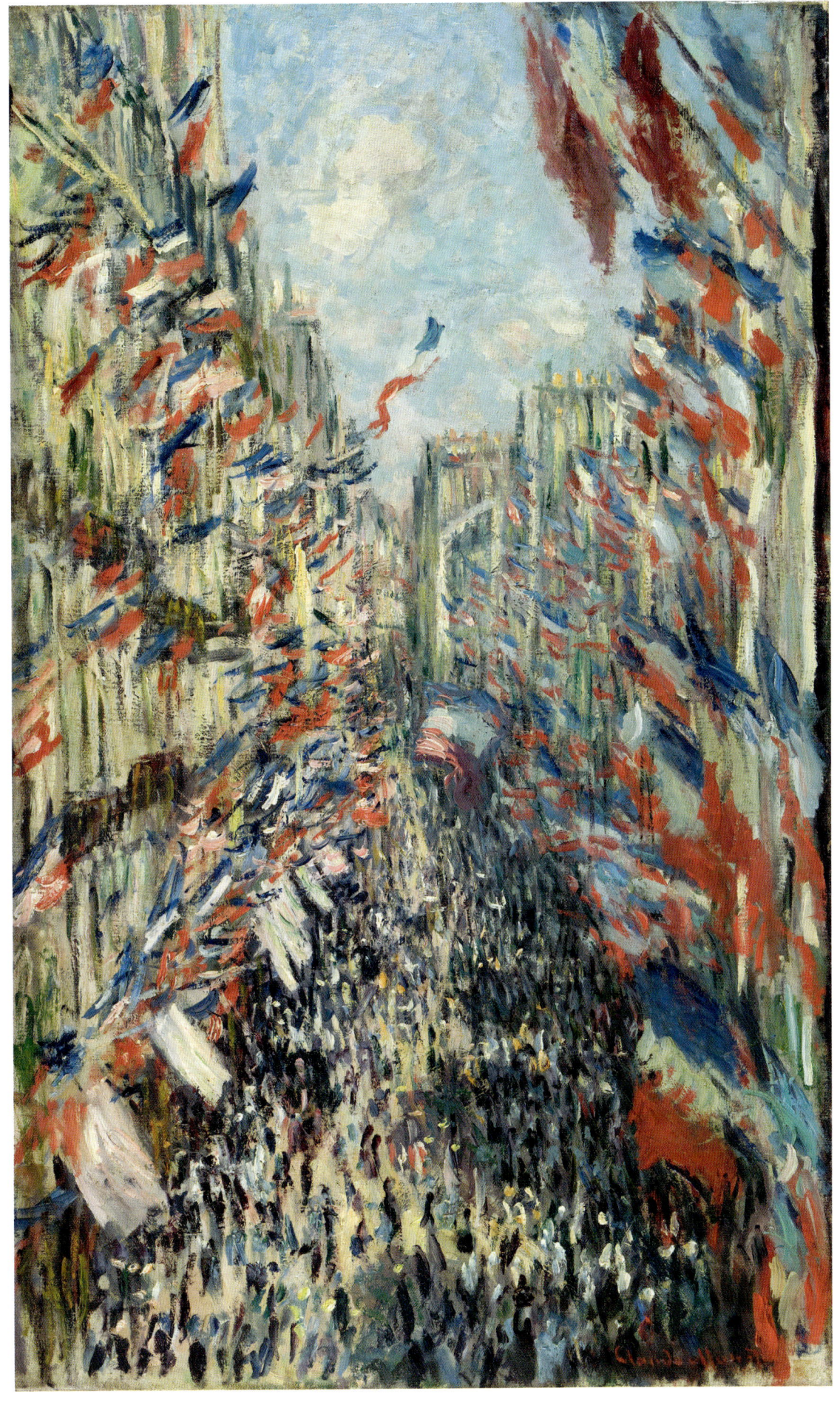

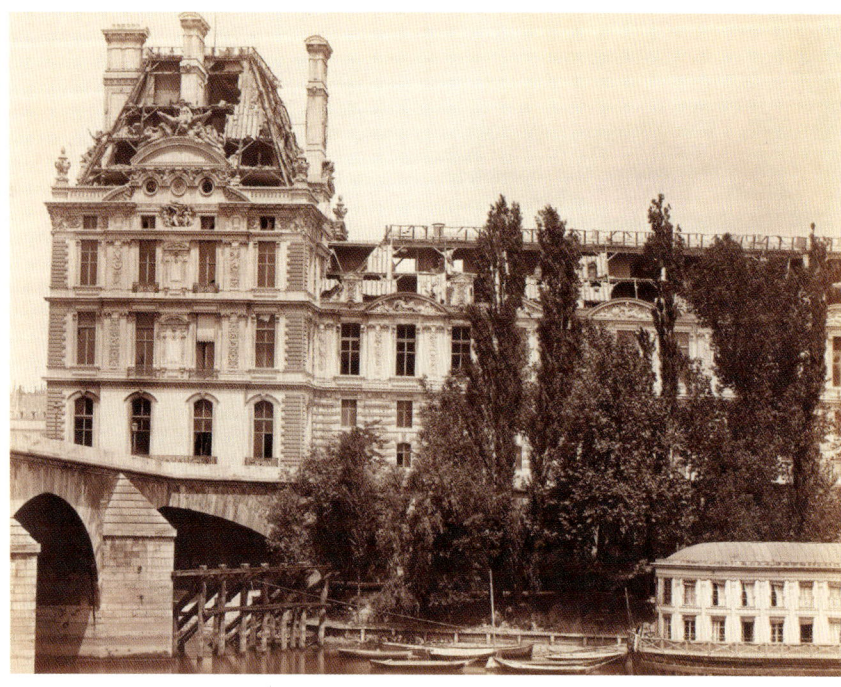

Charles Soulier (1840–1875), Damage to the Louvre, Pavillon de Flore,
at the time of the Commune, with the Seine in the foreground, 1871

Albumen print, 19.6 × 36.9 cm, Loan from the Rijksmuseum, Amsterdam

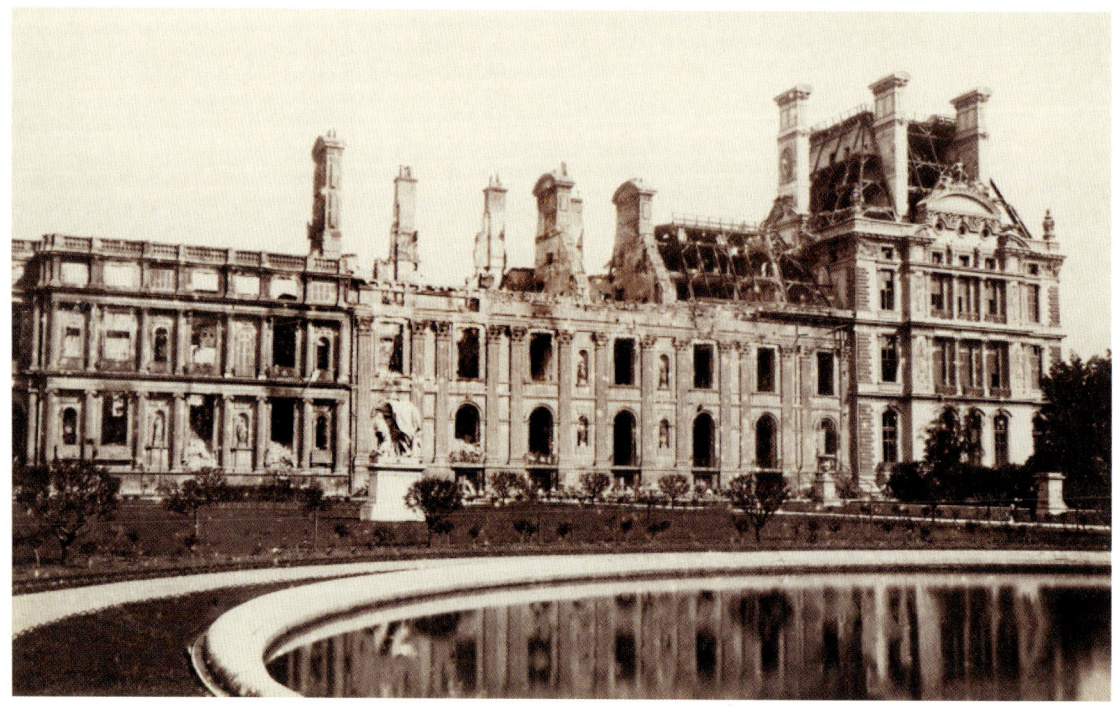

Anonymous, Paris after the Commune. The Tuileries Palace, 1871

Cabinet card, 11 × 16.5 cm, Kunstmuseum Den Haag

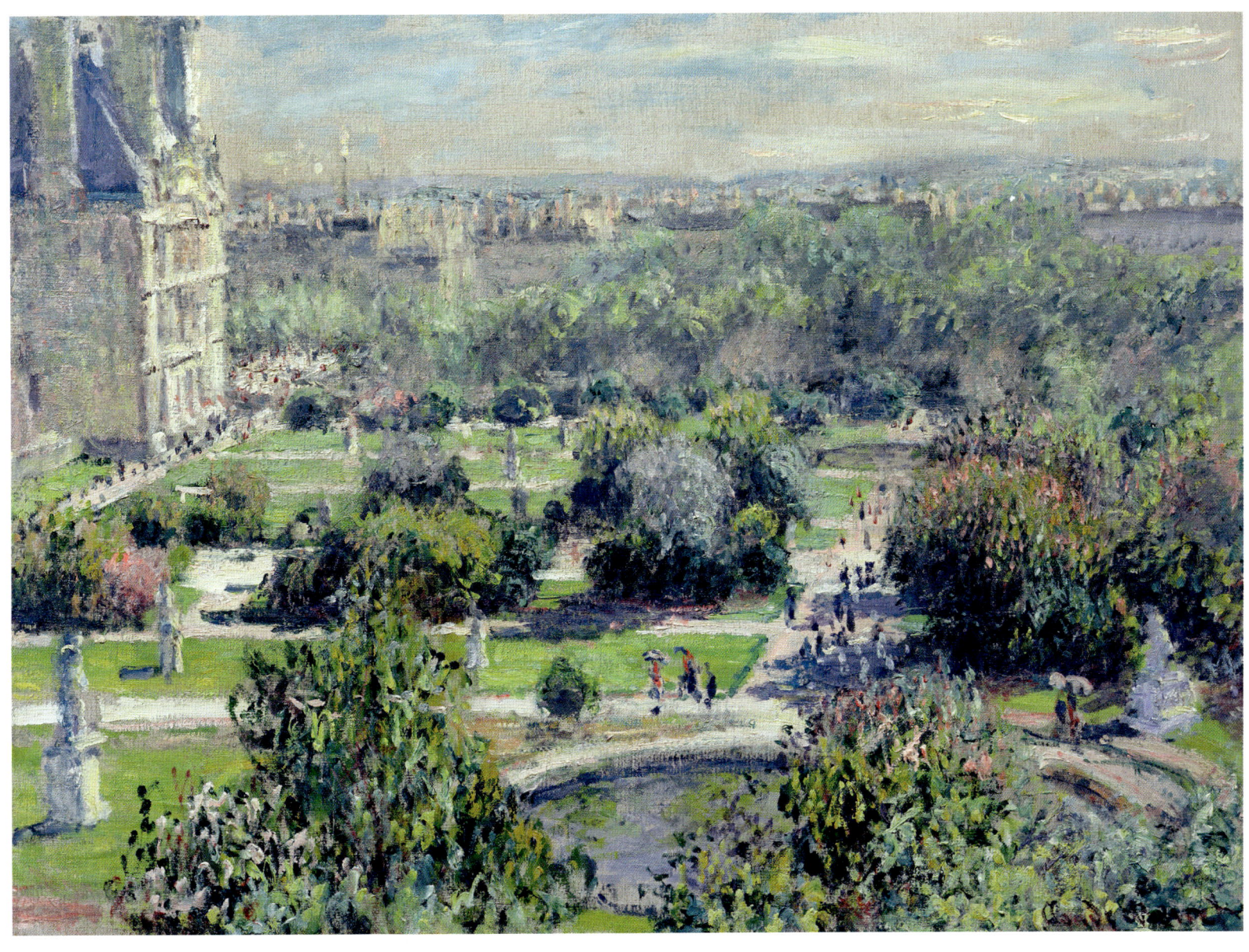

Claude Monet (1840–1926), *The Tuileries*, 1876
Oil on canvas, 54 × 73 cm, Musée Marmottan Monet, Paris, Gift of Eugène and Victorine Donop de Monchy, 1940

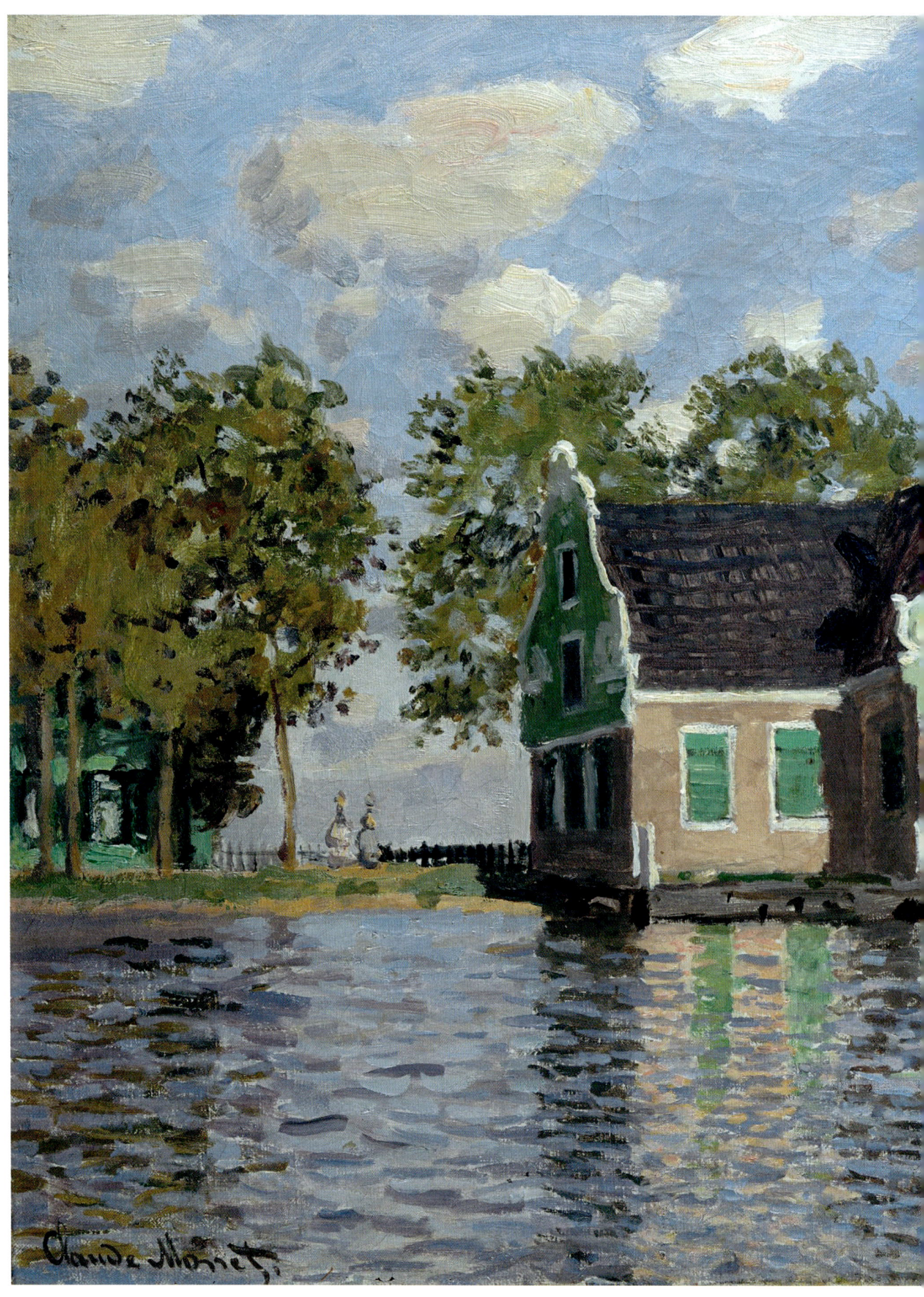

Claude Monet (1840–1926), *Houses by the Bank of the River Zaan*, 1871–72   Oil on canvas, 47.7 × 73.7 cm, Städel Museum, Frankfurt am Main

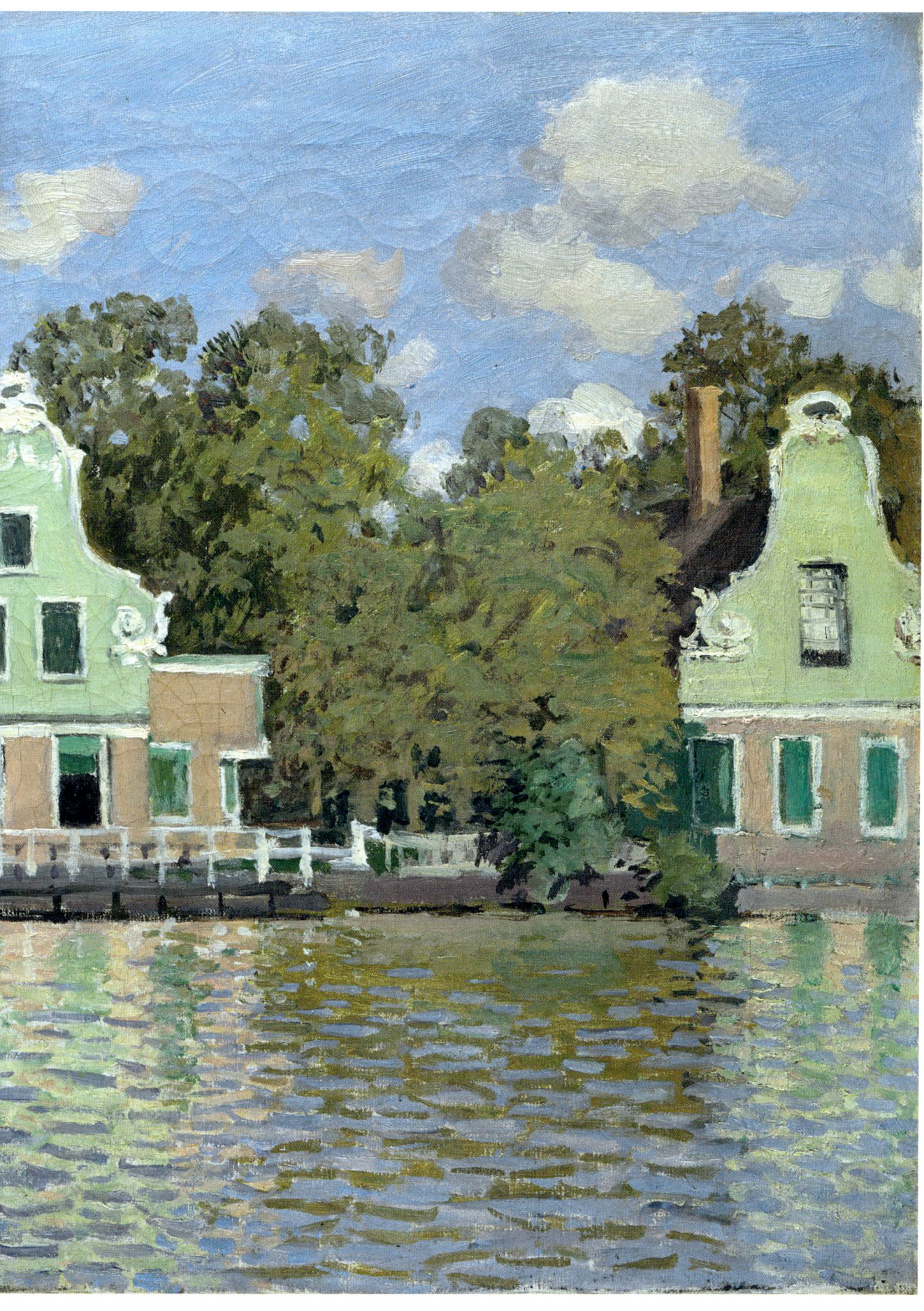

AUGUSTE RENOIR (1841–1919)

Pont Neuf, 1872

Pont Neuf by Auguste Renoir is a celebration of the modern metropolis viewed through an impressionist lens. While the image itself is static, the buzz of activity is palpable. Carriages and omnibuses traverse the scene while pedestrians move briskly around and across the canvas. Above, a clear blue sky dotted with fluffy white clouds suggests a perfect spring day. It is a joyous, almost utopian vision of daily life, rendered in the swift, energetic strokes of the artist's brush and a cheery palette of blues and yellows.

The choice of the Pont Neuf as a locus of modern life was astute. As the oldest extant bridge in Paris – it was completed in the early seventeenth century during the reign of Henri IV– and one of the city's most recognisable landmarks, the Pont Neuf is steeped in history. However, like so much of the city, it had been transformed in the 1850s under the direction of Georges-Eugène Haussmann. Old shops that once occupied the bridge were removed, the pavement was extended, and gas lights were installed. The result was a beautiful, modern thoroughfare capable of accommodating thousands of vehicles a day.[1]

Renoir depicts the bridge from Right Bank of the Seine facing south across the river towards the Île de la Cité. In the background, buildings stretch along the Quai des Augustins and the Quai de Conti. The bronze equestrian sculpture of Henri IV is clearly visible on the right-hand side of the composition.

Edmond Renoir, the artist's younger brother, later recalled how Renoir installed himself in a café on the corner of the Quai du Louvre, spending hours there sketching the scene before him.

> Auguste... took pleasure, after having outlined the ground, the parapets, the houses in the distance, the place Dauphine and the statue of Henri IV, in sketching the passers-by, vehicles and groups. Meanwhile, I scribbled, except when he asked me to go to the bridge and speak with passers-by to make them stop for a minute.[2]

It is clear from Edmond's account that Renoir was enthralled by the human spectacle. The artist populated his painting with an array of people and took great

delight in capturing the various types, from fashionably dressed ladies with bustles (gowns with a raised and accentuated skirt) and parasols to workers carrying baskets or pushing carts to soldiers in uniform. One can almost imagine Edmond himself as one – or all – of the elegant *flâneurs* with a straw hat and cane.

Perhaps the most alluring detail of all is the French flag standing proudly in the lower right corner. Painted in the aftermath of the Franco-Prussian War and the subsequent civil upheaval that had devastated the country in 1870 and 1871, Renoir's cityscape is aglow with optimism, the flag's presence a reminder of France's resilience and strength.

[KIMBERLY A. JONES]

1   See Colin B. Bailey, 'The greatest luminosity, colour and harmony', in Colin B. Bailey et al., *Renoir Landscapes 1865–1883*, exh. cat. London, Ottawa & Philadelphia (The National Gallery, The National Gallery of Canada & Philadelphia Museum of Art), 2007, p. 112.
2   John Rewald, 'Auguste Renoir and his Brother', *Gazette des Beaux-Arts*, XXXVI, 3 (1945), p. 181.

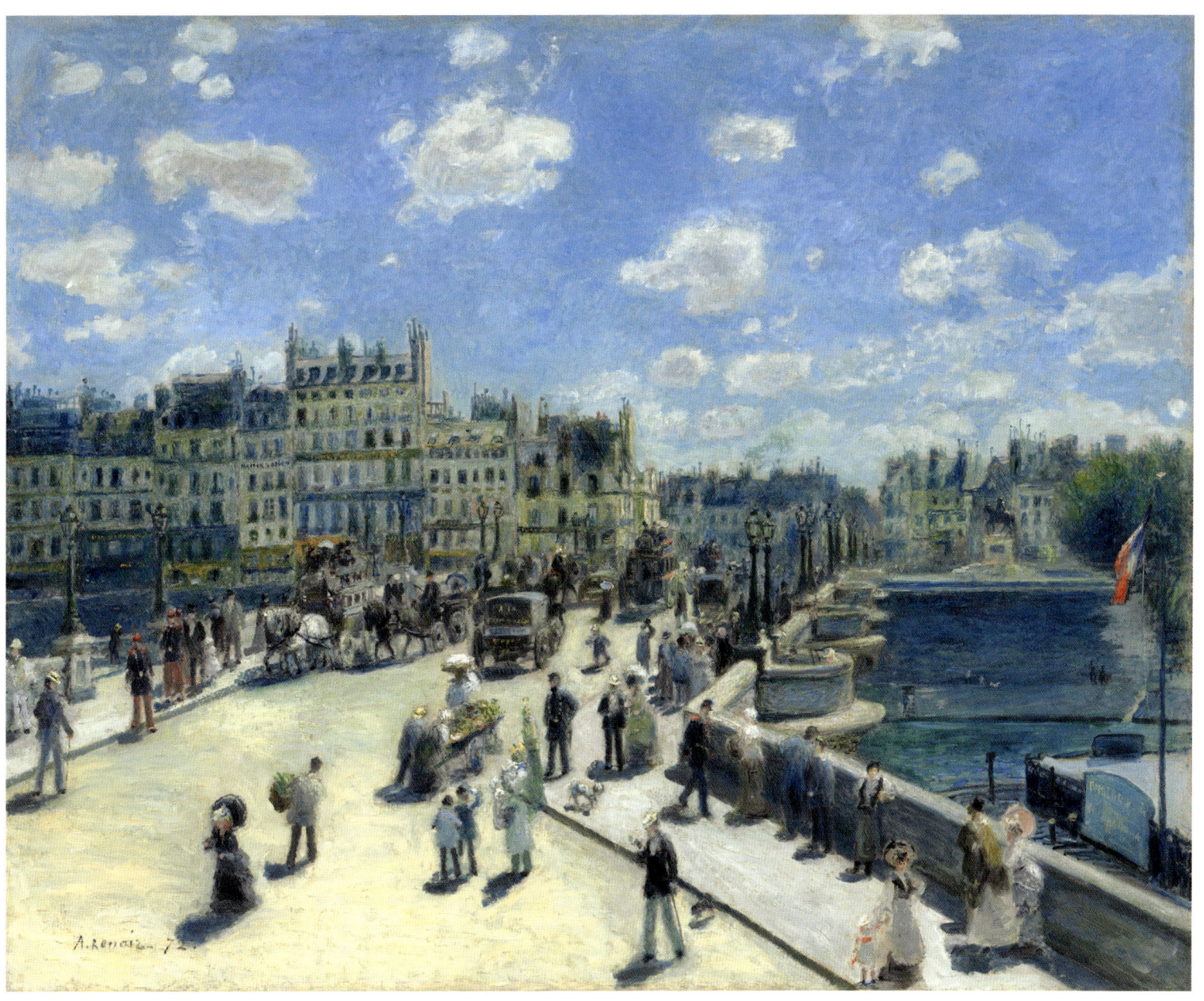

Auguste Renoir (1841–1919), *Pont Neuf*, 1872

Oil on canvas, 75.3 × 93.7 cm, National Gallery of Art, Washington, Ailsa Mellon Bruce Collection

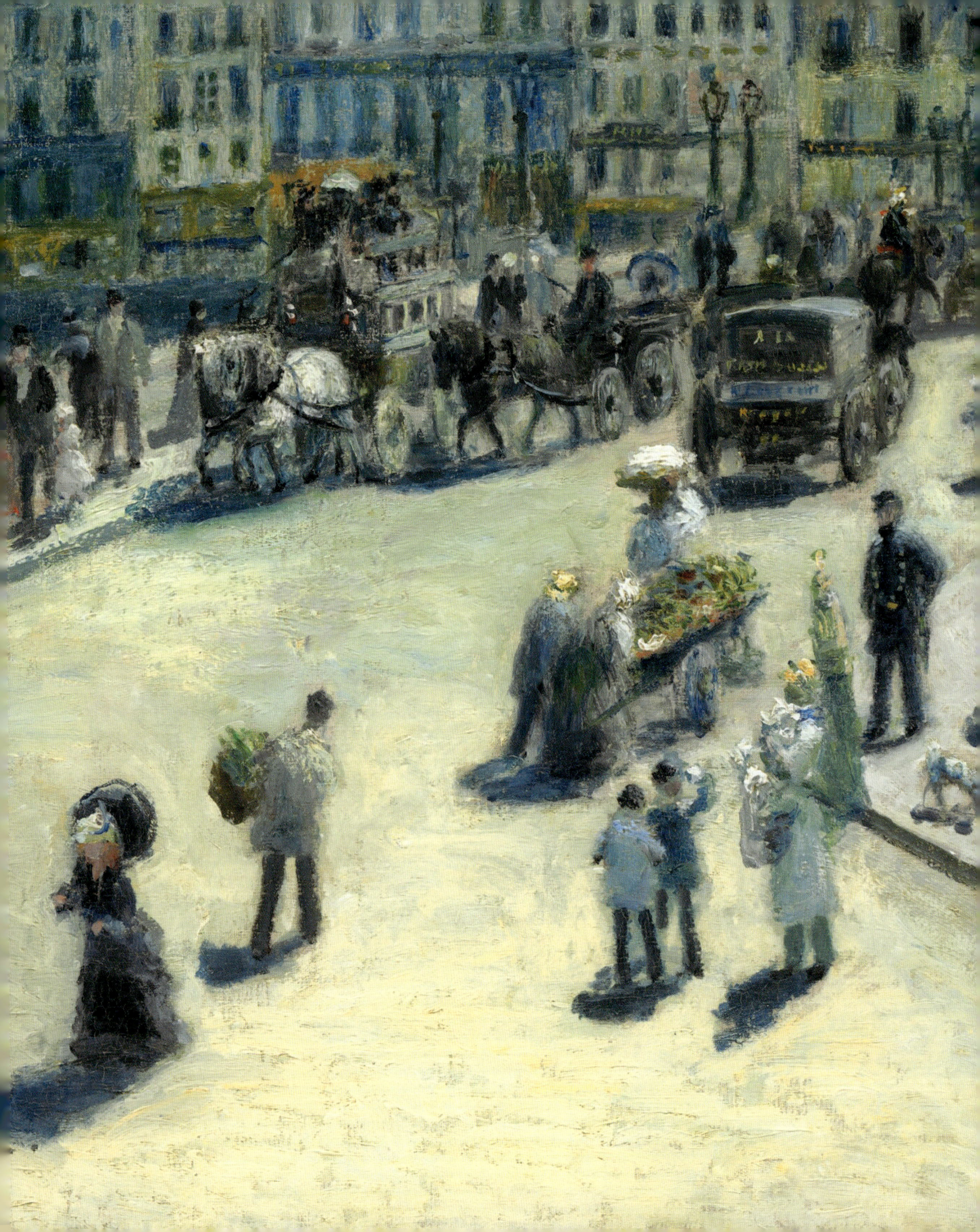

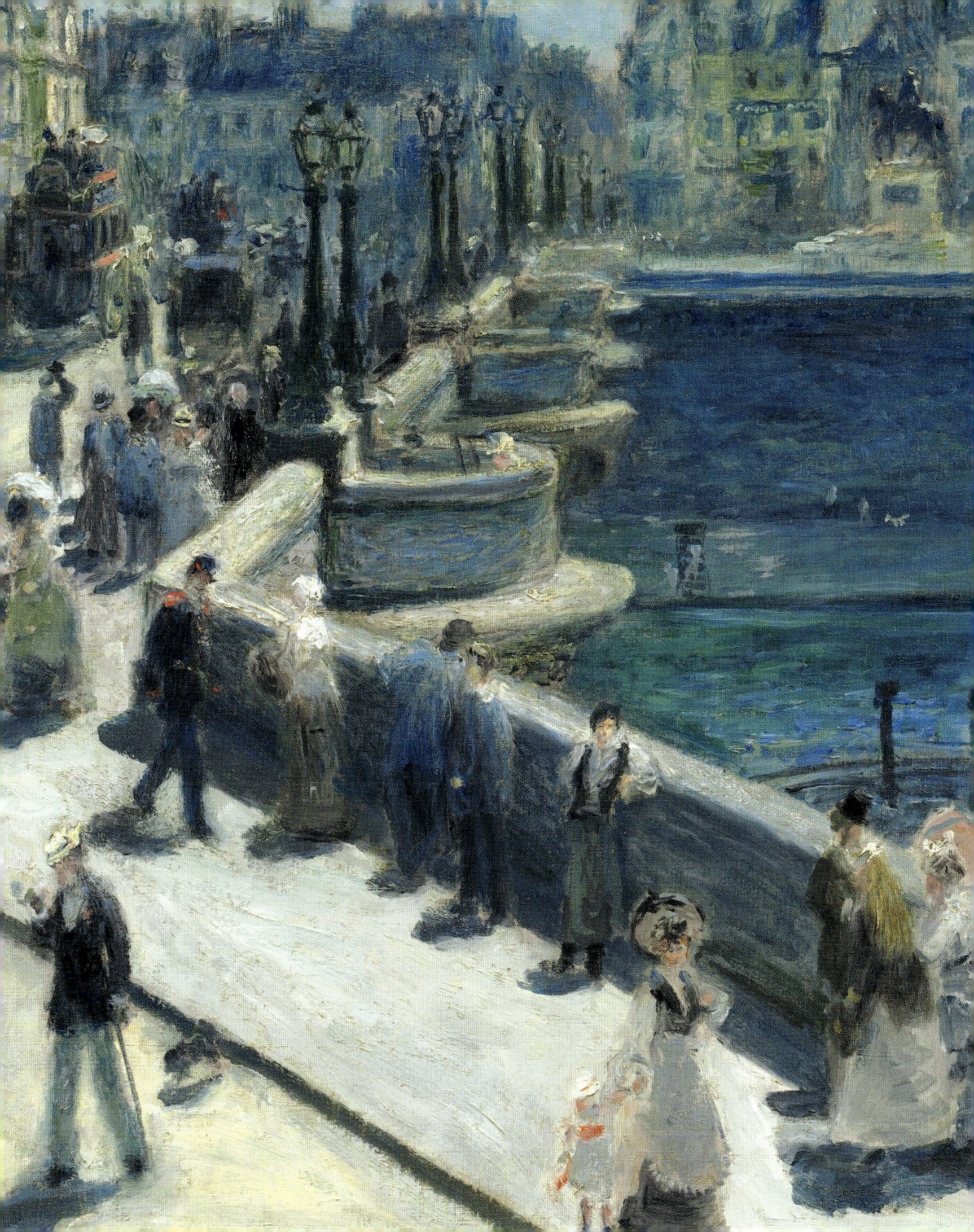

WITH THANKS TO

The exhibition has been supported by the Dutch government: an indemnity grant has been provided by the Cultural Heritage Agency of the Netherlands on behalf of the Minister of Education, Culture and Science.

Kunstmuseum Den Haag is grateful to the following lenders:
Allen Memorial Art Museum, Oberlin College, Oberlin
Amsterdam City Archives, Amsterdam
Archives nationales, Paris
Bibliothèque nationale de France, Paris
FAMM Museum, Mougins, The Levett Collection
Fondation Beyeler, Riehen (Basel)
Hamburger Kunsthalle, Hamburg
International Institute of Social History, Amsterdam
JK ART Foundation, 's-Hertogenbosch
Kröller-Müller Museum, Otterlo
Kunst Museum Winterthur, Winterthur
The Metropolitan Museum of Art, New York
Musée Carnavalet – Histoire de Paris, Paris
Musée Fabre, Montpellier
Musée Marmottan Monet, Paris
Musée d'Orsay, Paris
Museum Barberini, Potsdam
Museum Boijmans Van Beuningen, Rotterdam
Museum of Fine Arts, Reims
Museum Folkwang, Essen
National Gallery of Art, Washington, DC
Petit Palais, Musée des Beaux-Arts de la Ville de Paris, Paris
Rijksmuseum, Amsterdam
Royal Museum of Fine Arts in Antwerp, Antwerp
Staatliche Museen zu Berlin, Alte Nationalgalerie, Berlin
Staatsbibliothek zu Berlin, Berlin
Staatsgalerie Stuttgart, Stuttgart
Städel Museum, Frankfurt am Main
Szépművészeti Múzeum (Museum of Fine Arts), Budapest
Van Gogh Museum (Vincent van Gogh Foundation), Amsterdam

and all lenders who wish to remain anonymous.

The exhibition and book have been
realised with the financial support of:
het Cultuurfonds
Turing Foundation
Stichting Zabawas
Gravin van Bylandt Stichting

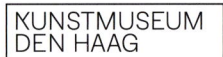
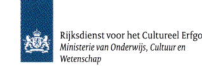
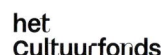
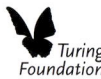
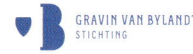
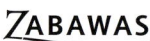

COLOPHON

This book is published on the occasion of the exhibition *New Paris: From Monet to Morisot* in Kunstmuseum Den Haag, from 15 February until 9 June 2025.

The exhibition was created in collaboration with the Alte Nationalgalerie in Berlin and the Allen Memorial Art Museum, Oberlin College, in Ohio.

Compilation and editing
Frouke van Dijke

Authors
Frouke van Dijke
Alexander Eiling
Judit Geskó
Kimberly A. Jones
Daniel Koep
Vera Merks
Paul Perrin
Michael Philipp
Joke de Wolf

Editing
Cath Phillips

Translation
Gerard Forde (from the Dutch)
Steve Kane (from the Hungarian)

Lithography
Séverine Lacante

Project management
Stephanie Van den bosch

Graphic design
Tim Bisschop

Printing & binding
Printer Trento, Italy

Publisher
Gautier Platteau

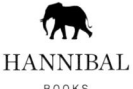

HANNIBAL
BOOKS

ISBN 978 94 6494 140 1
D/2025/11922/02
NUR 654

© Hannibal Books and
Kunstmuseum Den Haag, 2025
www.hannibalbooks.be
www.kunstmuseum.nl

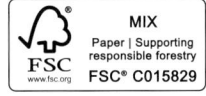

MIX
Paper | Supporting
responsible forestry
FSC® C015829

Cover: Claude Monet (1840–1926), *Quai du Louvre*, 1867, Kunstmuseum Den Haag

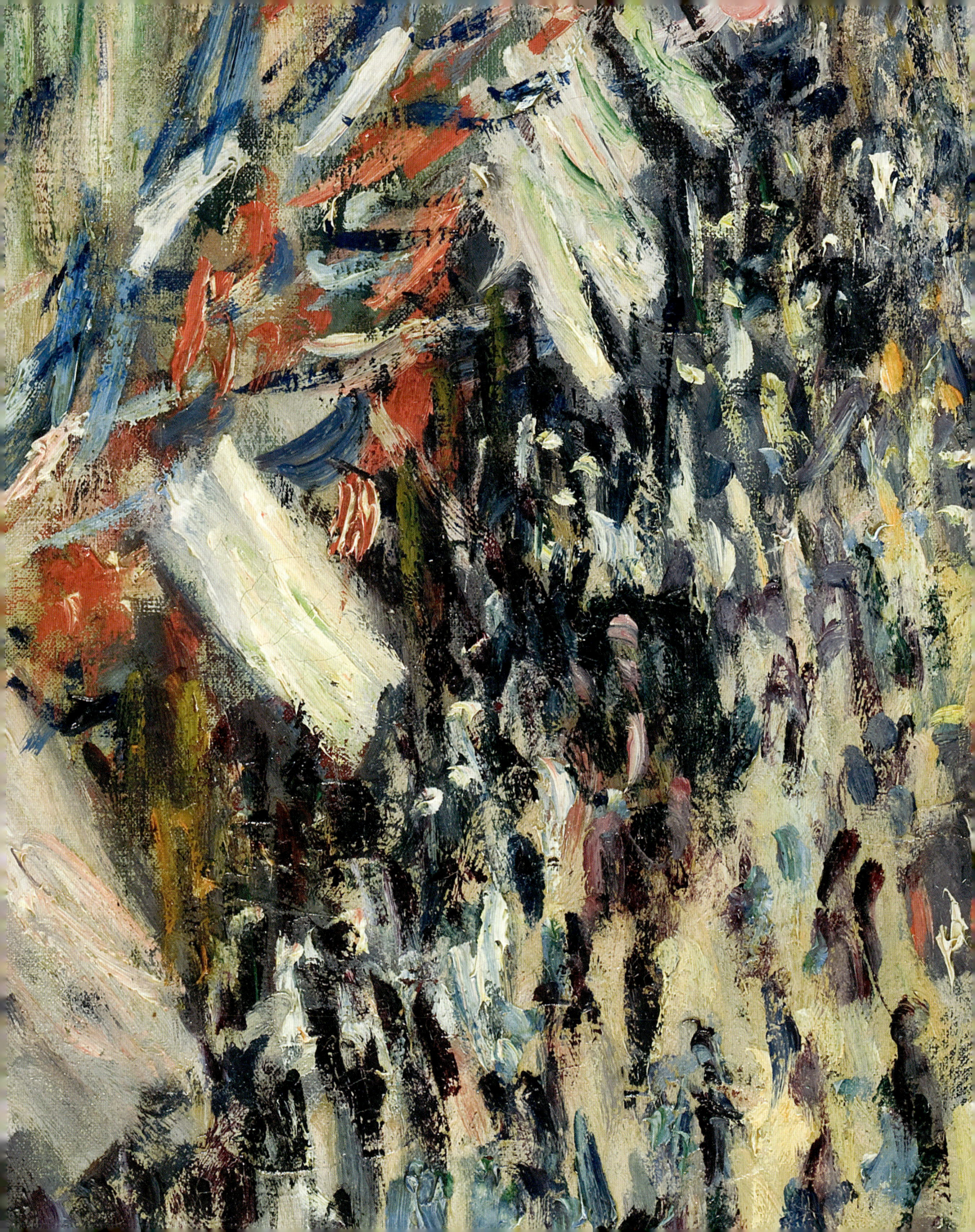

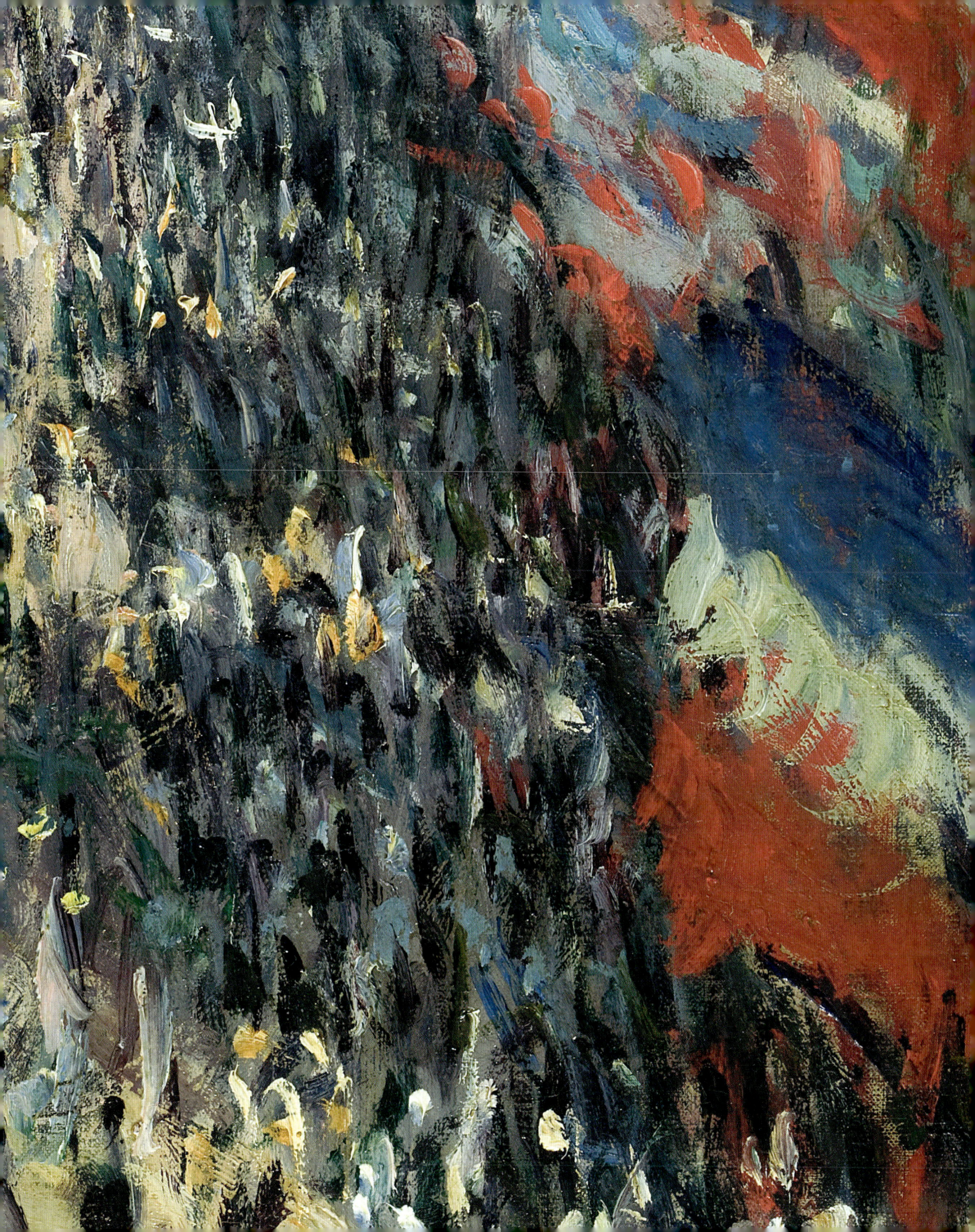